SWT/JFace in Action

SWT/JFace
in Action

MATTHEW SCARPINO
STEPHEN HOLDER
STANFORD NG
AND LAURENT MIHALKOVIC

MANNING

Greenwich
(74° w. long.)

Manning Publications Co.   Copyeditor: Tiffany Taylor
209 Bruce Park Avenue   Typesetter: Tony Roberts
Greenwich, CT 06830   Cover designer: Leslie Haimes

ISBN 1-932394-27-3

Printed in the United States of America

1 2 3 4 5 6 7 8 9 10 – VHG – 08 07 06 05 04

brief contents

contents

preface

We developed this book with one primary goal in mind: to introduce the SWT and JFace toolsets as simply and as thoroughly as possible. Although the available documentation covers many aspects of the two libraries, we were disappointed by the amount (particularly in graphics) that has gone undocumented. So, we came together in late 2003 to create an approachable book that covers both the high-level theory and the low-level details of the combined SWT/JFace development tools.

Thanks to the hard work of the folks at eclipse.org, SWT and JFace have recently received quite a bit of attention and debate within the Java community. Most of this discussion has focused on the relative merits of Swing as a standard component of the Java 2 platform, versus SWT as a nonstandard library that uses native code—an approach foreign to the "write once run anywhere" mantra embraced by most Java developers. Although Swing has many strengths, we believe that SWT and JFace together provide a compelling alternative for developing the user interface of many types of applications.

We wrote this book not only for Swing developers but also for new Java users who want to build applications that reach beyond the command line. Toward this end, we present code samples and also do our best to explain the general theories behind graphical user interface construction. In particular, we've gone into great depth concerning the Model-View-Controller paradigm, which greatly improves both the reliability and maintainability of graphical applications.

Our goal is to share our SWT experience with you, help you decide if SWT and JFace make sense for your project, and help you to make effective use of these technologies.

acknowledgments

The authors would like to acknowledge and thank the people who made this book a reality:

First, we'd like to express our appreciation to Marjan Bace, publisher of Manning, for this opportunity, and to his staff, Clay Andres, Susan Capparelle, and Dave Roberson, for their support throughout the process. Our heartfelt thanks go to Jacquelyn Carter, our beleaguered and ever-patient developmental editor who put up with all our whining and last-minute changes. We particularly want to recognize the hard work put in by the production team: Mary Piergies, Tiffany Taylor, and Tony Roberts. Their efforts have provided the professionalism and polish that has kept this book to its high production standard.

Next, we want to extend our sincere appreciation to our diligent reviewers: Phil Hanna, Christophe Avare, Frank Jania, Ted Neward, Dan Dobrin, Ryan Lowe, Steve Gutz, Carl Hume, Ed Burnette, Charles Bundy, Michael Caro, and Robert McGovern. Their feedback and encouragement helped us tremendously and in many cases guided the direction of the book's content. We're particularly grateful for the technical reviewing of Phil Hanna. There's nothing worse than a programming book with poor code, and his exacting tests ensured that our code will work as promised.

We also want to thank the Eclipse.org community in general. Not only have they produced a quality product, but this book wouldn't be possible without their dedication to technical support. Their programmers have promptly and thoroughly answered our many questions, and their documentation has provided a great deal of assistance. Of course, we're also indebted to the Eclipse developers for making their code open source, thereby giving us the means to look under the hood and discover exactly how the SWT/JFace mechanisms function.

Finally, we'd like to thank you for purchasing our book. We hope you enjoy it as much as we've enjoyed creating it, and we wish you the best of luck coding with SWT/JFace!

about this book

This book is written with the intermediate to advanced Java programmer in mind. We assume that you're familiar with the basics of Java syntax and comfortable considering design alternatives where there may not be a single choice that is superior in all situations.

Having some experience with developing graphical applications, whether in Java or any other language, will be helpful but isn't necessary. We define all terms as they're introduced and attempt to point out the purpose behind each widget as well as discuss the technical details of how to use it. However, this isn't a book about user interface design, so we won't attempt to cover the myriad details that go into assembling a compelling user experience out of the widgets we present.

We assume that most readers have some experience with Swing, but such experience isn't necessary to fully enjoy this book. We attempt to draw comparisons to Swing where we feel that doing so imparts additional understanding for Swing veterans, but these comparisons are secondary to the main discussion of each topic. We have made sure you can understand every topic in this book without having programmed a single line of Swing code.

Roadmap

This book is structured around the development of a sample application—the Widget Window—that shows off the details of each component included in SWT and JFace. The application consists of a series of tabs, one for each chapter. At the end of each chapter, we present code that you can drop into the overall project to add another tab. Where the initial chapters develop the foundation of the application, the code for the later chapters can stand on its own without needing that from the preceding chapters. We hope this approach lets you focus on the topics that are of particular interest to you, using the framework of the Widget Window application to play with the code and see the effects of different parameters on each component.

Beyond a general introduction to the tools, we cover several specific aspects of SWT/JFace:

- *The relationship between SWT and JFace*—When you first approach these two libraries, it's difficult to know when to use one over the other, or why JFace exists. We explain the seeming redundancies between the two libraries and demonstrate the trade-offs in coding with one or the other.

- *Rules of thumb concerning GUI development*—Having used these tools extensively, we've found a number of routines that simplify the process of creating GUIs. We've also encountered a number of places where SWT/JFace's operation differs from its documentation. In each case, we provide explanations and practical examples to help you avoid these pitfalls and create reliable SWT/JFace applications.

- *Cross-platform development*—Between SWT and JFace, you can find many different ways to build the same user interface. However, some methods translate well across operating systems, and some don't. Throughout this book, we present screenshots on multiple windowing platforms to show you how your application will appear.

- *Practical code examples*—When we came up with the example code in this book, we held two priorities in mind: We kept them concise, for hands-on readers; and we made them modular, so you can use them in SWT/JFace applications you build in the future.

- *Toolsets that build on SWT/JFace*—We're excited to present the first thorough walkthrough of the Draw2D and Graphical Editor Framework (GEF) toolsets. These libraries, which build on the capabilities of SWT and JFace, greatly extend the power and flexibility of GUI design.

Chapter 1, "Overview," presents the history of SWT and JFace and places these technologies in context. We present an overview of the history of graphical user interface development using Java and discuss the organization of the various classes and packages within SWT and JFace.

Chapter 2, "Getting started with SWT/JFace," shows you how to set up a project to use SWT and JFace, either within the Eclipse IDE or as a standalone project built from the command line. After showing how to implement a traditional "Hello World" application using SWT and JFace, we introduce the basic framework on which the Widget Window will be built.

Chapter 3, "Widgets: part 1," discusses the inheritance hierarchy used by the SWT and JFace classes. We also discuss several concepts common to all widgets within SWT and show how to use some basic, common widgets such as buttons and labels.

Chapter 4, "Working with events," explains how to enable your application to react appropriately when the user takes an action such as clicking a button on the screen. We show the details of low-level event classes in both SWT and JFace and discuss the higher-level Action framework that makes handling events easier.

Chapter 5, "More widgets," dives back in to the discussion of individual components provided by SWT. Most important, we discuss how to let users edit text within your application, and we cover a variety of useful widgets that are often used in user interfaces.

Chapter 6, "Layouts," takes a break from the details of individual widgets to discuss ways to organize widgets on the screen. After covering the built-in layout managers provided by SWT, we show how to create a custom layout manager if the default ones don't meet the needs of your application.

Chapter 7, "Graphics," covers low-level SWT facilities for drawing graphics by hand. In addition, we show how to programmatically manipulate colors, fonts, and images from within SWT.

Chapter 8, "Working with trees and lists," introduces the Viewer framework, a set of classes and interfaces provided by JFace to make working with data easier. We use this discussion of viewers and their related classes to show you how to easily work with tree and list widgets.

Chapter 9, "Tables and menus," continues the Viewer framework discussion from chapter 8 and includes several advanced features of the framework. We show how these features enable you to create tables that users can easily and intuitively edit. The chapter ends with a discussion of menus and how they tie into the action classes from chapter 4.

Chapter 10, "Dialogs," covers ways to create dialog boxes in both SWT and JFace. We discuss the dialog boxes provided by SWT and JFace and show how to create your own dialogs when necessary.

Chapter 11, "Wizards," shows how to use the framework provided by JFace to create a wizard that guides the user through a series of steps.

Chapter 12, "Advanced features," covers a variety of miscellaneous features. These are important topics to understand in order to fully master SWT and JFace, but they aren't essential to get a basic application running. We discuss subjects such as implementing drag and drop, interacting with the operating system's clipboard, and embedding a web browser in your application.

Chapter 13, "Looking beyond SWT/JFace: the Rich Client Platform," shows how to build custom workbench applications that contain editors and views. In addition, this chapter presents the new Eclipse Forms toolset for designing form-like applications.

Appendix A, "Creating projects with SWT/JFace," shows how set up a Java project that uses SWT and JFace. Specifically, it covers how to find the necessary libraries and set up common IDEs such as Eclipse.

Appendix B, "OLE and ActiveX in SWT/JFace," covers facilities provided by SWT for integrating with the Windows operating system. Obviously, the techniques we discuss in this appendix are relevant only to developers willing to tie themselves closely to one operating system; as such, they may not be of interest to some readers.

Appendix C, "Changeable GUIs with Draw2D," shows a framework you can use to create custom widgets for use in SWT. We cover the creation of a custom widget used in appendix D.

Appendix D, "The Graphical Editing Framework (GEF)," covers the most complicated topic in this book and requires knowledge of almost every aspect of JFace as well as the Eclipse Workbench. GEF is a powerful framework that you can use to create to create powerful graphical editors for your applications. This appendix uses the custom widget developed in appendix C to create a flowchart editor application.

If you have any questions or concerns about our content, visit the www.manning.com/scarpino web site. From there, we can answer questions and provide further explanations. We also provide our example code for download.

Conventions

Throughout this book, the text follows certain conventions. Method and variable names appear in `monotype` font in the text. Code snippets that illustrate a technique in context without necessarily covering every detail required to get the code to compile are also presented in `monotype` font, as are full code listings. Any code listing (preceded by a "Listing X.Y" header) can be typed in, compiled, and run as is.

We also present several UML diagrams in this book. These diagrams are in the spirit of what Martin Fowler refers to as "UML as sketch"—they aren't full-blown, comprehensive diagrams that cover every member variable and private method of the classes in question. Rather, they're intended to convey essential information about the relationship between certain classes and interfaces at a high level. The text and code samples around each diagram discuss the low-level details necessary to make effective use of the classes presented in the diagrams.

Source code downloads

Source code for the programming examples in this book is available for download from the publisher's web site at www.manning.com/scarpino.

Author Online

Purchase of *SWT/JFace in Action* includes free access to a private web forum run by Manning Publications where you can make comments about the book, ask technical questions, and receive help from the authors and from other users. To access the forum and subscribe to it, point your web browser to www.manning.com/scarpino. This page provides information on how to get on the forum once you are registered, what kind of help is available, and the rules of conduct on the forum.

Manning's commitment to our readers is to provide a venue where a meaningful dialog between individual readers and between readers and the authors can take place. It is not a commitment to any specific amount of participation on the part of the authors, whose contribution to the AO remains voluntary (and unpaid). We suggest you try asking the authors some challenging questions lest their interest stray!

The Author Online forum and the archives of previous discussions will be accessible from the publisher's web site as long as the book is in print.

about the authors

MATT SCARPINO has more than 10 years of software design and engineering experience. He uses Eclipse to build editing software for reconfigurable computing and has submitted code for Eclipse's graphical library. He lives in Fort Worth, Texas.

STEPHEN HOLDER is a software engineer who has worked as a consultant for several large commercial and government agencies on enterprise-level Java projects, including writing Eclipse plug-ins to streamline the development process. He currently resides in Tustin, California.

STANFORD NG is the cofounder of Nuglu, LLC and is currently working on improving back-end systems at Automotive.com, a top-5 automotive e-commerce site. He is also a co-conspirator with Dr. Robert Nideffer behind the International award-winning Proxy/MAM research project. He lives in Irvine, California.

LAURENT MIHALKOVIC is a technology consultant with 10 years' experience designing solutions in C/C++/Java/COM. He currently lives between Vancouver and Toronto, Canada.

about the title

By combining introductions, overviews, and how-to examples, the *In Action* books are designed to help learning and remembering. According to research in cognitive science, the things people remember are things they discover during self-motivated exploration.

Although no one at Manning is a cognitive scientist, we are convinced that for learning to become permanent it must pass through stages of exploration, play, and, interestingly, retelling of what is being learned. People understand and remember new things, which is to say they master them, only after actively exploring them. Humans learn *in action*. An essential part of an *In Action* guide is that it is example-driven. It encourages the reader to try things out, to play with new code, and to explore new ideas.

There is another, more mundane, reason for the title of this book: our readers are busy. They use books to do a job or to solve a problem. They need books that allow them to jump in and jump out easily and learn just what they want just when they want it. They need books that aid them in action. The books in this series are designed for such readers.

about the cover illustration

The figure on the cover of *SWT/JFace in Action* is a "Femme Patagonne," a woman from Patagonia, an area of breathtaking natural beauty in the southern regions of Argentina and Chile. From the towering tips of the Andes to the sweeping vistas of the central plains to the pristine beaches on both coasts, Patagonia is a land of stark contrasts. Sparsely populated even today, it has become the ultimate destination for modern-day adventurers.

The illustration is taken from a French travel book, *Encyclopedie des Voyages* by J. G. St. Saveur, published in 1796. Travel for pleasure was a relatively new phenomenon at the time and travel guides such as this one were popular, introducing both the tourist as well as the armchair traveler to inhabitants of faraway places.

The diversity of the drawings in the *Encyclopedie des Voyages* speaks vividly of the uniqueness and individuality of the world's towns and provinces just 200 years ago. This was a time when the dress codes of two regions separated by a few dozen miles identified people uniquely as belonging to one or the other. The travel guide brings to life a sense of isolation and distance of that period and of every other historic period except our own hyperkinetic present.

Dress codes have changed since then and the diversity by region, so rich at the time, has faded away. It is now often hard to tell the inhabitant of one continent from another. Perhaps, trying to view it optimistically, we have traded a cultural and visual diversity for a more varied personal life. Or a more varied and interesting intellectual and technical life.

We at Manning celebrate the inventiveness, the initiative, and the fun of the computer business with book covers based on the rich diversity of regional life two centuries ago brought back to life by the pictures from this travel guide.

Overview of SWT and JFace

This chapter covers

- The purpose of SWT and JFace
- The reasons for their creation
- How the two libraries differ from Swing
- Licensing and platform support

In March 2004, the *Java Developer's Journal* announced the results of its Readers' Choice Award for Best Java Component. More than 15,000 developers voted for one of many Java toolsets, including offerings from such established names as Oracle and Apple. But in the end, Eclipse's Standard Widget Toolkit (SWT) won handily, just as it did in 2003. Despite their late entry into the field of Java development, Eclipse and SWT have also won awards and recognition from *JavaWorld*, *JavaPro*, and *LinuxWorld*.

This well-earned applause goes a long way in showing the impact these tools have made on Java development. Java programmers around the world have embraced the power and versatility of SWT and JFace, deploying new plug-ins and standalone applications with each passing day. The goal of this book is to show you how this toolset functions and how you can use these tools for your own applications.

In particular, you'll be able to

- Develop SWT/JFace-based applications with hands-on code examples
- Create customized graphics with SWT's built-in graphical context
- Understand the structure and methodology behind the SWT/JFace API
- Further your knowledge of GUI (graphical user interface) design
- Build and deploy SWT/JFace applications for Eclipse and standalone usage

Most important, GUI development should be fun! No other branch of programming provides the same satisfaction as watching a new graphical interface spring to life. Therefore, we'll intersperse the theory of SWT and JFace with example code showing practical GUI development.

But before we start programming, we need to show you what this new technology is all about and what tasks it will help you perform.

1.1 What is SWT/JFace?

Although we refer to SWT and JFace as *tools* or *toolsets*, they're essentially software libraries. They consist of packages that contain Java classes and interfaces. But what makes these components so special is that you can combine them to form GUIs. And not just any GUIs, either! Your applications will run quickly, make effective use of computer memory, and, like chameleons, assume the look and feel of whichever Java-supported operating system they run on. No other GUI-building library can say that.

Although SWT and JFace accomplish the same goal, they follow different philosophies in creating user interfaces. Our favorite analogy involves automobile transmissions. SWT development is like using a standard transmission: It gives you greater control and access to the system internals, but it's more complicated to use. JFace, on the other hand, resembles an automatic transmission: It does most of the work for you, but you lose flexibility.

Of course, the truth is more complicated than any analogy. So, let's investigate these two libraries in greater depth.

1.1.1 Building GUIs with SWT

Every operating system contains a number of graphical components that make up its default user interface. These include buttons, windows, menus, and everything else you see on your computer screen. The goal of SWT is to give you, the Java programmer, direct access to these components so that you can configure and position them however you like.

You don't have to worry about the end user's operating system. When you add an SWT `Button` object to your application, it will look and act like a Windows button on Windows, a Macintosh button on Macintosh, and a Linux button on a Linux system. Users will think that you wrote the GUI specifically for their machines, and they'll have no idea that you wrote the code only once using SWT.

In addition to graphical components, SWT also provides access to events. This means you can keep track of what buttons your users have clicked and which menu items they've selected. This powerful capability makes it possible to receive and respond to nearly every form of user input, and we'll spend a great deal of time showing how this works.

Finally, if you want to add graphics to your application, SWT provides a large set of tools for creating images, working with new fonts, and drawing shapes. This feature not only allows you to build new graphics, but also lets you control how, when, and where they're displayed in your GUI. This book will show you how SWT manages colors, drawings, fonts, and images, and will present a great deal of example code.

SWT provides a wealth of capabilities for building user interfaces, but as you'll see in this book, the code can become lengthy and complex. For this reason, the Eclipse designers built a second library for GUI development: JFace.

1.1.2 Simplifying GUI development with JFace

Rather than write the same SWT code over and over again, the designers of the Eclipse Workbench created JFace. This library provides shortcuts around many of the tasks that can be time-consuming using SWT alone. But JFace is *not* a replacement for SWT, and many GUIs will need features from both toolsets.

An important example of JFace's increased efficiency involves events. In many user interfaces, you may have different events, such as button clicks, keystrokes, or menu selections, that all perform the same function. In SWT, each event needs to be received and handled separately. But JFace allows you to combine them into a single object, so you can concern yourself with the event's response instead of the component that triggered it. This simple but powerful concept makes it possible to add context menus, toolbars, and palettes to your GUIs without adding a lot of code.

JFace is also helpful when you're building large GUIs that require multiple windows and graphics. It provides registry classes that help you organize SWT components and manage their memory allocation. For example, in SWT, you need to specifically create and deallocate every `Font` and `Image` in your application. But with JFace, you can use built-in `FontRegistry` and `ImageRegistry` objects to take care of these tedious concerns for you.

Now that you understand the basic characteristics behind these two libraries, we need to dig a little deeper and show you the concepts behind their design. This discussion will explain why SWT/JFace GUIs are so fast, why they can take the appearance of whatever operating system they run on, and why they were created in the first place.

1.2   Looking under the hood

Adding components, events, and graphics to a user interface isn't a new idea. Therefore, to see why the SWT/JFace toolset has caused such a stir, you need to understand what its designers were thinking. This means investigating the principles behind Java GUI development and how these libraries make use of them.

But before we can investigate SWT/JFace in depth, we need to introduce Swing. SWT and JFace were created in response to this library, and by understanding the contrast between the two design philosophies, you'll better appreciate how SWT and JFace function. Further, in addition to recognizing the trade-offs between Swing and SWT/JFace, you'll be able to participate in the passionate debates concerning the two.

1.2.1   The old standby: Swing

When Sun released the Swing library in 1998, the Java community was delighted. Finally, Sun had backed up its "Write Once, Run Anywhere" credo with a toolset capable of building platform-independent user interfaces. Swing quickly became the most popular tool for creating GUIs in Java.

But as time went by, many developers became discontented. The qualities that made Swing so attractive initially also made for complex development and slow operation. For this reason, Java GUIs have found little use in desktop applications.

Swing rendering

In order to ensure consistent appearance and operation across operating systems, Swing takes complete control of rendering its user interfaces. That is, the Java Virtual Machine (JVM) specifies every pixel of its components and controls their behavior. It still communicates with the underlying platform, but instead of using the operating system's prebuilt objects, it creates everything from scratch.

Because these components are implemented at a high level, they're referred to as *lightweight components*. These components look the same on any operating system that supports the JVM. This cross-platform look-and-feel is shown graphically in figure 1.1, and it looks and behaves identically whether it's running on Windows, Macintosh, or *nix platforms.

But this approach has drawbacks. Because the JVM micromanages every aspect of the GUI's appearance and behavior, the application runs more slowly than if it relied on the operating system. Also, most users like the way their operating system looks and prefer that their Java applications resemble their other platform-specific (or *native*) applications.

Swing automatic garbage collection

Keeping with Java's promise of reliable computing, Swing uses Java's automatic garbage collection (AGC) for its applications. This process spawns a thread, or *daemon*, that runs beneath the application layer and deallocates memory for objects that are no longer needed. It activates during program execution and functions independently of the developer. AGC is an important capability: If programmers don't free their data, then other applications won't be able to reclaim memory for their objects.

The main advantage of AGC is that developers can concentrate on code design instead of keeping track of every object's lifetime. The downside involves the unpredictable nature of the garbage-collection thread. The deallocation process

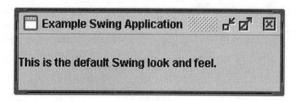

Figure 1.1
This application will act and appear similarly on every platform supported by Swing.

leaves you no idea as to when it will take place. Also, AGC capabilities change from one JVM to the next and from one platform to the next. Therefore, given the time-intensive nature of creating and disposing objects within large applications, programs may behave erratically from system to system.

Swing design architecture

Swing directs the GUI design process through an implementation of Model-View-Controller (MVC) architecture. MVC decomposes a user interface component into three parts: its state information, its displayed appearance, and its ability to react to outside events. These aspects are called the *Model, View,* and *Controller,* respectively. The Swing designers modified this methodology and created the *Model-Delegate* architecture, shown in figure 1.2. This architecture combines the component's View and Controller aspects into a UI-Delegate. So, for each element of the user interface—button, frame, and label—Swing allocates memory for a model that contains the component's state and the UI-Delegate, which controls its appearance and response to events.

By separating model information from appearance, Swing provides a programming methodology that ensures flexible, reusable code. But this capability also produces multiple objects for each widget that appears on the screen. As GUIs become more complex, this additional allocation and disposal can place a large burden on the processor.

1.2.2 *The newcomer: SWT/JFace*

The designers of Eclipse responded strongly to Swing's complexity and execution issues. They wanted a tool that would enable a Java user interface to run on a desktop with the same performance as a native application. In fact, they wanted it so badly that they created their own libraries: SWT and JFace.

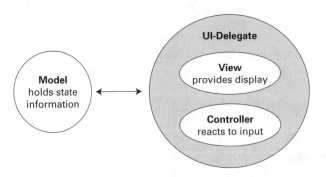

Figure 1.2
The design architecture of Swing GUIs. This diagram shows the relationship between classic MVC and Swing's Model-Delegate method.

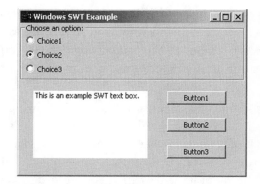
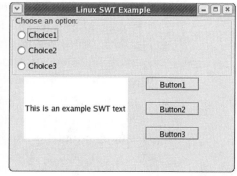

Figure 1.3 **Example Eclipse GUIs for Windows XP and Linux (GTK). By using heavyweight components, they take the appearance of their host operating system.**

Both Swing and SWT/JFace create Java-based, platform-independent GUIs. But their methods differ in nearly every other respect.

SWT/JFace rendering

The most prominent aspect of SWT/JFace involves its direct access to the operating system. Rather than reinventing graphics for its GUIs, it uses *heavyweight components* from the underlying platform. This decision makes possible the speed and appearance of SWT/JFace user interfaces, as shown in figure 1.3.

The communication between SWT/JFace and the operating system is performed using the *Java Native Interface* (JNI). We'll explore this topic in greater depth in the next chapter, but a short description here is helpful. Since the original creators of Java knew that its applications would eventually need to access legacy code and operating systems, they provided a library of methods to call procedures in other languages (such as C and Fortran) from within a Java class. SWT/JFace relies on JNI to manage the operating system's rendering instead of performing all the work by itself.

SWT/JFace resource management

Another important characteristic of SWT/JFace is that it doesn't rely on automatic garbage collection. At first, it may seem as though this will result in buggy code. However, you need to be careful when accessing operating system resources, and non-deterministic memory disposal can cause more problems than it solves. There are two reasons behind Eclipse's decision to remove AGC from SWT/JFace:

- The process of automatically deallocating memory during program operation is unpredictable, giving no indication when a freed resource will be available. If an irregularity occurs during the deallocation process, the process may not finish. This is a minor concern when you're dealing with simple data structures. But when these objects make up a large graphical application, memory allocation and deallocation become important tasks whose behavior you should fully understand.

■ Using AGC with operating system resources is difficult. Since Swing builds its lightweight components at such a high level, this isn't as large a concern. However, automatic disposal of low-level resources, such as SWT's widgets, is error-prone and erratic across different platforms. If these objects take too much time to be deleted, the memory leaks can crash the program. Or, if these resources are deallocated in the wrong order, then the system's operation can grind to a halt.

To prevent the errors associated with automatic object disposal, SWT/JFace lets you determine when your resources should be deallocated. The toolset simplifies this process by providing `dispose()` methods within the component classes. Also, once you have freed a parent resource, its child resources will automatically be disposed of. As you'll see in future chapters, this means that few explicit deallocation calls are necessary within most applications. You might call SWT/JFace's resource management *semi-automatic*.

Simplicity of design and development

GUI generation in Swing is performed with a Model-Delegate architecture, which creates different objects to represent different aspects of the GUI components. But this complexity isn't suitable for all cases. Developers building simple button-and-label interfaces, as well as those just ascending the learning curve, don't need this sophistication. At the other extreme, programmers building complex graphical editors and computer-aided design tools need more separation of GUI functions in order to allow for different views and designs.

SWT and JFace make no rules regarding the design architecture of their components. This means that you can build GUIs with as much sophistication or simplicity as you prefer. Because Eclipse is easily extensible and the source code is always available, you can add whatever tools or modifications you like. In fact, a number of plug-ins have been developed to provide MVC wrappers for SWT/JFace components.

1.2.3 *The SWT/Swing debate*

Any casual web search for *SWT* and *Swing* will bring up a number of heated arguments regarding which toolset is superior. This controversy is unnecessary and counterproductive. SWT was created as an alternative to Swing, not as a replacement.

Our goal in writing this section wasn't to praise one tool over the other, but to explain how and why they work. Infighting between Java developers can only harm the effort to build freely available, platform-independent applications. The world is big enough for both SWT and Swing, and we hope the two camps will be able to put aside their differences and concentrate on improving the Java community as a whole.

1.3 *SWT/JFace: licensing and platform support*

Before continuing with the code, we'd like to touch on two important concerns regarding building applications with SWT/JFace. The first involves the lack of strings attached to Eclipse and its development libraries, outlined in the Common Public License. This is important, and you should understand it if you're looking to build commercial applications. The second concern deals with the platforms currently supported by Eclipse in general and SWT/JFace in particular.

1.3.1 *The Common Public License*

The Eclipse consortium has released Eclipse to the public under the terms of the Common Public License (CPL). This license is fully compliant with the Open Source Initiative (OSI) licensing scheme and allows full commercial use of the software by granting royalty-free source code and worldwide redistribution rights. This means anyone can use the source code, modify it, and sell the resulting product. More information is available at www.eclipse.org/legal/main.html.

Although some components of the platform are distributed under specific licenses, the SWT and JFace toolsets are governed by the CPL. This makes it possible to develop commercial SWT/JFaces applications for all supported platforms.

1.3.2 *Platforms supported*

At the time of this writing, SWT/JFace development is available for a number of operating systems. Because it relies on particular windowing system functions, some platforms have multiple SWT implementations. Table 1.1 lists the operating systems and user interfaces supported by SWT/JFace.

Table 1.1   Platforms supported by SWT/JFace

Operating system	User interface
Microsoft Windows XP, 2000, NT, 98, ME	Windows
Microsoft Windows PocketPC 2002 Strong ARM	Windows
Microsoft Windows PocketPC 2002 Strong ARM (J2ME)	Windows
Red Hat Linux 9 x86	Motif, GTK 2.0
SUSE Linux 8.2 x86	Motif, GTK 2.0
Other Linux x86	Motif, GTK 2.0
Sun Solaris 8 SPARC	Motif
IBM PowerPC	Motif
HP-UX 11i hp9000 PA-RISC	Motif
QNX x86	Photon
Mac OS	Carbon

On Linux, KDE support isn't yet available. However, SWT/JFace applications can run under the KDE desktop provided that the GTK runtime libraries are also installed on the desktop. KDE is built on top of the Trolltech Qt toolkit, which is distributed under a more restrictive licence than the CPL. Should a KDE version of the SWT library be developed in the future, all existing SWT/JFaces applications would support it and inherit the native KDE look.

Support for Microsoft Pocket PC 2002 is one of the hidden treasures of SWT. The SWT distribution provides support for the StrongARM processor in both Pocket PC 2002 and Smartphone 2002 devices. Thanks to its great flexibility, the SWT Pocket PC version can be run against both the familiar J2SE (the standard distribution of Java) and the J2ME Connected Limited Device Configuration (CLDC) profile for embedded devices. Coverage of how to build the SWT library for the CDLC profile and use it in conjunction with the IBM J9 VM is beyond the scope of the book. If you're interested in exploring embedded development, visit the SWT newsgroup at the Eclipse Consortium web site (news://news.eclipse.org/eclipse.platform.swt).

Support for the Windows operating systems includes an unforeseen bonus: You can embed ActiveX controls directly inside SWT container widgets. The Eclipse platform uses this facility to include support for web browsing by embedding the

Microsoft WebBrowser control. You can find further details on ActiveX support in appendix B, "OLE and ActiveX in SWT/JFace."

1.4 The WidgetWindow

The best way to learn about the SWT/JFace toolset is to build GUIs that use its classes. With this priority in mind, we struggled to come up with an overarching project that would touch on the various aspects of SWT/JFace development. At first, we wanted to build something exciting, such as a web-enabled database display. But we decided that this would incorporate too much irrelevant code and place too large a burden on our hands-on readers.

So, we've opted for a simple application that incorporates as many GUI elements as possible while minimizing the amount of code. We feel that a `TabFolder` object (described in chapter 3) will be the clearest manner of presenting the information in this book. Then, with each following chapter, we'll add a new tab whose contents show the chapter's subject. The fully designed application is shown in figure 1.4. Not the savviest at marketing, we call it the `WidgetWindow`.

Development of the `WidgetWindow` application serves a number of purposes. Of course, it provides a single application for integrating the different components within the SWT and JFace libraries. But it also gives you a repository of reusable SWT/JFace code. Because it's a single project with multiple classes, as opposed to multiple projects with single classes, the `WidgetWindow` will ensure that you can reuse each part for your own user interfaces.

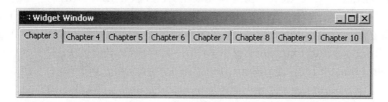

Figure 1.4 The `WidgetWindow` application. This overarching project will incorporate all the GUI and graphical elements presented in this book.

1.5 Summary

The contents of the SWT and JFace libraries are effective for building user interfaces, but by themselves, they don't constitute anything groundbreaking. There are still buttons, containers, labels, and menus that can be positioned and manipulated just as in other toolsets. Instead, the *philosophy* behind the toolset makes it revolutionary.

SWT/JFace may not conform to every rule of Java ideology, but it fulfills the goals of open-source software to a much greater extent than Java, with its pseudo-proprietary development. Not only doesn't SWT/JFace require any licences or royalties, but it also allows you, the developer, to charge these fees for software that you develop. If you have developed a new operating system and need a development tool to draw programmers to your platfrom, you can't do much better than tailoring SWT and JFace for your system. If you're building a new programming language and want something more than a command-line compiler and linker, the Eclipse platform, with SWT and JFace, is ideally suited to your task.

When Java developers debate the merits of SWT/JFace over those of other toolsets, they consider the capabilities available now or within the next six months. This mindset overlooks the fact that SWT/JFace, like Eclipse, is developed in a truly bazaar-like fashion, with companies and individuals providing improvements from across the world. If the abundance of programmer hours can be correlated with future improvement, then SWT/JFace will be the hands-down victor as its evolution continues.

Historically, software development has never been IBM's strong suit. Therefore, we'd like to express our appreciation to whichever lateral thinker realized that helping the open source effort is the best way to add value to IBM hardware. Given the freedom and extensibility of Eclipse and SWT/JFace and the enthusiasm of its developers, we feel confident that this toolset will continue to benefit the open source development community in years to come.

But enough backslapping. Let's start building applications!

Getting started with
SWT and JFace

2

This chapter covers

- The important classes of SWT: Display and Shell
- An SWT programming example
- The important class of JFace: ApplicationWindow
- An SWT/JFace programming example

GUI programming is one of the most rewarding aspects of software development, but when you rely on graphics instead of the command line, there are important questions to be asked. How can your program access the widgets, containers, and events of the operating system? What software classes represent the different components in a GUI, and how can you manipulate them?

The goal of this chapter is to answer the first question and begin answering the second. We'll discuss the fundamental classes of both the SWT and JFace libraries and how they access operating system resources. This chapter presents two main code examples—HelloSWT.java and HelloSWTJFace.java—that show how to use the Standard Widget Toolkit (SWT) with and without the JFace library. We'll examine these programs and draw conclusions about their underlying structures.

This chapter will also begin adding code to the WidgetWindow project. This is a graphical interface that will combine all the SWT and JFace topics discussed in this book. We'll build its frame here and update it in each chapter that follows. Because each chapter adds to this application, we recommend that you follow its development closely.

2.1 Programming in SWT

Although we'll use JFace shortly, this section focuses on programming with SWT alone. First, we'll present the code for a basic GUI and examine its structure. Then, this section will describe the two fundamental classes of the toolset: Display and Shell. These classes provide the foundation on which widgets, containers, and events can be added.

> **NOTE** In order to compile and execute the code in this book, you need to add the SWT/JFace Java libraries to the project and make the native graphic library available. This procedure is fully documented in appendix A, "Creating Projects with SWT/JFace."

2.1.1 The HelloSWT program

Before we explore SWT theory in detail, it will be helpful to prove in advance that it works. For this purpose, we present our first SWT GUI, HelloSWT.java, in listing 2.1. We encourage you to add this class to the com.swtjface.Ch2 package and execute the application.

Listing 2.1   HelloSWT.java

```java
package com.swtjface.Ch2;
import org.eclipse.swt.*;
import org.eclipse.swt.widgets.*;

public class HelloSWT
{
  public static void main (String [] args)
  {
    Display display = new Display();          ❶ Allocation and
    Shell shell = new Shell(display);            initialization

    Text helloText = new Text(shell, SWT.CENTER);  ❷ Adding widgets
    helloText.setText("Hello SWT!");                  to the shell
    helloText.pack();

    shell.pack();
    shell.open();
    while (!shell.isDisposed())
    {                                          ❸ GUI operation
      if (!display.readAndDispatch())
        display.sleep();
    }
    display.dispose();
  }
}
```

Although HelloSWT is a simple GUI, most SWT applications consist of the same three-part structure:

❶ The first part begins by creating an instance of the Display and Shell classes. As we'll show shortly, this allows the GUI to access the resources of the underlying platform and create a primary window for viewing widgets.

❷ The next section adds a Text widget to the shell. Although this is simple in Hello-SWT, this section usually requires the most effort in an SWT application. It deals with adding and configuring the building blocks necessary to provide the GUI's function. Widgets and groups of widgets (in containers) are added as *children* of the shell. Listeners and events are defined for each widget that the user can act on. The code in this section also sets the parameters for these widgets, containers, and events to make sure they look and act as required. In this case, the pack() methods tell the Shell and Text components to use only as much space as they need.

❸ The last part represents the operation of the GUI. Up to this point, all of the application's code has done nothing more than initialize variables. But when the Shell's open() method is invoked, the application's main window takes shape and its children are rendered in the display. So long as the Shell remains open, the Display instance uses its readAndDispatch() method to keep track of relevant user events in the platform's event queue. When one of these actions involves closing the window, the resources associated with the Display object (such as the Shell and its children) are deallocated.

Figure 2.1 shows an example of how the GUI should appear (in Linux/GTK).

Congratulations! You've created your first graphical user interface with the SWT library. Before moving on to an application that uses both SWT and JFace, it's important to further understand the classes we've used and the methods available for accessing and configuring them.

Figure 2.1
**Simple but effective:
the output of the**
HelloSWT code

2.1.2 The Display class

Although the Display class has no visible form, it keeps track of the GUI resources and manages communication with the operating system. That is, it concerns itself with how its windows are displayed, moved, and redrawn. It also ensures that events such as mouse clicks and keystroke actions are sent to the widgets that can handle them.

Operation of the Display class

Although the Display class may only appear in a few lines of your GUI code, it's important to respect and understand its operation. It's the workhorse of any SWT/JFace application, and whether you work with SWT/JFace or SWT alone, you must include an instance of this class in your program. This way, your interface will be able to use the widgets and containers of the operating system and respond to the user's actions. Although most applications do little more than create a Display object and invoke a few of its methods, the role played by this class is sufficiently important to be worth describing in detail.

The main task of the Display class is to translate SWT/JFace commands from your code into low-level calls to the operating system. This process comprises two parts and begins once the application creates an instance of the Display class. First, the Display object constructs an instance of the OS class, which represents the platform's operating system (OS). This class provides access to the computer's low-level resources through a series of special Java procedures called *native methods*.

Then, like a switchboard operator, this Display object uses these methods to direct commands to the operating system and convey user actions to the application.

As an example of a native method, the OS declaration for SetFocus() is shown here:

```
public static final native int SetFocus (int hWnd);
```

This method sets the focus on a window according to its handle, hWnd. Because of the native modifier, there is no Java code to specify its operation. Instead, this keyword tells the compiler that the method's code is written in another language and resides in another file. In the case of HelloSWT.java and all SWT/JFace applications, this other language is C and the other file is the native graphics library you included in your project. The C code in the graphic library corresponding to the SetFocus() method is presented here:

```
JNIEXPORT jint JNICALL OS_NATIVE(SetFocus)
  (JNIEnv *env, jclass that, jint arg0) {
  jint rc;
  NATIVE_ENTER(env, that, "SetFocus\n")
  rc = (jint)SetFocus((HWND)arg0);
  NATIVE_EXIT(env, that, "SetFocus\n")
  return rc;
}
```

As shown, the C implementation of the Java SetFocus() method calls the operating system function SetFocus(). This isn't a coincidence; this exact matching of SWT commands and operating system calls makes GUI debugging a straightforward process. As long as you can riddle out the Application Programming Interface (API) for your operating system, you can determine what is happening in your code. This example uses the Windows operating system, but the process is similar for all platforms supported by Eclipse.

Another important point to consider is that, if any features in your operating system aren't incorporated into SWT, you can use the Java Native Interface to add them yourself. All it requires is a native Java method in the SWT package and a C function in the native graphics library that calls the operating system.

Methods of the Display class

Table 2.1 identifies and describes a number of methods that belong to the Display class. This isn't a full listing, but it shows the methods vital for SWT/JFace GUIs to function and those necessary to implement particular capabilities in an application:

Table 2.1   Important methods of the `Display` class and their functions

Display method	Function
Display()	Allocates platform resources and creates a `Display` object
getCurrent()	Returns the user-interface thread
readAndDispatch()	`Display` object interprets events and passes them to receiver
sleep()	`Display` object waits for events

The first two methods must be used in any SWT-based GUI. The first, `Display()`, creates an instance of the class and associates it with the GUI. The second, get-Current(), returns the primary thread of the application, the *user-interface thread.* This method is generally used with the `dispose()` method to end the operation of the `Display`.

The next two methods in the table enable the application to receive notifications from the operating system whenever the user takes an action associated with the GUI. Event processing, handlers, and listeners will be fully discussed in chapter 4. However, it's important to understand the `readAndDispatch()` method, which accesses the operating system's event queue and determines whether any of the user's actions are related to the GUI. Using this method, the `HelloSWT` class knows whether the user has decided to dispose of the `Shell`. If so, the method returns TRUE, and the application ends. Otherwise, the `Display` object invokes its `sleep()` method, and the application continues waiting.

Although the `Display` class is important, there is no way to directly see the effects of its operation. Instead, you need to use classes with visual representations. The most important of these is the `Shell` class.

2.1.3   *The Shell class*

Just as the `Display` class provides window management, the `Shell` class functions as the GUI's primary window. Unlike the `Display` object, a `Shell` instance has a visual implementation, as shown in figure 2.1. The `Shell` class accesses the operating system through the `OS` class to an extent, but only to keep track of opening, activating, maximizing, minimizing, and closing the main window.

The main function of the `Shell` class is to provide a common connection point for the containers, widgets, and events that need to be integrated into the GUI. In this respect, `Shell` serves as the parent class to these components. Figure 2.2 shows the relationship between an application's operating system, `Display`, `Shell`, and their widgets.

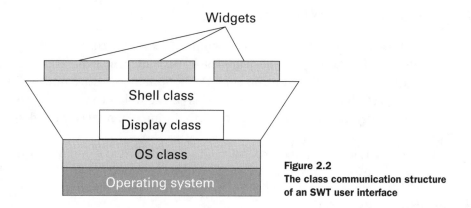

Figure 2.2
The class communication structure
of an SWT user interface

Every SWT/JFace application bases its widgets on a main Shell object, but other shells may exist in an application. They're generally associated with temporary windows or dialog boxes, which will be discussed further in chapter 10. Because these shells aren't directly attached to the Display instance, they're referred to as *secondary* shells. Shells that are attached to the Display are called *top-level* shells.

The Shell instance created in the HelloSWT application has a number of properties associated with it that allow users to alter its state or read information. These characteristics make up the component's *style*. You can control a Shell's style by adding a second argument to its constructor. Since the only argument in HelloSWT's Shell declaration is the display, it receives the default style for top-level windows, called SHELL_TRIM. This combines a number of individual style elements and tells the application that the window should have a title bar (SWT.TITLE) and that the user can minimize (SWT.MIN), maximize (SWT.MAX), resize (SWT.RESIZE), and close (SWT.CLOSE) the shell. The other default shell style, DIALOG_TRIM, ensures that dialog shells have title bars, a border around the active area (SWT.BORDER), and the ability to be closed.

Within your GUIs, you can set the style bits of the shell, or another widget, to whatever you prefer, and combine them with the | operator. In addition to the properties mentioned, you can also specify the shell's *modality*, which restricts the user's ability to alter the shell's state. A modal dialog box commands the user's attention by blocking all actions except those related to the dialog. It can't be moved or resized, and the user can only close or cancel it using the buttons provided. Finally, since not every platform can render these properties in GUI components, you must understand that SWT treats style settings as guidelines instead of strict rules.

2.2 *Programming in SWT/JFace*

With a clear understanding of SWT, learning JFace is straightforward. Although applications using both SWT and JFace have very different structures than those coded with SWT alone, the concepts underlying both libraries are similar. Like the preceding part, this section will provide a basic example of SWT/JFace code and explain its structure. Further, we'll delve into an important class provided in the JFace library: `ApplicationWindow`.

In chapter 1, we explained how JFace was constructed to simplify SWT development. We can now go into further depth by showing how its main classes work.

2.2.1 *Model-based adapters*

Eclipse documentation uses two terms to refer to JFace classes that work with SWT widgets: *helper classes* and *model-based adapters*. We've chosen to use the latter term in this book. This may be confusing because, in Java, an *adapter* is a class that provides additional event-handling capability to a widget. However, no self-respecting programmer will use helper classes, so we'll call them model-based adapters, or JFace adapters.

These adapters can be split into four categories, shown in table 2.2. We'll further elaborate on each in future chapters, but we'll briefly describe them here.

Table 2.2   Categories of JFace adapters

Adapter classification	Function
Viewers	Separate a widget's appearance and information
Actions and contributions	Simplify and organize event-handling procedures
Image and font registries	Manage the allocation/deallocation of fonts and images
Dialogs and wizards	Extend the capability of SWT `Dialogs` for user interaction

The first and most widely used category of model-based adapters includes the `Viewer` classes, fully described in chapter 9. In SWT, the information and appearance of a GUI component are bound together. However, viewers separate these aspects and allow for the same information to be presented in different forms. For example, the information in an SWT tree can't be separated from the tree object. But the same information in a JFace `TreeViewer` can be displayed in a `TableViewer` or a `ListViewer`.

The next category involves `Actions` and `Contributions`, which are described in chapter 4. These adapters simplify event handling, separating the response to a user's command from the GUI events that result in that response. This can be best explained with an example. In SWT, if four different buttons will close a dialog box, then you must write four different event-handling routines even though they accomplish the same result. In JFace, these four routines can be combined in an action, and JFace automatically makes the four buttons contributors to that action.

The third category involves image and font registries, which are further explained in chapter 7. In SWT, it's important to keep the number of allocated fonts and images to a minimum, since they require operating system resources. But with JFace registries, these resources can be allocated and deallocated when needed. Therefore, if you're using multiple images and fonts, you don't need to be concerned with manual garbage collection.

The last group comprises JFace dialogs and wizards, described in chapters 10 and 11. These are the simplest adapters to understand, since they extend the capability of SWT dialogs. JFace provides dialogs that present messages, display errors, and show the progress of ongoing processes. In addition, JFace provides a specialized dialog called a *wizard*, which guides the user through a group of tasks, such as installing software or configuring an input file.

2.2.2 *The HelloSWT_JFace program*

The best way to learn about JFace is to write a program that uses its library. The code for the HelloSWT_JFace class is shown in listing 2.2. The output is similar to that of HelloSWT, but the program structure is very different.

Listing 2.2   HelloSWTJFace.javaHelloSWTJFace.java

```
package com.swtjface.Ch2;
import org.eclipse.jface.window.*;
import org.eclipse.swt.*;
import org.eclipse.swt.widgets.*;

public class HelloSWT_JFace extends ApplicationWindow
{
  public HelloSWT_JFace()
  {                              ❶ Window allocation
    super(null);
  }

  protected Control createContents(Composite parent)
  {
    Text helloText = new Text(parent, SWT.CENTER);
    helloText.setText("Hello SWT and JFace!");       ❷ Window
    parent.pack();                                      presentation
    return parent;
  }
```

```
public static void main(String[] args)
{
    HelloSWT_JFace awin = new HelloSWT_JFace();
    awin.setBlockOnOpen(true);
    awin.open();
    Display.getCurrent().dispose();
}
}
```

❸ Window operation

Although the code for HelloSWTJFace.java is slightly longer than that of Hello-SWT.java, its structure is more clearly separated between the three class methods:

❶ The first method, HelloSWT_JFace(), constructs an instance of the main class. Any configuration or communication actions that need to be performed during allocation should be coded here. Because this is unnecessary for HelloSWT_JFace, this class only invokes the constructor of its superclass.

❷ The createContents() method deals with designing the presentation of the window. Since the visual aspect of an ApplicationWindow can't be directly accessed, this method associates a widget container called a Composite to control the GUI's appearance. This container object serves as the parent of any GUI components that need to be added to the application. After all the widgets are created, configured, and added to the parent, createContents() returns the Composite to the main window for display.

❸ The final part of this application, framed by the main() method, takes care of the actual operation of the GUI. After allocating resources for the ApplicationWindow, this method configures the window to appear until closed by invoking the set-BlockOnOpen() method with a TRUE argument. Then, the ApplicationWindow's open() method is called, displaying the window according to the Composite returned by the createContents() method. The code after the open() method only functions after the window is closed. Then, the program deallocates the GUI's Display instance by using its dispose() method. Because every widget in HelloSWT_JFace is a child of the display, this disposal also deallocates every GUI component in the program.

Once the code is compiled and the application is run, the result should look like the window shown in figure 2.3.

Figure 2.3
The `HelloSWTJFace.java` code is very different from that of `HelloSWT.java`, but the results are similar.

2.2.3 *Coding in JFace and SWT/JFace*

At this point, it's helpful to contrast the code behind `HelloSWT.java`, programmed with SWT alone, and that of `HelloSWTJFace.java`, which uses both SWT and JFace. The main difference is that SWT combines the GUI's appearance and operation in its `Shell` class, whereas SWT/JFace splits these aspects. This modular structure promotes code reuse and enables one developer to design the window's view while another determines its behavior. The appearance is controlled by the `Composite` configured in the `createContents()` method, and the operation is performed mainly through the instance of the `ApplicationWindow` class. Because this class is so crucial in SWT/JFace applications, it's important to examine its function in greater detail.

2.2.4 *The ApplicationWindow class*

Although we've just mentioned how the `ApplicationWindow` in `HelloSWT_JFace` differs from the `Shell` object in `HelloSWT`, both applications rely on `Shell` and `Display` objects to communicate with the operating system. An SWT/Face application still needs a separate `Display` instance, but the `ApplicationWindow` creates its own `Shell` whenever it's constructed with a `null` argument. This class relationship is shown in figure 2.4. Although this may seem like an unnecessary complication, the benefits of using JFace windows become apparent when you're building large user interfaces.

Like the model-based adapters mentioned in the beginning of this section, the `ApplicationWindow` serves as a JFace adapter on the `Shell` class and provides two main benefits. First, as mentioned, the `ApplicationWindow` separates the GUI's appearance from its behavior. Second, it provides a number of additional ways to configure the window that are useful for designers. Although the `Shell` class has methods that change its size and style, those of the `ApplicationWindow` class allow for much more useful customization. These methods, which include those from the `Window` class, are listed in table 2.3.

As shown in the table, the methods of an `ApplicationWindow` object make GUI programming much more convenient. You can quickly configure the window to include menu bars, toolbars, and status lines. These methods can also set the

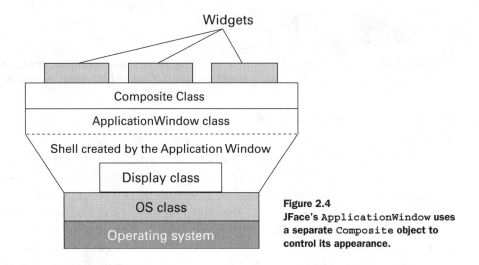

Figure 2.4
JFace's `ApplicationWindow` **uses a separate** `Composite` **object to control its appearance.**

application's exception handler and default image. In SWT, these capabilities need to be provided for and configured for each different shell you create. In JFace, this is performed automatically.

Table 2.3   Configuration methods of the `ApplicationWindow` **class**

`ApplicationWindow` method	Function
`addMenuBar()`	Configures the window with a top-level menu
`addToolBar()`	Adds a toolbar beneath the main menu
`addStatusLine()`	Creates a status area at the bottom of the window
`setStatus(String)`	Displays a message in the status area
`getSeparator()`	Returns the line separating the menu from the window
`setDefaultImage(Image)`	Displays an image when the application has no shell
`setExceptionHandler` `(IExceptionHandler)`	Configures the application to handle exceptions according to the specified interface

2.3 *Beginning the WidgetWindow application*

Although the `HelloSWT` and `HelloSWT_JFace` classes are helpful for learning the basics of SWT/JFace programming, the toolset offers a great deal more functionality that we need to explore. Rather than rewrite the same code in multiple projects, we thought it would be best to build a single project and add classes to it with each chapter.

To reduce the complexity of the WidgetWindow's design, we decided to use both SWT and JFace. In this chapter, we'll create the basic window, shown in listing 2.3. We strongly recommend that you add this class to your com.swtjface.Ch2 package.

Listing 2.3   WidgetWindow.java

```java
package com.swtjface.Ch2;
import org.eclipse.swt.widgets.*;
import org.eclipse.jface.window.*;

public class WidgetWindow extends ApplicationWindow
{
  public WidgetWindow()
  {
    super(null);
  }

  protected Control createContents(Composite parent)
  {
    getShell().setText("Widget Window");
    parent.setSize(400,250);
    return parent;
  }

  public static void main(String[] args)
  {
    WidgetWindow wwin = new WidgetWindow();
    wwin.setBlockOnOpen(true);
    wwin.open();
    Display.getCurrent().dispose();
  }
}
```

Figure 2.5 presents the unexciting but important output of the WidgetWindow class.

Figure 2.5
The blank-slate WidgetWindow application

2.4 Summary

Although you'll have to wait until the next chapter to build something fun and exciting, you should have a solid grasp of the internals of SWT and JFace at this point. These libraries make it possible to access platform-specific resources in a platform-independent manner, and it's important to understand the objects that make this possible.

The main object is the `Display`, which works behind the scenes to communicate with the operating system. This communication enables your SWT/JFace applications to use native components and process events. Although the `Display` has no appearance itself, other widgets require its operation to take shape.

SWT provides the `Shell` class as an overall container for GUI applications and dialog boxes. The `Shell` forms the GUI's parent window and makes it possible for child widgets to communicate with the `Display`. Using style bits, you can customize the `Shell`'s appearance and behavior.

In contrast, JFace applications use an `ApplicationWindow` as their main container. Unlike `Shell`s, `ApplicationWindow`s have no built-in form. This means you can specify what your top-level window should look like. Also, these objects provide methods for easily integrating other features, such as menus, toolbars, and status lines.

As you can see from the `Shell` and `ApplicationWindow` classes, the SWT and JFace libraries provide similar capabilities. This redundancy played a large role in determining the structure of this book. At first, we thought it would be best to present these toolsets in two separate parts: one covering SWT and the other covering SWT/JFace. But we realized that this approach wasn't feasible. First, because JFace provides so few widgets and containers of its own, most of the code between the two parts would be repeated. Second, as we'll show in later chapters, trying to build complex functionality with SWT requires a great deal of code, and the process is simplified by incorporating JFace.

Therefore, this book presents SWT and SWT/JFace development side by side. For the sake of being thorough and explaining basic concepts, we show how to implement GUI features in SWT. But when it comes to adding capability to the `WidgetWindow` application, we strongly recommend coding with both libraries. Doing so will not only improve your understanding of SWT and JFace, but also increase your appreciation for combining the two tools.

However, the best way to increase your appreciation is to start building real GUIs with real widgets. Let's see how they work!

Widgets: part 1

To the less enlightened, the term *widget* may suggest a gadget or gizmo—a mechanism that may or may not serve a useful purpose. But in studying SWT and JFace, you need to take widgets very seriously. These are the paints in your palette and the ingredients in your cupboard. Your understanding of the subject will determine how well your applications appear and perform.

The Eclipse designers define a widget as "any UI object that can be placed inside another widget." However, rather than use this recursive definition, we've come up with our own: A widget is "any object in a graphical user interface that displays information and/or allows the user to interface with an application."

We've used the word *object* on purpose, since every widget in an SWT/JFace GUI is the visual representation of an instance of a class. The goal of this chapter is to present many of these classes and show how you can configure their appearance. In particular, this chapter will cover three of the most important widget classes in SWT. We'll start with one of the most common widgets, the Label. Then, we'll add input capability to a label and learn about the Button class. Finally, we'll discuss Composites, which are widgets capable of containing other widgets.

But first, we need to examine the Widget class, which resides at the top of the widget hierarchy, and its most important subclass, Control.

3.1 *Introducing the Widget and Control classes*

Although our widget definition may be helpful from a conceptual standpoint, it's useless for writing programs. Therefore, this section will begin describing the classes behind these concepts. We'll start with the Widget class and its associated methods. Then, we'll focus on the Control class and the many ways its methods make our lives as GUI designers easier.

3.1.1 *Understanding the Widget class*

As the antecedent of all the widgets described in this book, the Widget class is very important when you're learning about SWT and JFace. It's the superclass of all classes that display information and allow user interface in SWT and JFace. However, not only is it an abstract class, but Eclipse.org strongly recommends against creating subclasses due to the complexity involved. Therefore, you won't be inheriting from Widget or using it directly in your code. Instead, this class is important because it unifies all widgets under one structure.

The methods in the `Widget` class represent the basic capabilities inherent in any SWT/JFace widget. Table 3.1 presents an important subset of these methods and their functions.

Table 3.1 Important methods of the `Widget` class and their functions

`Widget` method	Function
setData(String, Object)	Attaches an object to the widget, accessible through `String`
getData()	Returns the objects associated as data within the widget
getData(String)	Returns the data object corresponding to the `String`
getStyle()	Returns an `int` corresponding to the widget's style
getDisplay()	Returns the `Display` object associated with the widget
toString()	Returns a `String` representing the widget class
dispose()	Deallocates the widget and its resources
isDisposed()	Returns a boolean value regarding the widget's deallocation

The `setData()` method allows an application to attach information to a widget in the form of an `Object`. This may be particularly useful if a widget must be shared across different classes and must contain information beyond that normally provided by its class. It may also be helpful if a widget has a global scope and must provide information across procedures that can't directly communicate with each other. This method works by associating a `String` value to the `Object`, which will be deallocated when the widget is disposed of.

The next four methods allow an application to obtain information about the referenced `Widget`. The first, `getData()`, returns all the data associated with the widget through the `setData()` method, whereas the second only returns the `String` value of the data. The next method in the table, `getStyle()`, returns an `int` value that represents the appearance settings for the particular widget object. The fourth method in the table, `getDisplay()`, returns the `Display` object associated with the GUI; the final method, `toString()`, returns a `String` value corresponding to the class of the widget.

These capabilities are important, but GUI designers need much more to configure widgets for practical applications. For this reason, we need to investigate the `Control` class.

3.1.2   *Working with Control objects*

As we mentioned in chapter 2, SWT/JFace uses widgets provided by the operating system to render its graphical applications. Since different platforms offer different sets of GUI components, SWT can fully support only a subset of these widgets. Objects in the `Control` class have a direct counterpart in the operating system that you can access through the class's `handle` field. However, SWT still provides a number of widgets outside the `Control` class. This structure is displayed in figure 3.1.

The majority of the widgets you'll be working with, such as `Labels`, `Buttons`, and `Composites`, are members of the `Control` class. As a result, because of their associated `handles`, you can manipulate and configure these objects using a number of methods unavailable to the general `Widget` class. Although we won't cover all of them here, we'll present two categories of methods that allow you to obtain and specify the characteristics of a given `Control` object (see tables 3.2 and 3.3).

One of the most fundamental properties of a `Control` object is its size. The first method in table 3.2, `getSize()`, returns this value in the form of a `Point`. The next two methods set the widget's size either with the width and height or with a `Point` instance representing these dimensions.

The rest of the methods in the table deal with a `Control`'s *preferred size.* These are the minimum dimensions the `Control` needs in order to display its contents, which may comprise images, text, or other widgets. These coordinates can be obtained through the `computeSize()` method. Then, the program can resize the widget to these dimensions using the `pack()` method. You can also use both of these methods with a boolean argument to tell the layout manager that the widget's properties have changed.

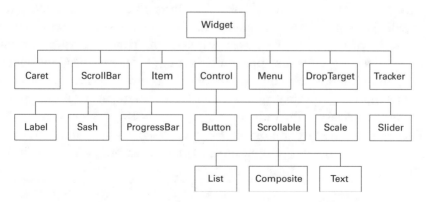

Figure 3.1   The `Widget` class and its primary subclasses

Table 3.2   Methods for acquiring and manipulating a `Control`'s size

`Control` method	Function
`getSize()`	Returns a `Point` object representing the widget's size
`setSize(int, int)`	Sets the widget's size based on the given length and width
`setSize(Point)`	Sets the widget's size according to a `Point` object
`computeSize(int, int)`	Returns the dimensions needed to fully display the widget
`computeSize(int, int, boolean)`	Returns the dimensions needed to fully display the widget, and indicates whether its characteristics have changed
`pack()`	Resizes the widget to its preferred size
`pack(boolean)`	Resizes the widget to its preferred size, and indicates whether its characteristics have changed

NOTE   Due to differences in resolution and platform rendering, we recommend that you use `pack()` instead of `setSize()` whenever possible. Doing so will ensure that your container will tailor its appearance to its contents, whose size may be controlled by the operating system. Also, you should invoke `pack()` only after the widgets have been added to the container.

The `getLocation()` method in table 3.3 returns a `Point` containing the coordinates of the `Control` relative to the widget that surrounds it. These coordinates can be specified with the `setLocation()` method. The next two methods refer to a widget's *bounds*, which incorporate both its size and location. The `getBounds()`

Table 3.3   Methods for setting and determining a `Control`'s location

`Control` method	Function
`getLocation()`	Returns the widget's location relative to its parent
`setLocation(int, int)`	Sets the widget's location relative to its parent
`getBounds()`	Returns the widget's size and location relative to its parent
`setBounds(int, int, int, int)`	Sets the widget's size and location relative to its parent
`toControl(int, int)`	Converts display-relative coordinates to a control-relative `Point`
`toControl(Point)`	Converts a display-relative `Point` to a control-relative `Point`
`toDisplay(int, int)`	Converts display-relative coordinates to a control-relative `Point`
`toDisplay(Point)`	Converts a display-relative `Point` to a control-relative `Point`

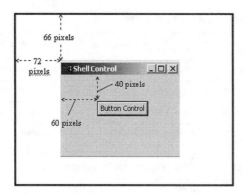

Figure 3.2
Different controls use different points of reference.

method returns the Control's x and y coordinates and its width and height. Similarly, the setBounds() method requires four integers to represent these quantities.

When describing any location, you need a point of reference. For the getLocation() method, this point is the upper-left corner of the widget's container, which is generally its Shell. For a Shell object, the getLocation() method returns its coordinates relative to the user's console, represented by the Display object. This is shown graphically in figure 3.2.

Using the dimensions shown in the figure, shell.getLocation() returns (72, 66), and button.getLocation() returns (60, 40).

Using the last methods in the table, Controls can also obtain their locations relative to the Display object. In this case, the application converts coordinates relative to the Shell, called *control-relative* coordinates, to those relative to the Display, called *display-relative* coordinates. This translation is performed by the toDisplay() method. The reverse process, which converts display-relative coordinates to control-relative coordinates, is performed through the toControl() method.

Although we haven't described all (or even half) of the methods associated with the Control class, we've presented enough to show how you can manipulate these objects in a user interface. Now all you need to know is what concrete Control subclasses you can add to your applications.

3.2 *Labels*

The Label class is the simplest of the Control classes. Labels display static information in a GUI, such as a String or Image, and receive no user input. Because they're used so frequently, you need to become familiar with their properties. This section will describe the styles and methods behind Labels, and how they're used in code.

3.2.1 Styles and separators

Fonts and Images will be fully explained in chapter 7; we'll focus here on the different methods of displaying basic information in Labels. The fundamental parameter in determining how a Label appears is its *style*, an integer value specified during construction. This is similar to the style of the Shell class, described in chapter 2.

The text-related styles of a Label object deal with the String's alignment and are represented by the values SWT.CENTER, SWT.LEFT, and SWT.RIGHT. In addition, you can configure Labels to display only a line—a *separator*—by setting the SWT.SEPARATOR style. These separators can be configured to appear horizontally or vertically (SWT.VERTICAL, SWT.HORIZONTAL) and shadowed or unshadowed (SWT.SHADOW_IN, SWT.SHADOW_OUT, and SWT.SHADOW_NONE).

Figure 3.3 shows how these different styles look inside a simple Shell.

To give you an idea how Labels (both text and separator Labels) are coded in an application, consider the following code:

Figure 3.3
Different separator styles provided by the Label class

```
Label shadow_label = new Label(shell, SWT.CENTER);
shadow_label.setText("SWT.SHADOW_OUT");
shadow_label.setBounds(30,60,110,15);

Label shadow_sep = new Label(shell, SWT.SEPARATOR |
   SWT.SHADOW_OUT);
shadow_sep.setBounds(30,85,110,5);
```

The first label declaration creates a Label object with center-aligned text. The next two methods set the label's display String, size, and location in the Shell. The next declaration uses the SWT.SEPARATOR style to create a separator and combines the SWT.SHADOW_OUT and SWT.HORIZONTAL styles to control its appearance.

The only Label-specific method in the code sample is setText(), which tells the object which String to display. However, there are other methods worth examining when working with Labels.

3.2.2 Label methods

Table 3.4 lists the primary methods for manipulating Label objects in a GUI. As you can see, most are straightforward.

Table 3.4   Methods for acquiring and manipulating a `Control`'s visibility

`Label` method	Function
`getText()`	Returns the `String` associated with the `Label`
`setText(String)`	Associates a `String` object with the `Label` for display
`getAlignment()`	Returns an `int` representing the `Label`'s text alignment
`setAlignment(int)`	Specifies text alignment according to an SWT constant
`getImage()`	Returns the `Image` object associated with the `Label`
`setImage(Image)`	Associates an `Image` object with the `Label`

It's important to remember that an application can set text alignment after constructing the `Label`. Also, when we discuss `Image` objects in a later chapter, the `getImage()` and `setImage()` methods will prove very helpful.

Labels are useful and frequently used in GUIs. But they're boring. They would be much more interesting if users had an opportunity to act. SWT provides this capability by adding an interface aspect to a `Label` and calling the combination a `Button`.

3.3   *Involving the user with buttons*

Outside of the menu, GUI users interface more with buttons than with any other type of component. `Button` objects are also the simplest interface components because they're strictly *binary*; they're either on or off. The `Buttons` presented in this chapter won't be able to react to the user's selection. But once we discuss the SWT/JFace event model in the next chapter, you'll be able to associate these objects with the `Listeners` and `Adapters` needed to react to user action.

Like `Shells` and `Labels`, a `Button`'s appearance in the GUI depends on the style bits used during their creation. Five of the available styles result in `Buttons` that look and act very differently from one another; we present them in the following subsections.

3.3.1   *Causing action with push buttons and SWT.PUSH*

The most common type of `Button` in a GUI is the push button, whose style is specified by the `SWT.PUSH` constant. This is the default style for the `Button` class. As with a `Label` object, a `Button`'s text is specified with the `setText()` method and acquired with the `getText()` method. It's simple to create and configure a push button, as shown in this code sample:

```
Button push = new Button(shell, SWT.PUSH);
push.setText("PUSH");
push.pack();
```

In addition to setting a `Button`'s text, an application can also control the alignment and appearance of the `String` in the `Button`. The `Button`'s constructor can combine any one of the `SWT.LEFT`, `SWT.CENTER`, and `SWT.RIGHT` styles with `SWT.PUSH` using the | operator. After the `Button` is allocated, you can use its `setAlignment()` method. These different alignments are shown in figure 3.4.

Figure 3.4 also shows another style available for any `Button` that appears as a raised surface. This is the `SWT.FLAT` style, which lowers the `Button` to the GUI's plane.

Figure 3.4
Push buttons with SWT.LEFT,
SWT.CENTER, SWT.RIGHT, and
SWT.FLAT styles

3.3.2 *Moving on with arrow buttons and SWT.ARROW*

Sometimes a simple picture is more appropriate than text for describing a `Button`'s purpose. A common picture is the arrow, which tells a user that he can navigate through a document, graphic, or map. An arrow button is simple to create, and you can specify the arrow's direction by combining the `SWT.ARROW` style with any one of the `SWT.UP`, `SWT.DOWN`, `SWT.LEFT`, and `SWT.RIGHT` constants. Here's a short code example:

```
Button push = new Button(shell, SWT.ARROW | SWT.RIGHT);
push.setText("RIGHT");
push.pack();
```

These styles are shown graphically in figure 3.5. Like push buttons, arrow buttons can also appear flat using the `SWT.FLAT` style.

Of course, if you want to customize the picture shown on a `Button` object, the `setImage()` method will attach an `Image` object for display. You'll create and manipulate these images in chapter 7.

Figure 3.5
Left, up, down, and right,
but no rewind or fast-
forward

3.3.3 *Changing state with toggle buttons and SWT.TOGGLE*

Push buttons and arrow buttons are used to perform actions, but sometimes all you need is a component to keep track of a binary state. SWT provides this capability using toggle buttons, which specify the `SWT.TOGGLE` style during allocation. Toggle buttons function similarly to push buttons, but they keep track of the application's state information instead of performing a routine. Also, once clicked, a toggle button remains pressed until selected again (see figure 3.6).

The toggle button is the first component we've discussed that maintains a change in appearance when selected. In this case, an application can set the `Button`'s state using the `set-Selection(boolean)` method, where the boolean value selects the button if `true` and deselects it when `false`. The two other buttons that share this capability are the check button and the radio button, which are described next.

Figure 3.6
Toggle buttons keep track of user preferences instead of performing an action.

3.3.4 *Choosing with check buttons and SWT.CHECK*

Check buttons work similarly to toggle buttons but are generally incorporated into lists. The user can select one or more options by marking check buttons in a collection. Because of their square selection area, these components are generally called *checkboxes*. For easier processing, we recommend using check buttons in an array, as shown in the following code:

```
Button[] checks = new Button[2];

checks[0] = new Button(shell, SWT.CHECK);
checks[0].setText("Choice 1");
checks[0].setLocation(10,5);
checks[0].pack();

checks[1] = new Button(shell, SWT.CHECK);
checks[1].setText("Choice 2");
checks[1].setLocation(10,30);
checks[1].pack();
```

By creating an array, an application can loop through the check button values by invoking the `getSelection()` method on each `Button`. Also, if the program needs to set any of the choices in advance, the `setSelection()` method marks the default options. In figure 3.7, the `setSelection()` method has been used to mark the first and third choices in the `Shell`.

Figure 3.7
Check buttons let the user select zero or more options from a group.

3.3.5 *Making a single choice with radio buttons and SWT.RADIO*

Sometimes a GUI only wants a single selection. In these situations, the open-ended nature of check buttons, which allow the user to pick as many or as few options as desired, is unacceptable. You need a capability similar to buttons on a radio, where selecting one immediately deselects the others. Appropriately, this capability is made possible by using what SWT/JFace calls *radio buttons*, which are created with the SWT.RADIO style.

Collecting radio buttons in arrays

Like check buttons, radio buttons are usually placed in a collection. A common method for manipulating these Button objects involves placing them in arrays; this technique allows the application to cycle through each object to acquire and set its parameters, as shown in the following code:

```
Button[] radios = new Button[3];

radios[0] = new Button(shell, SWT.RADIO);
radios[0].setSelected(true);
radios[0].setText("Choice 1");
radios[0].setLocation(10,5);
radios[0].pack();

radios[1] = new Button(shell, SWT.RADIO);
radios[1].setText("Choice 2");
radios[1].setLocation(10,30);
radios[1].pack();

radios[2] = new Button(shell, SWT.RADIO);
radios[2].setText("Choice 3");
radios[2].setLocation(10,55);
radios[2].pack();

for (int i=0; i<radios.length; i++)
  if (radios[i].getSelected())
    System.out.println(i);
```

Placing this code in a Shell produces the result shown in figure 3.8.

Containing radio buttons with RadioGroupFieldEditors

Many toolsets provide components specifically for collecting and managing groups of radio buttons. SWT/JFace provides a similar capability, but not in the Widget class or even in the org.eclipse. swt.widgets package. The RadioGroupField-Editor() class is hidden in the org.eclipse. jface.preference package; it provides a means of containing radio buttons in a single object.

Figure 3.8
With radio buttons, only one of the available alternatives can be selected.

We'll cover the topic of *preferences* in greater depth later in this book, but we'll provide a brief example here. This code sample creates a `RadioGroupFieldEditor` object and populates it with three radio button labels:

```
RadioGroupFieldEditor rgfe = new RadioGroupFieldEditor(
  "UserChoice", "Choose an option:", 1,
  new String[][] {{"Choice1", "ch1"},
                  {"Choice2", "ch2"},
                  {"Choice3", "ch3"}},
  shell, true);
```

The first argument in the constructor provides a name for the type of value returned by the editor. The second and third arguments specify the group's label and its number of columns. The fourth creates a set of option names with their associated values. In this manner, the `RadioGroupField-Editor` can display a series of radio buttons without allocating `Button` objects. The fifth argument adds the editor to a `Shell` object, which is shown in figure 3.9.

Figure 3.9
With a `RadioGroupField-Editor` **object, you can display a set of radio buttons without creating individual** `Button` **objects.**

The final argument in the `RadioGroupFieldEdi-tor` constructor specifies whether the radio buttons should be incorporated in a `Group` object. This object is categorized as a *container* widget because it collects a set of widgets and displays them in its boundaries. In SWT/JFace, these container widgets are provided by the `Composite` class.

3.4   *Containing components with Composites*

Although container widgets aren't as interesting as their contents, they're necessary in any SWT/JFace application. They make up the background structure of GUIs and provide for modular code, which means multiple `Composite` objects can be combined in a single `Composite`. Throughout this book, the majority of the classes in our code examples extend the `Composite` class.

In this section, we'll examine these container widgets in depth. First, we'll discuss the `Composite` class, its characteristics, and its parameters. Then, we'll describe three of its most prominent `Composite` subclasses: `Groups`, `SashForms`, and `TabFolders`. This last subclass will be particularly important in this book, since it forms the structure behind the `WidgetWindow` application.

3.4.1 *Understanding the Composite class*

We first discussed `Composites` when dealing with the `parent` object in chapter 2's `HelloSWT_JFace` application. There, the `ApplicationWindow` created a single `Composite` to provide its visual aspect. However, `Composite` objects are generally used to organize widgets in both the GUI and the application's code. Like any `Control`, they can be resized and repositioned in an application. `Composites` also have a number of capabilities particular to their class. These are represented by the methods listed in table 3.5.

Table 3.5   Methods provided by the `Composite` class

`Composite` method	Function
`getChildren()`	Returns an array of `Control` objects
`getLayout()`	Returns the layout associated with the `Composite`
`setLayout(Layout)`	Specifies the layout associated with the `Composite`
`getTabList()`	Returns an array of `Control` objects according to their tab order
`setTabList(Control[])`	Specifies the tab order of the widgets within the `Composite`

These methods give applications the ability to manage the widgets contained inside a `Composite`. The first method, `getChildren()`, lists the children of a `Composite` as an array of `Control` objects. The next two methods, `getLayout()` and `setLayout()`, deal with `Layout` objects, which specify how widgets are spatially arranged. (We'll discuss `Layouts` in chapter 6.) The `getTabList()` and `setTabList()` methods acquire and specify the *tab order* of widgets in a `Composite`; this refers to the order in which widgets will be selected if the user repeatedly presses the Tab key.

As shown in figure 3.1, the `Composite` class is a direct subclass of the `Scrollable` class. This means that all `Composite` objects in SWT/JFace can have `ScrollBars` (covered in chapter 5) associated with them. In addition, all `Scrollable` objects can use the methods listed in table 3.6 to access their dimensions and `ScrollBar` objects.

The first two methods deal with an important concern in GUI design. Although `getSize()` can tell you the total area of a `Control`, it can't tell you how much of that area is taken up by title bars, scrollbars, or status bars. This uneditable area of a `Composite` is called its *trim*, whereas the region available for use is its *client area*, which can be accessed using the `Composite`'s `getClientArea()` method. On the

Table 3.6 **Methods provided by the `Scrollable` class (superclass of `Composite`)**

`Composite` **method**	**Function**
`getClientArea()`	Returns the available display area of a `Scrollable` object
`computeTrim(int, int, int, int)`	Returns the necessary dimensions of the `Composite` for the desired client area
`getHorizontalBar()`	Returns the horizontal `ScrollBar` object
`getVerticalBar()`	Returns the vertical `ScrollBar` object

other hand, if you know how much client area your application needs, you can use the `computeTrim()` method to return the size of the `Composite` necessary to meet your specification.

Figure 3.10 graphically shows the relationship between the `Composite` class, the `Scrollable` class, and their many descendants.

3.4.2 *Groups*

Of all the `Composite` subclasses, the `Group` is the easiest to work with. It doesn't perform any action by itself, but it can improve the appearance and organization of an application. Essentially, it functions by drawing a rectangular border around its child widgets with a given label. You can specify this label with the `set-Text()` method.

The `Group`'s border closely resembles the separator (see section 3.2.1), in that it provides the same `SWT.SHADOW_IN`, `SWT.SHADOW_OUT`, and `SWT.SHADOW_NONE` styles.

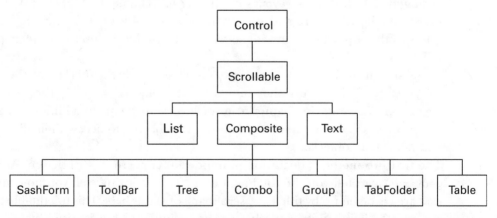

Figure 3.10 **The `Control`, `Scrollable`, and `Composite` classes and their hierarchical structure**

However, you can further customize this shadowing effect with *etching* by choosing the SWT.SHADOW_ETCHED_IN or SWT.SHADOW_ETCHED_OUT style.

Like many of the Widget subclasses, the Group class can't be extended. Therefore, our Ch3_Group, shown in listing 3.1, subclasses the Composite class and creates a Group object in it. This class will be integrated into the WidgetWindow application at the end of the chapter, so we recommend that you create a package named com.swtjface.Ch3 and insert Ch3_Group.

Listing 3.1 Ch3_Group.java

```
package com.swtjface.Ch3;
import org.eclipse.swt.*;
import org.eclipse.swt.widgets.*;

public class Ch3_Group extends Composite
{
  public Ch3_Group(Composite parent)
  {
    super(parent, SWT.NONE);

    Group group = new Group(this, SWT.SHADOW_ETCHED_IN);
    group.setText("Group Label");

    Label label = new Label(group, SWT.NONE);
    label.setText("Two buttons:");
    label.setLocation(20,20);
    label.pack();

    Button button1 = new Button(group, SWT.PUSH);
    button1.setText("Push button");
    button1.setLocation(20,45);
    button1.pack();

    Button button2 = new Button(group, SWT.CHECK);
    button2.setText("Check button");
    button2.setBounds(20,75,90,30);

    group.pack();
  }
}
```

This straightforward code creates the straightforward container displayed in figure 3.11.

The Ch3_Group class can't be directly executed: It needs an application to invoke its constructor method and add its object to a Shell or ApplicationWindow. Since most of the example code in this book is structured in Composite classes, you need to create a short application specifically for viewing Composite objects.

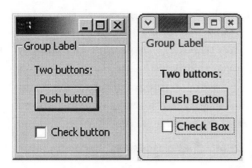

Figure 3.11
Group objects organize child widgets in a labeled border.

This application, called CompViewer, is presented in listing 3.2. This class creates an instance of Ch3_Group, adds it to the window's parent Composite, and displays it in the ApplicationWindow.

Listing 3.2   CompViewer.java

```java
package com.swtjface.Ch3;
import org.eclipse.jface.window.*;
import org.eclipse.swt.widgets.*;

public class CompViewer extends ApplicationWindow
{
  public CompViewer()
  {
    super(null);
  }

  protected Control createContents(Composite parent)
  {
    Ch3_Group cc1 = new Ch3_Group(parent);
    return parent;
  }

  public static void main(String[] args)
  {
    CompViewer cv = new CompViewer();
    cv.setBlockOnOpen(true);
    cv.open();
    Display.getCurrent().dispose();
  }
}
```

The Group class performs the main functions of a Composite object, but other containers provide additional capability. This can be seen with the SashForm, which allows users to manipulate the sizes of the Composite's children.

3.4.3 *SashForms*

Although the Group container is suitable for static displays, sometimes applications need controls that can be dynamically resized. Such GUIs may present multiple panels in a limited space, making it necessary for the user to expand one and reduce others. The SashForm provides this capability by creating a moveable barrier between child widgets. This barrier, called a Sash, allows the user to increase the size of one widget while reducing the size of the other widgets in the Composite. The Sash class is located in the org.eclipse.swt.widgets package with the majority of your widgets, but the SashForm class can be found in the org.eclipse.swt.custom package.

The styles and methods associated with the SashForm are mainly concerned with the position of the Sash and the degree of expansion and reduction of the form's child widgets. You can specify the Sash's orientation using the SWT.HORIZONTAL or SWT.VERTICAL constant, or by incorporating one of these constants in the setOrientation() method. The SashForm class provides a method called getMaximizedControl(), which returns the Control object that has been expanded the most. Similarly, the getWeights() method returns an int array containing the weight of each of the SashForm's children. The setWeights() method uses an int array to specify weights for each of the widgets in the Composite.

Listing 3.3 presents the second Composite example in this chapter: Ch3_SashForm. This class shows the capability of the SashForm by creating two arrow buttons separated by a Sash.

Listing 3.3 Ch3_SashForm.java

```java
package com.swtjface.Ch3;
import org.eclipse.swt.*;
import org.eclipse.swt.custom.SashForm;
import org.eclipse.swt.widgets.*;

public class Ch3_SashForm extends Composite
{
  public Ch3_SashForm(Composite parent)
  {
    super(parent, SWT.NONE);

    SashForm sf = new SashForm(this, SWT.VERTICAL);
    sf.setSize(120,80);
```

```
        Button button1 = new Button(sf, SWT.ARROW | SWT.UP);
        button1.setSize(120,40);

        Button button2 = new Button(sf, SWT.ARROW | SWT.DOWN);
        Button2.setBounds(0,40,120,40);
    }
}
```

When this `Composite` is instantiated in an application such as `CompViewer`, you get the result shown in figure 3.12. This figure also displays how the GUI reacts when the user raises and lowers the `Sash` object.

Figure 3.12
`SashForms` **allow the user to specify the relative sizes of the** `Composite`'s **children.**

`SashForms` give you a certain amount of control over the GUI, but you may want to do more than just expand or reduce child widgets. For example, if there are too many GUI elements to fit in a given display, then you need a `Composite` to arrange them into logical groups. This functionality is provided by the last `Composite` we'll present in this chapter, the `TabFolder`.

3.4.4 *TabFolders*

The `TabFolder` class extends the capability of `Composites` to incorporate multiple `Composite` objects in a single container. Instances of this class hold other containers in a structure resembling a filing cabinet, each accessible through a tabbed index.

The process of creating and populating a `TabFolder` is simple. After creating the main instance, the application constructs a `TabItem` object for each page in the `TabFolder`, also called a *tab*. Then, it invokes the `setText()` method with a `String` argument that will serve as the tab's label. Finally, using the `setControl()` method, the application associates a `Control` that will be displayed when its tab is selected.

A brief example of this configuration is shown here. Although the `TabFolder`'s constructor takes an `int` argument, there are no styles particular to this class:

```
TabFolder folder = new TabFolder(parent, SWT.NONE);
TabItem item1 = new TabItem(folder, SWT.NONE);
item1.setText("Tab Label");
item1.setControl(new SashForm(folder));
```

In addition to the methods used to configure the tabs, the `TabFolder` class provides methods to acquire information about its `TabItems`:

- `getItemCount()`—Returns the number of `TabItems` in the `TabFolder`
- `getItems()`—Returns an array of the `TabItem` objects
- `getSelection()`—Determines which `TabItem` the user has picked
- `setSelection()`—Makes this decision from within the application

Because of this function and the modular manner in which new `Composites` can be added, we decided to base the `WidgetWindow` application on a `TabFolder` object. Therefore, rather than present a short `TabFolder` example here, we'll proceed to add this class to this book's main application.

3.5 Updating WidgetWindow

From this point on, each chapter will contain a section devoted to adding graphical components to the `WidgetWindow` GUI created in chapter 2. We'll now update this application by performing two tasks. First, we'll add the two `Composites` from this chapter (`Ch3_Group` and `Ch3_SashForm`) into a final container, `Ch3_Composite`. Then, we'll create a `TabFolder` object in the `WidgetWindow` and create its first `TabItem`.

3.5.1 Creating the Ch3_Composite class

Now that you're familiar with programming with `Composites`, integrating two containers in a larger object will be simple. Listing 3.4 creates the `Ch3_Composite` class for this purpose.

Listing 3.4   Ch3_Composite.java

```
package com.swtjface.Ch3;
import org.eclipse.swt.*;
import org.eclipse.swt.widgets.*;

public class Ch3_Composite extends Composite
{
  public Ch3_Composite(Composite parent)
  {
    super(parent, SWT.NONE);
    parent.getShell().setText("Chapter 3 Composite");

    Ch3_Group cc1 = new Ch3_Group(this);
    cc1.setLocation(0,0);
    cc1.pack();
```

```
        Ch3_SashForm cc2 = new Ch3_SashForm(this);
        cc2.setLocation(125,25);
        cc2.pack();

        pack();
    }
}
```

As shown, adding `Composites` to a `Composite` is as simple as adding a normal `Control`. Each container maintains its features and functions. To see the result, let's add an instance of this class to the `WidgetWindow` application.

3.5.2 Creating the WidgetWindow TabFolder

As you've seen, working with `TabFolders` is a straightforward process. You need to perform two steps to add the `Ch3_Composite` class to `WidgetWindow`: import the `com.swtjface.Ch3` package and then create a `TabFolder` with a `TabItem` representing the `Ch3_Composite` class. This can be accomplished by updating the `WidgetWindow` program in `com.swtjface.Ch2` with the code shown in bold in listing 3.5.

Listing 3.5 WidgetWindow.java

```java
package com.swtjface.Ch2;
import org.eclipse.swt.*;
import org.eclipse.swt.widgets.*;
import org.eclipse.jface.window.*;

import com.swtjface.Ch3.*;

public class WidgetWindow extends ApplicationWindow
{
    public WidgetWindow()
    {
        super(null);
    }

    protected Control createContents(Composite parent)
    {
        TabFolder tf = new TabFolder(parent, SWT.NONE);

        TabItem chap3 = new TabItem(tf,SWT.NONE);
        chap3.setText("Chapter 3");
        chap3.setControl(new Ch3_Composite(tf));

        getShell().setText("Widget Window");
        return parent;
    }

    public static void main(String[] args)
    {
```

```
        WidgetWindow wwin = new WidgetWindow();
        wwin.setBlockOnOpen(true);
        wwin.open();
        Display.getCurrent().dispose();
    }
}
```

When you execute `WidgetWindow`, the result should appear similar to figure 3.13.

Although this simple application may not seem exciting yet, you have our word that `WidgetWindow` will grow more interesting and more complex with each chapter.

Figure 3.13
The updated `WidgetWindow` application

3.6 *Summary*

This chapter has delved deeply into the `Widget` class and its many subclasses and methods. In addition to describing individual components, we have clarified the class structure behind SWT/JFace widgets. This is important since a component's place in the hierarchy will determine what methods are available for use.

This has been a relatively simple chapter, focusing on the `Label` widget, the `Button` widget, and a small set of `Composite` subclasses. In each case, we've shown you the styles and methods available and used them in code samples. But along with being straightforward, these classes are necessary for any serious GUI programmer. Later chapters of this book will assume that you understand this material thoroughly.

The main drawback of this chapter is that its GUIs are so static. All the buttons change with user selection, but the application doesn't do anything. The `Controls` in this chapter may as well be images for all they accomplish. Similarly, a `Tab-Folder` with only one tab might as well be a plain `Composite`.

What we need are *events*: We need to make these applications active instead of passive. The theory behind this topic can become complex, but the capability it provides is well worth the effort. Without further ado, let's learn about the SWT/JFace event model.

Working with events

4

This chapter covers

- Event processing with SWT
- Typed and untyped listeners
- Mouse and keyboard events
- Event processing with JFace
- Actions and contributions

Without events, the widgets and containers we've looked at are only good for decoration. This chapter focuses on how to configure these components to understand and respond to user actions. In particular, it describes the SWT/JFace framework that acquires these actions and translates them into software constructs called *events*. The process of using a toolset to generate, receive, and respond to these events is the toolset's *event model*. Many books on GUIs leave the event model until later chapters, but we feel the subject's importance demands an early introduction.

The first part of this chapter describes the SWT data structures that enable applications to process events. These include the event classes, which are created when a user carries out actions, and the *listener* interfaces, which receive event objects. By combining these appropriately, an application can provide multiple responses to nearly every form of event that can occur. However, SWT's powerful event-processing mechanisms can make coding more complicated than it needs to be. For this reason, we need to examine how JFace simplifies the process.

This chapter's second part deals with using both SWT and JFace to interface with the user. The JFace library replaces events and listeners with *actions* and *contributions*, which perform the same function as their SWT counterparts but in very different ways. These new classes simplify the process of event programming by separating the event-processing methods from the GUI's appearance. Also, actions and contributions are meant for performing window-oriented interfacing, and this narrowed scope reduces the developer's programming burden.

4.1 Event processing in SWT

The SWT event-processing cycle is depicted in figure 4.1. It begins with the operating system's event queue, which records and lists actions taken by the user. Once an SWT application begins running, its `Display` class sorts through this queue using its `readAndDispatch()` method and `msg` field, which acts as a handle to the underlying OS message queue. If it finds anything relevant, it sends the event to its top-level `Shell` object, which determines which widget should receive the event. The `Shell` then sends the event to the widget that the user acted on, which transfers this information to an associated interface called a *listener*. One of the listener's methods performs the necessary processing or invokes another method to handle the user's action, called an *event handler*.

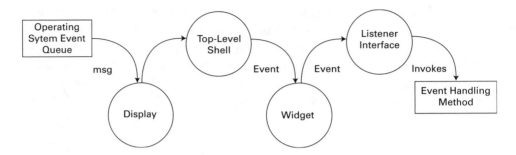

Figure 4.1   Acquiring events from the operating system and processing them in an SWT application

When making a widget responsive to events, the main tasks of the GUI designer are determining which events need to be acted on, creating and associating listeners to sense these events, and then building event handlers to perform the necessary processing. This section will show how to accomplish these tasks using the SWT data structures contained in the `org.eclipse.swt.events` package.

4.1.1   *Using typed listeners and events*

Most of the listener interfaces in SWT only react to a particular set of user actions. They're called *typed listeners* for this reason, and they inherit from the `TypedListener` class. Similarly, the events corresponding to these specific actions are *typed events*, which subclass the `TypedEvent` class. For example, a mouse click or double-click is represented by a `MouseEvent`, which is sent to an appropriate `MouseListener` for processing. Keyboard actions performed by the user are translated into `KeyEvents`, which are picked up by `KeyListeners`. A full list of these typed events and listeners is shown in table 4.1.

In order to function, these listeners must be associated with components of the GUI. For example, a `TreeListener` will only receive `TreeEvents` if it's associated with a `Tree` object. But not every GUI component can use each listener. For example, as shown in the GUI component column of the table, a `Control` component broadcasts many more types of events than a `Tracker` object. There are also listeners, such as `MenuListeners` and `TreeListeners`, that can only be attached to very specific widgets. This attachment is performed by invoking the component's `add...Listener()` method with the typed listener as the argument.

Table 4.1 SWT Event classes and their associated listeners

Event	Listener	Listener methods	GUI component
ArmEvent	ArmListener	widgetArmed()	MenuItem
ControlEvent	ControlListener	controlMoved() controlResized()	Control, TableColumn, Tracker
DisposeEvent	DisposeListener	widgetDisposed()	Widget
FocusEvent	FocusListener	focusGained() focusLost()	Control
HelpEvent	HelpListener	helpRequested()	Control, Menu, MenuItem
KeyEvent	KeyListener	keyPressed() keyReleased()	Control
MenuEvent	MenuListener	menuHidden() menuShown()	Menu
ModifyEvent	ModifyListener	modifyText()	CCombo, Combo, Text, StyledText
MouseEvent	MouseListener	mouseDoubleClick() mouseDown() mouseUp()	Control
MouseMoveEvent	MouseMoveListener	mouseMove()	Control
MouseTrackEvent	MouseTrackListener	mouseEnter() mouseExit() mouseHover()	Control
PaintEvent	PaintListener	paintControl()	Control
SelectionEvent	SelectionListener	widgetDefaultSelected() widgetSelected()	Button, CCombo, Combo, CoolItem, CTabFolder, List, MenuItem, Sash, Scale, ScrollBar, Slider, StyledText, TabFolder, Table, TableCursor, TableColumn, TableTree, Text, ToolItem, Tree
ShellEvent	ShellListener	shellActivated() shellClosed() shellDeactivated() shellDeiconified() shellIconified()	Shell

continued on next page

Table 4.1 SWT Event classes and their associated listeners *(continued)*

Event	Listener	Listener methods	GUI component
TraverseEvent	TraverseListener	keyTraversed()	Control
TreeEvent	TreeListener	treeCollapsed() treeExpanded()	Tree, TableTree
VerifyEvent	VerifyListener	verifyText()	Text, StyledText

Understanding Event classes

The Event column in table 4.1 lists the subclasses of TypedEvent that the Display and Shell objects send to typed listeners. Although programmers generally don't manipulate these classes directly, the classes contain member fields that provide information regarding the event's occurrence. This information can be used in event handlers to obtain information about the environment. These fields, inherited from the TypedEvent and EventObject classes, are shown in table 4.2.

Table 4.2 Data fields common to all typed events

TypedEvent field	Function
data	Information for use in the Event handler
display	The display in which the Event fired
source	The component that triggered the Event
time	The time that the Event occurred
widget	The widget that fired the Event

In addition to these, many event classes have other fields that provide more information about the user's action. For example, the MouseEvent class also includes a button field, which tells which mouse button was pressed, and x and y, which specify the widget-relative coordinates of the mouse action. The ShellEvent class contains a boolean field called doit, which lets you specify whether a given action will result in its intended effect. Finally, the PaintEvent class provides additional methods that we'll discuss in chapter 7.

Programming with listeners

There are two main methods of incorporating listeners in code. The first creates an anonymous interface in the component's add...Listener() method, which narrows the scope of the listener to the component only. This method is shown in the following code snippet:

```
Button button = new Button(shell, SWT.PUSH | SWT.CENTER);
button.addMouseListener(new MouseListener()
{
  public void mouseDown(MouseEvent e)
  {
    clkdwnEventHandler();
  }
  public void mouseUp(MouseEvent e)
  {
    clkupEventHandler();
  }
  public void mouseDoubleClick(MouseEvent e)
  {
    dblclkEventHandler();
  }
});
static void dblclkEventHandler()
{
  System.out.println("Double click.");
}
static void clkdwnEventHandler()
{
  System.out.println("Click - down.");
}
static void clkupEventHandler()
{
  System.out.println("Click - up.");
}
```

In the first line, a `Button` widget is created and added to the application's `Shell`. Then, the `addMouseListener()` method creates an anonymous `MouseListener` interface and associates it with the button. This interface contains three methods—`mouseDown()`, `mouseUp()`, and `mouseDoubleClick()`—which must be implemented in any instance of a `MouseListener`. If the user presses the mouse button, releases the button, or double-clicks, a `MouseEvent` is sent to one of these methods, which invokes the appropriate event-handling method. These event handlers complete the event processing by sending a message to the console. Although the event-handling routines are simple in this example, they generally demand more effort than any other aspect of event processing.

An anonymous interface can be helpful if you need to access objects (declared with the `final` keyword) in the outer class. However, the listener can't be associated with other components. You can solve this problem by declaring a separate interface that inherits from MouseListener. An example is shown here:

```
Button button = new Button(shell, SWT.PUSH | SWT.CENTER);
button.addMouseListener(ExampleMouseListener);

MouseListener ExampleMouseListener = new MouseListener()
{
  public void mouseDoubleClick(MouseEvent e)
  {
    System.out.println("Double click.");
  }

  public void mouseDown(MouseEvent e)
  {
    System.out.println("Click - down.");
  }

  public void mouseUp(MouseEvent e)
  {
    System.out.println("Click - up.");
  }
};
```

The previous code samples declare all three of the MouseListener's member methods. But what if you're only concerned with the double-click event, and you only want to work with the mouseDoubleClick() method? If you use the MouseListener interface, you have to declare all of its methods, just as in any interface. However, you can eliminate this unnecessary code by using special classes called *adapters*.

4.1.2 Adapters

Adapters are abstract classes that implement Listener interfaces and provide default implementations for each of their required methods. This means that when you associate a widget with an adapter instead of a listener, you only need to write code for the method(s) you're interested in. Although this may seem like a minor convenience, it can save you a great deal of programming time when you're working with complex GUIs.

> **NOTE** The *adapters* mentioned in this section are very different from the *model-based adapters* provided by the JFace library, first mentioned in chapter 2. Here, adapters reduce the amount of code necessary to create listener interfaces. Although model-based adapters can simplify event processing, as you'll see in section 4.2, they also help with many other aspects of GUI programming.

Adapters are only available for events whose listeners have more than one member method. The full list of these classes is shown in table 4.3, along with their associated Listener classes.

Table 4.3 SWT adapter classes and their corresponding listener interfaces

Adapter	Listener
ControlAdapter	ControlListener
FocusAdapter	FocusListener
KeyAdapter	KeyListener
MenuAdapter	MenuListener
MouseAdapter	MouseListener
MouseTrackAdapter	MouseTrackListener
SelectionAdapter	SelectionListener
ShellAdapter	ShellListener
TreeAdapter	TreeListener

Adapter objects are easy to code and are created with the same add...Listener() methods. Two examples are shown here:

```
button.addMouseListener(new MouseAdapter()
{
  public void mouseDoubleClick(MouseEvent e)
  {
    dblclkEventHandler();
  }
)};
static void dblclkEventHandler()
{
  System.out.println("Double click.");
}
```

As shown, using the MouseAdapter class allows you to disregard the other methods associated with the MouseListener interface and concentrate on handling the double-click event. Similar to listener interfaces, adapters can be coded as anonymous classes or local classes.

4.1.3 Keyboard events

Although most of the events in table 4.1 are straightforward to understand and use, the keyboard event classes require further explanation. Specifically, these events include the KeyEvent class, which is created any time a key is pressed, and its two subclasses, TraverseEvent and VerifyEvent. A TraverseEvent results when the user presses an arrow key or the Tab key in order to focus on the next widget. A VerifyEvent fires when the user enters text that the program needs to check before taking further action.

In addition to the fields inherited from the TypedEvent and EventObject classes, the KeyEvent class has three member fields that provide information concerning the key that triggered the event:

- *character*—Provides a char value representing the pressed key.

- *stateMask*—Returns an integer representing the state of the keyboard modifier keys. By examining this integer, a program can determine whether any of the Alt, Ctrl, Shift, and Command keys are currently pressed.

- *keyCode*—Provides the SWT public constant corresponding to the typed key, called the *key code*. These public constants are presented in table 4.4.

The following code snippet shows how to use a KeyListener to receive and process a KeyEvent. It also uses the fields (character, stateMask, and keyCode) to acquire information about the pressed key:

```
Button button = new Button(shell, SWT.CENTER);
button.addKeyListener(new KeyAdapter()
{
  public void keyPressed(KeyEvent e)
  {
    String string = "";
    if ((e.stateMask & SWT.ALT) != 0) string += "ALT-";
    if ((e.stateMask & SWT.CTRL) != 0) string += "CTRL-";
    if ((e.stateMask & SWT.COMMAND) != 0) string += "COMMAND-";
    if ((e.stateMask & SWT.SHIFT) != 0) string += "SHIFT-";
    switch (e.keyCode)
    {
      case SWT.BS:  string += "BACKSPACE"; break;
      case SWT.CR:  string += "CARRIAGE RETURN"; break;
      case SWT.DEL: string += "DELETE"; break;
      case SWT.ESC: string += "ESCAPE"; break;
      case SWT.LF:  string += "LINE FEED"; break;
      case SWT.TAB: string += "TAB"; break;
      default:      string += e.character; break;
    }
    System.out.println (string);
  }
});
```

Table 4.4 Keyboard entries and their SWT code constants

Key	Key code
Alt	SWT.ALT
Arrow (down)	SWT.ARROW_DOWN
Arrow (left)	SWT.ARROW_LEFT
Arrow (right)	SWT.ARROW_RIGHT
Arrow (up)	SWT.ARROW_UP
Backspace	SWT.BS
Mouse button 1	SWT.BUTTON1
Mouse button 2	SWT.BUTTON2
Mouse button 3	SWT.BUTTON3
Carriage return	SWT.CR
Ctrl	SWT.CTRL
End	SWT.END
Esc	SWT.ESC
F1–F12	SWT.F1-SWT.F12
Home	SWT.HOME
Insert	SWT.INSERT
Line feed	SWT.LF
Mod1–Mod4	SWT.MOD1-SWT.MOD4
Page Down	SWT.PAGE_DOWN
Page Up	SWT.PAGE_UP
Shift	SWT.SHIFT
Tab	SWT.TAB

This code uses the KeyEvent fields and the public constants to create a String that displays the name of the pressed key and any associated modifier keys. The first step in the event handler's operation involves checking the event's stateMask field to see whether the Alt, Ctrl, Shift, and Command keys are pressed. If so, the name of the modifier key is added to the String. The method continues by checking whether the event's keyCode corresponds to an alphanumeric character or one of the support keys. In either case, the name of the key is appended to the `String`, which is sent to the console.

The `TraverseEvent` fires when the user presses a key to progress from one component to another, such as in a group of buttons or checkboxes. The two fields contained in this class let you control whether the traversal action will change the focus to another control, or whether the focus will remain on the widget that fired the event. The simplest field, `doit`, is a boolean value that allows (`TRUE`) or disallows (`FALSE`) traversal for the given widget. The second field of the `TraverseEvent` class, `detail`, is more complicated. It's an integer that represents the identity of the key that caused the event. For example, if the user presses the Tab key to switch to a new component, the `detail` field will contain the SWT constant `TRAVERSE_TAB_NEXT`.

Each type of control has a different default behavior for a given traversal key. For example, a `TraverseEvent` that results from a `TRAVERSE_TAB_NEXT` action will, by default, cause a traversal if the component is a radio button, but not if it's a `Canvas` object. Therefore, by setting the `doit` field to `TRUE`, you override the default setting and allow the user to traverse. Setting the field to `FALSE` keeps the focus on the component.

The use of the `VerifyEvent` is similar to that of the `TraverseEvent`. The goal is to determine beforehand whether the user's action should result in the usual or default behavior. In this case, you can check the user's text to determine whether it should be updated or deleted in the application. Two of the class fields, `start` and `end`, specify the range of the input, and the `text` field contains the input `String` under examination. Having looked at the user's text, you set the boolean `doit` field to allow (`TRUE`) or disallow (`FALSE`) the action.

4.1.4 *Customizing event processing with untyped events*

Typed events and listeners enable event processing with classes and interfaces expressly suited to their tasks. Further, typed listeners provide specific methods to receive and handle these events. By narrowing the scope of listeners and events to handle only particular actions, the use of typed components reduces the possibility of committing coding errors.

However, if you prefer coding flexibility over safety, SWT provides untyped events and listeners. When an untyped listener, represented by the `Listener` class, is associated with a GUI component, it receives every class of event that the component is capable of sending. Therefore, you have to manipulate the catch-all event, represented by the `Event` class, to determine which action the user performed. The proper event-handling method can then be invoked.

It's important to note that Eclipse.org recommends against using untyped events and listeners. In fact, it mentions that they are "not intended to be used by applications." These mechanisms also aren't included with their typed counterparts in the org.eclipse.swt.events package. Instead, both the untyped Listener interface and the Event class are located in the org.eclipse.swt.widgets package.

Despite this, the SWT code snippets provided by the Eclipse website use untyped listeners and events exclusively. This makes coding convenient, since you can create a customized listener that reacts to a specified set of events. An example is shown here:

```
Listener listener = new Listener ()
{
  public void handleEvent (Event event)
  {
    switch (event.type)
    {
      case SWT.KeyDown:
        if (event.character == 'b')
          System.out.println("Key"+event.character);
        break;
      case SWT.MouseDown:
        if (event.button == 3)
          System.out.println("Right click");
      break;
      case SWT.MouseDoubleClick:
        System.out.println("Double click");
      break;
    }
  }
};
Button button = new Button(shell, SWT.CENTER);
button.addListener(SWT.KeyDown, listener);
button.addListener(SWT.MouseDown, listener);
button.addListener(SWT.MouseDoubleClick, listener);
```

In this code, the Listener object sends any Event instance to its single method, handleEvent(). Then, the Event's type field determines what processing needs to be done. If the event has type SWT.Keydown and the character is the letter *b*, then a statement is sent to the console. If the type is SWT.MouseDown and the third mouse button was pressed (that is, the user right-clicked), then the statement *Right click* is shown. If an SWT.MouseDoubleClick event fires, then *Double click* is displayed.

You can obtain this capability using typed listeners and events, but the process is more involved. The button needs to add both a MouseListener and KeyListener, with corresponding adapters. Then, you need to place the event-handling routines in the appropriate listener method. Clearly, untyped event processing is not only more convenient in this case, but also reduces the number of classes necessary to handle the event.

In order to take the place of typed events, the Event class contains all the fields in each typed event. It has the same character field as a KeyEvent and the same button field as a MouseEvent. As shown in the previous code, it also has a field called type, which refers to the nature of the event. A listing of these types is presented in table 4.5.

Table 4.5 SWT type values for the Event class

Values for type field			
SWT.Activate	SWT.FocusIn	SWT.KeyUp	SWT.Move
SWT.Arm	SWT.FocusOut	SWT.MenuDetect	SWT.None
SWT.Close	SWT.Expand	SWT.Modify	SWT.Paint
SWT.Collapse	SWT.HardKeyDown	SWT.MouseDoubleClick	SWT.Resize
SWT.Deactivate	SWT.HardKeyUp	SWT.MouseEnter	SWT.Selection
SWT.DefaultSelection	SWT.Help	SWT.MouseExit	SWT.Show
SWT.Deiconify	SWT.Hide	SWT.MouseHover	SWT.Traverse
SWT.Dispose	SWT.Iconify	SWT.MouseMove	SWT.Verify
SWT.DragDetect	SWT.KeyDown	SWT.MouseUp	

4.1.5 *An SWT listener/event application*

Before we discuss the JFace event model, we'll present an SWT Composite that integrates and summarizes the material covered. This class, shown in listing 4.1, contains two buttons, a label, and the necessary event processing. We recommend creating a com.swtjface.Ch4 package to your project and adding this class to it.

Listing 4.1 Ch4_MouseKey.java

```
package com.swtjface.Ch4;
import org.eclipse.swt.events.*;
import org.eclipse.swt.widgets.*;
import org.eclipse.swt.*;

public class Ch4_MouseKey extends Composite
{
  Label output;

  Ch4_MouseKey(Composite parent)
  {
    super(parent, SWT.NULL);
```

```
Button typed = new Button(this, SWT.PUSH);
typed.setText("Typed");
typed.setLocation(2,10);
typed.pack();

typed.addKeyListener(new KeyAdapter()
{
  public void keyPressed(KeyEvent e)
  {
    keyHandler();
  }
});

Button untyped = new Button(this, SWT.PUSH);
untyped.setText("Untyped");
untyped.setLocation(80,10);
untyped.pack();
untyped.addListener(SWT.MouseEnter, UntypedListener);
untyped.addListener(SWT.MouseExit, UntypedListener);

output = new Label(this, SWT.SHADOW_OUT);
output.setBounds(40,70,90,40);
output.setText("No Event");

pack();
}

Listener UntypedListener = new Listener()
{
  public void handleEvent(Event event)
  {
    switch (event.type)
    {
      case SWT.MouseEnter:
        output.setText("Mouse Enter");
        break;
      case SWT.MouseExit:
        output.setText("Mouse Exit");
        break;
    }
  }
};

void keyHandler()
{
  output.setText("Key Event");
}
}
```

The first button is associated with an anonymous typed listener that receives keyboard events when selected. An untypedListener interface is added to the second

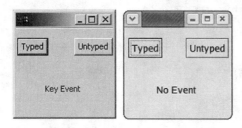

Figure 4.2
The Ch4_MouseKey Composite.
This example combines many types of
SWT classes and interfaces used for
event handling.

button, which catches events that occur when the mouse pointer enters and exits the button. Whenever either button fires an event, a String is sent to the label.

By integrating this Composite in the CompViewer application from the previous chapter, the displayed Shell should resemble figure 4.2.

The SWT structure of this code allows a widget to receive many types of events and provides for many different responses. But in the majority of GUIs, this isn't necessary. In these cases, SWT's broad capabilities only increase the complexity of coding event processing. Those willing to trade power for simplicity will find the JFace event model very helpful.

4.2 *Event processing in JFace*

A listener interface can provide the same event handling for different controls, but its usage depends on the component that launched the event. Listeners that receive MouseEvents can't be used for menu bar selections. Even untyped Events are only useful after the program determines which type of control triggered the event.

But when you're dealing with complex user interfaces, it's helpful to separate the event-handling capability from the GUI components that generated the event. This allows one group to work on a GUI's event handling independently from the group designing its appearance. Also, if a listener's capability can be attached to any component, then its code can be reused more often. Finally, if one section of a program deals strictly with the GUI's view and another is concerned only with event processing, then the code is easier to develop and understand.

JFace provides this separation with its Action and ActionContributionItem classes. Put simply, an ActionContributionItem combines the function of a GUI widget and its attached listener class. Whenever the user interfaces with it, it triggers its associated Action class, which takes care of handling the event. Although this may seem similar to SWT's listener/event model, these classes are more abstract, simpler to use, and narrower in scope.

Because these classes are more abstract than their SWT counterparts, it may take time to appreciate their merits. However, once you understand them, we feel certain that you'll use them regularly when handling repetitive event processing. This can be best proven through coding examples. But first, a technical introduction is in order.

4.2.1 *Understanding actions and contributions*

Although it's interesting to know that you can handle TraverseEvents and ArmEvents if they occur, few applications use them. Also, it may be fascinating to attach multiple listeners and event handlers to a widget, but GUI components usually perform only a single function in response to a single input type. Because SWT's structure provides for every conceivable component and combination of events, even the simplest listener/event code requires complexity.

It would make event programming easier if a toolset concentrated on only those few widgets and events that are used most often and made their usage as simple as possible. JFace's event-processing structure does exactly this: Its goal is to make event processing more straightforward, allowing programmers to receive and use common events with fewer lines of code. In reaching this goal, JFace makes three assumptions:

- The user's actions will involve buttons, toolbars, and menus.
- Each component will have only one associated event.
- Each event will have only one event handler.

By taking these assumptions into account, JFace simplifies event processing considerably. The first assumption means that contributions only need to take one of three forms. The second assumption provides the separation of contributions from their associated actions; that is, if each contributing component triggers only one event, then it doesn't matter what action is triggered or which component fired the event. The third assumption means that each action needs only one event-handling routine. This simplified event model for SWT/JFace is shown in figure 4.3.

Like the SWT event model, the interface process begins with the Display class keeping track of the operating system's event queue. This time, though, it passes information to the ApplicationWindow, which contains the Display's Shell object. The ApplicationWindow creates an Actionb class and sends it to the contribution that generated the original event. The contribution then invokes the run() method of the Action class as the single event handler.

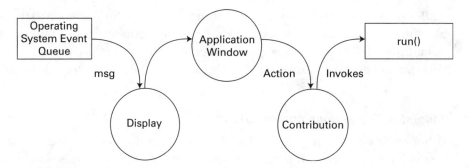

Figure 4.3   By combining listeners and widgets into contributions, this event model is much easier to code.

The `Action` class behaves similarly to SWT's `Event` class, but the contribution capability is more complicated. The two main contribution classes are the `Contribution-` `tionItem` class and the `ContributionManager` class. The `ContributionItem` class provides individual GUI components that trigger actions, and the `Contribution-` `Manager` class produces objects capable of containing `ContributionItem`s. Because these are both abstract classes, event handling is performed with their subclasses. Figure 4.4 shows these inheritance relationships.

Although the `ActionContributionItem` class is one of many concrete subclasses of `ContributionItem`, it's the most important. This class is created and implemented in an `ApplicationWindow` to connect an action to the GUI. It has no set appearance, but instead takes the form of a button, menu bar item, or toolbar item, depending on your use of the `fill()` method.

The second way to incorporate contributions in an application involves the use of a `ContributionManager` subclass. These subclasses serve as containers for

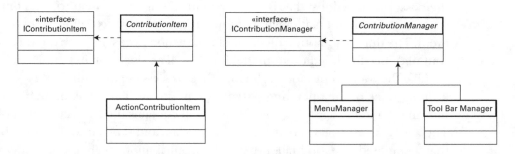

Figure 4.4   The classes and interfaces that provide contribution capability in the SWT/JFace model

ContributionItems, combining them to improve GUI organization and simplify programming. The MenuManager class combines ContributionItems in a window's top-level menu, and the ToolBarManager class places these objects in a toolbar located just under the menu.

4.2.2 Creating Action classes

Listing 4.2 creates a subclass of the abstract Action class called Ch4_StatusAction. This class functions by sending a String to an ApplicationWindow's status line whenever it triggers. We recommend that you add this class to your project directory.

Because this class will be implemented in a toolbar, it needs an associated image. The simplest way to do this is to enter the $ECLIPSE_HOME/plugins/ org.eclipse.platform_x.y.z directory, copy the eclipse.gif file, and paste it into the current project folder.

Listing 4.2 Ch4_StatusAction.java

```java
package com.swtjface.Ch4;

import org.eclipse.jface.action.*;
import org.eclipse.jface.resource.*;

public class Ch4_StatusAction extends Action
{
  StatusLineManager statman;
  short triggercount = 0;

  public Ch4_StatusAction(StatusLineManager sm)
  {
    super("&Trigger@Ctrl+T", AS_PUSH_BUTTON);
    statman = sm;
    setToolTipText("Trigger the Action");
    setImageDescriptor(ImageDescriptor.createFromFile
      (this.getClass(),"eclipse.gif"));
  }

  public void run()
  {
    triggercount++;
    statman.setMessage("The status action has fired. Count: " +
      triggercount);
  }
}
```

The first thing to observe in this class is what *isn't* present. Although the constructor receives a StatusLineManager object to display output, the Ch4_StatusAction class has no idea what components are firing its action. Therefore, any control that can generate actions can have an associated Ch4_StatusAction without additional code. Also, there is only one event-handling routine, run(), as opposed to the multiple handlers associated with SWT events.

The run() method handles the event processing, but the main work in this class is performed in the constructor. First, it invokes the constructor of its superclass, Action, and initializes its TEXT and STYLE fields. This way, if the Ch4_StatusAction is incorporated in a menu, the item label will read Trigger. The *&* before the *T* means that this letter will serve as the accelerator key for the action. The *Ctrl+T* in the TEXT field ensures that the action will fire if the user presses the Ctrl and T keys simultaneously.

Beneath the Action constructor, further methods are invoked to configure its appearance in the GUI. If it's implemented in a Composite, the Ch4_StatusAction class will take its form according to the AS_PUSH_BUTTON style, as opposed to the AS_RADIO_BUTTON or AS_CHECK_BOX style. Next, the setToolTipText() method initializes the TOOL_TIP_TEXT field of the class, creating the String that will appear when a mouse pointer hovers over the toolbar item. Finally, the constructor associates an image with the Ch4_StatusAction class, which will appear on the toolbar item and button.

Every time the Ch4_StatusAction is generated, the run() method is invoked. In this case, the triggercount accumulator is updated, and a message is sent to the StatusLineManager object. In most applications, however, this method will be much more involved in order to serve your event-processing needs.

4.2.3 *Implementing contributions in an ApplicationWindow*

Because actions and contributions can only be associated with buttons, toolbar items, and menu items, any application demonstrating their capability must rely on these components. So, although a formal introduction to these widgets will have to wait until later chapters, we must include them here for that purpose.

Listing 4.3 shows how ContributionItem and ContributionManager classes are added to a window. Three contributor classes, ActionContributionItem, MenuManager, and ToolBarManager, all trigger the Ch4_StatusAction when acted on. This action sends a message to the status line at the bottom of the window.

We recommend that you create the Ch4_Contributions class in com.swtjface.Ch4 and run the executable with the Ch4_StatusAction class in the same directory.

NOTE On many platforms, the Contribution operation can't take place unless the OSGi library is added. For this reason, we recommend that you create an OSGI_LIB variable and match it to the osgi.jar file located at $ECLIPSE/plugins/osgi_x.y.z/. The full process for adding classpath variables is described in appendix A.

OSGi refers to the Open Services Gateway Initiative, which was formed to enable networking for smart devices in consumer electronics, cars, and homes. Although its widespread adoption seems uncertain at the time of this writing, it's certain that IBM wants it to succeed very badly.

Listing 4.3   Ch4_Contributions.java

```java
package com.swtjface.Ch4;
import org.eclipse.swt.*;
import org.eclipse.swt.widgets.*;
import org.eclipse.jface.window.*;
import org.eclipse.jface.action.*;

public class Ch4_Contributions extends ApplicationWindow
{
  StatusLineManager slm = new StatusLineManager();
  Ch4_StatusAction status_action = new Ch4_StatusAction(slm);
  ActionContributionItem aci = new
    ActionContributionItem(status_action);        ❶ Assign status_action
                                                      contribution
  public Ch4_Contributions()    ❷ Add resources to
  {                                 ApplicationWindow
    super(null);
    addStatusLine();
    addMenuBar();
    addToolBar(SWT.FLAT | SWT.WRAP);
  }

  protected Control createContents(Composite parent)
  {
    getShell().setText("Action/Contribution Example");
    parent.setSize(290,150);
    aci.fill(parent);     ❸ Create button
    return parent;            within window
  }

  public static void main(String[] args)
  {
    Ch4_Contributions swin = new Ch4_Contributions();
    swin.setBlockOnOpen(true);
    swin.open();
    Display.getCurrent().dispose();
  }

  protected MenuManager createMenuManager()
  {
```

```
        MenuManager main_menu = new MenuManager(null);
        MenuManager action_menu = new MenuManager("Menu");
        main_menu.add(action_menu);
        action_menu.add(status_action);
        return main_menu;
      }
```
❶ **Assign status_action contribution**

```
    protected ToolBarManager createToolBarManager(int style)
    {
        ToolBarManager tool_bar_manager = new ToolBarManager(style);
        tool_bar_manager.add(status_action);    ❶
        return tool_bar_manager;
      }

    protected StatusLineManager createStatusLineManager()
    {
        return slm;
      }
  }
```

The only difference between this JFace application and those in prior chapters is the introduction of actions and contributions.

❶ Beneath the class declaration, the program constructs an instance of the Ch4_StatusAction with a StatusLineManager object as its argument. Then, it creates an ActionContributionItem object and identifies it with the Ch4_StatusAction instance. This contribution has no form yet, but is simply a high-level means of connecting an action to the user interface.

❷ The constructor method creates an ApplicationWindow object and adds a menu, toolbar, and status line.

❸ The createContents() method sets the title and size of the window and then invokes aci.fill(). This method is important since it places the ActionContributionItem object in the GUI. In this case, because the fill() argument is a Composite object, the contributor takes the form of a button that triggers a StatusEvent whenever it's pressed.

The last three methods in Ch4_Contributions are also straightforward. The main() method takes care of creating and opening the window and then disposing of the GUI resources. Then, the createMenuManager() method creates a menu instance at the top of the window. Because it's a subclass of ContributionManager, an Action object can be associated with it, and the status_action object is added with the add() method. This method is also used in the createToolBarManager() method to associate the action instance. In both cases, an ActionContributionItem is

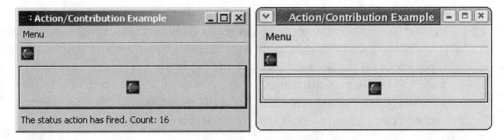

Figure 4.5 `Ch4_Contributions`. **This application shows the three ways a** `ContributionItem` **can be incorporated in a window.**

implicitly created and added to the menu in the form of a menu item and to the toolbar as a toolbar item.

Figure 4.5 shows the user interface of `Ch4_Contributions`. The status line at the bottom keeps a running count of the number of `Ch4_StatusActions` that trigger.

4.2.4 *Interfacing with contributions*

There are two main ways of incorporating an `ActionContributionItem` in a GUI. The first method is to use the `add()` method of a `ContributionManager` subclass, as performed by the `MenuManager` and `ToolBarManager` in the `Ch4_Contributions` application. The second is to use the `fill()` method associated with the `Action-ContributionItem` class and add an SWT widget as its argument. If the argument is a `Composite`, as in `Ch4_Contributions`, then the contributor will appear as determined by the `STYLE` property of the action. If the argument is an SWT `Menu` object, then the contributor will take the form of a menu item. Finally, if the argument is an SWT `ToolBar` object, then the contributor will appear as an item in a toolbar. The characteristics of the `fill()` method are shown in table 4.6.

Table 4.6   Overloaded fill() methods of the `ActionContributionItem` **and their associated appearances**

`fill()` method	GUI implementation (appearance)
`fill(Composite)`	According to Action's STYLE property
`fill(Menu, index)`	`MenuItem` with index position
`fill(ToolBar, index)`	`ToolBarItem` with index position

An interesting characteristic of the ContributionManager class is that its add() method is overloaded to accept arguments of both Action and ActionContribution-Item classes. So, you can associate a ContributionItem with a ContributionManager implicitly (with the Action) or explicitly (with the ActionContributionItem). But there's a fundamental difference: You can perform implicit contribution association repeatedly with the same Action object, as shown in the Ch4_Contributions class. Explicit contribution association can be performed only once.

4.2.5 *Exploring the Action class*

Although Ch4_StatusAction was simple to code and understand, you need to keep in mind many more aspects of the Action class. The Action class contains a large number of methods to enhance the capability of your user interface. These have been divided into categories and listed in the tables that follow.

The first set of methods, shown in table 4.7, is important in any implementation of the Action class. The first and most important method is run(). As we mentioned earlier, this is the single event-handling routine in an Action class, and it's invoked every time the action is triggered. The next method in the table serves as the default constructor. In addition, constructor methods initialize the member fields associated with the Action class, which we'll fully describe shortly.

Table 4.7 **Important methods of the Action class**

Action method	Function
run()	Performs event processing associated with the Action
Action()	Default constructor
Action(String)	Constructor that initializes the TEXT field
Action(String, ImageDescriptor)	Constructor that initializes the TEXT field and associates an image with the Action
Action(String, int)	Constructor that sets the TEXT and STYLE fields

As shown in the Ch4_StatusAction code sample, an instance of the Action class contains a number of fields that provide information about displaying the Action in a GUI. You can access and manipulate these fields using the methods listed in table 4.8. The TEXT field, set and accessed by the first two methods, contains a String that displays a title or menu item description in a contributor. The next two deal with the DESCRIPTION field, which is generally written to a status line to provide additional help. When the user rests the pointer on a contributor, the

String in the TOOL_TIP_TEXT field is shown. The last two methods in this table set and access the IMAGE property of the Action class, which contains a String representing an object of the ImageDescriptor class. As we'll further explain in chapter 7, an ImageDescriptor isn't an image, but an object that holds information needed to create one.

Table 4.8   Property methods for the Action class

Action property method	Function
setText(String)	Sets the TEXT field
getText()	Returns the TEXT field
setDescription(String)	Sets the DESCRIPTION field
getDescription()	Returns the DESCRIPTION field
setToolTipText(String)	Sets the TOOL_TIP_TEXT field
getToolTipText()	Returns the TOOL_TIP_TEXT field
setImageDescriptor(ImageDescriptor)	Sets the IMAGE field
getImageDescriptor()	Returns the IMAGE field

The final field contained in the Action class is the STYLE. This integer value is set by a constructor and accessed through the getStyle() method listed at the top of table 4.9. The next two methods, setEnabled() and getEnabled(), determine whether the component(s) associated with the Action object can be acted on by the user. If not, they are grayed out by default. The final methods, setChecked() and isChecked(), are useful if the Action is associated with a radio button or checkbox. They're used to set the default state of the button or determine whether the user has checked it.

Table 4.9   Style methods for the Action class

Action style method	Function
getStyle()	Returns the STYLE field
setEnabled(boolean)	Sets the ENABLED field
getEnabled()	Returns the ENABLED field
setChecked(boolean)	Sets the CHECKED field
isChecked(void)	Returns the CHECKED field

Table 4.10 shows the methods that deal with accelerator keys and keyboard conversion. *Accelerator keys* are keyboard shortcuts that accomplish the same function as a mouse click. As mentioned in section 4.1.4, pressed keys are represented in SWT with integer key codes, which include all alphanumeric keys and modifier keys (Alt, Ctrl, Shift, Command). The first method creates an accelerator key for the Action object and associates it with an SWT key code. The next method provides the key code for the Action's accelerator key. The next two methods convert back and forth between an accelerator key's key code and its String representation. The removeAcceleratorKey() method parses text and deletes occurrences of the Action's accelerator key. The last four methods in the table provide conversion between Strings representing keyboard characters and modifier keys, and their SWT code representations.

Table 4.10 Accelerator key / keyboard methods for the Action class

Keyboard method	Function
setAccelerator(int)	Set the key code as the Action's accelerator key
getAccelerator()	Returns the key code for the Action's accelerator key
convertAccelerator(int)	Converts the accelerator key to a String
convertAccelerator(String)	Converts the String to an accelerator key
removeAcceleratorText(String)	Removes the accelerator keys from a given String
findKeyCode(String)	Converts the key name to an SWT key code
findKeyString(int)	Converts the key code to a key name
findModifier(String)	Converts the modifier name to a modifier key code
findModifierString(int)	Converts the modifier key code to a modifier name

Although JFace uses actions to replace the SWT listener/event mechanism, the Action class can still incorporate listeners for special-purpose event handling. These methods are shown in table 4.11; they mainly concern the IProperty-ChangeListener interface. This interface pays attention to user-customized PropertyChangeEvents, which fire whenever a given Object changes into a different Object in a manner you describe. Although dealing with property changes may seem complicated, they let you create custom listener/event relationships instead of being limited to those provided by SWT.

The first two methods in table 4.11 take care of associating and disassociating PropertyChangeListeners. You can use the next two methods to test these listeners by triggering property changes, based on a precreated event class or a specified change in a given `Object`. The final methods in this table relate to `HelpListeners`, which deal with the user's attempt to obtain information concerning a given component.

Table 4.11 Listener methods for the `Action` class

`Action` listener method	Function
`addPropertyChangeListener` `(IPropertyChangeListener)`	Associates a property change listener with the `Action`
`removePropertyChangeListener` `(IPropertyChangeListener)`	Removes a property change listener from the `Action`
`firePropertyChange(Event)`	Changes a property according to an event
`firePropertyChange` `(String, Object, Object)`	Changes a property according to old and new objects
`setHelpListener(HelpListener)`	Associates a help listener with the `Action`
`getHelpListener()`	Returns a help listener associated with the `Action`

Table 4.12 lists a group of diverse methods contained in the `Action` class. The first four are used to obtain and access identifiers for both the `Action` class and its definition. The next two, `setMenuCreator()` and `getMenuCreator()`, work with `IMenuCreator` interfaces that can be associated with an `Action` object. This interface provides a simple way of creating a drop-down or pop-up menu when a particular action triggers. The last four methods concern more images that can be linked to an action. When an `Action`'s `ENABLED` field is set to `FALSE`, you can specify which image will represent the action by using the `setDisabledImageDescriptor()` method and retrieve the image with the `getDisabledImageDescriptor()` method. Also, if you want to change an image while a pointer hovers above it, the `setHoverImageDescriptor()` method will set this property.

Table 4.12 Miscellaneous methods of the `Action` class

Method	Description
`setID(String)`	Sets an `Action` identifier
`getID()`	Returns an `Action` identifier
`setActionDefinitionID(String)`	Sets an `Action` definition identifier
`getActionDefinitionID()`	Returns an `Action` definition identifier

continued on next page

Table 4.12   Miscellaneous methods of the `Action` class *(continued)*

Method	Description
`setMenuCreator(IMenuCreator)`	Sets a menu creator for the `Action`
`getMenuCreator()`	Returns a menu creator for the `Action`
`setDisabledImageDescriptor(ImageDescriptor)`	Sets the disabled `Action` image
`getDisabledImageDescriptor()`	Returns the disabled `Action` image
`setHoverImageDescriptor(ImageDescriptor)`	Sets the mouse-hovering image
`getHoverImageDescriptor()`	Returns the mouse hovering image

With these methods, the JFace toolset broadens the functionality of the `Action` class far beyond the simple `Ch4_StatusAction` class. Although you may not need all of them, it's important to know how they function and how they can be used in applications.

4.3   *Updating the WidgetWindow*

To continue populating the `WidgetWindow` application, this chapter provides a `Composite` subclass containing widgets that receive and respond to user actions. This will incorporate code presented earlier in the chapter.

4.3.1   *Building the chapter 4 Composite*

Listing 4.4 presents the `Ch4_Composite` class, which subclasses the `Ch4_MouseKey` class from section 4.1 and launches the `Ch4_Contributions` class developed in section 4.2. We recommend that you add this class to the `com.swtjface.Ch4` package.

Listing 4.4   Ch4_Composite.java

```
package com.swtjface.Ch4;
import org.eclipse.swt.*;
import org.eclipse.swt.widgets.*;
import org.eclipse.swt.events.*;

public class Ch4_Composite extends Ch4_MouseKey
{
  public Ch4_Composite(Composite parent)
  {
    super(parent);
    Button launch = new Button(this, SWT.PUSH);
    launch.setText("Launch");
    launch.setLocation(40,120);
    launch.pack();
```

```
      launch.addMouseListener(new MouseAdapter()
      {
        public void mouseDown(MouseEvent e)
        {
          Ch4_Contributions sw = new Ch4_Contributions();
          sw.open();
        }
      });
    }
  }
```

The operation of Ch4_Composite is simple to understand. By extending the Ch4_MouseKey class, it incorporates the typed and untyped SWT listeners associated with that Composite. It also adds a third button labeled Launch. When clicked, this button creates an instance of the JFace window that uses actions and contributors to perform event processing.

4.3.2 Adding Ch4_Composite to the WidgetWindow

Next a tab is added to the WidgetWindow Tabfolder that comprises the Composite created in this chapter. The code for the main WidgetWindow application is shown in listing 4.5, with the lines added in this chapter in boldface.

Listing 4.5 The updated WidgetWindow

```
package com.swtjface.Ch2;

import org.eclipse.swt.*;
import org.eclipse.swt.widgets.*;
import org.eclipse.jface.window.*;

import com.swtjface.Ch3.*;
import com.swtjface.Ch4.*;

public class WidgetWindow extends Window {

  public WidgetWindow() {
    super(null);
  }

  protected Control createContents(Composite parent) {
    TabFolder tf = new TabFolder(parent, SWT.NONE);

    TabItem chap3 = new TabItem(tf,SWT.NONE);
    chap3.setText("Chapter 3");
    chap3.setControl(new Ch3Comp(tf));

    TabItem chap4 = new TabItem(tf,SWT.NONE);
    chap4.setText("Chapter 4");
    chap4.setControl(new Ch4_Composite(tf));
```

```
      getShell().setText("Widget Window");
      return parent;
    }

  public static void main(String[] args) {
    WidgetWindow wwin = new WidgetWindow();
    wwin.setBlockOnOpen(true);
    wwin.open();
    Display.getCurrent().dispose();
    }
  }
```

Once updated, the WidgetWindow should appear similar to the GUI shown in figure 4.6. Ch4_Contributions appears when the Launch button is clicked.

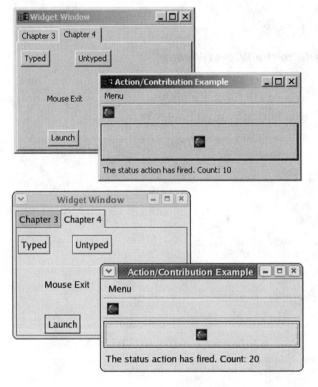

Figure 4.6
The updated WidgetWindow

4.4 *Summary*

Event handling is simple in theory but complicated in practice. It's obvious that when a user clicks a button or enters text, a software routine should respond. But the process of keeping track of which widget fired the event, what type of event occurred, and which software routine should execute isn't obvious and requires effort. To an extent, the degree of effort depends on the toolset. If the toolset provides processing of as many events as possible, for as many widgets as possible, then you'll pay for this vast scope by having to comply with a complicated code structure.

This is the situation with SWT's event model. Because there are so many different types of events, you need tables 4.1 and 4.5 in order to write responsive code. So many methods are available for responding to events that a separate adapter class becomes necessary. This event processing demands a fair amount of understanding, but when you need to keep track of right-click events and whether the user can traverse a widget, SWT is the best toolset available.

The developers of JFace, on the other hand, used the Pareto Rule in designing the toolset. This rule, applied to GUI programming, states that 80% of the code needed for event processing will deal with only 20% of the available events. Similarly, the majority of these events will be fired by a small set of widgets. By following these rules, the developers of JFace concluded that there is no need for listeners, adapters, or widgets. Instead, JFace performs event processing with actions, which are triggered when a user interfaces the GUI, and contributors, which can take multiple forms but trigger a single action.

Clearly, a user interface of any complexity must incorporate both event-processing methods. Although JFace will provide rapid coding for menus, toolbars, and buttons, SWT is needed to process keyboard actions as well as events related to widgets like Shells and tables. Also, JFace's classes won't help you when you need to distinguish between a left click and a right click. Therefore, a GUI developer seeking to provide a maximum of capability with a minimum of code should be familiar with both toolsets.

As shown by the tables in this chapter, effective event programming depends on keeping track of a myriad of rules, classes, and details. Because of this complexity, we thought long and hard about where to present this material in this book. We first planned to present the SWT/JFace event model in the later chapters, but then all of the preceding code would be static. So, to ensure that future code examples will be more helpful to readers, we decided to introduce this convoluted subject early on.

Let's start building dynamic GUIs!

5

More widgets

Now that you know how to tie together widgets with events and listeners, we'll continue our tour of JFace/SWT widgets. The controls we discuss in this chapter will round out your toolbox of widgets and give you an understanding of the majority of controls you'll be using in a GUI application.

We'll explore two (mostly) separate approaches to text editing in this chapter. First we'll discuss in some detail the text widgets built into SWT. We'll follow this discussion with an overview of the enhanced text support available in JFace. Although the JFace text packages offer more advanced options, they're also much more complicated to use.

Once we've covered the details of text editing, we'll move on to a demonstration of several commonly used widgets. We'll cover combo boxes, toolbars, sliders, and progress indicators, as well as discussing the coolbar, which allows you to group several toolbars and let users rearrange them in whatever configuration they find most convenient.

In a break from the way we've been doing things, we won't build a single example for the `WidgetWindow` application. Instead, due to the wide variety of widgets we cover, we'll create several smaller examples that demonstrate a single widget or concept at a time. These examples will each be structured the same as the `Composites` you've seen before, and they can be plugged in to the `WidgetWindow` like any of our other examples.

5.1 Editing text with SWT

SWT provides two controls for your text-editing needs: `Text` allows text to be entered with no style or formatting; `StyledText`, on the other hand, lets you change the color and style of both the entered text and the control itself. Although `StyledText` is very similar to `Text`, with the addition of methods to control styles, the classes are unrelated other than the fact that both extend `Composite` (as most widgets do).

The editing facilities provided by these classes are rudimentary. They provide convenience methods to copy text to or from the clipboard, but you'll need to write code to call these methods at the appropriate times.

5.1.1 The basic Text widget

The `Text` control allows the user to enter unformatted text. `Text` can be instantiated and used in its basic form; however, a few more interesting capabilities are available. `Text` exposes several events, and by listening to them, you can affect the widget's behavior. A brief example will demonstrate: Ch5Capitalizer, presented in listing 5.1, capitalizes text as the user enters it.

Listing 5.1   Ch5Capitalizer.java

```
package com.swtjface.Ch5;

import org.eclipse.swt.SWT;
import org.eclipse.swt.events.VerifyEvent;
import org.eclipse.swt.events.VerifyListener;
import org.eclipse.swt.layout.FillLayout;
import org.eclipse.swt.widgets.Composite;
import org.eclipse.swt.widgets.Text;

public class Ch5Capitalizer extends Composite
{
  public Ch5Capitalizer(Composite parent)
  {
    super(parent, SWT.NONE);
    buildControls();
  }

  private void buildControls()
  {
    this.setLayout(new FillLayout());
    Text text = new Text(this, SWT.MULTI | SWT.V_SCROLL);

    text.addVerifyListener(new VerifyListener() {
      public void verifyText(VerifyEvent e) {
        if( e.text.startsWith("1") )
        {
          e.doit = false;    ❶ Validate
        }
        else
        {
          e.text = e.text.toUpperCase();  ❷ Modify text
        }
    } } );
  }
}
```

For the sake of this example, assume that in addition to capitalizing all text, we also need to reject anything that starts with a number one (1). This example accomplishes both tasks by using the VerifyListener interface. Any registered VerifyListeners are called whenever the text is modified and given the chance to react to the new text being inserted.

❶ First the `VerifyListener` checks to make sure the new text doesn't start with 1. If it does, the `doit` field of the event is set to `false`, causing the edit to be rejected by the `Text` control. For the user typing at his keyboard, this method will be called once for each keypress, effectively preventing any 1s from being entered but allowing any other character through. However, if more than one character is inserted at a time, programmatically or through pasting text, the listener is called only once for the entire block of text that's inserted. Therefore, it will be rejected only if the first character is a 1—any others will make it through.

❷ After validating that the text should be allowed, we capitalize it by assigning the new text to insert to the text field of the event. Initially this field holds the `String` being inserted, but as shown here, we can modify that string to be whatever we want.

To run this example, add it to the `WidgetWindow` by adding the following lines to the `createContents()` method:

```
TabItem chap5Capitalizer = new TabItem(tf, SWT.NONE);
chap5Capitalizer.setText("Chapter 5 Capitalizer");
chap5Capitalizer.setControl(new Ch5Capitalizer(tf));
```

Table 5.1 summarizes the important methods controlling an instance of `Text`. These methods allow you to modify the text, control its appearance, and attach listeners to be notified of events you're interested in.

Table 5.1 Important `Text` methods

Method	Description
`addModifyListener()`	Adds a listener to be notified when the text is modified
`addSelectionListener()`	Adds a listener to be notified when this control is selected
`addVerifyListener()`	Adds a listener to validate any changes to the text
`append()`	Appends the given `String` to the current text
`insert()`	Replaces the current contents with the given `String`
`copy()`, `cut()`, `paste()`	Moves the current selection to the clipboard, or replaces the current selection with whatever currently is in the clipboard
`setSelection()`, `selectAll()`	Programmatically modifies the current selection
`setEchoCharacter()`	Displays the character passed to this method instead of the text typed by the user (useful for hiding passwords, for example)

continued on next page

Table 5.1 Important `Text` methods *(continued)*

Method	Description
`setEditable()`	Turns editing on or off
`setFont()`	Sets the font used to display text, or uses the default if passed null (the font can only be set for the widget as a whole, not for individual sections)

For the most part, these methods are straightforward. The only thing you need to pay attention to is that `insert()` replaces the entire contents of the widget—it doesn't allow you to insert text into the existing content.

Now that we've covered simple text entry, we'll move on to more visually interesting options using the `StyledText` widget.

5.1.2 The StyledText widget

Although the `Text` control can be useful for text entry, often you'll want more control over the presentation of text. Toward that end, SWT provides the `Styled-Text` widget.

`StyledText` provides all the methods present on `Text` and adds capabilities to modify the displayed font, text color, font style, and more. Additionally, `Styled-Text` provides support for basic operations expected of an edit control, such as cutting and pasting.

`StyledText` includes a large set of predefined actions that can be applied to the widget; these are common things such as cut, paste, move to the next word, and move to the end of the text. Constants representing each of these actions are defined in the `ST` class in the `org.eclipse.swt.custom` package. The constants are useful in two cases: First, you can use them to programmatically invoke any of these actions by using the `invokeAction()` method; second, you can bind these actions to keystrokes by using the `setKeyBinding()` method. `setKeyBinding()` takes a key (which can be optionally modified by one of the SWT constants for modifier keys such as Shift or Ctrl) and binds it to the action specified. The following example binds the key combination Ctrl-Q to the paste action. Note that this doesn't clear the default key binding; either one will now work.

```
StyledText.setKeyBinding( 'Q' | SWT.CONTROL, ST.PASTE );
```

`StyledText` also broadcasts many events that you can listen for. In addition to the same ones defined by `Text`, `StyledText` adds events for drawing line backgrounds and line styles. You can use them to modify the style or background color of an entire line as it's drawn by setting the attributes on the event to match the way you wish the line to be displayed. However, be aware that if you use a LineStyleListener, it's no longer valid to call the get/setStyleRange() methods (discussed in the next section) on the StyledText instance. Likewise, using a LineBackgroundListener means that you can't call getLineBackground() or setLineBackground().

You modify the styles displayed by a StyledText through the use of StyleRanges.

Updating text styles with StyleRange

StyledText uses the class StyleRange to manage the different styles it's currently displaying. A StyleRange holds information about the styled attributes of a range of text. All fields of a StyleRange are public and may be modified freely, but the modified style won't be applied until setStyleRange() is called on the StyledText instance.

StyleRanges specify a region of text by using a start offset and length. Each StyleRange tracks both background and foreground colors (or null, to use the default) and a font style, which may be either SWT.NORMAL or SWT.BOLD.

StyleRange also has a similarTo() method, which you can use to check whether two StyleRanges are *similar* to each other. Two StyleRanges are defined as being similar if they both contain the same foreground, background, and font style attributes. This can be useful when you're trying to combine adjacent StyleRanges into a single instance.

To demonstrate the use of StyleRange, we'll present snippets from a simple text editor that is capable of persisting both the text and style information to a file. Due to space constraints, we won't show the complete code listing here, but it's included in the code you can download from this book's website.

We'll first consider how to persist the style information. After we've saved the text, we can obtain the style information by calling styledText.getStyleRanges(), which gives an array of StyleRange representing every style currently in the document. Because this is a simple example, we assume that the only possible style is bold text; we loop through the array and save the start offset and length of each StyleRange to our file. This example could easily be expanded to query each StyleRange and persist additional information such as the background and foreground colors. The following snippet demonstrates:

```
StyledText styledText = ...
StyleRange[] styles = styledText.getStyleRanges();
for(int i = 0; i < styles.length; i++)
{
   printWriter.println(styles[i].start + " " + styles[i].length);
}
```

Once the styles have been saved, they need to be loaded when the file is reopened. We read the styles one line at a time and parse each line to retrieve the style information:

```
StyledText styledText = ...
String styleText = ... //read line from the file
StringTokenizer tokenizer = new StringTokenizer(styleText);
int startPos = Integer.parseInt(tokenizer.nextToken());
int length = Integer.parseInt(tokenizer.nextToken());

StyleRange style = new StyleRange(startPos, length, null, null, SWT.BOLD);
styledText.setStyleRange(style);
```

Again, in this example the only possible style is bold text, so we can assume that each style line represents a length of text that should be made bold starting at the given offset. We instantiate a new StyleRange using the offset and length values read from the file, mark it as bold, and add it to our StyledText control. Alternatively, we could have built an array of all the StyleRanges to be used and used set-StyleRanges() to apply them all at once.

The following method, toggleBold(), switches between entering text in bold and normal font. It's called from a KeyListener that listens when the F1 key is pressed:

```
private void toggleBold()
{
    doBold = !doBold;
    styledText = ...
    if(styledText.getSelectionCount() > 0)
    {
      Point selectionRange = styledText.getSelectionRange();
      StyleRange style = new StyleRange(selectionRange.x,
                                        selectionRange.y,
                                        null, null,
                                        doBold ? SWT.BOLD
                                               : SWT.NORMAL);
        styledText.setStyleRange(style);
    }
}
```

After toggleBold() switches the current text mode, it checks whether there is currently selected text. If so, it ensures that the selected text matches the new mode. getSelectionRange() returns a Point object whose x field represents the offset of the start of the current selection; the y field holds the length of the selection. We use these values to create a StyleRange, and we apply it to the currently selected text.

Finally, there remains the question of how the text is made bold in the first place. We once again use an ExtendedModifyListener:

```
public void modifyText(ExtendedModifyEvent event)
{
  if(doBold)
  {
    StyleRange style = new StyleRange(event.start,
                                     event.length,
                                     null, null,
                                     SWT.BOLD);
    styledText.setStyleRange(style);
  }
}
```

modifyText() is called after text has been newly inserted. If bold mode is currently on (toggled by pressing F1), we use the information about the recent modification included in the event to create a new StyleRange with bold text attributes and apply it to the document. Calling setStyleRange() applies our new style to the document. StyledText tracks the styles of adjacent text and, where possible, combines multiple smaller ranges into a single larger range.

A StyledText example

Our detailed StyledText example (listing 5.2) demonstrates how you can use the events published by StyledText to implement undo/redo functionality. The example presents a text area with scrollbars, where the user may type. Pressing F1 undoes the last edit, and pressing F2 redoes the last undone edit. Notice that cut, copy, and paste functionality is provided automatically with no explicit code required on our part; it's tied to the standard keyboard shortcuts for our platform.

ExtendedModifyListener differs from ModifyListener, which is also present on StyledText, in the amount of information that is sent as part of the event. Whereas ExtendedModifyListener is provided with details about exactly what was done, ModifyListener is given notification that an edit occurred without details of the exact modification.

In the interest of keeping the code shorter, this example makes the assumption that all edits occur at the end of the buffer. Inserting text anywhere else in the buffer will therefore cause undo/redo to behave strangely. Tracking actual edit locations, as well as style information, is left as an exercise for the reader.

Listing 5.2   Ch5Undoable.java

```
package com.swtjface.Ch5;

import java.util.LinkedList;
import java.util.List;

import org.eclipse.swt.SWT;
```

```java
import org.eclipse.swt.custom.*;
import org.eclipse.swt.events.KeyAdapter;
import org.eclipse.swt.events.KeyEvent;
import org.eclipse.swt.layout.FillLayout;
import org.eclipse.swt.widgets.Composite;

public class Ch5Undoable extends Composite
{
  private static final int MAX_STACK_SIZE = 25;
  private List undoStack;
  private List redoStack;

  private StyledText styledText;

  public Ch5Undoable(Composite parent)
  {
    super(parent, SWT.NONE);
    undoStack = new LinkedList();
    redoStack = new LinkedList();
    buildControls();
  }

  private void buildControls()
  {
    this.setLayout(new FillLayout());
    styledText = new StyledText(this, SWT.MULTI | SWT.V_SCROLL);

    styledText.addExtendedModifyListener(         ❶ ExtendedModifyListener
      new ExtendedModifyListener() {
        public void modifyText(ExtendedModifyEvent event)
        {
          String currText = styledText.getText();
          String newText = currText.substring(event.start,
                                     event.start + event.length);
          if( newText != null && newText.length() > 0 )
          {
            if( undoStack.size() == MAX_STACK_SIZE )
            {
              undoStack.remove( undoStack.size() - 1 );
            }
            undoStack.add(0, newText);
          }
    } } );

    styledText.addKeyListener(new KeyAdapter() {
      public void keyPressed(KeyEvent e)        ❷ KeyListener
      {
        switch(e.keyCode)
        {
          case SWT.F1:
            undo(); break;
          case SWT.F2:
            redo(); break;
```

```
        default:
          //ignore everything else
        }
    } } );
  }
  private void undo()
  {
    if( undoStack.size() > 0 )
    {
      String lastEdit = (String)undoStack.remove(0);
      int editLength = lastEdit.length();
      String currText = styledText.getText();
      int startReplaceIndex = currText.length() - editLength;
      styledText.replaceTextRange(startReplaceIndex,    ❸  Undo
                                  editLength, "");
      redoStack.add(0, lastEdit);
    }
  }
  private void redo()
  {
    if( redoStack.size() > 0 )
    {
      String text = (String)redoStack.remove(0);
      moveCursorToEnd();
      styledText.append(text);    ❹  Redo
      moveCursorToEnd();
    }
  }
  private void moveCursorToEnd()
  {
    styledText.setCaretOffset(styledText.getText().length());
  }
}
```

❶ This is the key section of this example: An ExtendedModifyListener is added to the StyledText object so that we can track edit events. The ExtendedModifyListener is called each time the text is edited. The event that's passed contains information about the newly inserted text. In the example, we use the start offset and length to retrieve the new text from the StyledText and save it in case the user wants to undo her edit later. The event also provides information about the text that was replaced, if any, in the replacedText field. A more robust implementation could save this text along with the new edit and reinsert it if the edit was undone.

❷ A KeyListener listens for keypresses, which are reported using a KeyEvent. We check the keyCode field to see if it matches one of the keys we're interested in.

Constants for the keys are defined in the SWT class. Additionally, we can query the state of modifier keys such as Ctrl or Alt by masking the stateMask field of the event against the appropriate constants defined in the SWT class.

❸ Undo pops the top entry of the undo stack, which holds a record of all edits that have been made. We then use replaceTextRange() to replace the last n characters in the buffer with the empty string, where n is the length of the edit we retrieved from the stack.

❹ To redo an edit, we pop the top entry off the redo stack. It's then inserted at the end of the document using append().

The following lines added to WidgetWindow will let you test the undoable editor:

```
TabItem chap5Undo = new TabItem(tf, SWT.NONE);
chap5Undo.setText("Chapter 5 Undoable");
chap5Undo.setControl(new Ch5Undoable(tf));
```

There are some complexities to editing text in SWT, but once you understand the events that are broadcast by the widget, it isn't difficult to add basic types of validation or control logic to your application. Certain features, however, are difficult to implement with the facilities provided by SWT. JFace text editing, although more complex, is also more powerful; it offers a host of new options that we'll discuss in the next section.

5.2 JFace text support

As an alternative to using the StyledText control provided by SWT, JFace offers an extensive framework for text editing. More than 300 classes and interfaces are spread between 7 jface.text packages and subpackages. Rather than try to cover them all in the limited space we have available, we'll provide an overview of the key classes in org.eclipse.jface.text and develop a small example showing some of the advanced capabilities available.

5.2.1 Obtaining the JFace text packages

Before you can use the JFace text packages, you need to extract a couple of jar files from your Eclipse installation: text.jar, located in $ECLIPSE_HOME/plugins/org.eclipse.text_x.y.z; and jfacetext.jar, in $ECLIPSE_HOME/plugins/org.eclipse.jface.text_x.y.z. Make sure both of them are in your classpath before you try any of the examples in this section.

5.2.2 *TextViewer and Document*

JFace text support is implemented by a core set of classes and augmented by a variety of extensions that add specific advanced features. We'll discuss the core first and then provide an overview of the available extensions.

Two interfaces form the core of JFace's text support: IDocument and IText-Viewer. Each has a default implementation provided by JFace.

An instance of IDocument holds the actual text that's being edited. The primary implementation of IDocument is the class Document, although AbstractDocument provides a partial implementation that you can extend if you decide to write your own. In addition to standard methods to set or retrieve text, IDocument also allows for listeners to receive notification of content edits through the IDocumentListener interface.

IDocument also supports several more advanced features:

- *Positions*—You can assign a "sticky" marker known as a Position to a region of text. A Position object is given an offset and a length of text when it's assigned to the document. As the document's text is updated, the Position is kept in sync with the text changes so that it always points to the same section of text, no matter how it moves in the document. You can use this to implement features such as bookmarks, which allow the user to jump to a marked location in the document. The base Position class offers little beyond basic tracking of an offset and length; you'll usually need to subclass it in order to build useful behavior for your application.

- *Partition content types*—Conceptually, a document is composed of one or more partitions represented by the ITypedRegion interface. Each partition can have a different content type, such as plain text, rich text, or HTML. To use this feature, you need to create an IDocumentPartitioner and assign it to your document. The document partitioner is then responsible for responding to queries about the content type of specific locations in the document, and it must implement computePartitioning() to return an array of all the ITypedRegions present in the document. It isn't necessary to implement your own document partitioner; if you don't assign one, the entire document will be treated as a single region with type IDocument.DEFAULT_CONTENT_TYPE.

- *Searching*—IDocument provides search facilities to clients through the search() method. Although it doesn't support regular expressions or other patterns in the search, it does give you control over the search start location, direction, and case sensitivity and whether to match whole words only.

ITextViewer is intended to turn a standard text widget into a document-based text widget. The default implementation is TextViewer, which uses a StyledText under the hood to display data. ITextViewer supports listeners for both text modifications and visual events, such as changes in the currently visible region of text (known as the *viewport*). Although the default implementation of ITextViewer, TextViewer, allows direct access to the StyledText if you wish to modify the display, it's intended that you use TextPresentation instead; it collects the various StyleRanges present in the document.

ITextViewer also supports a number of different types of plug-ins that can be used to modify the behavior of the widget. The functionality that can be customized includes undo support, through IUndoManager; how to react to double clicks, through ITextDoubleClickStrategy; automatic indentation of text, supplied by IAutoIndentStrategy; and text to display when the mouse is left on a section of the document, through ITextHover. You use each of these plug-ins by assigning an appropriate instance of the interface to the text viewer and then calling activatePlugins().

Finally, a variety of subpackages of org.eclipse.jface.text provide useful extensions; they're summarized in table 5.2.

Table 5.2 The subpackages of org.eclipse.jface.text provide a variety of advanced functionality.

Package	Description
org.eclipse.jface.text.contentassist	Provides a framework for automatic completion of text as it's being typed, such as is found in many Java IDEs. IContentAssistant and IContentAssistantProcessor work together to provide ICompletionProposals at appropriate times.
org.eclipse.jface.text.formatter	Provides utilities to format text. IContentFormatter registers instances of IFormattingStrategy with different content types. When text needs formatting, the appropriate formatting strategy is given a String representing the text to be modified.
org.eclipse.jface.text.presentation	Used to update the visual appearance of the document in response to changes. After a change, an IPresentationDamager is used to calculate the region of the document that needs to be redrawn, and that information is given to an IPresentationRepairer along with a TextPresentation to reset the styles on the damaged region.

continued on next page

Table 5.2 The subpackages of `org.eclipse.jface.text` provide a variety of advanced functionality. *(continued)*

Package	Description
`org.eclipse.jface.text.reconciler`	Used to synchronize a document with an external store of its text. The default `Reconciler` runs periodically in the background, delegating to instances of `IReconcilingStrategy` as it finds dirty regions that need to be kept in sync.
`org.eclipse.jface.text.rules`	Defines classes to scan and match text based on configurable `IRules`. This framework is used to implement the presentation package and document partitioner and includes built in rules to match common occurrences such as words, numbers, whitespace, or ends of lines.
`org.eclipse.jface.text.source`	Used to attach visual markers to text, such as the red Xs used in Eclipse to denote compilation errors. To employ these features, you must use `ISource-Viewer` instead of `ITextViewer`, which it extends. You'll then need to subclass `Annotation` to draw appropriate images.

5.2.3 *A JFace example*

We'll now build a simple text editor that uses some of `TextViewer`'s features. Inspired by a feature in OpenOffice and other word processors, this editor tracks individual words as the user types. At any time, the user can press F1 to obtain a list of suggested completions for the word he's currently typing, drawn from the list of all words he has typed so far that start with the text currently under the cursor.

To implement this functionality, we'll use the classes in `org.eclipse.jface.text.contentassist`. We've created a utility class called `WordTracker`, which is responsible for tracking the user's most recently typed words and is capable of suggesting completions for a string. An instance of `IContentAssistProcessor`, `RecentWordContentAssistProcessor`, presents the possible completions to the framework. Finally, `CompletionTextEditor` is our main class: It configures the `TextViewer` and attaches the appropriate listeners. We'll discuss each of these classes in detail, followed by the complete source code.

A `ContentAssistant` is responsible for suggesting possible completions to the user. Each `ContentAssistant` has one or more instances of `IContentAssistProcessor` registered; each processor is associated with a different content type.

When the TextViewer requests suggestions, the ContentAssistant delegates to the assist processor that is appropriate for the content type of the current region of the document.

You can often use ContentAssistant as is. However, we need to define an IContentAssistProcessor. The processor's main responsibility is to provide an array of possible completions when computeCompletionProposals() is called. Our implementation is straightforward: Given the current offset of the cursor into the document, it looks for the first occurrence of whitespace to determine the current word fragment, if any, by moving backward through the document one character at a time:

```
while( currOffset > 0
  && !Character.isWhitespace(
    currChar = document.getChar(currOffset)) )
{
  currWord = currChar + currWord;
  currOffset--;
  }
```

Once it has the current word, it requests completions from the WordTracker and uses those completions to instantiate an array of ICompletionProposal in the buildProposals() method:

```
int index = 0;
for(Iterator i = suggestions.iterator(); i.hasNext();)
{
  String currSuggestion = (String)i.next();
  proposals[index] = new CompletionProposal(
                                    currSuggestion,
                                    offset,
                                    replacedWord.length(),
                                    currSuggestion.length());
  index++;
}
```

Each proposal consists of the proposed text, the offset at which to insert the text, the number of characters to replace, and the position where the cursor should be afterward. The ContentAssistant will use this array to display choices to the user and insert the proper text once she chooses one.

In this example, we always activate the ContentAssistant programmatically by listening for a keypress. However, IContentAssistProcessor also contains methods that allow you to specify a set of characters that will serve as automatic triggers for suggestions to be displayed. You implement the getCompletionProposalAutoActivationCharacters() method to return the characters that you wish to serve as triggers. Listing 5.3 shows the complete implementation of the IContentAssistProcessor.

Listing 5.3   RecentWordContentAssistProcessor

```java
package com.swtjface.Ch5;

import java.util.Iterator;
import java.util.List;

import org.eclipse.jface.text.*;
import org.eclipse.jface.text.contentassist.*;

public class RecentWordContentAssistProcessor
  implements IContentAssistProcessor
{
  private String lastError = null;
  private IContextInformationValidator contextInfoValidator;
  private WordTracker wordTracker;

  public RecentWordContentAssistProcessor(WordTracker tracker)
  {
    super();
    contextInfoValidator = new ContextInformationValidator(this);
    wordTracker = tracker;
  }

  public ICompletionProposal[] computeCompletionProposals(
    ITextViewer textViewer,
    int documentOffset)
  {
    IDocument document = textViewer.getDocument();
    int currOffset = documentOffset - 1;

    try
    {
      String currWord = "";
      char currChar;
      while( currOffset > 0            ❶ Find current word
              && !Character.isWhitespace(
                    currChar = document.getChar(currOffset)) )
      {
        currWord = currChar + currWord;
        currOffset--;
      }

      List suggestions = wordTracker.suggest(currWord);
      ICompletionProposal[] proposals = null;
      if(suggestions.size() > 0)
      {
        proposals = buildProposals(suggestions, currWord,
                          documentOffset - currWord.length());
        lastError = null;
```

```
      }
      return proposals;
    }
    catch (BadLocationException e)
    {
      e.printStackTrace();
      lastError = e.getMessage();
      return null;
    }
  }

  private ICompletionProposal[] buildProposals(List suggestions,
                                               String replacedWord,
                                               int offset)
  {
    ICompletionProposal[] proposals =
                 new ICompletionProposal[suggestions.size()];
    int index = 0;
    for(Iterator i = suggestions.iterator(); i.hasNext();)
    {
      String currSuggestion = (String)i.next();
      proposals[index] = new CompletionProposal(    ❷  Build proposals
                                    currSuggestion,
                                    offset,
                                    replacedWord.length(),
                                    currSuggestion.length());
      index++;
    }
    return proposals;
  }

  public IContextInformation[] computeContextInformation(
    ITextViewer textViewer,
    int documentOffset)
  {
    lastError = "No Context Information available";
    return null;
  }

  public char[] getCompletionProposalAutoActivationCharacters()
  {
    //we always wait for the user to explicitly trigger completion
    return null;
  }

  public char[] getContextInformationAutoActivationCharacters()
  {
    //we have no context information
    return null;
  }

  public String getErrorMessage()
  {
```

```
    return lastError;
  }

  public IContextInformationValidator getContextInformationValidator()
  {
    return contextInfoValidator;
  }
}
```

1 We move backward through the document a character at a time until we hit whitespace or the beginning of the document.

2 Each proposal contains the text to propose, as well as information about where to insert the text into the document. Theoretically, you could insert the proposed text wherever you wish, although doing so could be confusing for the user if the text isn't inserted at the cursor's current position.

WordTracker is a utility class used to maintain and search a list of words (see listing 5.4). Our implementation isn't particularly efficient, but it's simple and fast enough for our purposes. Each word is added to a List, and when suggestions are needed, the List is traversed looking for any item that starts with the given String. WordTracker doesn't contain any SWT or JFace code, so we won't examine it in detail.

Listing 5.4   WordTracker.java

```
package com.swtjface.Ch5;

import java.util.*;

public class WordTracker
{
  private int maxQueueSize;
  private List wordBuffer;
  private Map knownWords = new HashMap();

  public WordTracker(int queueSize)
  {
    maxQueueSize = queueSize;
    wordBuffer = new LinkedList();
  }

  public int getWordCount()
  {
    return wordBuffer.size();
  }

  public void add(String word)
```

```
    {
      if( wordIsNotKnown(word) )
      {
        flushOldestWord();
        insertNewWord(word);
      }
    }

    private void insertNewWord(String word)
    {
      wordBuffer.add(0, word);
      knownWords.put(word, word);
    }

    private void flushOldestWord()
    {
      if( wordBuffer.size() == maxQueueSize )
      {
        String removedWord =
                (String)wordBuffer.remove(maxQueueSize - 1);
        knownWords.remove(removedWord);
      }
    }

    private boolean wordIsNotKnown(String word)
    {
      return knownWords.get(word) == null;
    }

    public List suggest(String word)
    {
      List suggestions = new LinkedList();
      for( Iterator i = wordBuffer.iterator(); i.hasNext(); )
      {
        String currWord = (String)i.next();
        if( currWord.startsWith(word) )
        {
          suggestions.add(currWord);
        }
      }
      return suggestions;
    }

}
```

Ch5CompletionEditor brings together the components we've discussed. In build-
Controls(), we instantiate and configure a TextViewer. The ContentAssistant is
created, and our custom processor is assigned to the default content type:

```
final ContentAssistant assistant = new ContentAssistant();
assistant.setContentAssistProcessor(
            new RecentWordContentAssistProcessor(wordTracker),
            IDocument.DEFAULT_CONTENT_TYPE);
assistant.install(textViewer);
```

Once the assistant has been configured, it's installed on the viewer. Note that the assistant is given the viewer to install itself to, instead of the viewer receiving a ContentAssistant as you might expect.

To be notified about edits, we use an ITextListener, which is similar to the ExtendedModifyListener used by StyledText:

```
textViewer.addTextListener(new ITextListener() {
  public void textChanged(TextEvent e)
  {
    if(isWhitespaceString(e.getText()))
    {
      wordTracker.add(findMostRecentWord(e.getOffset() - 1));
    }
  }
});
```

Listening for keystrokes here uses the same listener classes that StyledText did. When we find the completion trigger key, we programmatically invoke the content assistant:

```
case SWT.F1:
    assistant.showPossibleCompletions();
```

ContentAssistant does all the work from this point on, displaying the possible completions and inserting the selected one into the document; see listing 5.5.

Listing 5.5 Ch5CompletionEditor

```
package com.swtjface.Ch5;

import java.util.StringTokenizer;

import org.eclipse.jface.text.*;
import org.eclipse.jface.text.contentassist.ContentAssistant;
import org.eclipse.swt.SWT;
import org.eclipse.swt.events.KeyAdapter;
import org.eclipse.swt.events.KeyEvent;
import org.eclipse.swt.layout.FillLayout;
import org.eclipse.swt.widgets.Composite;

public class Ch5CompletionEditor extends Composite
{
  private TextViewer textViewer;
  private WordTracker wordTracker;
```

```
private static final int MAX_QUEUE_SIZE = 200;

public Ch5CompletionEditor(Composite parent)
{
  super(parent, SWT.NULL);
  wordTracker = new WordTracker(MAX_QUEUE_SIZE);
  buildControls();
}

private void buildControls()
{
  setLayout(new FillLayout());
  textViewer = new TextViewer(this, SWT.MULTI | SWT.V_SCROLL);

  textViewer.setDocument(new Document());        ❶ Assign an IDocument instance

  final ContentAssistant assistant = new ContentAssistant();
  assistant.setContentAssistProcessor(
          new RecentWordContentAssistProcessor(wordTracker),
          IDocument.DEFAULT_CONTENT_TYPE);       ❷ Assign content
                                                   assist processor
  assistant.install(textViewer);

  textViewer.getControl().addKeyListener(new KeyAdapter() {
    public void keyPressed(KeyEvent e)
    {
      switch(e.keyCode)
      {
        case SWT.F1:
          assistant.showPossibleCompletions();   ❸ Display completions
          break;
        default:
          //ignore everything else
      }
    }
  });

  textViewer.addTextListener(new ITextListener() {
    public void textChanged(TextEvent e)
    {
      if(isWhitespaceString(e.getText()))        ❹ Capture new words
      {
        wordTracker.add(findMostRecentWord(e.getOffset() - 1));
      }
    }
  });
}

protected String findMostRecentWord(int startSearchOffset)
{
  int currOffset = startSearchOffset;
  char currChar;
  String word = "";
  try
```

```
{
  while(currOffset > 0
       && !Character.isWhitespace(        ⑤  Find last word
            currChar = textViewer.getDocument()
                                  .getChar(currOffset)
         ))
  {
    word = currChar + word;
    currOffset--;
  }
  return word;
}
catch (BadLocationException e)
{
  e.printStackTrace();
  return null;
}
}

protected boolean isWhitespaceString(String string)
{
  StringTokenizer tokenizer = new StringTokenizer(string);
  //if there is at least 1 token, this string is not whitespace
  return !tokenizer.hasMoreTokens();
}
}
```

❶ Each `TextViewer` needs an `IDocument` to store its text. Here we use the default `Document` class, which is sufficient for most needs. You must set the document on a `TextViewer` before it's used, or `NullPointerExceptions` will be generated.

❷ Each `ContentAssistant` can have a variety of `IContentAssistProcessors` assigned; the appropriate one will be selected based on the content type of the document. Here we assign our processor to the default content type, which is defined in the `IDocument` interface.

❸ When we detect that the proper key has been pressed, we programmatically invoke the `ContentAssistant`.

❹ We examine each edit as it's made. When we find an edit that consists only of whitespace, we assume that a new word has been added, retrieve it from the Document, and store it in our `WordTracker`.

❺ Here we cycle backward through the document one character at a time, starting from the current editing position. When we find whitespace, we grab the word for the `WordTracker`.

To see this in action, add the following to `WidgetWindow`:

```
TabItem chap5Completion = new TabItem(tf, SWT.NONE);
chap5Completion.setText("Chapter 5 Completion Editor");
chap5Completion.setControl(new Ch5CompletionEditor(tf));
```

As you can see, SWT and JFace provide a wide variety of text-editing options. Although we've only touched on the possibilities offered by JFace, by understanding the overall design you should be able to use the extensions without much trouble. Now we'll move on to several less complicated widgets, starting with combo boxes.

5.3 *The Combo widget*

The `Combo` control is used to create a combo box. Typically, the `Combo` control lets the user select an option from a list of choices. There are three styles of `Combo` controls:

- *Simple*—Contains an editable text field at the top and a list box with the choices on the bottom. This is the default combo style.
- *Drop-down*—An editable text field with an arrow at the right side. Clicking the arrow reveals a list of choices and allows the user to select one.
- *Read-only*—A drop-down combo whose text field can't be edited. This style is used when you want to limit the choices the user can input. The read-only combo defaults to an empty selection, so most of the time you'll call `select( 0 )` to default the combo to the first choice available.

These styles are set via the usual `STYLE.*` attributes in the constructor and, slightly unexpectedly, are mutually exclusive. Figure 5.1 shows the available styles of combos; you can use the code in listing 5.6 to generate these results.

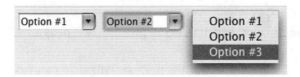

Figure 5.1
Combo styles, from left to right: simple, drop-down, and read-only

Listing 5.6 Ch5ComboComposite.java

```java
package com.swtjface.Ch5;

import org.eclipse.swt.SWT;
import org.eclipse.swt.layout.RowLayout;
import org.eclipse.swt.widgets.Combo;
import org.eclipse.swt.widgets.Composite;

public class Ch5ComboComposite extends Composite {

    public Ch5ComboComposite(Composite parent) {
        super(parent, SWT.NONE);
        buildControls();
    }

    protected void buildControls() {
        setLayout(new RowLayout());

        int[] comboStyles = { SWT.SIMPLE,
                              SWT.DROP_DOWN,
                              SWT.READ_ONLY };

        for (int idxComboStyle = 0;
            idxComboStyle < comboStyles.length;
            ++idxComboStyle) {
            Combo combo = new Combo(this,
                              comboStyles[idxComboStyle]);
            combo.add("Option #1");
            combo.add("Option #2");
            combo.add("Option #3");
        }
    }
}
```

Run this example by adding the following code to `WidgetWindow`:

```java
TabItem chap5Combos = new TabItem(tf, SWT.NONE);
chap5Combos.setText("Chapter 5 Combos");
chap5Combos.setControl(new Ch5ComboComposite(tf));
```

5.4 *ToolBarManager*

The `ToolBarManager` is a JFace class that simplifies the construction of toolbars by making use of the action framework we discussed in chapter 4. It's the toolbar equivalent of the `MenuManager`, and the interfaces are similar. This class is also derived from the `ContributionManager` class. As such, objects implementing either the `IAction` or `IContribution` interface can be added to the `ToolBarManager`. The `ToolBarManager` will generate the appropriate SWT Controls when required, so you don't have to get involved with the gritty details. Most of the time you'll be adding `Action` objects to the `ToolBarManager`, which will then automatically generate instances of the `Toolbar` and `ToolItem` classes that we discuss later.

You can easily add a toolbar to your application by calling the `ApplicationWindow`'s `createToolBarManager()` method. Unlike its `MenuManager` counterpart, `createToolBarManager()` requires a style parameter. This style parameter determines the style of buttons to be used by the `ToolBar`: either flat or normal pushbuttons. As we mentioned earlier, it's handy to use the same `Actions` to generate items on both the menu and the toolbar—for example, actions such as `OpenFile` are normally found on both. By reusing `Actions`, you simplify the code and ensure that menu and toolbar are always in sync.

5.4.1 *ControlContribution*

In addition to the `ContributionItems` that `MenuManager` works with, there is a new `ContributionItem` that can only be used with a `ToolBarManager`: the `ControlContribution`. This is a cool class that wraps any `Control` and allows it to be used on a `ToolBar`. You can even wrap a `Composite` and throw it onto the toolbar.

To use the `ControlContribution` class, you must derive your own class and implement the abstract `createControl()` method. The following code snippet demonstrates a simple implementation of such a class. We create a custom `ControlContribution` class that can be used by the JFace `ToolBarManager`:

```
toolBarManager.add(new ControlContribution("Custom") {
    protected Control createControl(Composite parent) {
        SashForm sf = new SashForm(parent, SWT.NONE);
        Button b1 = new Button(sf, SWT.PUSH);
        b1.setText("Hello");
        Button b2 = new Button(sf, SWT.PUSH);
        b2.setText("World");
        b2.addSelectionListener(new SelectionAdapter() {
            public void widgetSelected(SelectionEvent e) {
                System.out.println("Selected:" + e);
            }
        });
        return sf;
    }
});
```

Note that you must implement the `SelectionListeners` on your controls if you want anything to happen. For all intents and purposes, the `ControlContribution` class lets you place anything you want on the `ToolBar`.

5.4.2 *Creating toolbars by hand*

Although it's often easiest to create a toolbar by using a `ToolBarManager`, you may occasionally wish to create one manually, if it's simple or if you aren't using JFace. In this case, you'll need to use two classes: `ToolBar` and `ToolItem`.

ToolBar

The `Toolbar` is a composite control that holds a number of `ToolItems`. The `ToolBar` is rendered as a strip of small iconic buttons, typically 16-by-16 bitmap graphics. Each of these buttons corresponds to a `ToolItem`, which we'll discuss in the next section. By clicking the button, the user triggers an action represented by the `ToolItem`.

A `ToolBar` may be oriented either horizontally or vertically, although it's horizontal by default. In addition, it's possible for `ToolItems` to wrap around and form additional rows.

Typically, `ToolBars` are used to organize and present sets of related actions. For example, there might a `ToolBar` representing all text operations with buttons for paragraph alignment, typeface, font size, and so on.

ToolItem

The `ToolItem` represents a single item in a `ToolBar`. Its role with respect to the `ToolBar` is similar to that of the `MenuItem` to a `Menu`. Unlike `MenuItems`, `ToolItems` aren't text but iconic in nature. As such, an image should always be assigned to a `ToolItem`. A `ToolItem` on a `ToolBar` ignores the text label and displays only a small red square if no image is assigned. When the user selects a `ToolItem` from the menu, it broadcasts the event to any registered `SelectionListeners`. Your application should register a listener with each `ToolItem` and use that listener to perform whatever logic corresponds to the menu item.

5.5 *CoolBar*

The `CoolBar` control is like the `ToolBar` control with upgraded functionality. The primary distinction between the two is that the items on a `CoolBar` can be repositioned and resized at runtime. Each of these items is represented by a `CoolItem` control, which can contain any sort of control. The most common uses of a `CoolBar` are to hold toolbars or buttons.

The next snippet shows the creation of a `CoolBar` that holds multiple toolbars. Each child `ToolBar` contains items that are grouped together by function. In this case, we have one `ToolBar` with file functions, another with formatting functions, and a third with search functions, each of which is wrapped in a `CoolItem` control

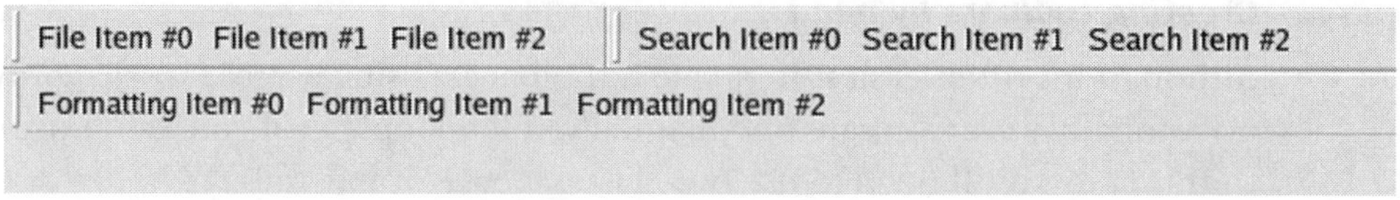

Figure 5.2   The initial toolbars, controlled by a `CoolBar`. Notice that the File and Search items are adjacent.

and contained in a single parent `CoolBar`. This example is representative of a typical `CoolBar`; there are many ways to layer and organize controls to create striking user interfaces. Figure 5.2 shows what the toolbars look like before moving them around; notice that initially, the file and search items are next to each other. The code to create the `CoolBar` looks like this:

```
String[] coolItemTypes = {"File", "Formatting", "Search"};
CoolBar coolBar = new CoolBar(parent, SWT.NONE);
for(int i = 0; i < coolItemTypes.length; i++)
{
  CoolItem item = new CoolItem(coolBar, SWT.NONE);
  ToolBar tb = new ToolBar(coolBar, SWT.FLAT);
  for(int j = 0; j < 3; j++)
  {
    ToolItem ti = new ToolItem(tb, SWT.NONE);
    ti.setText(coolItemTypes[i] + " Item #" + j);
  }
}
```

Notice that each `CoolItem` has a handle on the left side: Double-clicking the handle expands the `CoolItem` to the full width of the `CoolBar`, minimizing the other `CoolItems` if necessary. By clicking the handle and dragging it, the user can move a `CoolItem` to different parts of the `CoolBar`. To create additional rows, drag a `CoolItem` below the current `CoolBar`. To reorder a `CoolItem`, drag it to the new position—other `CoolItems` will be bumped out of the way to accommodate it. Figure 5.3 shows our example after we've repositioned the `CoolItems`.

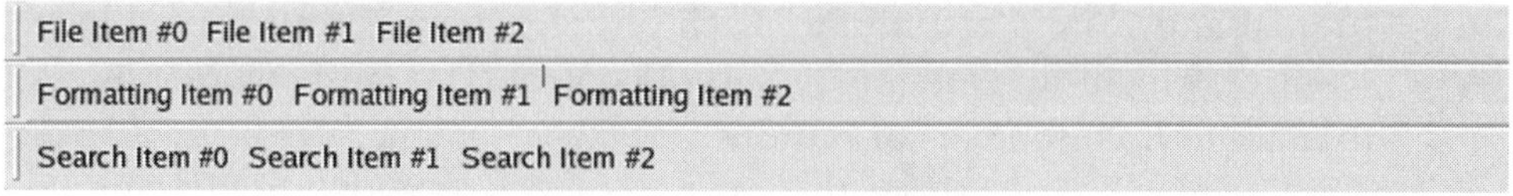

Figure 5.3   The same toolbars have been repositioned by the user.

5.6 *Slider*

The Slider control is similar to the scrollbars you see on a window. Although it seems logical to assume that scrollbars are implemented with Slider controls, they're different. Scrollbars are associated with the item they're scrolling and aren't available for use outside of that context. This is where the Slider comes in.

You can use the Slider as a control to select any value along an integral range. This range is set via the setMinimum() and setMaximum() methods.

The rectangular slider you can click and drag is officially referred to as the *thumb*. You set the size of the thumb via setThumb(); it should be an integral number. Visually, the size of the thumb is depicted realistically as a percentage of the entire range. Thus, if the range is from 0 to 100 and the size of the thumb is 10, then the thumb will take up 10% of the Slider control.

> **NOTE** Some operating systems have native scrollbars that feature a constant-sized thumb. On these platforms, the size of the thumb is ignored for visual purposes but used in other calculations.

Arrows at each end move the thumb by a set amount referred to as the *increment*. You specify this increment via the setIncrement() method. Clicking the area between the thumb and an endpoint arrow causes the thumb to jump by a larger set amount. This amount is referred to as the *page increment* and is set via the set-PageIncrement() method. Figure 5.4 shows a typical slider; notice that it appears similar to a vertical scrollbar.

There is also a convenience method called setValues() that takes in all these values at once. The method signature is as follows:

```
void setValues( int selection, int minimum, int maximum, int thumb,
                int increment, int pageIncrement)
```

The selection is the starting point for the thumb. This is again represented by an integral number that specifies a value along the range of the Slider. The example in listing 5.7 demonstrates a Slider control with a range of 400 to 1600, as might be needed to represent a standardized test score.

Figure 5.4   A typical Slider control

```
package com.swtjface.Ch5;

import org.eclipse.swt.SWT;
import org.eclipse.swt.layout.FillLayout;
import org.eclipse.swt.widgets.Composite;
import org.eclipse.swt.widgets.Slider;

public class Ch5Slider extends Composite {
    public Ch5Slider(Composite parent) {
        super(parent, SWT.NONE);
        setLayout(new FillLayout());
        Slider slider = new Slider(this, SWT.HORIZONTAL);
        slider.setValues(1000, 400, 1600, 200, 10, 100);    ❶ Create Slider
    }
}
```

❶ The code sets the selection to 1000, the minimum to 400, the maximum to 1600, the thumb size to 200, the increment value to 10, and the page increment to 100.

The Slider also takes a style attribute that lets you specify whether it should be vertical or horizontal. By default, a horizontal Slider is constructed.

The following code adds the slider example to WidgetWindow:

```
TabItem chap5Slider = new TabItem(tf, SWT.NONE);
chap5Slider.setText("Chapter 5 Slider");
chap5Slider.setControl(new Ch5Slider(tf));
```

5.7 *ProgressBar*

The ProgressBar control lets you convey the progress of a lengthy operation. Its simplified counterpart, the ProgressIndicator, is recommended in most cases. Occasionally, you may need more control than a ProgressIndicator allows; if you decide that you need to use a ProgressBar directly, you're taking responsibility for changing the display of the bar yourself. The following code snippet shows an example:

```
//Style can be SMOOTH, HORIZONTAL, or VERTICAL
ProgressBar bar = new ProgressBar(parent, SWT.SMOOTH);
bar.setBounds(10, 10, 200, 32);
bar.setMaximum(100);
...
for(int i = 0; i < 10; i++) {
    //Take care to only update the display from its
    //own thread
    Display.getCurrent().asyncExec(new Runnable() {
        public void run() {
```

```
            //Update how much of the bar should be filled in
            bar.setSelection((int)(bar.getMaximum() * (i+1) / 10));
        }
    });
}
```

As you examine this code, note that in addition to needing to calculate the amount to update the bar, the call to setSelection() causes the widget to be updated every time. This behavior is unlike that of ProgressIndicator or ProgressMonitorDialog, which will update the display only if it has changed by an amount that will be visible to the end user.

As you can see, more work is involved with using ProgressBars than the other widgets we've discussed, and in general we recommend avoiding them unless you have no choice. However, a ProgressBar may occasionally be necessary—for example, if you need to unfill the bar, there is no way to do it with the higher-level controls.

5.8 *ProgressIndicator*

The ProgressIndicator widget allows you to display a progress bar without worrying much about how to fill it. Like the ProgressMonitorDialog, it supports abstract units of work—you need only initialize the ProgressIndicator with the total amount of work you expect to do and notify it as work is completed:

```
ProgressIndicator indicator = new ProgressIndicator(parent);
...

indicator.beginTask(10);
...
Display.getCurrent()display.asyncExec(new Runnable() {
  public void run() {
    //Inform the indicator that some amount of work has been done
    indicator.worked(1);
  }
});
```

As this example shows, there are two steps to using a ProgressIndicator. First you let the indicator know how much total work you intend to do by calling beginTask(). The control won't be displayed on the screen until this method is called. Then you call worked() each time some work has been completed. As we discussed in chapter 4, there are several threading issues to pay attention to here. Doing the actual work in the UI thread will cause the display to lock up and defeats the purpose of using a ProgressIndicator in the first place. However, you aren't allowed to update widgets from a non-UI thread. The solution is to use asyncExec() to schedule the code that updates the widget to be run from the UI thread.

The `ProgressIndicator` also provides an *animated* mode, where the total amount of work isn't known. In this mode, the bar continually fills and empties until `done()` is called. To use animated mode, call `beginAnimatedTask()` instead of `beginTask()`; there is no need to call the `worked()` method. Assuming your work is being correctly done in a non-UI thread, this implies that you don't have to worry about the `asyncExec()` call, either.

5.9 *Summary*

SWT and JFace provide many options for editing text. The SWT controls are fairly easy to use, but implementing anything beyond simple text editing using them can quickly become painful. The JFace controls, on the other hand, offer enough power to create sophisticated text editors, such as the one in Eclipse. However, they're much more complicated to understand and use.

We've now covered many useful widgets. We've discussed creating combo boxes and toolbars, combining controls with coolbars, adding sliders to a control, and several ways of displaying the progress of a task to the user. As you may have noticed, the code examples have also become more complex and closer to how real-world usage may look. The points we've discussed in relation to threading issues are important to keep in mind always, not just when you're using progress bars or indicators.

In the next chapter, we'll cover layouts and explain how you can control the overall presentation of controls in a GUI application.

6

Layouts

We've used layouts throughout the course of this book. Now that you have a firm grasp of widgets and controls, we'll delve into the complexities of how to use layouts to arrange widgets into a pleasant interface.

Layouts are associated with a composite and help organize the controls within it. One way to think about the process is to imagine each widget as a book and the layout as shelving. You can stack books up on the shelf or lay them side by side in a horizontal row. Layouts can consist of partitions to separate the books or new layers to hold them more efficiently. Unlike real-world shelving, SWT layouts are dynamic: the container and its contents can be resized, reflowed, and laid out according to rules you specify. These rules are known as *constraints* in SWT.

Building a wooden bookshelf can be a lot of work, taking days or weeks. Although creating a UI can also be time consuming, the many options available in SWT's layouts can make the job much easier. You may not ever make a nice oak bookshelf, but this chapter will show you how to exercise your imagination in creating virtual cabinets.

NOTE   Before we get into the details, it's worth taking a moment to compare SWT's approach with Swing's design. Swing also has layouts, such as the ubiquitous `BorderLayout`. Unfortunately, SWT's layouts typically differ from the Swing layouts, and knowledge of Swing doesn't ease the learning curve much. The layout algorithms have a tangibly different feel. SWT's approach minimizes layouts, using attributes and modifiers on widgets to control their position. By contrast, Swing uses a recursive approach that nests layouts. The drawback is that the nesting can quickly become deep, leading to inefficiency and high resource costs. Compared to Swing, SWT layouts require you to do more advance planning and map where the `Controls` will go, often breaking out paper and pencil to sketch your ideas in advance. With Swing, it's possible to use a divide-and-conquer approach, laying out small sections at a time and then nesting them to form the overall GUI. Ultimately, the two toolkits chose to emphasis different strengths: design-time simplicity versus runtime simplicity. Neither holds a marked advantage, but this difference shapes our approach as GUI designers.

6.1 The fill layout

Our desks are often littered with books stacked in gigantic piles; this system is simple, easy, and useful in many cases. The *fill layout* is the layout equivalent of a stack of books. It's a simple layout that takes the child controls and lays them out at equal intervals to fill the space in a composite. By default, the controls are stacked side by side, from left to right. Each control is given the space it needs, and any leftover space in the composite is divided among the child controls.

Figure 6.1 shows buttons in a `FillLayout`; the code in listing 6.1 demonstrates how to create this layout. You add a series of buttons to a composite, and the layout resizes them to take up all the available space.

Listing 6.1   Ch6FillLayoutComposite.java

```
package com.swtjface.Ch6;

import org.eclipse.swt.*;
import org.eclipse.swt.widgets.*;
import org.eclipse.swt.layout.*;

public class Ch6FillLayoutComposite extends Composite {

    public Ch6FillLayoutComposite(Composite parent) {
        super(parent, SWT.NONE);

        FillLayout layout = new FillLayout( SWT.VERTICAL);
        setLayout(layout);
        for (int i = 0; i < 8; ++i) {
            Button button = new Button(this, SWT.NONE);
            button.setText("Sample Text");
        }
    }
}
```

Notice the `setLayout()` method call. This method in `Composite` is used to associate a layout with the composite that will be used to arrange all the child controls. Without this call, SWT won't know how to size or position any of the child controls, so nothing will be displayed. (If you're having trouble getting your widgets to appear, forgetting to set a layout is a common cause.)

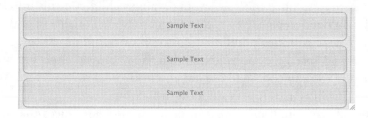

Figure 6.1
Buttons in a
`FillLayout`, **before**
resizing

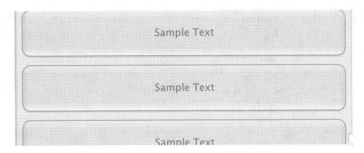

Figure 6.2
The same buttons,
after resizing

Resizing the window changes the buttons to look like figure 6.2. There is little visible difference between the two images, because the FillLayout always expands the buttons to fill all available space.

You can call the FillLayout constructor with no parameters or with a single style parameter. The default constructor uses the SWT.HORIZONTAL style, in which case the layout arranges child controls from left to right. Using SWT.VERTICAL causes the controls to be arranged from top to bottom.

Add the following code to WidgetWindow to see how the FillLayout works:

```
TabItem fillLayoutItem = new TabItem(tf, SWT.NONE);
fillLayoutItem.setText("Chapter 6 FillLayout");
fillLayoutItem.setControl(new Ch6FillLayoutComposite(tf));
```

Like a stack of books, the fill layout is good only for simple situations. As you gather more books—or controls, in the case of JFace/SWT—the stack becomes unmanageable. Books get lost in the clutter, and your eyes become distracted. To organize more effectively, you need the GUI equivalent of a bookcase.

6.2 *The row layout*

If the fill layout is like a stack of books, then the row layout is a basic bookcase. Instead of being limited to one pile, you can organize controls into a number of rows, much like shelves. Since the row layout arranges child controls into single row by default, you need to pass in SWT.WRAP to get the functionality of additional rows. The row layout provides additional customization options by giving you access to margin and spacing options. (Note that the name *row layout* is a bit of a misnomer, because you can choose to use either a horizontal row or a vertical row. The vertical row layout is therefore really a column layout.)

Let's see how having multiple rows can facilitate user interfaces that have a large number of controls. The code for the WidgetWindow pane in figure 6.3 is

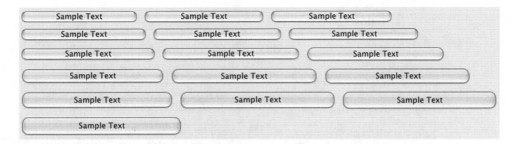

Figure 6.3 Buttons positioned by a `RowLayout,` **before resizing**

almost the same as for the fill layout, but the child controls are laid out differently. The code to produce this layout appears in listing 6.2.

Listing 6.2   Ch6RowLayoutComposite.java

```
package com.swtjface.Ch6;

import org.eclipse.swt.*;
import org.eclipse.swt.widgets.*;
import org.eclipse.swt.layout.*;

public class Ch6RowLayoutComposite extends Composite {

    public Ch6RowLayoutComposite(Composite parent) {
        super(parent, SWT.NONE);

        RowLayout layout = new RowLayout(SWT.HORIZONTAL);
        setLayout(layout);
        for (int i = 0; i < 16; ++i) {
            Button button = new Button(this, SWT.NONE);
            button.setText("Sample Text");
        }
    }
}
```

Add the next three lines to `WidgetWindow`, and resize the window showing the buttons:

```
TabItem rowLayoutItem = new TabItem(tf, SWT.NONE);
rowLayoutItem.setText("Chapter 6 RowLayout");
rowLayoutItem.setControl(new Ch6RowLayoutComposite(tf));
```

As you can see, instead of using all available space for each child, the row layout combines multiple buttons into each row. The layout does so dynamically, so

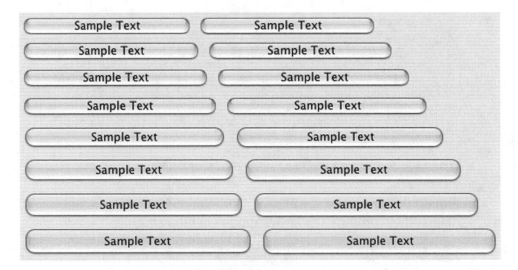

Figure 6.4 **After resizing, the** `RowLayout` **rearranges the buttons into two columns.**

when you reduce the width of the window, the buttons shift downward, as figure 6.4 shows.

Much of the other behavior in a `RowLayout` is specified through property values. We're mainly concerned with the following properties:

- *wrap*—A boolean value that defaults to `true`. You'll probably want to keep the default. Switching it off will result in all the controls staying on a single row, with the controls cut off at the end of the visible edge of the parent composite.

- *pack*—A boolean value that defaults to `true`. This property keeps child controls the same size, which typically is desirable in the context of a row layout. You get even rows of controls by setting `pack`; on the other hand, keeping `pack` off lets controls retain their natural sizing.

- *justify*—A boolean value that defaults to `false`. This property distributes controls evenly across the expanse of the parent composite. If `justify` is on and the parent is resized, then all the child controls pick up the slack and redistribute themselves evenly across the empty space.

6.2.1 *Customizing individual layout cells*

You've seen how to control the overall behavior of the layout. However, it's also possible to tinker with each individual child control's sizing in the layout by using the RowData class. Many layouts use the layout data mechanism. The idea is that you can help guide the parent layout by associating hints with each control using the setLayout() method, which takes an instance of LayoutData. An examination of the class hierarchy reveals that RowData is derived from LayoutData and therefore all the layouts have the potential to understand the associated layout data. In practice, though, you need to use the exact layout data class that each layout expects in order to get tangible results. Layouts will ignore hints from layout data they don't recognize. By convention, for each layout class that supports data for individual children, there is a data class whose name matches: FooLayout has a data class called FooData, and so on.

Creating row data hints for the row layout is simple. All the information is passed in through the row data's constructor. Let's expand our WidgetWindow example to give more room for the first couple controls. Add the line in bold in listing 6.3 to the existing code.

Listing 6.3 Ch6RowLayoutComposite.java

```java
package com.swtjface.Ch6;

import org.eclipse.swt.*;
import org.eclipse.swt.widgets.*;
import org.eclipse.swt.layout.*;

public class Ch6RowLayoutComposite extends Composite {

    public Ch6RowLayoutComposite(Composite parent) {
        super(parent, SWT.NONE);

        RowLayout layout = new RowLayout(SWT.HORIZONTAL);
        setLayout(layout);
        for (int i = 0; i < 16; ++i) {
            Button button = new Button(this, SWT.NONE);
            button.setText("Sample Text");
            button.setLayoutData(new RowData(200 + 5 * i, 20 + i));
        }
    }
}
```

The figures have illustrated the effects of having row data set. Remember, the best way to learn what these options do and how they interact is to tinker with the code. Often, to get the result you want, you'll need a combination of style hints, properties, and layout data.

6.3 *The grid layout*

The grid layout builds on the row layout model by allowing you to explicitly create multiple rows and columns. In effect, the grid layout offers a nicely partitioned bookcase with multiple shelves and clean divisions on each shelf to further organize your controls. Factor in a flexible grid data object, and the end result is that the grid layout is the most useful and widely used layout. Figure 6.5 shows a series of buttons, this time controlled by a GridLayout.

Listing 6.4 demonstrates a simple grid layout example in the WidgetWindow framework. We create a GridLayout with four columns and allow the layout to create as many rows as necessary.

Listing 6.4   Ch6GridLayoutComposite.java

```java
package com.swtjface.Ch6;

import org.eclipse.swt.*;
import org.eclipse.swt.widgets.*;
import org.eclipse.swt.layout.*;

public class Ch6GridLayoutComposite extends Composite {

    public Ch6GridLayoutComposite(Composite parent) {
        super(parent, SWT.NONE);
        GridLayout layout = new GridLayout(4,false);    ◁──┐  GridLayout
        setLayout(layout);                                     constructor
        for (int i = 0; i < 16; ++i) {
            Button button = new Button(this, SWT.NONE);
            button.setText("Cell " + i);
        }
    }
}
```

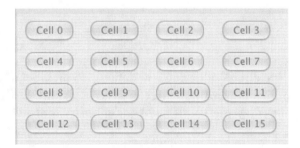

Figure 6.5
Buttons controlled by a GridLayout

Note that the constructor takes two parameters: the number of columns and a boolean to indicate whether the columns should take up an even amount of space. By passing `false`, you tell the layout to only use the minimum amount of space needed for each column.

You can run the composite by adding the following lines to `WidgetWindow`:

```
TabItem gridLayoutItem = new TabItem(tf, SWT.NONE);
gridLayoutItem.setText("Chapter 6 GridLayout");
gridLayoutItem.setControl(new Ch6GridLayoutComposite(tf));
```

6.3.1 *GridData*

At first, the notion of having a grid may seem contrary to a flexible layout. The key to using the grid layout is understanding that a single child control can span more than one grid cell at a time. You do this through layout data. In this case, let's turn to the `GridData` object, which provides additional hints for the `GridLayout` on how to lay out a `Control`.

Using GridData styles

`GridData` is in many ways similar to the `RowData` object that we examined in the previous section. The constructor takes a series of style constants, which when combined determine how the layout will position an individual widget. These styles fall into three categories: `FILL`, `HORIZONTAL_ALIGN`, and `VERTICAL_ALIGN`.

The various `FILL` styles determine whether the cell should be expanded to fill available space. Valid values include `FILL_HORIZONTAL`, which indicates that the cell should be expanded horizontally; `FILL_VERTICAL`, to expand the cell vertically; and `FILL_BOTH`, which effectively causes the cell to fill all the space available.

The `ALIGN` styles, on the other hand, determine where the control should be positioned in the cell. Values include `BEGINNING`, `END`, `CENTER`, and `FILL`. `BEGINNING` positions the control at the left or topmost edge of the cell, whereas `END` puts the control at the right or bottommost edge. `CENTER` centers the control, and `FILL` causes the control to expand to fill all available space.

Table 6.1 summarizes the available style combinations for a `GridData` object.

Using GridData size attributes

Unlike `RowData`, `GridData` also has a number of public attributes that can be set to control its behavior. Several of these are boolean values that are automatically managed when the different styles are set, so it isn't typically necessary to manipulate them directly. Some, however, are integer values used to precisely control the size of individual cells. These attributes are summarized in table 6.2.

Table 6.1 Style combinations for GridData

Style Constant	Description
FILL_HORIZONTAL	Expand the cell to fill any empty space horizontally. Implies HORIZONTAL_ALIGN_FILL.
FILL_VERTICAL	Expand the cell to fill any empty space vertically. Implies VERTICAL_ALIGN_FILL.
FILL_BOTH	Expand the cell both vertically and horizontally. Equivalent to FILL_HORIZONTAL | FILL_VERTICAL.
HORIZONTAL_ALIGN_BEGINNING	Align the cell's contents at the leftmost edge of the cell.
HORIZONTAL_ALIGN_END	Align the cell's contents at the rightmost edge of the cell.
HORIZONTAL_ALIGN_CENTER	Center the cell's contents horizontally.
HORIZONTAL_ALIGN_FILL	Expand the cell's contents to fill all empty horizontal space in the cell.
VERTICAL_ALIGN_BEGINNING	Align the cell's contents at the top of the cell.
VERTICAL_ALIGN_END	Align the cell's contents at the bottom of the cell.
VERTICAL_ALIGN_CENTER	Center the cell's contents vertically.
VERTICAL_ALIGN_FILL	Expand the cell's contents to fill all empty vertical space in the cell.

Of particular importance are the horizontalSpan and verticalSpan attributes. As we mentioned earlier, by setting a certain control to cover more than one cell, you can make your UI look less like a spreadsheet so it's more visually appealing. Figure 6.6 demonstrates this concept. We've created a grid layout with three

Table 6.2 GridData size attributes

Attribute	Description	Default Value
widthHint	Minimum width for the column. SWT.DEFAULT designates that there is no minimum width.	SWT.DEFAULT
heightHint	Minimum height for the row. SWT.DEFAULT designates that there is no minimum height.	SWT.DEFAULT
horizontalIndent	Number of pixels to be placed between the control and the left edge of the cell.	0
horizontalSpan	Number of columns in the grid that this cell should cover.	1
verticalSpan	Number of rows in the grid that this cell should cover.	1

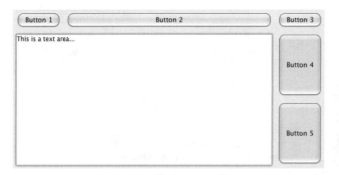

Figure 6.6
A more advanced `GridLayout`.
The text area covers two
columns and two rows. All the
other controls are contained in
one cell each.

columns and three rows. The text area in the lower-left corner has been configured to cover two columns and two rows, allowing it to expand to cover much more area than the buttons. Note that button 2 along the top and buttons 4 and 5 on the right have been set to FILL_HORIZONTAL and FILL_VERTICAL, respectively.

For reference, the snippet of code that configures the text area is shown here:

```
Text t = new Text(this, SWT.MULTI);
GridData data = new GridData(GridData.FILL_BOTH);
data.horizontalSpan = 2;
data.verticalSpan = 2;
t.setLayoutData(data);
```

We set both span attributes to 2 and tell the GridData that we wish to expand as much as possible in both directions.

6.4 *The form layout*

You've seen a steady progression in capability as we've discussed the fill layout, the row layout, and finally the grid layout. Those layouts share the same underlying layout algorithm—laying out controls in rows and columns—albeit in varying degrees of complexity. The form layout is a departure from that path. Instead of partitioning sections, the form layout lets you create a UI based on gluing together controls relative to each other or the parent composite.

This makes it much easier to create resizable forms with controls of differing sizes. A typical dialog box, for example, has a large central text area and two buttons located just below and to the right. In this case, the most natural way to think of how the controls should be positioned is by envisioning them relative to each other. It's easier to say "the buttons should be below the text area, and the Cancel button should be to the right of the Ok button" and let SWT worry about the details than to try to calculate how many rows and columns each control should

Figure 6.7
A `FormLayout` **has been used to position the two buttons relative to the text area.**

span. Figure 6.7 shows an example of this setup; in the following sections, we'll discuss the elements necessary to create it.

The `FormLayout` class is fairly simple. The only configuration options come from attributes that control the height and width of the margins around the edge of the layout, and the `spacing` attribute, which lets you specify the amount of space (in pixels) to be placed between all controls. Similar to the layouts we examined previously, you configure individual controls using instances of `FormData`.

6.4.1 Using FormData

A `FormData` instance is typically associated with each child control in a composite. Even more so than with other layouts, it's important to provide configuration data for each child, because the whole idea of a form layout is to specify positions of child controls relative to each other. If a given control doesn't have a `FormData` instance describing it, it will default to being placed in the upper-right corner of the composite, which is rarely what you want.

The `width` and `height` attributes specify the dimensions of a control in pixels. More important are the `top`, `bottom`, `right`, and `left` attributes, each of which holds an instance of `FormAttachment`. These attachments describe the control's relations to other controls in the composite.

6.4.2 Specifying relations using FormAttachment

Understanding the `FormAttachment` class is the most important part of using a form layout. As mentioned earlier, each instance of `FormAttachment` describes the positioning of one side of a control. You can use `FormAttachment` two different ways.

First, you can specify a `FormAttachment` using a percentage of the parent composite. For example, if the `left` side of a `FormData` is set to a `FormAttachment` with 50%, then the left edge of the control will be placed at the horizontal middle of the parent. Likewise, setting the top edge to 75% positions the control three quarters of the way down the composite. Table 6.3 summarizes the FormAttachment constructors that can be used to specify percentages.

Table 6.3 Percentage-based FormAttachment constructors

Constructor signature	Description
FormAttachment(int numerator)	Assumes a denominator of 100, meaning that the argument will be treated as a percentage. Only available in SWT 3.0.
FormAttachment(int numerator, int offset)	Assumes a denominator of 100, meaning that the argument will be treated as a percentage. The offset is the number of pixels that the control should be offset from the percentage position.
FormAttachment(int numerator, int denominator, int offset)	The numerator divided by the denominator gives the percentage used to position the control. The offset is the number of pixels that the control should be offset from the percentage position.

Specifying FormAttachments in terms of percentages can be useful, but you shouldn't use this approach often. Specifying all your controls using percentages isn't much different from assigning them absolute pixel positions: It quickly becomes difficult to visualize the positions of each element; and when the composite is resized, it's unlikely that the controls will still be in the positions you desire. The point of using a FormLayout is to position controls relative to each other, which the second form of FormAttachment allows.

The second series of FormAttachment constructors are based on passing in other controls. They're used to position the edge of one control next to another. By setting the right attribute of the FormData for button1 to a FormAttachment constructed with button2, you're saying that button1 should always be positioned such that button2 is immediately to its right. Laying out most or all of your controls in this fashion has several benefits. The intent of your layout code becomes easier to understand: Instead of your having to guess which controls are meant to be next to each other based on percentages or pixels, it becomes obvious that, for example, control foo should always be below bar. Second, the form layout is also aware of your intent. However the composite may be resized, it will always be able to maintain the correct relative positions.

Again, there are several different forms of the FormAttachment constructor for specifying relative positions; they're summarized in table 6.4.

Table 6.4 `FormAttachment` **constructors that accept relative positions**

Constructor signature	Description
`FormAttachment(Control control)`	Attach the current widget to the adjacent side of the control parameter.
`FormAttachment(Control control, int offset)`	Attach the current widget to the adjacent side of the control parameter, offset by the number of pixels in the `offset` parameter.
`FormAttachment(Control control, int offset, int alignment)`	`alignment` must be one of `SWT.TOP`, `SWT.BOTTOM`, `SWT.LEFT`, `SWT.RIGHT`, or `SWT.CENTER`. Attach the current widget to the side of the `control` parameter specified by `alignment`, offset by the number of pixels in the `offset` parameter.

6.4.3 *Laying out controls using a form layout*

Now that we've discussed the classes that work together to drive a form layout, we'll look at the code we used to produce the screenshot in figure 6.7. Listing 6.5 creates a text area and two buttons. The text control is anchored to the top and left edges of the composite. Both buttons are placed below the text control, and the Ok button is placed to the left of the Cancel button.

Listing 6.5   Ch6FormLayoutComposite.java

```
package com.swtjface.Ch6;

import org.eclipse.swt.*;
import org.eclipse.swt.widgets.*;
import org.eclipse.swt.layout.*;

public class Ch6FormLayoutComposite extends Composite {

    public Ch6FormLayoutComposite(Composite parent) {
    super(parent, SWT.NONE);

    FormLayout layout = new FormLayout();
    setLayout(layout);

    Text t = new Text(this, SWT.MULTI);
    FormData data = new FormData();
    data.top = new FormAttachment(0, 0);         ❶ Text goes at upper left
    data.left = new FormAttachment(0, 0);
    data.right = new FormAttachment(100);
    data.bottom = new FormAttachment(75);
    t.setLayoutData(data);

    Button ok = new Button(this, SWT.NONE);
    ok.setText("Ok");
```

```
    Button cancel = new Button(this, SWT.NONE);
    cancel.setText("Cancel");

    data = new FormData();                    Ok button positioned
    data.top = new FormAttachment(t);     ❷  relative to other widgets
    data.right = new FormAttachment(cancel);
    ok.setLayoutData(data);

    data = new FormData();
    data.top = new FormAttachment(t);
    data.right = new FormAttachment(100);  ❸  Cancel button on right side
    cancel.setLayoutData(data);
    }
}
```

❶ Here we position the text widget, which is the main control that everything else will be positioned relative to. By setting both the top and left fields to FormAttachments with a percentage of 0, we anchor the text widget to the upper-left corner. The right field is 100, so the text widget expands horizontally to fill the available area; and the bottom field's value of 75 causes it to take up the top three quarters of the available area.

❷ The Ok button must follow two rules: It should always be immediately below the text area and immediately to the left of the Cancel button. We specify this using the top and right fields of the FormData, giving each a FormAttachment instance with a reference to the appropriate control.

❸ After positioning the Cancel button below the text area, we force it to the right side of the composite by using a FormAttachment with a percentage of 100.

However you resize the window, the buttons and the text area always maintain their correct positions.

You may have noticed that although we use the line

```
    data.right = new FormAttachment(cancel);
```

when we set up the data for the Ok button, there is no corresponding

```
    data.left = new FormAttachment(ok);
```

statement for the Cancel button. The second line is implied by the first, but SWT forbids you from creating such circular attachments. Whenever you have a control foo that refers to control bar, bar must not refer back to foo. According to the SWT documentation, if you create such an attachment, the result of the layout algorithm will be undefined, although it's guaranteed to terminate and not leave your program stuck in an infinite loop.

Add the following lines to `WidgetWindow` to see for yourself how `FormLayout` works:

```
TabItem formLayoutItem = new TabItem(tf, SWT.NONE);
formLayoutItem.setText("Chapter 6 FormLayout");
formLayoutItem.setControl(new Ch6FormLayoutComposite(tf));
```

6.5 *Custom layouts*

The standard layouts serve a variety of roles and are suitable for most situations. Sometimes, though, you need to build a custom layout to deal with the exceptions to the rule. Like a finely crafted piece of custom cabinetry, a custom layout can make everything it contains look better.

It's relatively rare that you'll need to create a custom layout implementation—the existing layouts can handle most situations, especially when they're used with a `ResizeListener` to tweak the positions of widgets after the window has been resized. It's only appropriate to create a new layout class if the same layout logic will be reused in several places in your application, or if manually adjusting positions after resize events proves to be more awkward than laying them out precisely in the first place.

To demonstrate the process of creating a custom layout manager, we'll create a `RadialLayout` class that positions its widgets in a circle. You wouldn't often use this layout in an application, but the fairly straightforward algorithm lends itself to being used as an example. When we're done, the final result will look like figure 6.8.

Custom layouts are derived from the abstract `Layout` class. You need to write only two methods: `computeSize()` and `layout()`. (These are the only methods

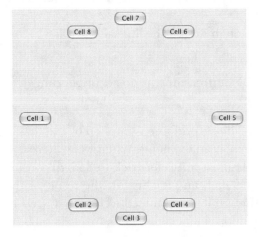

Figure 6.8
Buttons laid out using `RadialLayout`

that Layout defines; it's more of an interface than a true abstract class.) The computeSize() method is called when the parent composite is instantiated to calculate how much space the layout requires. This is followed by a call to layout() to position all the controls.

6.5.1 *Calculating the layout's size*

The first method we'll examine is computeSize(). The relevant bits of this method are as follows:

```
protected Point computeSize(Composite composite,
                            int wHint, int hHint,
                            boolean flushCache)
{
  Point maxDimensions =
          calculateMaxDimensions(composite.getChildren());
  int stepsPerHemisphere =
          stepsPerHemisphere(composite.getChildren().length);

  int maxWidth = maxDimensions.x;
  int maxHeight = maxDimensions.y;

  int dimensionMultiplier = (stepsPerHemisphere + 1);
  int controlWidth = maxWidth * dimensionMultiplier;
  int controlHeight = maxHeight * dimensionMultiplier;
  int diameter = Math.max(controlWidth, controlHeight);
  Point preferredSize = new Point(diameter,
                                  diameter);
  ... // code to handle case when our calculations
      // are too large
  return preferredSize;
}
```

The parameters to this method are straightforward:

- *composite*—The object we're going to populate. At the time this method is called, it has children, but neither the composite nor the children have been sized or positioned on the screen.

- *wHint* and *hHint*—Suggestions for the width and height, respectively. These values represent the largest size the layout should request. They may also have the special value SWT.DEFAULT, which signifies that the layout is free to use whatever sizes it decides it needs.

- *flushCache*—A simple flag to tell the layout whether it's safe to use any cached values that it may be maintaining. In our example, we don't cache anything, so it's safe to ignore this flag.

The purpose of `computeSize()` is to calculate how large the composite we're laying out should be. In particular, this method shouldn't modify the sizes of any components—the system will set the parent composite's size when it's ready and call `layout()` when it's time to position the children. Because our example lays out the controls in a circle, we need to figure out an appropriate radius to fit all the controls without having them overlap and then return a size for the composite that will accommodate a circle of that size.

The calculations are simple. We first find the largest child by calling `calculateMaxDimensions()`, which asks each child for its preferred size and returns the largest. In order to keep the code simple, we assume that each child is as large as the largest one. (This approach works fine when you're laying out objects that are all approximately the same size, but it would cause trouble in a real system if some widgets were significantly larger than the others.) Once we have a size for our child objects, we multiply that size by half the number of children. Because one hemisphere of the circle will contain half the child objects, this gives us the diameter of the circle. We create a `Point` object representing a square of this size (plus some padding) and return it as the preferred size of our composite.

6.5.2 Laying out the widgets

Once we've recommended a size for our composite, the `layout()` method is called. This is our cue to position each of the children in the parent composite.

The parameters are even simpler this time. We're given the composite that's being populated and the same `flushCache` flag as before. The logic, however, is a bit more complex, because we have to calculate the exact position of each child object. To do so, we use an equation you may remember from geometry:

$$X^2 + Y^2 = R^2$$

We can easily calculate R (the radius), so for any X coordinate we might choose, Y can be calculated as:

$$Y = \pm\sqrt{R^2 - X^2}$$

Starting at the leftmost point of the circle, the layout method traverses the list of children, regularly spacing each along the X axis and using this X coordinate to calculate the appropriate Y coordinate. The work is done in the `calculateControlPositions()` method, which is called by `layout()`. Here's a summary of the code:

```
private Point[] calculateControlPositions(Composite composite)
{
  ... // set up control counts, max width, etc.
  Rectangle clientArea = composite.getClientArea();

  int radius = (smallestDimension / 2) - maxControlWidth;
  Point center = new Point(clientArea.width / 2,
                           clientArea.height / 2);
  long radiusSquared = radius * radius;

  int stepXDistance = ...

  int signMultiplier = 1;
  int x = -radius;
  int y;
  Control[] controls = composite.getChildren();
  for(int i = 0; i < controlCount; i++)
  {
    Point currSize = controls[i].getSize();
    long xSquared = x * x;

    int sqrRoot = (int)Math.sqrt(radiusSquared - xSquared);
    y = signMultiplier * sqrRoot;

    ... // translate coordinates to be relative to
        // actual center, instead of the origin

    positions[i] = new Point(translatedX - (currSize.x  / 2),
                             translatedY - (currSize.y / 2) );

    x = x + (signMultiplier * stepXDistance);
    //we've finished the upper hemisphere, now do the lower
    if(x >= radius)
    {
      x = radius - (x - radius);
      signMultiplier = -1;
    }
  }

  return positions;
}
```

This method is mostly a straightforward implementation of the algorithm mentioned earlier. The only tricky part is that we lay out one hemisphere at a time. Once the X value has reached the rightmost point of the circle, we switch the X coordinates to decrease back along the same path and reverse the sign on the Y coordinates (which accounts for the +/- part of our equation earlier). The sign-Multiplier variable takes care of this for us. It has the value of either 1 or –1, and it controls both whether the X value is increasing or decreasing and whether the Y values are positive or negative.

The other "gotcha" in this code is remembering that the equation we're using assumes that the center of the circle is at the origin. It's therefore necessary to translate each point to be relative to the actual center of the circle instead.

Once we have `calculateControlPositions()` working, writing `layout()` is easy. We take the list of positions that we've calculated and apply them to the children of the parent composite:

```
protected void layout(Composite composite, boolean flushCache)
{
  Point[] positions = calculateControlPositions(composite);
  Control[] controls = composite.getChildren();
  for(int i = 0; i < controls.length; i++)
  {
    Point preferredSize = controls[i].computeSize(SWT.DEFAULT,
                                                  SWT.DEFAULT);
    controls[i].setBounds(positions[i].x, positions[i].y,
                          preferredSize.x, preferredSize.y);
  }
}
```

Because the complete class has already grown rather large, we ask each control to calculate its preferred size and use that value, plus the positions calculated earlier, to place each control in the composite. Giving each control a size is critical: If you don't set the size, the control will default to having a width and height of 0, meaning that it will be invisible.

6.5.3 *Updating WidgetWindow*

The complete code for `RadialLayout` is shown in listing 6.6. The listing is long, but we've already examined the complicated parts in detail, so it should be easy to follow.

Listing 6.6   RadialLayout.java

```
package com.swtjface.Ch6;

import org.eclipse.swt.SWT;
import org.eclipse.swt.graphics.Point;
import org.eclipse.swt.graphics.Rectangle;
import org.eclipse.swt.widgets.*;

public class RadialLayout extends Layout
{
  public RadialLayout()
  {
    super();
  }

  protected Point computeSize(Composite composite,
```

```
                              int wHint, int hHint,
                              boolean flushCache)
{
    Point maxDimensions =
            calculateMaxDimensions(composite.getChildren());
    int stepsPerHemisphere =
            stepsPerHemisphere(composite.getChildren().length);

    int maxWidth = maxDimensions.x;
    int maxHeight = maxDimensions.y;

    int dimensionMultiplier = (stepsPerHemisphere + 1);
    int controlWidth = maxWidth * dimensionMultiplier;
    int controlHeight = maxHeight * dimensionMultiplier;
    int diameter = Math.max(controlWidth, controlHeight);
    Point preferredSize = new Point(diameter,
                                    diameter);

    if(wHint != SWT.DEFAULT)
    {
        if(preferredSize.x > wHint)
        {
            preferredSize.x = wHint;
        }
    }

    if(hHint != SWT.DEFAULT)
    {
        if(preferredSize.y > hHint)
        {
            preferredSize.y = hHint;
        }
    }

    return preferredSize;
}

protected void layout(Composite composite, boolean flushCache)
{
    Point[] positions = calculateControlPositions(composite);
    Control[] controls = composite.getChildren();
    for(int i = 0; i < controls.length; i++)
    {
        Point preferredSize = controls[i].computeSize(SWT.DEFAULT,
                                                      SWT.DEFAULT);
        controls[i].setBounds(positions[i].x, positions[i].y,
                              preferredSize.x, preferredSize.y);
    }
}

private Point[] calculateControlPositions(Composite composite)
{
    int controlCount = composite.getChildren().length;
```

```
int stepsPerHemisphere = stepsPerHemisphere(controlCount);
Point[] positions = new Point[controlCount];

Point maxControlDimensions =
        calculateMaxDimensions(composite.getChildren());
int maxControlWidth = maxControlDimensions.x;

Rectangle clientArea = composite.getClientArea();
int smallestDimension =
        Math.min(clientArea.width, clientArea.height);
int radius = (smallestDimension / 2) - maxControlWidth;
Point center = new Point(clientArea.width / 2,
                            clientArea.height / 2);
long radiusSquared = radius * radius;

int stepXDistance =
        calculateStepDistance(radius * 2, stepsPerHemisphere);

int signMultiplier = 1;
int x = -radius;
int y;
Control[] controls = composite.getChildren();
for(int i = 0; i < controlCount; i++)
{
  Point currSize = controls[i].getSize();
  long xSquared = x * x;

  int sqrRoot = (int)Math.sqrt(radiusSquared - xSquared);
  y = signMultiplier * sqrRoot;
  int translatedX = x + center.x;
  int translatedY = y + center.y;
  positions[i] = new Point(translatedX - (currSize.x  / 2),
                            translatedY - (currSize.y / 2) );

  x = x + (signMultiplier * stepXDistance);
  //we've finished the upper hemisphere, now do the lower
  if(x >= radius)
  {
    x = radius - (x - radius);
    signMultiplier = -1;
  }
}

return positions;
}

private Point calculateMaxDimensions(Control[] controls)
{
  Point maxes = new Point(0, 0);

  for(int i = 0; i < controls.length; i++)
  {
    Point controlSize =
            controls[i].computeSize(SWT.DEFAULT, SWT.DEFAULT);
```

```
      maxes.x = Math.max(maxes.x, controlSize.x);
      maxes.y = Math.max(maxes.y, controlSize.y);
    }

    return maxes;
  }
  private int stepsPerHemisphere(int totalObjects)
  {
    return (totalObjects / 2) - 1;
  }
  private int calculateStepDistance(int clientAreaDimensionSize,
                                    int stepCount)
  {
    return clientAreaDimensionSize / (stepCount + 1);
  }
}
```

Now that we have our custom layout, using it is easy, as shown by the class in listing 6.7.

Listing 6.7   Ch6RadialLayoutComposite.java

```
package com.swtjface.Ch6;

import org.eclipse.swt.SWT;
import org.eclipse.swt.widgets.Button;
import org.eclipse.swt.widgets.Composite;

public class Ch6RadialLayoutComposite extends Composite
{
  public Ch6RadialLayoutComposite(Composite parent)
  {
    super(parent, SWT.NONE);
    setLayout(new RadialLayout());

    for(int i = 0; i < 8; i++)
    {
      Button b = new Button(this, SWT.NONE);
      b.setText("Cell " + (i + 1));
    }

  }
}
```

When you add this class to the WidgetWindow with the following code, it creates a series of buttons laid out in a circle, as you saw earlier:

```
TabItem radialLayoutItem = new TabItem(tf, SWT.NONE);
radialLayoutItem.setText("Chapter 6 RadialLayout");
radialLayoutItem.setControl(new Ch6RadialLayoutComposite(tf));
```

6.6 *Summary*

When you're using SWT, choosing a layout is often an exercise of weighing flexibility versus complexity. The available options range from the simple `FillLayout`, which makes all your controls as large as can be such that they all fit; to `RowLayout`, which lets you position controls in rows or columns; to the more complicated `GridLayout` and `FormLayout`, which allow more advanced positioning but require more planning and more code to use. No single layout is the correct choice for all situations, but by knowing the options that are available, you can make appropriate trade-offs for your application. You can use simple layouts to get quick results when the UI isn't complicated, and advanced layouts can create a good-looking interface when required.

In addition to the layouts, you'll be using a variety of data classes. Each data class is associated with a specific layout that knows how to use it. Instances of these data classes are attached to individual controls to fine-tune the way they're laid out by the algorithms embedded in the layout classes.

Graphics

7

The main reason for the popularity of the SWT/JFace toolset is its use of the operating system's native widgets. Most users, accustomed to their operating system, prefer applications that resemble their environment. They want widgets that look and operate similarly from one GUI to the next. But sometimes, a developer needs to go beyond built-in parts and create components of his own. Customized controls add a sense of individuality to a user interface, and images may be necessary for visually oriented applications. In these situations, it's necessary to understand the graphics capabilities of the SWT/JFace toolset.

This chapter's goal is to provide that understanding. To meet this goal, we'll proceed from general concepts to specific applications. The first section will describe the class that makes the toolset's graphical capability possible: the *graphic context*. Then, we'll explain how SWT works with colors and how JFace makes this easier. The third section will show how SWT and JFace allow applications to use text with different fonts and graphical properties. Finally, we'll show how the SWT and JFace libraries create and modify images, and when to use the methods of one library over the other.

7.1 The graphic context

The graphic context functions like a drawing board on top of a `Control`. It lets you add custom shapes, images, and multifont text to GUI components. It also provides event processing for these graphics by controlling when the `Control`'s visuals are updated.

In SWT/JFace, the graphic context is encapsulated in the `GC` class. `GC` objects attach to existing `Control`s and make it possible to add graphics. This section will deal with how this important class and its methods operate.

7.1.1 Creating a GC object

The first step in building a graphically oriented application is creating a graphic context and associating it with a component. The `GC` constructor method performs both tasks. The two available constructor methods are shown in table 7.1.

Table 7.1   The constructor methods of the GC class and their functions

Color constructor	Function
GC(Drawable)	Creates a GC and configures it for the Drawable object
GC(Drawable, int)	Creates and configures a GC and sets the text-display style

The style constant mentioned in the second constructor determines how text appears in the display. The two values are RIGHT_TO_LEFT and LEFT_TO_RIGHT; the default style is LEFT_TO_RIGHT.

The first argument requires an object that implements the Drawable interface. This interface contains methods that relate to the internals of a graphic context. SWT provides three classes that implement Drawable: Image, Device, and Control. Unless you create your own Drawable objects, you can only add graphics to instances of these classes or their subclasses. A diagram describing these relationships is presented in figure 7.1. Since Image objects will be covered in a later section, we'll discuss Devices and Controls here.

The Device class represents any mechanism capable of displaying SWT/JFace objects. This is easier to understand if you consider its two main subclasses: Printer, which represents print devices, and Display, which accesses a computer's console. The Display class, the base class of any SWT/JFace application, is described in chapter 2. But since this chapter deals with adding graphics to individual components, we'll associate our GC with the third Drawable class, Control.

As we mentioned in chapter 3, a Control object is any widget that has a counterpart in the underlying operating system. Instances of this class and its subclasses can be resized, traversed, and associated with events and graphics. Figure 7.1 shows some of the Control subclasses provided in SWT. Although of all them can contain graphics, only one class is particularly suited for GC objects: Canvas, shown at the bottom of figure 7.1. This class not only provides the

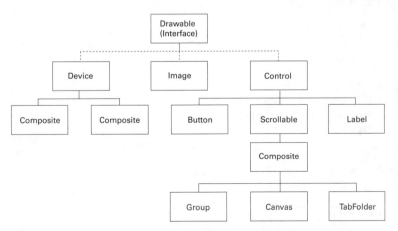

Figure 7.1 Only classes that implement the Drawable interface can have graphic contexts associated with them.

containment property of a Composite, but also can be customized with a number of styles that determine how graphics are shown in its region.

Because of this, the code in this chapter will focus on creating images in Canvas objects. Since we have a means of creating graphics (the GC class) and a means of seeing them displayed (the Canvas class), let's see how these classes work together.

7.1.2 *Drawing shapes on a Canvas*

A full graphical application, DrawExample.java, is shown in listing 7.1. It uses a GC object to draw lines and shapes on a Canvas instance.

Listing 7.1 DrawExample.java

```java
package com.swtjface.Ch7;
import org.eclipse.swt.SWT;
import org.eclipse.swt.graphics.*;
import org.eclipse.swt.widgets.*;

public class DrawExample
{
  public static void main (String [] args)
  {
    Display display = new Display();
    Shell shell = new Shell(display);
    shell.setText("Drawing Example");

    Canvas canvas = new Canvas(shell, SWT.NONE);   // Create Canvas object in shell
    canvas.setSize(150, 150);
    canvas.setLocation(20, 20);
    shell.open ();
    shell.setSize(200,220);
                                                   // Create graphic context in Canvas
    GC gc = new GC(canvas);
    gc.drawRectangle(10, 10, 40, 45);
    gc.drawOval(65, 10, 30, 35);
    gc.drawLine(130, 10, 90, 80);
    gc.drawPolygon(new int[] {20, 70, 45, 90, 70, 70});
    gc.drawPolyline(new int[] {10,120,70,100,100,130,130,75});
    gc.dispose();                                  // Deallocate Color object when finished

    while (!shell.isDisposed())
    {
      if (!display.readAndDispatch())
        display.sleep();
    }
    display.dispose();
  }
}
```

Figure 7.2 shows the GUI created by the DrawExample class.

This example demonstrates two important concerns to keep in mind when you work with GCs. First, the program constructs its Canvas object before invoking the shell.open() method; it creates and uses the GC object afterward. This sequence is necessary since open() clears the Canvas display. This also means that graphic contexts must be created in the same class as the Shell object. Second, the program deallocates the GC object immediately after its last usage. Doing so frees up computer resources quickly without affecting the drawing process.

Figure 7.2
Creating shapes on a Canvas
using the graphic context

Along with those used in DrawExample.java, the GC class provides a number of methods that draw and fill shapes on a Drawable object. These are listed in table 7.2.

Table 7.2   Drawing methods of the GC **class**

Method	Function
drawArc(int x, int y, int width, int height, int startAngle, int arcAngle)	Draws a curve with the given starting point and parameters
fillArc(int x, int y, int width, int height, int startAngle, int arcAngle)	Draws and fills an arc with the background color
drawFocus(int x, int y, int width, int height)	Draws a focus rectangle with the given vertices
drawLine(int x1, int y1, int x2, int y2)	Draws a line between coordinates
drawOval(int x, int y, int width, int height)	Draws an oval with the given center point and dimensions
fillOval(int x, int y, int width, int height)	Fills an oval with the given dimensions
drawPolygon(int[] pointArray)	Draws a closed figure with the given vertices
fillPolygon(int[] pointArray)	Fills a closed figure with points
drawPolyline(int[] pointArray)	Draws a line with multiple segments and the specified endpoints
drawRectangle(int x, int y, int width, int height)	Draws a rectangle with the given starting point and coordinates

continued on next page

Table 7.2   Drawing methods of the GC **class** *(continued)*

Method	Function
`fillRectangle(int x, int y, int width, int height)`	Draws and fills a rectangle with the given coordinates
`drawRectangle(Rectangle rect)`	Draws a rectangle based on an object
`fillRectangle(Rectangle rect)`	Fills a rectangle based on an object
`drawRoundRectangle(int x, int y, int width, int height, int arcWidth, int arcHeight)`	Creates a rounded rectangle with the given width, height, and arc dimensions
`fillGradientRectangle(int x, int y, int width, int height, boolean vertical)`	Draws and fills a rectangle with a gradient from the foreground to the background color

One problem with DrawExample is that its shapes are erased whenever the shell is obscured or minimized. This is an important concern, since we need to make sure the graphics remain visible despite windowing changes. For this purpose, SWT lets you control when a Drawable object is refreshed. This updating process is called *painting*.

7.1.3 *Painting and PaintEvents*

When a GC method draws an image on a Drawable object, it performs the painting process only once. If a user resizes the object or covers it with another window, its graphics are erased. Therefore, it's important that an application maintain its appearance whenever its display is affected by an external event.

These external events are called PaintEvents, and the interfaces that receive them are PaintListeners. A Control triggers a PaintEvent any time its appearance is changed by the application or through outside activity. These classes are used in a similar manner to the events and listeners mentioned in chapter 4. The following snippet shows an example; because a PaintListener has only one event-handling method, no adapter class is necessary:

```
Canvas canvas = new Canvas(shell, SWT.NONE);
canvas.setSize(150, 150);
canvas.setLocation(20, 20);
canvas.addPaintListener(new PaintListener()
{
  public void paintControl(PaintEvent pe)
  {
    GC gc = pe.gc;
    gc.drawPolyline(new int[] {10,120,70,100,100,130,130,75});
  }
```

```
});
shell.open();
```

An interesting aspect of using `PaintListeners` is that each `PaintEvent` object contains its own `GC`. This is important for two reasons. First, because the `GC` instance is created by the event, the `PaintEvent` takes care of its disposal. Second, the application can create the `GC` before the shell is opened, which means that graphics can be configured in a separate class.

SWT optimizes painting in `PaintListener` interfaces, and its designers strongly recommend painting with `Controls` only in response to `PaintEvents`. If an application must update its graphics for another reason, they recommend using the control's `redraw()` method, which adds a paint request to the queue. Afterward, you can invoke the `update()` method to process all the paint requests associated with the object.

It's important to remember that, although painting in a `PaintListener` is recommended for `Control` objects, `Device` and `Image` objects can't use this interface. If you need to create graphics in an image or device, you must create a separate `GC` object and dispose of it when you're finished.

7.1.4 *Clipping and Canvas styles*

By default, the area available for drawing with a graphic context is the same as that of its associated `Control`. However, the `GC` provides methods that establish bounds for its own graphical region, called the *clipping* region. The `setClipping()` method specifies the limits for the `GC`'s graphics, and the `getClipping()` method returns the coordinates of the clipping region.

The concept of clipping is also important when you're dealing with `PaintEvents`. Not only do these events fire whenever a `Drawable` object is covered by another window, but they also keep track of the area being obscured. That is, if a user covers part of a `Canvas` with a second window, the `PaintEvent` determines which section has been clipped and sets its `x`, `y`, `height`, and `width` fields according to the smallest rectangle that encloses the concealed region. This is necessary since repainting refreshes only this clipped region, not the entire object.

If multiple sections of a `Control` object are obscured, then by default, the object merges these sections into a single region and requests that it be repainted. However, if an application requires that separate requests be made for each concealed area, then the `Control` should be constructed with the `NO_MERGE_PAINTS` style. This is the first of the styles associated with the `Composite` class but specifically intended for `Canvas` objects. The rest of these styles are shown in table 7.3.

Table 7.3 Style options for `Canvas` objects

Style	Function
`NO_MERGE_PAINTS`	Keeps concurrent paint requests separate
`NO_FOCUS`	Specifies that `Canvas` can't receive focus
`NO_REDRAW_RESIZE`	Specifies that `Canvas` doesn't repaint itself if resized
`NO_BACKGROUND`	Specifies that `Canvas` has no default background color

Normally, when a user clicks a window, any keyboard input is directed to it. This property is called *focus behavior*, and you can remove it from a `Canvas` object by constructing the object with the `NO_FOCUS` style. Similarly, when a `Canvas` is resized, a `PaintEvent` is triggered by default and the display is repainted. You can change this default behavior by using the `NO_REDRAW_RESIZE` style. It's important to note, though, that using this style may cause graphical artifacts during a resize operation.

Before a graphic context draws its images, its `Canvas` paints itself with the color of its shell, the default background color. These paint operations can cause screen flicker on certain displays. You can prevent this by using the `NO_BACKGROUND` style, which prevents the first painting. Without a background color, the graphic context must cover every pixel of the `Canvas`, or it will take the appearance of the screen behind the shell.

Now that we've begun discussing the colors associated with graphic contexts, let's pursue this important topic in detail.

7.2 Programming with colors

One of the fundamental aspects of any graphical toolset is its use of colors. The theory behind colors is straightforward, but their practical usage requires explanation. This section will discuss how colors are represented in SWT and how to allocate and deallocate them in a program. It will also discuss two classes provided by the JFace library that simplify the process of working with colors.

7.2.1 Color development with SWT

Because monitors use light to provide color, it makes sense to use light's primary colors—red, green, and blue (RGB)—to represent the colors of a display. This color system is *additive*, which means that colors are generated by adding red, green, and blue elements to a black field. For example, if 24 bits are used to specify the RGB value at a point, then black (the absence of light) is represented in hexadecimal as 0x000000, and white (the combination of light) as 0xFFFFFF. SWT follows this course by providing classes and methods that access and use RGB objects.

This concept may seem simple, but SWT's designers faced a serious challenge in implementing it on multiple platforms. The problem involved providing a standard set of colors despite variations in display resolution and color management policy. In the end, they decided on a two-part solution.

First, SWT provides a set of 16 basic colors (called *system colors*) using the display's getSystemColor() method. This method takes an integer representing one of SWT's color constants and returns a Color object. These constants are listed in table 7.4 with their RGB representations.

Table 7.4   Default system colors provided by SWT

SWT color constant	Color hex value
SWT.COLOR_BLACK	0x000000
SWT.COLOR_DARK_GRAY	0x808080
SWT.COLOR_GRAY	0xC0C0C0
SWT.COLOR_WHITE	0xFFFFFF
SWT.COLOR_RED	0xFF0000
SWT.COLOR_DARK_RED	0x800000
SWT.COLOR_MAGENTA	0xFF00FF
SWT.COLOR_DARK_MAGENTA	0x800080
SWT.COLOR_YELLOW	0xFFFF00
SWT.COLOR_DARK_YELLOW	0x808000
SWT.COLOR_GREEN	0x00FF00
SWT.COLOR_DARK_GREEN	0x008000
SWT.COLOR_CYAN	0x00FFFF
SWT.COLOR_DARK_CYAN	0x008080
SWT.COLOR_BLUE	0x0000FF
SWT.COLOR_DARK_BLUE	0x000080

If you want to use colors that fall outside this set, you must allocate a Color object according to its RGB values. You do so by invoking one of two constructor methods associated with the `Color` class, shown in table 7.5. If a display's resolution is too low to show this color, then it will use the system color with the nearest RGB value.

Table 7.5   The constructor methods of the `Color` class

Color constructor	Function
`Color(Device, int, int, int)`	Allocates a color according to separate RGB values
`Color(Device, RGB)`	Allocates a color according to a given RGB object

In both constructors, the first argument is an object of the `Device` class. Afterward, the color's RGB value is set according to three integers between 0 and 255, or an instance of the `RGB` class. This `RGB` class, whose constructor is `RGB(int, int, int)`, is used to describe a color according to the values of its elements. It's important to remember that creating an `RGB` instance doesn't create a color and that an `RGB` object doesn't require disposal.

The code in listing 7.2 creates a `Canvas` that displays colored two shapes. At this point, we recommend that you create a package named `com.swtjface.Ch7` in the `WidgetWindow` project and add the `Ch7_Colors` class.

Listing 7.2   Ch7_Colors.java

```java
package com.swtjface.Ch7;
import org.eclipse.swt.SWT;
import org.eclipse.swt.graphics.*;
import org.eclipse.swt.widgets.*;
import org.eclipse.swt.events.*;

public class Ch7_Colors extends Canvas
{
  public Ch7_Colors(Composite parent)
  {
    super(parent, SWT.NONE);
    setBackground(this.getDisplay().
      getSystemColor(SWT.COLOR_DARK_GRAY));          ◁──┤ Use system color for
    addPaintListener(drawListener);                        Canvas background
  }

  PaintListener drawListener = new PaintListener()
  {
    public void paintControl(PaintEvent pe)
    {                                                       Create Color
      Display disp = pe.display;                            object based
      Color light_gray = new Color(disp, 0xE0, 0xE0, 0xE0);  ◁──┤ on RGB
      GC gc = pe.gc;                                        value
      gc.setBackground(light_gray);
```

```
        gc.fillPolygon(new int[] {20, 20, 60, 50, 100, 20});
        gc.fillOval(120, 30, 50, 50);
        light_gray.dispose();        ◁─┐ Deallocate Color object
    }                                   │ when finished
  };
}
```

This code demonstrates the two ways that applications can obtain and use color. In the constructor, the getSystemColor() method returns a basic color, SWT.COLOR_DARK_GRAY, which doesn't need to be disposed of. The graphic context created by the PaintEvent allocates resources for a new color using the Color() constructor. This color, light_gray, is created using three hexadecimal values corresponding to the desired amounts of red, green, and blue. After its last use, the light_gray color is deallocated. These colors are shown in figure 7.3.

In both cases, a Display object is needed in order to generate a color. This is done by using the getDisplay() method associated with the Canvas. But the PaintListener interface can't access the constructor's members. Instead, it uses the PaintEvent's display field.

The two uses of setBackground() play significant roles in assigning colors. In the class constructor, this method sets the background color of the Canvas, which is DARK_GRAY. This method is used again to add color to the PaintEvent's GC, which is the color of the triangle and oval. It's worth noting that the setForeground() method isn't needed at all.

Working with SWT colors is a straightforward process, but there are ways to make it even simpler. For this purpose, JFace provides classes that reduce the work of managing colors.

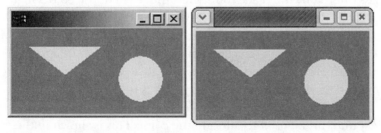

Figure 7.3 The program uses the system color SWT.COLOR_DARK_GRAY and creates the color light_gray according to its RGB values.

7.2.2 *Additional color capability with JFace*

JFace uses the same color methodology as SWT. It also provides two interesting classes to simplify color manipulation: JFaceColors, located in the org.eclipse.jface.resource package; and ColorSelector, located in the org.eclipse.jface.preference package.

The JFaceColors class

The JFaceColors class contains a number of static methods that you can use to obtain colors in an Eclipse Workbench application. getBannerBackground() returns the color of an application's banner, and getErrorBorder() returns the border color of widgets that display errors. There are also methods that return colors of different kinds of text.

The JFaceColors class also provides a useful method that can be invoked in both SWT and JFace applications: setColors(), which you can use to set both the foreground and background colors of a widget at once. The following code snippet makes the button's foreground color red and its background color green:

```
Button button = new Button(parent, SWT.NONE);
red = display.getSystemColor(SWT.COLOR_RED);
green = display.getSystemColor(SWT.COLOR_GREEN);
JFaceColors.setColors(button,red,green);
```

There is also a disposeColors() method, which despite its described capability of deallocating all colors at once, can't replace the dispose() method in the Color class. Instead, it's meant to perform additional tasks when the workbench disposes of its color resources.

The ColorSelector class

Another class offered by the JFace toolset lets the user choose colors in an application. Although the ColorSelector is part of JFace's Preference framework, we felt it necessary to mention its capability here. In essence, this class adds a button to an instance of SWT's ColorDialog class. An example is shown in figure 7.4.

The ColorSelector sets and retrieves the RGB value corresponding to the user's selection. The setColorValue() method sets the default selection as the dialog box is created. The getColorValue() method converts the user's selection into an RGB object that can be used to allocate the color. This is shown in the following code snippet:

```
ColorSelector cs = new ColorSelector(this);
Button button = cs.getButton();
RGB RGBchoice = cs.getColorValue();
```

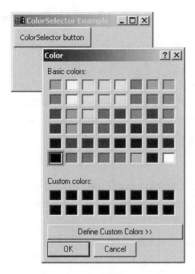

Figure 7.4
The ColorSelector **allows users to select an RGB object.**

```
Color colorchoice = new Color(display, RGBchoice);
```

Colors improve the appearance of a GUI, but they don't convey useful information. A proper user interface needs to communicate with the user. This means adding text, which means working with resources that control how text is presented. These resources are called *fonts*.

7.3 *Displaying text with fonts*

Like working with colors, programming with fonts is simple to understand, but there are important details to consider. This section will present the means of choosing, allocating, and deallocating fonts with the SWT toolset. Then, we'll show you how to simplify these tasks with JFace.

In keeping with its goal of maintaining a native look and feel, the SWT/ JFace toolkit relies primarily on fonts provided by the operating system. Unfortunately, these fonts vary from one platform to another. Therefore, when this section describes a font's *name*, it means the name of one of the fonts installed on your system.

7.3.1 *Using fonts with SWT*

SWT provides a number of font-related classes that perform one of three functions. The first involves font management—allocating and deallocating Font objects. The second function is implementing fonts in objects to change the display of their text. Finally, SWT contains methods that provide measurements of text dimensions for use in graphical applications.

Font management

Just as RGB objects contain the information needed to create Color objects, Font-Data objects provide the basic data for creating Font instances. This data consists of three parts, which are also the three arguments to the most common FontData constructor method:

```
FontData(String name, int height, int style)
```

The first argument represents the name of the font, such as Times New Roman or Arial. The height refers to the number of points in the font, and the style represents the type of font face: SWT.NORMAL, SWT.ITALIC, or SWT.BOLD.

In addition, you can customize a FontData object by specifying its *locale* (the application's geographic location and the set of characters that should be used). A font's locale can be determined by invoking the getLocale() method and specified with setLocale().

Neither RGB or FontData instances need to be disposed of, but Font objects require allocation and deallocation. Table 7.6 presents the constructor methods available for the Font class.

Table 7.6 Constructor methods of the Font class

Font constructor	Function
Font(Device, FontData)	Allocates a font according to its FontData object
Font(Device, FontData[])	Allocates a font according to an array of FontData
Font(Device, String, int, int)	Allocates a font based on its name, size, and style

There is only one deallocation method for the Font class: dispose(). You should invoke it shortly after the Font's last usage.

Implementing fonts in objects

In SWT, fonts are generally associated with one of two GUI objects: Controls and GCs. When you use the setFont() method associated with Controls, any text presented with a setText() method is displayed with the specified font. Graphic contexts also use the setFont() method, but they provide a number of different methods for painting text in its clipping region. These methods are shown in table 7.7.

Table 7.7 Text methods of the graphic context (GC) class

Graphic context text method	Function
`drawString(String, int, int)`	Displays `String` with the given coordinates
`drawString(String, int, int, Boolean)`	Displays `String` with the given coordinates and background
`drawText(String, int, int)`	Displays `String` with the given coordinates
`drawText(String, int, int, Boolean)`	Displays `String` with the given coordinates and background
`drawText(String, int, int, int)`	Displays `String` with the given coordinates and flags

Because of the overloaded `drawString()` and `drawText()` methods, this table requires some explanation. Although implementations of `drawString()` and `drawText()` have the same argument types and functions, the difference is that `drawText()` processes carriage returns and tab expansions, whereas `drawString()` disregards them. Also, the two integers following the `String` argument represent the coordinates of the text display.

The `Boolean` argument in the second and fourth methods indicates whether the text background should be transparent. If this value is set to `TRUE`, then the color of the rectangle containing the text won't be changed. If it's `FALSE`, the color of the rectangle will be set to that of the graphic context's background.

The third integer in the last `drawText()` method represents a flag that changes the text display. These flags are as follows:

- *DRAW_DELIMITER*—Displays the text as multiple lines if necessary
- *DRAW_TAB*—Expands tabs in the text
- DRAW_MNEMONIC—Underlines accelerator keys
- *DRAW_TRANSPARENT*—Determines whether the text background will be the same color as its associated object

Many of these flags are implemented in the code that follows.

Measuring font parameters

When incorporating text in GUIs, you may want to know the text's dimensions, which means knowing the measurements of a given font. SWT provides this information through its FontMetrics class, which contains a number of methods for determining these parameters. These are shown in table 7.8.

Table 7.8 Measurement methods of the FontMetrics class

FontMetrics text method	Function
getAscent()	Returns the distance from the baseline to the top of the characters
getAverageCharWidth()	Returns the width of an average character
getDescent()	Returns the distance from the baseline to the bottom of the characters
getHeight()	Returns the sum of the ascent, the descent, and the leading area
getLeading()	Returns the distance between the top of the characters and raised marks

This class has no constructor methods. Instead, the GC object must invoke its get-FontMetrics() method. It returns a FontMetrics object for the font used in the graphic context and lets you use the listed methods. Each returns an integer that measures the given dimension according to the number of pixels.

Now that we've described the management, integration, and measurement of fonts, it's important to use these classes and methods in actual code.

7.3.2 *Coding with fonts*

The class Ch7_Fonts, shown in listing 7.3, extends Canvas and creates a graphic context that draws text with a chosen font. When the user clicks a button, a Font-Dialog instance opens. This dialog determines which fonts are available on the platform and lets the user choose the name, size, and style of the text in the Canvas. Once the user has chosen, the graphic context displays the text dimensions by invoking its getFontMetrics() method.

This class will be added to WidgetWindow, so we recommend placing Ch7_Fonts in the com.swtjface.Ch7 package.

Listing 7.3   Ch7_Fonts.java

```java
package com.swtjface.Ch7;
import org.eclipse.swt.SWT;
import org.eclipse.swt.graphics.*;
import org.eclipse.swt.widgets.*;
import org.eclipse.swt.events.*;

public class Ch7_Fonts extends Canvas
{
  static Shell mainShell;
  static Composite comp;
  FontData fontdata;

  public Ch7_Fonts(Composite parent)
  {
    super(parent, SWT.BORDER);
    parent.setSize(600, 200);
    addPaintListener(DrawListener);
    comp = this;
    mainShell = parent.getShell();

    Button fontChoice = new Button(this, SWT.CENTER);
    fontChoice.setBounds(20,20,100,20);
    fontChoice.setText("Choose font");
    fontChoice.addMouseListener(new MouseAdapter()
    {
      public void mouseDown(MouseEvent me)
      {
        FontDialog fd = new FontDialog(mainShell);      ◄──┐ Open FontDialog
        fontdata = fd.open();                              │ box in Canvas
        comp.redraw();
      }
    });
  }

  PaintListener DrawListener = new PaintListener()
  {
    public void paintControl(PaintEvent pe)
    {
      Display disp = pe.display;
      GC gc = pe.gc;
      gc.setBackground(pe.display.getSystemColor(SWT.COLOR_DARK_GRAY));
      if (fontdata != null)
      {                                                 ┌ Create Font based
        Font GCFont = new Font(disp, fontdata);    ◄────┘ on user choice
        gc.setFont(GCFont);                             ┌ Measure properties of
        FontMetrics fm = gc.getFontMetrics();      ◄────┘ chosen font
        gc.drawText("The average character width for this font is " +
          fm.getAverageCharWidth() + " pixels.", 20, 60);
        gc.drawText("The ascent for this font is " +
          fm.getAscent() + " pixels.", 20, 100, true);
```

```
        gc.drawText("The &descent for this font is " + fm.getDescent()+
          " pixels.", 20, 140, SWT.DRAW_MNEMONIC|SWT.DRAW_TRANSPARENT);
        GCFont.dispose();
      }
    }
  };
}
```

Once the user clicks the Choose Font button, the MouseEvent handler creates an instance of a FontDialog and makes it visible by invoking the dialog's open() method. This method returns a FontData object, which is used in the DrawListener interface to create a font for the graphic context. This GC object, created by the PaintEvent, then invokes its getFontMetrics() method to measure the parameters of the font.

When the graphic context sets its foreground color to SWT.COLOR_DARK_GRAY, this usually means that all text created by the GC will be surrounded by this color. However, as you can see in figure 7.5, only the first drawText() method is surrounded by the foreground color; this is because the second and third invocations are considered transparent and take the color of the underlying Canvas. The third drawText() method also enables mnemonic characters, which means that an ampersand (&) before a letter results in the display underlining this character. This is shown in figure 7.5 by the underlined *d* in the third sentence.

In the DrawListener interface, a great deal of the processing is performed only after the FontData object has been set by the FontDialog. This is necessary since errors will result if the FontData argument is null. Also, since the graphic context only draws its text after a PaintEvent, the MouseAdapter ends by invoking the redraw() method, which causes the Canvas to repaint itself.

7.3.3 *Improved font management with JFace*

As we mentioned in section 7.3.1, one of the main functions of SWT's graphics is to provide font management—the allocation and deallocation of font resources. This can be accomplished with the Font constructor and dispose() methods, but there is no efficient way to manage multiple fonts in a single application. JFace provides this capability with its FontRegistry class, located in the org.eclipse.jface.resource package.

By using a FontRegistry, you don't need to worry about the creation or disposal of Fonts. Instead, the FontRegistry's put() method lets you match a String value with a corresponding FontData[] object. This method can be invoked multiple times to add more Fonts to the registry. Then, when the application needs a

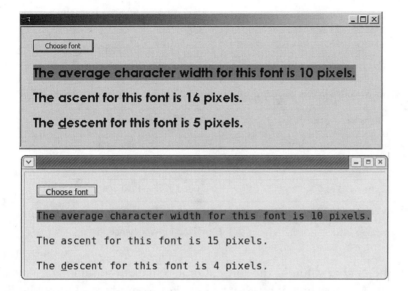

Figure 7.5 **The user interface for** `Ch7_Fonts.java`**. This application combines the many elements of SWT font manipulation.**

new `Font` to change its text display, it calls the registry's `get()` method, which returns a `Font` object based on the argument's `String` value. This is shown in the following example code:

```
FontRegistry fr = JFaceResources.getFontRegistry();
fr.put("User_choice", fontdialog.getFontList());
fr.put("WingDings", WDFont.getFontData());
Font choice = fr.get("User_choice");
```

Rather than create an empty registry, this code uses the preexisting `FontRegistry` associated with JFace and adds two more fonts. The first font is placed in the registry from the result of a `FontDialog` selection, and the second is taken from a font that existed previously in the application. In the last line, the `FontRegistry` converts the `FontData[]` object associated with the `FontDialog` into a `Font` instance. Just as the `FontRegistry` manages the creation of this font, it also performs its disposal, as well as that of every font in its registry.

The fonts in the `FontRegistry` include those used in the Eclipse Workbench's banners and dialog boxes. However, you need the `JFaceResources` class to access them. The following code shows how this can be performed. It's important to note that the `Strings` used to invoke the registry's `get()` method, as well as the `FontRegistry` itself, are member fields in `JFaceResources`:

```
FontRegistry fr = JFaceResources.getFontRegistry();
Font headFont = fr.get(JFaceResources.HEADER_FONT);
Font dialogFont = fr.get(JFaceResources.DIALOG_FONT);
```

Table 7.9 lists these fonts with their `String` values and functions.

Table 7.9 Fonts available in the JFace `FontRegistry`

Access `String`	Font function
JFaceResources.BANNER_FONT	Font used in JFace banners
JFaceResources.DEFAULT_FONT	Standard JFace font
JFaceResources.DIALOG_FONT	Font used in JFace dialogs
JFaceResources.HEADER_FONT	Font used in JFace headers
JFaceResources.TEXT_FONT	Font used for Workbench text

Although the `String` value in the left column remains the same across multiple platforms, the font to which it refers may vary. For example, on Linux, the Banner font is Adobe Courier, Boldface, at 14 pitch. On MacOS, the default Banner font is Lucida Grande, Bold, at 12 pitch.

Having progressed from colors to fonts, we need to discuss graphics that convey even more information: *images*. After all, a picture is worth a thousand words...

7.4 *Incorporating images in graphics*

Although the subject of manipulating images is more complicated than fonts or colors, there are fewer concerns with platform dependence. Different operating systems and applications may support divergent file types, but many image formats have become so prevalent that they are supported on nearly all systems. The code examples in this section work exclusively with these common image types.

As this section will make clear, working with images is similar to working with fonts. SWT provides classes and methods for image management and integration in much the same way that it provides for font handling. Also, JFace provides built-in resources and registries that reduce the amount of complexity involved with image management.

7.4.1 *Allocating images*

Most applications only create `Image` objects to add existing image files to a user interface. In this case, you should use the first and simplest of the `Image` constructor methods:

```
Image(Device, String)
```

Applications seeking to present the image in a GUI invoke this method using the `Display` object as the first argument and the image file's pathname as the second. As of the time of this writing, SWT accepts *.jpg, *.gif, *.png, *.bmp, and *.ico file types.

If the image file resides in the same directory as a known class, then an `Input-Stream` can be generated by invoking the class's `getResourceAsStream()` method. With this `InputStream`, you can use the second constructor method:

```
InputStream is = KnownClass.getResourceAsStream("Image.jpg");
Image Knownimage = new Image(Display, is);
```

The full list of overloaded `Image` constructor methods is shown in table 7.10.

Table 7.10 Constructor methods for the `Image` class

Constructor method	Function
`Image(Device, String)`	Creates an `Image` using an existing file
`Image(Device, InputStream)`	Creates an `Image` using an `InputStream` from an existing image
`Image(Device, int, int)`	Creates an empty `Image` with the given dimensions
`Image(Device, Rectangle)`	Creates an empty `Image` with the dimensions of a `Rectangle`
`Image(Device, Image, int)`	Creates an `Image` based on another `Image` and a set parameter
`Image(Device, ImageData)`	Creates an `Image` according to information in the `ImageData`
`Image(Device, ImageData, ImageData)`	Creates an `Image` (icon) according to an `ImageData` object and a second `ImageData` object that determines transparency

The third and fourth constructor methods create empty `Image` instances with dimensions set by the method's arguments. The two integers specify the x and y parameters of the image, and the `Rectangle` object in the fourth method frames the image according to its boundaries. The fifth creates an `Image` based on a second `Image` instance and an integer flag that determines whether the image should appear disabled or in grayscale.

The last two constructor methods construct `Image` instances using objects of the `ImageData` class. This class provides device-independent information about an `Image` object and contains methods to manipulate the image. Like the `FontData` class, instances of `ImageData` don't use operating system resources and don't require deallocation. Image instances, however, need to invoke their dispose() methods when they're no longer in use.

The ImageData class and its ability to incorporate effects in images will be explored in greater depth shortly. First, it's important for you to understand how images are integrated in applications.

7.4.2 Coding graphics with images

The process of adding an Image to a GUI begins with creating a graphic context. This GC object then calls its drawImage() method, which takes one of two forms, based on whether the image will be presented with its original dimensions. This method is presented in the code that follows.

In chapter 4, we used a standard Eclipse image to show how the Action class functions. To fully show SWT's image capabilities, we need a larger image. There-fore, we recommend that you copy eclipse_lg.gif from $ECLIPSE_HOME/ plugins/org.eclipse.platform_x.y.z and add it to the com.swtjface.Ch7 package. This way, any class in the package will be able to work with this image.

However, the following snippet is presented only to demonstrate how an Image object works in a graphic context:

```
public class ImageTest extends Composite
{
  public ImageTest(Composite parent)
  {
    super(parent, SWT.NONE);
    parent.setSize(320,190);
    InputStream is = getClass().getResourceAsStream("eclipse_lg.gif");
    final ImageData eclipseData = new ImageData(is).scaledTo(87,123);   ◁──┐  Create ImageData
    this.addPaintListener(new PaintListener()                                  object from file
    {
      public void paintControl(PaintEvent pe)                              Create Image
      {                                                                    from ImageData
        GC gc = pe.gc;
        Image eclipse = new Image(pe.display, eclipseData);   ◁───────────┘
        gc.drawImage(eclipse, 20, 20);
        gc.drawText("The image height is: " + eclipseData.height +
        " pixels.",120,30);
        gc.drawText("The image width is: " + eclipseData.width +
        " pixels.",120,70);
          gc.drawText("The image depth is: " + eclipseData.depth +
        " bits per pixel.",120,110);
        eclipse.dispose();
      }
    });
  }
}
```

This code begins by constructing an ImageData object using an InputStream. In this case, it makes sense to start with an ImageData instance since Image objects can't be resized or recolored. This resizing process is performed using the scaleTo() method, which shrinks the image for the GUI. This new image is shown in figure 7.6.

When a PaintEvent occurs, the program invokes the paintControl() method. This method creates the window's graphic context and an Image object based on the ImageData. To the right of the image, three statements provide information regarding the fields of the ImageData instance. It's worth noting that by changing the coordinates, you can superimpose the text (or any graphic) on the image.

The code shows how you can ue the ImageData class to obtain information about images and change their size. However, this class is capable of much more. But before we can discuss how ImageData creates image effects, you need to fully understand this class and how it represents images.

7.4.3 Creating a bitmap with ImageData

The easiest way to learn about ImageData is to design, build, and display an instance of this class. In this case, you'll create a bitmap and use it to form an Image. Doing so will introduce many of the fields and methods associated with the ImageData class and provide a better idea why this class is necessary.

The first step involves determining which colors will be used. Given this book's grayscale presentation, we'll restrict ourselves to shades of gray. To reduce the amount of programming, we'll keep the number of different colors to a minimum. With this in mind, this example uses three colors—white, black, and gray— and combines them into a racing flag bitmap. This isn't terribly exciting, but it will be sufficient to show you how to generate ImageData.

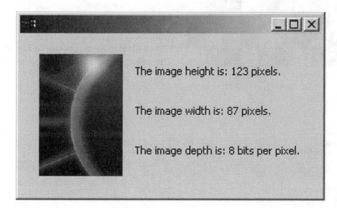

Figure 7.6
Although an Image object can be displayed in a window, the ImageData instance provides the information.

To tell `ImageData` about the colors you'll be using, you need to create an instance of the `PaletteData` class. This object contains an array of the RGB values in the image. For the image sketched in figure 7.7, this consists of three elements: 0x000000 (black), 0x808080 (gray), and 0xFFFFFF (white).

Each pixel in an image has three pieces of information: its x coordinate, or *offset*; its y coordinate, or *scanline*; and the pixel's color, which is referred to as its *value* or *index*. Because this image contains only three colors, you don't need to assign each pixel its full RGB value (0x000000, 0x808080, 0xFFFFFF). Instead, it's simpler and less memory-intensive to use the color's index in the `PaletteData` array and assign pixel values of (0, 1, 2). This simplified mapping between a pixel's value and color is referred to as an *indexed palette*. For example, because the `eclipse_lg.gif` file used in the last code snippet has a depth of only 8 bits per pixel, each pixel is assigned a value between 1 and 2^8 (255).

However, for images with depth greater than 8 bits per pixel, the additional processing needed to translate between an index and its color isn't worth the reduced memory. These images use a *direct palette*, which directly assigns a pixel's value to its RGB value. The `isDirect()` method in the `PaletteData` class tells whether an instance uses direct or indexed conversion.

If you understand how the `PaletteData` class functions, then coding a bitmap is straightforward, as shown in listing 7.4. Because this `ImageData` object will be integrated in an animated graphic, we recommend that you add this `FlagGraphic` class to the `com.swtjface.Ch7` package.

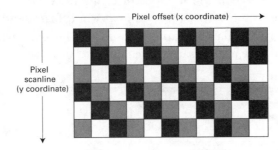

Figure 7.7
Each pixel in an image can be identified by its offset, scanline, and color value.

Listing 7.4 FlagGraphic.java

```java
package com.swtjface.Ch7;
import org.eclipse.swt.graphics.*;

public class FlagGraphic
{
  public FlagGraphic()
  {
    int pix = 20;
    int numRows = 6;
    int numCols = 11;

    PaletteData pd = new PaletteData(new RGB[]
    {
      new RGB(0x00, 0x00, 0x00),
      new RGB(0x80, 0x80, 0x80),
      new RGB(0xFF, 0xFF, 0xFF)
    });

    final ImageData flagData = new ImageData(pix*numCols,
      pix*numRows, 2, pd);

    for(int x=0; x<pix*numCols; x++)
    {
      for(int y=0; y<pix*numRows; y++)
      {
        int value = (((x/pix)%3) + (3-((y/pix)%3))) % 3;
        flagData.setPixel(x,y,value);
      }
    }
  }
}
```

Create color palette with black, gray, and white

Set value of each pixel in image

This example begins by creating a `PaletteData` object as an array of `RGB` objects corresponding to black, gray, and white colors. Then, an `ImageData` instance is constructed with the dimensions of the image, the depth of the image, and the `PaletteData`. Because there are three possible colors, the depth is set to 2, which provides support for up to 2^2 (4) colors. If an image's color depth is 1, 2, 4, or 8, then the application creates an indexed palette for the `ImageData` object during its allocation process. For images with greater depth, the application will create a direct palette.

NOTE If the user attempts to create a palette with a depth outside the set of {1, 2, 4, 8, 16, 24, 32}, the compiler will throw an ERROR_INVALID_ARGUMENT.

In this example, the setPixel() method assigns values to all the pixels in the 220x120 image. This is only one of many bitmap methods provided by the Image-Data class; table 7.11 provides a complete list.

Table 7.11   Bitmap methods for the ImageData class

Method	Function
getPixel(int, int)	Returns the pixel value at the specified coordinates
getPixels(int, int, int, int[], int)	Returns a specified number of pixels beginning at a given offset and scanline
getPixels(int, int, int, byte[], int)	Returns a specified number of pixels beginning at a given offset and scanline
getRGBs()	Returns the array of RGB objects in the indexed palette; returns null if a direct palette is used
setPixel(int, int, int)	Sets the value of the pixel located at the given coordinates
setPixels(int, int, int, int[], int)	Sets the values of a specified number of pixels beginning at a given offset and scanline
setPixels(int, int, int, byte[], int)	Sets the values of a specified number of pixels beginning at a given offset and scanline

It's important to remember that, because flagData only works with RGB, Palette-Data, and ImageData objects, no dispose() methods need to be invoked. Deallocation is only necessary when an ImageData instance is used to create an Image or if the RGB values are used to create Colors. However, if an Image was constructed from the flagData information, it would resemble that shown in figure 7.8.

Now that we've covered the basics of working with ImageData objects, we can progress to more advanced topics. It will take some time before an SWT application can compete with a commercial photo-editing tool, but the toolset provides a number of impressive ways to manipulate images.

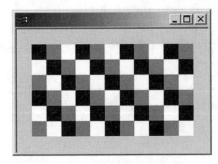

Figure 7.8
Bitmap of an example ImageData object

7.4.4 *Manipulating images with ImageData*

Along with the bitmap methods described so far, the ImageData class also contains methods that provide graphical effects. You can set pixels in an image to provide transparency instead of a color. Using alpha blending, two images can be combined into an image that contains elements of both. Finally, using the ImageData and ImageLoader classes, you can sequence images into animated GIF files.

Transparency

With sufficient color depth, the RGB system can provide any color in the visible spectrum. However, this won't help if you want sections of the image to be transparent. No combination of red, green, and blue elements will add up to a see-through color, so you need to set a specific pixel value to represent transparency. This way, any pixel with this value will instead take the color of the background behind it. This capability is provided with the transparentPixel field of the ImageData class. This is simple to use in code, as the following snippet shows:

```
flagData.transparentPixel = 2;
Image flagImage = new Image(pe.display, flagData);
gc.drawImage(flagImage, 20, 20);
```

In this code, any pixels in FlagImage with the value of 2 (representing white) take the color of the image's background. This is shown on the left image in figure 7.9. The right image is the result of setting the transparentPixel value to 1 (representing gray).

In addition to the transparentPixel field, the ImageData class contains a number of methods that provide information about transparency. The getTransparencyMask() method returns an ImageData object with its transparent pixels separated in a mask array. The getTransparencyType() method returns an integer

Figure 7.9 Image transparency. On the left, all white pixels are made transparent. On the right, all gray pixels are transparent.

representing the type of transparency used. In many image-editing toolsets, a program can specify different degrees of transparency in an image. However, since there is no setTransparencyType() method at the time of this writing, this feature has yet to be integrated in SWT.

Transparency is a helpful capability, but it's still *static*. It would be much more striking to create a series of images and display them at short time intervals to provide the illusion of continuous motion. We'll now cover this king of computer graphic effects: *animation*.

Saving and animating images

Of the many common types of images, the Graphics Interchange Format (GIF) is the only one that supports animation. Therefore, before we can discuss animation in depth, we need to describe how SWT's Image objects are saved as image files. This means looking into SWT's ImageLoader class.

Like the ImageData constructors, the ImageLoader class contains methods that accept image files and streams and return ImageData[] objects. However, this class's main purpose involves converting ImageData[] instances into Output-Streams and image files. This way, graphics can be persisted instead of being disposed with their Image objects. Table 7.12 shows the formats accepted for loading and saving files with SWT.

Table 7.12   Image file formats accepted for SWT access

SWT constant	Image type
SWT.IMAGE_JPEG	Joint Photographic Experts Group (*.jpg)
SWT.IMAGE_GIF	Graphics Interchage File (*.gif)
SWT.IMAGE_PNG	Portable Native Graphic (*.png)
SWT.IMAGE_BMP	Windows Bitmap (*.bmp)—No compression
SWT.IMAGE_BMP_RLE	Windows Bitmap (*.bmp)—RLE compression
SWT.IMAGE_ICO	Windows Icon format (*.ico)

There are two steps in the process of building an image file in SWT:

1 The application creates an instance of the ImageLoader class and sets its data field equal to the ImageData or ImageData[] object that contains the image information.

2 The image file is created by invoking the ImageLoader's save() method. This method can also be used to create an OutputStream for the image.

However, an application seeking to create an animated GIF file must perform several additional tasks:

3   Each `ImageData` object, or frame, in the sequence must be configured to display itself for a specified amount of time and then dispose of itself appropriately. In code, this is done using the `delayTime` and `disposal-Method` fields of the `ImageData` class.

4   The application must combine these frames in an `ImageData` array and load this array into an `ImageLoader`.

5   The application must initialize the `repeatCount` field of the `ImageLoader` instance in order to specify how many times the animated sequence should repeat itself.

6   The `ImageLoader`'s `save()` method is used with the `SWT.IMAGE_GIF` tag to save the image array as an animated GIF file.

The `Ch7_Images` class, shown in listing 7.5, demonstrates the process of integrating multiple instances of the `ImageData` class into a single animated GIF.

NOTE   This GIF works best if you open it in a browser that supports animation.

Listing 7.5   Ch7_Images.java

```
package com.swtjface.Ch7;
import java.io.*;
import org.eclipse.swt.*;
import org.eclipse.swt.graphics.*;

public class Ch7_Images {

  public static void main(String[] args) {

    int numRows = 6, numCols = 11, pix = 20;          Initialize color
    PaletteData pd = new PaletteData(new RGB[]    ←   palette
    {
      new RGB(0x00, 0x00, 0x00),
      new RGB(0x80, 0x80, 0x80),
      new RGB(0xFF, 0xFF, 0xFF)
    });                                               Create three
                                                      images
    ImageData[] flagArray = new ImageData[3];   ←
    for(int frame=0; frame<flagArray.length; frame++)
    {
      flagArray[frame]= new ImageData(pix*numCols, pix*numRows, 4, pd);
      flagArray[frame].delayTime = 10;
      for(int x=0; x<pix*numCols; x++)
      {
        for(int y=0; y<pix*numRows; y++)
```

```
        {
          int value = (((x/pix)%3) + (3 - ((y/pix)%3)) + frame) % 3;
          flagArray[frame].setPixel(x,y,value);
        }
      }
    }

    ImageLoader gifloader = new ImageLoader();
    ByteArrayOutputStream flagByte[] = new ByteArrayOutputStream[3];
    byte[][] gifarray = new byte[3][];
    gifloader.data = flagArray;                    ┌─── Convert images
                                                   │    to bytes
    for (int i=0; i<3; i++)      ◄─────────────────┘
    {
      flagByte[i] = new ByteArrayOutputStream();
      flagArray[0] = flagArray[i];
      gifloader.save(flagByte[i],SWT.IMAGE_GIF);
      gifarray[i] = flagByte[i].toByteArray();
    }                                         ┌─── Prepare output
                                              │    GIF stream
    byte[] gif = new byte[4628];      ◄───────┘
    System.arraycopy(gifarray[0],0,gif,0,61);
    System.arraycopy(new byte[]{33,(byte)255,11},0,gif,61,3);
    System.arraycopy(new String("NETSCAPE2.0").getBytes(),0,gif,64,11);
    System.arraycopy(new byte[]{3,1,-24,3,0,33,-7,4,-24},0,gif,75,9);

    System.arraycopy(gifarray[0],65,gif,84,1512);  ◄──┐ Add images to
    for (int i=1; i<3; i++)                           │ GIF stream
    {
      System.arraycopy(gifarray[i],61,gif,1516*i + 80,3);
      gif[1516*i + 83] = (byte) -24;
      System.arraycopy(gifarray[i],65,gif,1516*i + 84,1512);
    }

    try                                       ┌─── Create GIF file
    {                                         │    from stream
      DataOutputStream in = new DataOutputStream  ◄──┘
        (new BufferedOutputStream(new FileOutputStream
          (new File("FlagGIF.gif")))));
      in.write(gif, 0, gif.length);
    }
    catch (FileNotFoundException e)
    {
      e.printStackTrace();
    }
    catch (IOException e)
    {
      e.printStackTrace();
    }
  }
}
```

The complexity of this code is due to the fact that the `ImageLoader.save()` method can't convert an `ImageData` array into an animated GIF. However, this method can create a GIF `OutputStream` from an individual `ImageData` object, and this capability is used for each image in the array. Then, after a great deal of byte manipulation, these three `OutputStream`s are fused into a final `OutputStream` that creates the FlagGIF.gif file.

If this file doesn't immediately appear in Eclipse, right-click the project name (`WidgetWindow`) and select the Refresh option. The file will appear in the project.

Now that we've discussed SWT's image-handling capability in excruciating detail, let's look at JFace. Although the JFace library can't create incredible special effects, it can greatly simplify the process of working with images.

7.4.5 *Managing images with JFace*

Just as JFace's `FontRegistry` class simplifies font management, the `ImageRegistry` class lets you incorporate multiple images in an application without worrying about resource deallocation. It also uses the same access methods as the `FontRegistry` class. To place an image in the registry, you use the `put()` method with an `Image` object and a `String`. When the image needs to be displayed, the `get()` method returns the image based on the key. Here's an example that uses the eclipse_lg.gif file:

```
ImageRegistry ir = new ImageRegistry();
ir.put("Eclipse", new Image(display, "eclipse_lg.gif"));
Image eclipse = ir.get("Eclipse");
```

In this case, you still need to allocate resources for the `Image` object. This may cause a problem if the application places many images in the registry but only needs to display a few. For this reason, JFace created the `ImageDescriptor` class. Like SWT's `ImageData` class, the `ImageDescriptor` contains the information needed for an image without requiring allocation of system resources. The `get()` and `put()` methods associated with the `ImageRegistry` class are also available for `ImageDescriptor` objects, as shown in the following code sample:

```
ImageRegistry ir = new ImageRegistry();
ImageDescriptor id = createFromFile(getClass(),"eclipse_lg.gif");
ir.put("Eclipse", id);
Image eclipse = ir.get("Eclipse");
```

If you use `ImageDescriptor`s, the `put()` and `get()` operations can be performed without allocating for `Image` objects. This way, you can add a large number of `ImageDescriptor`s to an application's `ImageRegistry` without worrying about image creation. Finally, since an `ImageRegistry` disposes of its contents when its `Display` object is closed, you don't need to concern yourself with image deallocation.

7.5 *Updating the WidgetWindow*

To add graphics to the `WidgetWindow` application, in this section you'll create a `Composite` subclass containing colors, fonts, and images. This container incorporates the `Ch7_Colors` and `Ch7_Fonts` classes, as well as the animated image created by the `Ch7_Images` class.

7.5.1 *Building the chapter 7 composite*

Listing 7.6 presents the `Ch7_Composite` class, which extends the `Canvas` class and combines the drawing from section 7.2.1 with the font dialog box from section 7.3.2 and the animated image from section 7.4.4. In order for this to function properly, you must add the FlagGIF.gif file to the `com.swtjface.Ch7` package.

Listing 7.6   Ch7_Composite.java

```java
package com.swtjface.Ch7;
import java.io.*;
import org.eclipse.swt.*;
import org.eclipse.swt.widgets.*;
import org.eclipse.swt.events.*;
import org.eclipse.swt.graphics.*;

public class Ch7_Composite extends Canvas
{
  public Ch7_Composite(Composite parent)
  {
    super(parent, SWT.BORDER);
    Ch7_Colors drawing = new Ch7_Colors(this);        Add figure
    drawing.setBounds(20,20,200,100);                  drawing
    Ch7_Fonts fontbox = new Ch7_Fonts(this);
    fontbox.setBounds(0,150,500,200);
    Ch7_Images flagmaker = new Ch7_Images();          Add font
    addPaintListener(new PaintListener()              dialog button
    {
      public void paintControl(PaintEvent pe)
      {
        Display disp = pe.display;                     Add GIF
        GC gc = pe.gc;                                 to Canvas
        InputStream is=getClass().getResourceAsStream("FlagGIF.gif");
```

```
            Image flag = new Image(disp, is);
            gc.drawImage(flag, 255, 10);
            flag.dispose();
         }
      });
   }
}
```

The operation of Ch7_Composite is simple to understand: It creates a Ch7_Colors Composite in the upper-left corner of the Canvas and a Ch7_Fonts Composite at the bottom of the display. It also constructs a graphic context that displays the Flag-GIF.gif file in the upper-right corner of the window.

7.5.2 Adding Ch7_Composite to the WidgetWindow

Let's add a tab to the WidgetWindow Tabfolder that comprises the Ch7_Composite class created in this chapter. As in previous chapters, the only parts of the code that need to be updated are the import statements and the createContents() method. To conserve space, these are the only sections presented in listing 7.7.

Listing 7.7   WidgetWindow.java (updated)

```
...Previous import statements...
import com.swtjface.Ch6.*;
import com.swtjface.Ch7.*;

protected Control createContents(Composite parent) {
   getShell().setText("Widget Window");
   TabFolder tf = new TabFolder(parent, SWT.NONE);

   ...Previous tab items...

   TabItem chap7 = new TabItem(tf,SWT.NONE);
   chap7.setText("Chapter 7");
   chap7.setControl(new Ch7_Composite(tf));

   return parent;
}
```

Once it's been updated, the WidgetWindow should appear similar to the GUI shown in figure 7.10. Unfortunately, although the FlagGIF.gif file is an animated GIF, the image loaded in the application remains static.

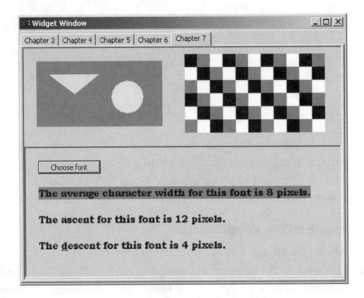

Figure 7.10 The updated `WidgetWindow` **combines the color, font, and image-handling capabilities of SWT/JFace.**

7.6 *Summary*

The SWT/JFace graphics library allows applications to display significantly more than the widgets described in chapters 3 and 5. This capability isn't perfect, but it's incredible for such a young toolset. Not only does it let you manage and manipulate colors, images, and fonts, it also provides numerous classes to hold their information. These are particularly helpful for running graphical applications on systems with limited resources.

It's difficult to keep track of `ImageData`, `ImageDescriptor`, and `ImageLoader` objects, but SWT/JFace separates the roles of the graphical classes clearly. Also, although the registries provided by JFace may seem complicated to work with, they perform helpful functions, so we hope you remember them when building your applications.

The special-effects methods in SWT/JFace need work, but the potential for future capabilities is enormous. We hope that in a few years' time, Eclipse applications will be used to create and manipulate professional-quality graphical editing applications, which can be used not only to create images and animation, but also to incorporate full audio/visual aspects.

Working with trees and lists

In this chapter and the next, we'll explore some of the most useful widgets provided by JFace. However, the framework that goes along with those widgets is also one of the most complicated that we'll cover in this book, so pay attention.

Certain widgets' main purpose is to display sets of data. Although the data can be anything from rows in a database to a list of your most frequently played mp3s, certain common ways of structuring that data for display occur frequently. Even when the final display is very different, many common tasks must be done to make sure the data is ready to be shown to the user. The data must be obtained from a source; it's often sorted into a certain order or has elements filtered out; and you need a way to associate a text string or image with each domain object. JFace provides the *Viewer framework* to deal with these common issues; we'll need to discuss the common elements of that framework before we get into the details of particular widgets.

After we provide a foundation for understanding viewers and their related classes, this chapter will show you how to display data in a list or tree. We'll follow that up with a discussion of tables in chapter 9.

8.1 *Viewers and the Viewer framework*

JFace provides the Viewer framework to enable easy manipulation of certain widgets. This framework includes many classes and interfaces with complex relationships, as shown in figure 8.1. As we discuss each section of this framework in turn, you may find it helpful to refer to this diagram frequently.

As we discuss these classes, it's important to keep the big picture in mind. The Viewer framework is an implementation of the design pattern known as Model-View-Controller (MVC). The core of the idea is to separate domain objects (the Model) from the user interface (the View) and the logic that controls them (the Controller).

At the heart of the framework is the abstract class `Viewer` and its descendants. The path of the inheritance hierarchy we're concerned with here involves `ContentViewer` and `StructuredViewer`.

An appropriate `Viewer` provides a layer of abstraction between a widget and the data it displays and forms the View portion of the MVC triad, creating a display for a domain object. To the client programmer, a `Viewer` provides an interface that is much more natural to manipulate than is provided by the widget itself. The widget, on the other hand, is given a way to obtain data without having to worry about its source. By manipulating a collection of objects through the interface

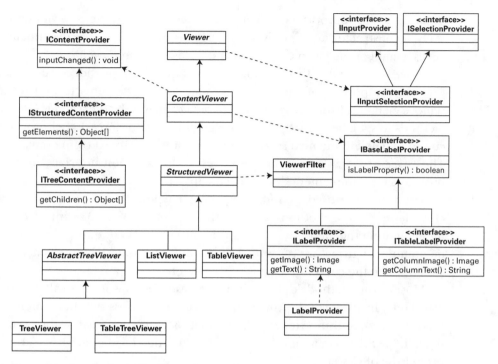

Figure 8.1 An overview of the Viewer framework

provided by the Viewer, the widget can rearrange the data into a form most convenient for its own internal use without affecting the original data structure.

ContentViewer adds functionality to deal with data in the form of domain objects by making use of a variety of interfaces, which by JFace convention have an *I* at the beginning of their names. These interfaces, which we'll discuss in more detail later in the chapter, represent extension points, which you can use to plug your application's custom logic into the framework.

StructuredViewer imposes a structure on the data provided to ContentViewer. The specifics of the structure can vary widely, but methods to perform common tasks such as filtering or sorting are implemented at this level of the hierarchy.

Each widget—Tree, List, Table, and so on—has a matching Viewer subclass, such as ListViewer or TableViewer. The widget is intended to be matched with at most one instance of its Viewer, and once the Viewer has been associated with the widget, all manipulation should be done through the viewer instead of to the widget directly. Trying to mix calls between the widget and its viewer will have unpredictable results. All concrete Viewer subclasses provide a constructor that takes an instance of the appropriate widget and associates it with the new viewer. Alternatively, a constructor taking only a Composite is provided, which instantiates a widget as a child of the given Composite and binds it to the viewer.

Once associated with the widget, viewers typically provide several methods. The most important of these are easy ways to add elements to and retrieve or remove elements from the collection of data displayed by the widget. Additionally, methods to set label providers are implemented at this level. Label providers, discussed in detail in the next section, generate suitable UI text from domain objects. The IBaseLabelProvider interface serves as the common interface that all label providers must implement. More specific interfaces then derive from IBaseLabel-Provider and are used by individual widget types. The abstract ContentViewer class defines these methods to take the IBaseLabelProvider interface; but by implementing the methods here, you can insert checks to ensure that only implementations of IBaseLabelProvider that are appropriate to the given widget are added, while the common logic is performed by the superclass.

Most of the methods defined in these base classes won't be called directly by your code. Instead, you'll provide the viewer with a class that implements one of the interfaces, and the viewer will call methods on your class at the appropriate time. Table 8.1 summarizes the methods you'll need to be familiar with to make proper use of viewers.

Table 8.1   Important viewer methods

Method	Defined in...
getControl()	Viewer
getSelection()	Viewer
refresh()	Viewer
setInput()	Viewer
setContentProvider()	ContentViewer
setLabelProvider()	ContentViewer
addFilter()	StructuredViewer
reveal()	StructuredViewer
setSorter()	StructuredViewer

8.1.1   Providers

The first subclass of Viewer, ContentViewer, adds functionality for dealing with the data displayed by a widget, thereby providing the M (Model) in MVC. It's the role of a provider to perform application-specific work to make a piece of data available to the widget—for example, to return the text that should be displayed to represent a given domain object in a list. There are two types of providers: `Label-Providers` and `ContentProviders`. The class hierarchies we discuss here are both shown in figure 8.1; you'll probably find it helpful to refer back to the diagram as we explore the various interfaces and classes.

Label providers

Label providers implement either `ILabelProvider` or `ITableLabelProvider`, both of which extend `IBaseLabelProvider`. `ILabelProvider` and `ITableLabelProvider` are similar in spirit, the only difference being that `ITableLabelProvider` deals with table columns, whereas `ILabelProvider` assumes one-dimensional data.

The logic for label providers revolves around three methods. The first is `isLabelProperty()`, defined in `IBaseLabelProvider`. Given an object and the name of a property, the method returns a boolean indicating whether a change to the given property requires a corresponding update to a visible label. It isn't mandatory, but properties typically conform to JavaBean naming standards: that is, if the bean has a property `name`, then a `getName()` and possibly a `setName()` method is defined for the object. `isLabelProperty()` is called when an object has been updated by an `Editor` (see the next section) to optimize drawing operations. If `isLabelProperty()` returns false, `ContentViewer` knows that it isn't necessary to redraw the widget.

Subinterfaces of `IBaseLabelProvider` also provide `getText()` and `getImage()` methods in various forms. Each is given an object, and it's the responsibility of the provider to return the text and/or image that should be displayed for that object. Returning `null` results in no text or image being displayed. The only difference between standard label providers and table label providers is that the methods in `ITableLabelProvider` take an additional parameter indicating the index of the column being populated; the concept is otherwise exactly the same.

JFace provides a default implementation of `ILabelProvider` called `LabelProvider`, which returns `null` for all images, along with the result of calling `toString()` on the given object for the text. This can be useful for debugging or getting a prototype running quickly, but you'll usually need to subclass `LabelProvider` or provide a new implementation of the interface that performs logic appropriate to your application. The data returned by `toString()` typically isn't appealing for users to look at.

Content providers

In addition to label providers, `ContentViewer` concerns itself with content providers. Whereas a label provider provides the text or image to display for an element, a content provider provides the actual elements to be displayed. `IStructuredContentProvider` defines the `getElements()` method, which is given an `Object` as input and returns an array of `Object`s to display in the widget. When `setInput()` is called on the `Viewer`, the object given as a parameter is passed to the content viewer. The content provider is then responsible for using that input parameter to return a collection of domain objects to be displayed by the widget.

A simple example is a content provider that displays information from an XML file. It could take an input stream as a parameter, parse the XML from the stream, and then return objects representing various elements of the XML data to be displayed by the viewer. It isn't necessary to use a content provider, however; if you `add()` the elements that you wish to display, it will work fine.

Two other methods on `IStructuredContentProvider` can often be left empty. The first is `dispose()`, which the viewer calls when it's being disposed of; you can use this method to clean up any allocated resources that the content provider may be hanging on to. The last method is `inputChanged(Viewer viewer, Object oldInput, Object newInput)`, which the viewer uses to notify the content provider that the root input object has changed. Although many applications can safely ignore this method, the Javadocs suggest its intended use. Suppose your application contains domain objects that broadcast events, such as a network resource that sends notifications when it becomes unavailable. When the viewer's input is changed from one of these objects to another, `inputChanged()` can be used to unregister the content provider from listening to the old input object and register for events from the new one.

8.1.2 Listeners

The various viewer classes provide support for a variety of event listeners. The base `Viewer` class offers notification of help request and selection changed events. Moving down the hierarchy, `StructuredViewer` adds support for double-click events, and `AbstractTreeViewer` adds default selections and tree events. Events and listeners were already discussed in detail in chapter 4; the same principles that we talked about earlier apply here as well. Listeners are used to implement the logic behind the application; they make up the Controller portion of MVC.

8.1.3 Filters and sorters

As we mentioned earlier, it's common to want to sort items before they are displayed. This sorting can be done by an infinite variety of parameters, from alphabetically sorting contact information in an address book to listing emails by data received. To perform sorting or similar manipulations of data, the elements need some sort of structure. Knowledge of this structure comes from the Structured-Viewer class. The key functionality offered by a StructuredViewer is the ability to run objects through a filter and sort them before they're displayed.

Filters are an elegant idea; they help decouple the creation of a group of items from the act of deciding which ones should be displayed. A natural first inclination would be to create only the items that should be displayed. However, this approach lacks flexibility. For each set of objects to display, you must rewrite the retrieval logic. Additionally, for efficiency reasons, it may make more sense to load the entire set of objects once and cache them. Making constant round trips to a database is a sure way to slow your application to a crawl.

In order to use a filter, you'll load the entire collection once, either by using a ContentProvider or by add()ing the objects. When it's time to display the data, you call StructuredViewer's addFilter() method, giving it an implementation of ViewerFilter that only accepts the items to be displayed.

For example, assume we have a list of words. The user can choose to display only words that start with a certain string. The code is simple. It first defines a filter:

```
public class SubstringFilter extends ViewerFilter
{
  private String filterString;

  public SubstringFilter( String s )
  {
    filterString = s;
  }

  public boolean select( Viewer viewer,
                   Object parentElement, Object element )
  {
    return element.toString().startsWith( filterString );
  }
}
```

Now we can use it on the viewer:

```
StructuredViewer viewer = ...
//set content provider, etc for the viewer
SubstringFilter filter = new SubstringFilter( "" );
viewer.addFilter( filter );
```

By default, this displays every element, because any string starts with the empty string. When the user enters a string to filter by, these lines of code update the display:

```
viewer.removeFilter( filter );
filter = new SubstringFilter( userEnteredString );
viewer.addFilter( filter );
```

Calling addFilter() automatically triggers refiltering of the elements, and now only strings that start with the string entered by the user are displayed. Notice that there was no need to worry about the original collection of objects. The viewer still maintains the entire collection; it chooses to display only the ones for which the filter returns true when select() is called. It's even possible to have multiple filters on a viewer; in this case, only items that pass all the filters are displayed.

There is one caveat to be aware of when you're using a design that revolves around filters: Although it's conceptually simpler to load an entire collection and let the filters handle selection, this approach won't scale well if your collection potentially contains millions of items. In this case, you'll probably have to fall back on the "load only what you need" method. As always, carefully consider the demands of your specific application.

Similar in spirit to filters, StructuredViewer also allows custom sorting of its elements using setSorter() and a ViewerSorter. After all elements have been filtered, the sorter is given a chance to reorder the elements before they are displayed. To continue our earlier example, you could use a sorter to alphabetize the words in the list. The default implementation of ViewerSorter sorts the labels for each element in a case-insensitive manner. The easiest way to implement your own ViewerSorter is to override the compare() method, which acts identically to the compare() method in java.util.Comparator. compare() is given two objects and returns a negative integer, zero, or a positive integer, to denote less than, equals, or greater than, respectively.

You can use the isSorterProperty() method to avoid resorting if a given change wouldn't change the sort order. If you need more complex comparisons, you can use the category() method to break elements into different categories, each of which will be sorted independently. For example, if you have a list of Order objects, category() could return 1 for inbound orders and 2 for outbound orders, whereas compare() sorts based upon the order number. The list will then group all the inbound orders together, sorted by order number, followed by all the outbound orders, also sorted by order number. This technique is most effective if there is also a visual cue that corresponds to the different categories. The following example shows the code used to implement such an approach:

```
public class OrderSorter extends ViewerSorter
{
  public int category(Object element)
  {
    //assumes all objects are either InboundOrder
    //or OutboundOrder
    return (element instanceof InboundOrder) ? 1 : 2;
  }
  public int compare(Viewer viewer, Object e1, Object e2)
  {
    int cat1 = category(e1);
    int cat2 = category(e2);
    if( cat1 != cat2 ) return cat1 - cat2;
    //Order is the superclass of both InboundOrder
    //and OutboundOrder
    int firstOrderNumber = ((Order)e1).getOrderNumber();
    int secondOrderNumber = ((Order)e2).getOrderNumber();
    return firstOrderNumber - secondOrderNumber;
  }
}
```

Notice that this example manually calls category(). This is necessary because we've overridden the compare() method, so if we don't call category() ourselves, it won't be called at all.

Unlike filters, it's only possible to have one sorter at a time on a given StructuredViewer. Multiple sorters wouldn't make sense, because each would clobber the work done by the others.

The default implementation of compare() generates labels for each item and sorts based on those generated labels. For this reason, the Viewer is passed to the compare() method. By casting the Viewer to a ContentViewer, the label provider can be retrieved using getLabelProvider() and used to get the text that will be displayed for the given element. In the previous example, overriding compare() thus becomes unnecessary if the label provider is implemented such that it returns the order number in String form. In that case, you could get away with implementing category() to differentiate between inbound and outbound orders and trust the default compare() to correctly group the orders. However, doing so would introduce coupling between the label provider and the sorter, since if the label provider changes, the orders may not be sorted correctly. How serious an issue this might be will vary from application to application.

Now that we have all the background out of the way, let's see some examples of using these widgets.

8.2 Trees

A tree control displays data in a hierarchal format, allowing a user to easily see the relationship between different elements. You're probably familiar with using Windows Explorer or a similar tool on your platform of choice to navigate your machine's file system. The folders on your machine are displayed, with each subfolder displayed beneath its parent. Sections of this hierarchy can be expanded or hidden, allowing you to focus on the section of the file system that interests you. A tree control lets you provide similar functionality for any group of objects that has a parent/child relationship, the way folders and subfolders do. Figure 8.2 shows a simple tree.

**Figure 8.2
A tree showing
parent/child
relationships**

We'll first discuss the SWT `Tree` widget, followed by the `TreeViewer` from JFace, which you can use to simplify use of the `Tree`.

8.2.1 SWT trees

`Tree` doesn't have a particularly useful interface. It extends `Scrollable` and provides the basic operations outlined in table 8.2.

Table 8.2 Operations available on a tree

Method	Description
addSelectionListener()	Enables notification of selection events.
addTreeListener()	The `TreeListener` interface provides callbacks for notification when a level of the tree is expanded or collapsed.
select()/deselect()	Modifies the current selection.
getSelection()	Retrieves the current selection.
show()	Forces the control to scroll until the given item is visible.

The items in the tree are a bit more interesting.

TreeItem

`TreeItem` is the class used to add items to a `Tree`. In addition to displaying content, `TreeItems` maintain a relationship with both parent and child items. A given item's parent can be retrieved with getParentItem(), which returns null for an item at the root of the Tree; getItems() returns the children in the form of an array of TreeItem.

Two style options are relevant for a Tree. The first is a choice between SWT.SINGLE or SWT.MULTI, which affects how many items may be selected at a time. Tree defaults to SWT.SINGLE, which means that each time an item is selected, the previous selection disappears. Using SWT.MULTI lets the user select multiple options in whatever way is supported by the operating system (usually by Ctrl- or Shift-clicking multiple entries).

The last style that may be applied is SWT.CHECK, which causes checkboxes to be drawn to the left of each item in the tree. If checkboxes have been enabled, the status of any given TreeItem can be queried using the getChecked() method, which returns a boolean indicating whether the item has been checked. Note that on some platforms, an item can be selected without being checked.

A parent is set by passing it to the constructor of TreeItem and can't be modified from either end of the relationship. Because of the way these relationships are maintained, removing a single item from a Tree is awkward: You must call removeAll() to empty the Tree and rebuild its contents, minus the items you wish to remove.

TreeItems provide methods to modify the text or image displayed in the form of setText() and setImage(). A TreeItem can be forced to expand or contract itself using setExpanded(boolean).

You're welcome to build and display a tree by directly creating and manipulating TreeItems, but doing so forces you to deal with widgets on a lower level than is necessary. By using a TreeViewer to handle your tree, you can focus on the logic of your application rather than on the details of user interface elements.

8.2.2 JFace TreeViewers

A TreeViewer offers the filtering and sorting capabilities common to all Viewers, as well as the ability to use a label provider. Additionally, a TreeViewer can use an ITreeContentProvider to populate itself. The ITreeContentProvider interface extends IStructuredContentProvider to add methods for querying the parent or children of a given node.

As we mentioned in our earlier discussion of general Viewer features, a content provider provides an interface to business object relationships. For example, suppose you need to display the elements of an XML document in a tree to allow the user to easily navigate between them. Using a Tree and TreeItems directly, this would require you to loop through all elements in the document, building the items by hand. Using the DOM parsing facilities in JDK 1.4, the resulting pseudocode looks something like this:

```
Document document = ... //parse XML
Tree tree = ...
NodeList rootChildren = document.getChildNodes();
for(int i = 0; i < rootChildren.getLength(); i++)
{
  Element rootElement = (Element)rootChildren.item(i);
  TreeItem item = new TreeItem(tree, NODE_STYLE);
  item.setText(rootElement.getTagName());
  buildChildren(rootElement, item);
}

...

/*
Recursively builds TreeItems out of the child
nodes of the given Element
*/
private void buildChildren(Element element,
                          TreeItem parentItem)
{
  NodeList children = element.getChildNodes();
  for(int i = 0; i < children.length(); i++)
  {
    Element child = (Element)children.item(i);
    TreeItem childItem = new TreeItem(parentItem, NODE_STYLE);
    buildChildren(child, childItem);
  }
}
```

In contrast, the code to use a content provider consists of trivial implementations of methods defined in ITreeContentProvider:

```
Document document = ... //parse XML document
TreeViewer viewer = ...
viewer.setContentProvider(new XMLContentProvider());
viewer.setInput(document);
viewer.setLabelProvider(XMLLabelProvider());

...

class XMLContentProvider
      implements ITreeContentProvider
{
  public Object[] getChildren(Object parentElement) {
    return toObjectArray(((Node)parentElement).getChildren());
  }

  public Object[] getElements(Object inputElement) {
    return toObjectArray(((Node)inputElement).getChildren())
  }
```

```
private Object[] toObjectArray(NodeList list){
  Object[] array = new Object[list.getLength()];
  for(int i = 0; i < list.getLength(); i++) {
    array[i] = list.item(i);
  }
  return array;
}

public Object getParent(Object element) {
  return ((Node)element).getParentNode();
}

public boolean hasChildren(Object element) {
  return ((Node)element).getChildNodes().getLength() > 0;
}

... //additional methods with empty implementations
}
```

At first glance, the content provider code takes more space, and in terms of lines of code it's longer. However, we would argue that the content provider is both conceptually simpler and easier to maintain. getChildren() and getElements() call getChildren() on the current Node and convert the result to an array. Using Tree, you're forced to handle the top-level elements differently than the rest of the items, creating two separate sections of code that must be updated if the requirements change. More importantly, by using a TreeViewer, content provider, and label provider, you're operating directly on your domain objects (in this case, Nodes of an XML document). If the document changes, the display can be updated by calling refresh() on the viewer. At runtime, if more detail should be displayed at each node, an alternate implementation of ILabelProvider can be assigned to the viewer. If you're creating a Tree and TreeItems by hand, these cases require you either to manually traverse the tree to find and update the relevant nodes or to rebuild the entire Tree from scratch. On the whole, use of a content provider results in a design that is both simpler and more flexible.

It's worth discussing the hasChildren() method briefly. It's provided as an optimization hint for the tree. It would be possible to call getChildren() and check the size of the returned array, but in some cases it may be expensive to get the children of a given element. If a content provider can determine whether there are children for a node without having to compute all the children, then returning false here enables the tree to skip calling getChildren() when there aren't any children to display. If there is no easy way to calculate this, it's safe to always return true from hasChildren() and let getChildren() return an empty array when there are no children to display.

8.3 *Using the List widget*

A List widget presents a sequence of items. An mp3 player could use a List to present playlists to the user, whereas Eclipse uses a List to display possible matching classes when you choose Open Type. The user can select one or more values from the list, as shown in figure 8.3.

Figure 8.3
A simple list

Again, we'll cover building lists with the basic SWT classes and then dive into the more powerful capabilities offered by ListViewers.

8.3.1 *SWT lists*

Because the widget is so simple, it's easy to use a List without an attached Viewer and still obtain useful results. For example, building a list of Strings requires nothing more than the following:

```
List list = new List(parent, SWT.SINGLE);
for( int i = 0; i < 20; i++ )
{
   list.add( "item " + i);
}
```

Like Tree, List supports SWT.SINGLE or SWT.MULTI to control how many items may be selected simultaneously. No other styles (other than the ones supported by superclasses) are supported by Tree.

> **NOTE** If you're developing an SWT application that will run on Motif, you should be aware that it isn't possible to absolutely prevent the vertical scrollbar from being shown on a list. Accordingly, in Motif, SWT.V_SCROLL is added to whatever other styles you specify for a List in order to ensure that the style bits match what is displayed.

The List inherits scrolling capability from its superclass, Scrollable. Unless you specifically change it, the style is assumed to be SWT.V_SCROLL. This means that if the list of items exceeds the space available, a vertical scrollbar appears to allow the user to navigate the list. No horizontal scrollbar is available unless you add SWT.H_SCROLL to the style.

The drawback in our example is that List only accepts instances of String. Consequently, there is no way to display an image in the list, and updating a domain object requires searching the List for its old value, removing it, and replacing with the new one. This approach works fine for simple situations like the one shown previously, but eventually you'll most likely want to do something more interesting with your List. For that, you'll need to use a ListViewer.

8.3.2 JFace ListViewers

Using a ListViewer is the preferred way to interact with a List. At its most basic level, using the viewer allows more options for controlling the behavior of the widget, such as adding an image to each element or changing the order of the items on the fly without having to rebuild the entire list. It also allows decoupling of your model data from the way it's presented.

A ListViewer is instantiated with a parent Composite and an SWT style. The viewer supports the same styles as the basic List: SWT.SINGLE and SWT.MULTI, which designate how many items may be selected at the same time.

Although ListViewer provides an add() method that you can use to insert objects directly into the list, using a ContentProvider, as we did with the Tree-Viewer, is a good idea. ListViewer uses the IStructuredContentProvider interface. This interface is simple, generally requiring only that the method Object[] getElements(Object inputElement) be implemented. After setInput() is called in the viewer, getElements() is called and passed the same object that was set the input to the viewer.

With all the various helper classes operating on the viewer—content providers, label providers, filters, sorters—it's important to understand the way they interact. Everything starts with the content provider, which returns the entire set of items that may be displayed. This set is then passed to any filters attached to the viewer, which have the opportunity to remove items. Any items that pass all filters are then sorted and finally given to the label provider to determine what to display.

Retrieving items with IStructuredSelection

Up to this point, we haven't discussed how to retrieve the selected items from a ListViewer or TreeViewer. Any time you wish to query which items are selected, JFace provides an interface, IStructuredSelection, to manage the results.

getSelection(), which returns an instance of IStructuredSelection, is provided by the StructuredViewer class. Being an IStructuredSelection implies that there is some structure to the data returned—namely, an order. The interface provides a method to retrieve an iterator for the selected items, the same as the objects in the Collections framework. This iterator returns items in the same order in which they appear in the List. Typically, you'll loop through the items, as shown here:

```
...
IStructuredSelection selection =
    (IstructuredSelection)viewer.getSelection();
for( Iterator i = selection.iterator();
     i.hasNext(); )
{
    Object item = i.next();
    //process item
}
...
```

If necessary, however, the interface also provides toArray() and toList() methods to retrieve the entire collection of selected items at once.

8.4 *Updating WidgetWindow*

Let's add two new composites to the WidgetWindow, one to demonstrate trees and the second for lists. First add Ch8TreeComposite, which appears in listing 8.1.

Listing 8.1   Ch8TreeComposite.java

```
package com.swtjface.Ch8;

import java.util.ArrayList;
import java.util.List;

import org.eclipse.jface.viewers.ITreeContentProvider;
import org.eclipse.jface.viewers.TreeViewer;
import org.eclipse.jface.viewers.Viewer;
import org.eclipse.swt.SWT;
import org.eclipse.swt.layout.FillLayout;
import org.eclipse.swt.widgets.Composite;

public class Ch8TreeComposite extends Composite
{
  public Ch8TreeComposite(Composite parent)
  {
    super(parent, SWT.NULL);
    populateControl();
  }

  protected void populateControl()
  {
    FillLayout compositeLayout = new FillLayout();
    setLayout(compositeLayout);

    int[] selectionStyle = {SWT.SINGLE, SWT.MULTI};    ❶ Styles
    int[] checkStyle = {SWT.NONE, SWT.CHECK};

    for(int selection = 0;
            selection < selectionStyle.length;
```

```
              selection++)
   {
     for(int check = 0; check < checkStyle.length; check++)
     {
       int style = selectionStyle[selection] | checkStyle[check];
       createTreeViewer(style);
     }
   }
 }

 private void createTreeViewer(int style)
 {
   TreeViewer viewer = new TreeViewer(this, style);

   viewer.setContentProvider(new ITreeContentProvider() {    ❷ ContentProvider
     public Object[] getChildren(Object parentElement) {
       return ((TreeNode)parentElement).getChildren().toArray();
     }

     public Object getParent(Object element) {
       return ((TreeNode)element).getParent();
     }

     public boolean hasChildren(Object element) {
       return ((TreeNode)element).getChildren().size() > 0;
     }

     public Object[] getElements(Object inputElement) {
       return ((TreeNode)inputElement).getChildren().toArray();
     }

     public void dispose() {}

     public void inputChanged(Viewer viewer,
                              Object oldInput,
                              Object newInput) {}
   });

   viewer.setInput(getRootNode());    ❸ setInput()
 }
 private TreeNode getRootNode()      ❹ getRootNode()
 {
   TreeNode root = new TreeNode("root");
   root.addChild(new TreeNode("child 1")
         .addChild(new TreeNode("subchild 1")));
   root.addChild(new TreeNode("child 2")
         .addChild( new TreeNode("subchild 2")
           .addChild(new TreeNode("grandchild 1"))) );

   return root;
 }
}

class TreeNode    ❺ TreeNode
```

```
    {
      private String name;
      private List children = new ArrayList();
      private TreeNode parent;

      public TreeNode(String n)
      {
        name = n;
      }

      protected Object getParent()
      {
        return parent;
      }

      public TreeNode addChild(TreeNode child)
      {
        children.add(child);
        child.parent = this;
        return this;
      }

      public List getChildren()
      {
        return children;
      }

      public String toString()
      {
        return name;
      }
    }
```

1 These two orthogonal style sets cover all possible styles available for a `Tree`. The code loops through and combines them to make several sample tree instances, demonstrating all the different styles.

2 Here the code defines a `ContentProvider`, which is used to provide data to the `TreeViewer`. Notice that it can assume the parameters to each method are an instance of the appropriate domain object (`TreeNode`, in this case) and cast them accordingly.

3 Calling `setInput()` on the viewer starts the process of populating the tree with the given data.

4 This method builds the initial collection of domain objects.

5 This simple class serves as the domain object for the example.

This pane creates simple trees three levels deep. We use the class `TreeNode` to act as the domain objects. `TreeNode`'s only function is to maintain a list of children.

The key method to pay attention to is `createTreeViewer()`, which creates a new `TreeViewer` instance and assigns it an `ITreeContentProvider`. This content provider receives `TreeNodes` and knows how to return the children for each node. Because the domain objects naturally know about their own relationships, implementing the content provider consists of trivially asking each node for its parent or children and calling `toArray()` when appropriate. There is no need to convert objects to `Strings` in `getChildren()` or `getElements()`. You can return the full domain object and let the label provider (in this case, the default `BaseLabelProvider`, which calls `toString()`) worry about how to display them.

After assigning the content provider, you must remember to call `setInput()` and pass it the `TreeNode` to use as the base of the tree. This step associates actual domain objects with the viewer; otherwise the viewer can't know which objects to display. This root object is passed to `getElements()` to retrieve the first level of children. Each element in the array returned by `getElements()` is in turn passed to `getChildren()` to build the next level of the hierarchy. This process continues until `has-Children()` returns false or no more children are returned by `getChildren()`. Figure 8.4 shows the results when you run this example.

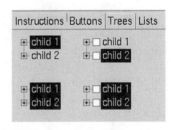

Figure 8.4   Tree pane

To run this example, you must add the following three lines to `WidgetWindow`:

```
TabItem chap8Tree = new TabItem(tf, SWT.NONE);
chap8Tree.setText("Chapter 8 Tree");
chap8Tree.setControl(new Ch8TreeComposite(tf));
```

Next, listing 8.2 presents the `Ch8ListComposite`, which uses some of the more advanced viewer features.

Listing 8.2   Ch8ListComposite.java

```
package com.swtjface.Ch8;

import java.util.ArrayList;
import java.util.List;

import org.eclipse.jface.viewers.IStructuredContentProvider;
import org.eclipse.jface.viewers.LabelProvider;
import org.eclipse.jface.viewers.ListViewer;
import org.eclipse.jface.viewers.Viewer;
```

```
import org.eclipse.jface.viewers.ViewerFilter;
import org.eclipse.jface.viewers.ViewerSorter;
import org.eclipse.swt.SWT;
import org.eclipse.swt.layout.FillLayout;
import org.eclipse.swt.widgets.Composite;
public class Ch8ListComposite extends Composite
{
  public Ch8ListComposite(Composite parent)
  {
    super(parent, SWT.NULL);
    populateControl();
  }

  protected void populateControl()
  {
    FillLayout compositeLayout = new FillLayout();
    setLayout(compositeLayout);

    int[] styles = {SWT.SINGLE, SWT.MULTI};       ❶ Styles

    for(int style = 0; style < styles.length; style++)
    {
      createListViewer(styles[style]);
    }
  }

  private void createListViewer(int style)
  {
    ListViewer viewer = new ListViewer(this, style);

    viewer.setLabelProvider(new LabelProvider() {
        public String getText(Object element) {
            return ((ListItem)element).name;
        }
    });

    viewer.addFilter(new ViewerFilter() {         ❷ Filter
        public boolean select(Viewer viewer,
                              Object parent,
                              Object element) {
            return ((ListItem)element).value % 2 == 0;
        }
    });

    viewer.setSorter( new ViewerSorter() {         ❸ Sorter
      public int compare(Viewer viewer,
                         Object obj1,
                         Object obj2) {
        return ((ListItem)obj2).value - ((ListItem)obj1).value;
      }
    });

    viewer.setContentProvider(new IStructuredContentProvider() {
```

```
      public Object[] getElements(Object inputElement)
      {
        return ((List)inputElement).toArray();
      }

      public void dispose() {}

      public void inputChanged(Viewer viewer,
                               Object oldInput,
                               Object newInput)
      {
      }
    });

    List input = new ArrayList();
    for( int i = 0; i < 20; i++ )
    {
      input.add(new ListItem("item " + i, i));
    }

    viewer.setInput(input);
  }

}

class ListItem      ❹  ListItem
{
  public String name;
  public int value;

  public ListItem(String n, int v)
  {
    name = n;
    value = v;
  }
}
```

❶ These two styles are the only ones available for lists. The code creates one of each.

❷ This simple `ViewerFilter` selects only items whose value field is even. If two divides cleanly into the value, you return true, which allows the item to be displayed.

❸ This `ViewerSorter` sorts domain objects by their value field, from high to low.

❹ `ListItem` acts as the domain object for this example.

This code creates a class `ListItem` to act as domain objects. `ListItem` stores a name and an integer value, which are used for ordering and filtering.

Because a `List` handles only simple data with no relationships between elements, implementing the `IStructuredContentProvider` requires only a single line in `getElements()`. To make up for the boring implementation of the content provider, we've added a label provider, a filter, and a sorter. We'll consider these in the order in which they're executed.

After the viewer has retrieved the list of items from the content provider, the filter is given first shot at the items. For the sake of this example, we decided to only display items whose value field is even. This can be accomplished by implementing the select() method of the filter and returning true or false depending on whether the value is even. Only items that you return true for will eventually be displayed. If you added more than one filter to the viewer, they would each be called in turn.

Next the sorter is used to determine the order of items in the list. The compare() method sorts ListItems by their value, from high to low. Again, this requires a single line of code.

Finally, once the items have been filtered and sorted, the text to display is determined by calling a label provider. Because the results of calling toString() on objects wouldn't be pretty, you create a label provider that returns the name field of each ListItem. The final result is shown in figure 8.5; add these lines to WidgetWindow, compile, and run:

```
TabItem chap8List = new TabItem(tf, SWT.NONE);
chap8List.setText("Chapter 8 List");
chap8List.setControl(new Ch8ListComposite(tf));
```

The elegance of the viewer design becomes apparent when you consider that all these operations are cleanly decoupled from each other. The content provider doesn't care what will be done with the objects it provides. Filters don't need to know about each other or how the items will be sorted. The label provider displays objects without having to care how the sorter ordered them. And any one of these can be swapped for a completely different implementation without affecting the rest of the code.

Figure 8.5 The list pane

8.5 Summary

Understanding the relationships between the various widgets and their viewers is key to using these controls effectively. Simple use of the controls is possible without the viewers, but being able to use filters, sorters, label providers, and content providers will enable you to separate the concerns of your application much more cleanly. Above all, decide whether you're going to use the viewers, and stick to that decision. Mixing direct creation of `TreeItems` (or any other item class) with use of a content provider will cause unpredictable results and make understanding your code very difficult.

Tables and menus

9

This chapter covers

- SWT tables
- JFace tables
- Editing table data
- Creating menus

Just about every time we want to go out to eat, we find ourselves sitting in the car, wracking our brains as we try to think of somewhere to go. We end up naming different styles of food—"Japanese?" "Not bad, but not really what I'm in the mood for." "Italian?" "Not tonight." "Indian?" "That's a good idea, but let's keep thinking." Especially when we're hungry, we have a hard time thinking about what restaurants are nearby and coming up with good options.

Eventually, we came up with a plan: One afternoon, when we weren't hungry and had time to think, we wrote up a list of restaurants in the area, organized by price and type of food. Now, when we decide to go out, we can look at the list and have concrete options to discuss. It doesn't help when we're in the mood for different things, but it makes the process of deciding where to go easier.

In a software application, a menu provides a function similar to our list of restaurants. A finite list of options is presented to users to guide them in deciding what tasks they wish to perform. Just as we sometimes rediscover a favorite place to eat that we haven't visited in a while, users can discover functionality they didn't know existed in your application by seeing it listed in a pull-down or context menu.

We'll cover two tasks in this chapter. First, we'll continue our discussion of the Viewer framework from the previous chapter by covering the last of the basic viewer widgets, the table. The concepts you've already learned are just as applicable to tables as they were to trees and lists, but JFace also provides advanced options in the form of cell editors to make it easy to implement user-editable tables. Once you're familiar with the editing framework, we'll revisit the `Actions` we discussed in chapter 4 and show how to apply them to the creation of menus, so that you can present functions to your users instead of leaving them to guess or remember what your application is capable of. Finally, our example in this chapter shows how to apply a context menu to a table by presenting a small user-editable widget that could be used to edit data in a relational database.

9.1 Tables

To the user, a table looks like a two-dimensional grid composed of many cells. Often this is a convenient way to display items such as the result of a database query—each row of the result set maps nicely to a single row in the table. As you'll see, however, JFace provides advanced facilities for editing table data as well.

9.1.1 Understanding SWT tables

Continuing SWT's trend of intuitive widget names, a table is represented by a class named `Table`. The `Table` class isn't terribly interesting. In general, if you're using

JFace, you'll be better off interacting with a `Table` through the interface provided by a `TableViewer`, which we discuss later in the chapter. However, if you need to manipulate the currently selected table items directly, or you aren't using JFace, you'll need to use the underlying `Table`.

The first thing you'll notice when looking at the methods available on `Table` is that although there are plenty of accessor methods to query its state, there is a distinct lack of setters that would let you customize the `Table`. In fact, rather than adding data or columns directly to the `Table`, you'll pass a `Table` instance to the appropriate dependent class when that dependent is instantiated, similar to the way `Composites` are passed to other widgets rather than the widget being added to the `Composite`. Other than a few setters for straightforward display properties, such as header visibility, the critical methods to be aware of when manipulating a `Table` are summarized in table 9.1.

Table 9.1 Important `Table` methods

Method	Description
addSelectionListener()	Notifies you when the table's selection changes
select()/deselect()	Overloaded in several ways to let you programmatically add or remove the selection on one or more items
getSelection()	Retrieves an array of the currently selected items
remove()	Removes items from the table
showItem()/showSelection()	Forces the table to scroll until the item or selection is visible

It's also important to remember that `Table` extends `Scrollable` and will therefore automatically come equipped with scrollbars unless you turn them off.

TableItems

To add data to a table, you must use a `TableItem`. Each instance of `TableItem` represents an entire row in the table. Each `TableItem` is responsible for controlling the text and image to display in each column of its row. These values can be set using the `setText()` and `setImage()` methods, each of which takes an integer parameter designating which column to modify.

As we mentioned, `TableItems` are associated with a `Table` in their constructor, as shown here:

```
Table t = ...
//Create a new TableItem with the parent Table
//and a style
```

```
TableItem item = new TableItem(t, SWT.NONE);
item.setText(0, "Hello World!");
...
```

According to the Javadocs, no styles are valid to be set on a `TableItem`, but the constructor accepts a style parameter anyway. This seems rather unnecessary to us, but it's at least consistent with the other widgets we've seen.

TableColumn

The final class you'll need to work directly with tables is `TableColumn`, which creates an individual column in the table. As with `TableItem`, you must pass a `Table` to the constructor of `TableColumn` in order to associate the two objects.

Each `TableColumn` instance controls one column in the table. It's necessary to instantiate the `TableColumns` you need, or the `Table` will default to having only one column. Several methods are available to control the behavior and appearance of each column, such as the width, alignment of text, and whether the column is resizable. You can add header text by using the `setText()` method. Instead of setting the attributes directly on a column, however, it's usually easier to use a `TableLayout`. By calling `TableLayout`'s `addColumnData()` method, you can easily describe the appearance of each column in the table. The ability to pass `addColumnData()` instances of `ColumnWeightData` is key; doing so lets you specify a relative weight for each column without having to worry about the exact number of pixels required for each one.

The following snippet shows how to create a table using a `TableLayout`. The code creates three columns of equal width and fills two rows with data. The code produces a table that looks similar to figure 9.1.

```
//Set up the table layout
TableLayout layout = new TableLayout();
layout.addColumnData(new ColumnWeightData(33, 75, true));
layout.addColumnData(new ColumnWeightData(33, 75, true));
layout.addColumnData(new ColumnWeightData(33, 75, true));

Table table = new Table(parent, SWT.SINGLE);
table.setLayout(layout);

//Add columns to the table
TableColumn column1 = new TableColumn(table, SWT.CENTER);
TableColumn column2 = new TableColumn(table, SWT.CENTER);
TableColumn column3 = new TableColumn(table, SWT.CENTER);

TableItem item = new TableItem(table, SWT.NONE);
item.setText( new String[] { "column 1",
                             "column 2",
                             "column 3" } );
item = new TableItem(table, SWT.NONE);
item.setText( new String[] { "a", "b", "c" } );
```

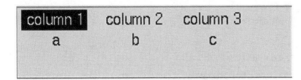

Figure 9.1
A simple three-column table

The first thing to do is set up the structure for this table using a `TableLayout`. Each time you call `addColumnData()`, it adds a new column to the table. We'll have three columns, so we add a `ColumnWeightData` to describe each. The parameters to the constructor that we use here are `weight`, `minimumWidth`, and `resizeable`. `weight` indicates the amount of screen space this column should be allocated, as a percentage of the total space available to the table. `minimumWidth` is, as the name indicates, the minimum width in pixels to use for this column. The `resizeable` flag determines whether the user can resize this column.

After we've set up the table, we need to instantiate three columns so they will be added to the table. It's important to keep in mind that adding columns is a two-step process: create a `TableLayout` that describes how large each column will be, and then create the columns themselves. Because we allow the `TableLayout` to control sizing, we don't need to use the columns after they've been created.

9.1.2 JFace TableViewers

Although it's possible to use a `Table` directly in your code, as you can see, doing so is neither intuitive nor convenient. Similarly to `List`, however, JFace provides a viewer class to make using tables easier. The following snippets demonstrate a basic `TableViewer` that displays data from a database. The same concepts of filters, sorters, and label providers that we discussed in chapter 8 apply here as well. Additionally, we'll use a `ContentProvider` to supply the data to our table, because the same arguments presented in the previous chapter apply here.

First, the table must be set up. This is similar to the process of setting up a `Table`, which you saw in the previous section, using `addColumnData()` for each column that will be created:

```
final TableViewer viewer = new TableViewer(parent,
                     SWT.BORDER | SWT.FULL_SELECTION);

//configure the table for display
TableLayout layout = new TableLayout();
layout.addColumnData(new ColumnWeightData(33, true));
layout.addColumnData(new ColumnWeightData(33, true));
layout.addColumnData(new ColumnWeightData(33, true));

viewer.getTable().setLayout(layout);
```

```
viewer.getTable().setLinesVisible(true);
viewer.getTable().setHeaderVisible(true);
```

Once the table has been configured, we attach the appropriate providers. The most important one in this example is the content provider, which is responsible for retrieving data from the database and passing it back to the viewer. Note that you never return `null` from `getElements()`—instead, return an empty array if there are no more children:

```
viewer.setContentProvider(new IStructuredContentProvider() {
  public Object[] getElements(Object input)
  {
    //Cast input appropriately and perform a database query
    ...
    while( results.next() )
    {
      //read results from database
    }
    if(resultCollection.size() > 0)
    {
      return new DBRow[] { ... };
    }
    else
    {
      return new Object[0];
    }
  }
  //... additional interface methods
});
viewer.setLabelProvider(new ITableLabelProvider() {
  public String getColumnText(Object element, int index) {
      DBRow row = (DBRow)element;
      switch(index)
      {
      //return appropriate attribute for column
      }
  }
  //... additional interface methods
});
```

Once the providers have been set up, we can add the columns. The text we set on each column will appear as a header for that column when the table is displayed:

```
TableColumn column1 = new TableColumn(viewer.getTable(),
                                      SWT.CENTER);
column1.setText("Primary Key");
TableColumn column2 = new TableColumn(viewer.getTable(),
                                      SWT.CENTER);
column2.setText("Foreign Key");
```

```
TableColumn column3 = new TableColumn(viewer.getTable(),
                                      SWT.CENTER);
column3.setText("Data");
```

Finally, we need to provide input to drive the content provider. The input object (in this case, a `String` describing a query) is set on the viewer, which passes it to the content provider when it's ready to display the table:

```
viewer.setInput(QUERY);
```

This example simulates retrieving multiple rows from a database and displaying the results. However, it suffices to get our point across about content providers. The role of the `IStructuredContentProvider` implementation is straightforward: Given an input element, return all the children elements to be displayed. A table doesn't maintain parent/child relationships, so this method is called only once and is given the current input object. The final issue to be aware of when using a content provider is that it will always execute in the UI thread. This means updates to the interface will be waiting for your methods to complete, so you definitely shouldn't query a database to get your updates. The content provider should traverse a graph of already-loaded domain objects to select the appropriate content to display.

A word about error handling

When you're using JFace—especially the providers that the widgets call internally—it pays to be careful with your error handling. When JFace makes the callback to your class, it typically does so inside a `try/catch` block that catches all exceptions. JFace does some checks to see whether it knows how to handle the exception itself before letting the exception propagate. Unfortunately, these checks rely upon the `Platform` class, which is tightly coupled with Eclipse; it's practically impossible to initialize `Platform` correctly unless you're running Eclipse. This leads to internal assertion failures when JFace tries to use `Platform` outside of Eclipse, and these exceptions end up masking your own errors.

In practical terms, you shouldn't ever let an exception be thrown out of a provider method. If it happens, you're in for strange "The application has not been initialized" messages. If you ever see one of these, check your code carefully—things such as `ClassCastExceptions` can be hard to spot, and locating them is even more difficult when JFace hides them from you.

Editing table data

Displaying data can be useful on its own, but eventually you'll want to let the user edit it. Often, the most user-friendly way to enable editing is to allow the user to change it directly in the table as it's presented. JFace provides a means to support this editing through CellEditors.

As we mentioned in the chapter overview, CellEditors exist to help decouple the domain model from the editing process. In addition, using these editors can make your UI more user friendly: Users won't be able to enter values your application doesn't understand, thus avoiding confusing error messages further down the line. The framework assumes that each domain object has a number of named properties. Generally, you should follow the JavaBeans conventions, with property foo having getFoo() and setFoo() methods; but doing so isn't strictly necessary as long as you can identify each property given only its name. You begin by attaching an instance of ICellModifier to your TableViewer. The ICellModifier is responsible for retrieving the value of a given property from an object, deciding whether a property can currently be edited, and applying the updated value to the object when the edit has been completed. The actual edit, if allowed, is performed by a CellEditor. JFace provides CellEditors for editing via checkbox, combo box, pop-up dialog, or directly typing the new text value. In addition, you can subclass CellEditor if you need a new form of editor. After registering CellEditors, you associate each column with a property. When the user clicks on a cell to change its value, JFace does all the magic of matching the proper column with the property to edit and displaying the correct editor, and it notifies your ICellModifier when the edit is complete.

We'll show examples of the important parts of the process here. The rest of the snippets in this section are taken from the Ch9TableEditorComposite, which is presented in full at the end of the chapter.

The first snippet sets up data that the rest of the code will reference. The array of Strings in VALUE_SET holds the values that will be displayed by our ComboBox-CellEditor. We'll need to convert between indices and values several times (see the discussion later in the chapter):

```
private static final Object[] CONTENT = new Object[] {
            new EditableTableItem("item 1", new Integer(0)),
            new EditableTableItem("item 2", new Integer(1))
            };
private static final String[] VALUE_SET = new String[] {
                            "xxx", "yyy", "zzz"
                            };
```

```
private static final String NAME_PROPERTY = "name";
private static final String VALUE_PROPERTY = "value";
```

Our class contains several different methods that are each responsible for setting up a different facet of the cell editor. They are called in turn from `buildControls`. The first thing this method does is set up the table and the classes required by the viewer:

```
protected Control buildControls()
{
  final Table table = new Table(parent, SWT.FULL_SELECTION);
  TableViewer viewer = new TableViewer(table);
  ... //set up a two column table
```

Once the table has been initialized, we continue by adding an instance of `ITable-LabelProvider` to our viewer. The idea is similar to the label providers we discussed in chapter 8. However, because each row of a table has many columns, the signature of our methods must change slightly. In addition to the element, each method now takes the integer index of the column that is being requested. The label provider must therefore contain the logic to map column indices to properties of the domain objects. The next snippet shows how this is done:

```
viewer.setLabelProvider(new ITableLabelProvider() {
  public String getColumnText(Object element,
                              int columnIndex) {
    switch(columnIndex)
    {
      case 0:
        return ((EditableTableItem)element).name;
      case 1:
        Number index = ((EditableTableItem)element).value;
        return VALUE_SET[index.intValue()];
      default:
        return "Invalid column: " + columnIndex;
    }
  }
});

attachCellEditors(viewer, table);
return table;
}
```

The `attachCellEditors()` method is where we set up our `ICellModifier`, which is responsible for translating a property name into data to be displayed, deciding whether a given property can be edited, and then applying whatever changes the user makes. When the user double-clicks a cell to edit it, `canModify()` is called to determine whether the edit should be allowed. If it's allowed, `getValue()` is called next to retrieve the current value of the property being edited. Once the edit is complete, `modify()` is called; it's `modify()`'s responsibility to apply the changes the user made back to the original domain object. While in `getValue()` and `canModify()`, it's safe to cast parameters directly to the domain objects; this doesn't work in `modify()`. `modify()` receives the `TableItem` that's displaying the row. This `TableItem` has had the domain object set as its data, so we must retrieve it using `getData()` before we can update it:

```
private void attachCellEditors(final TableViewer viewer,
                              Composite parent)
{
  viewer.setCellModifier(new ICellModifier() {
    public boolean canModify(Object element,
                             String property) {
      return true;
    }

    public Object getValue(Object element, String property) {
      if( NAME_PROPERTY.equals(property))
        return ((EditableTableItem)element).name;
      else
        return ((EditableTableItem)element).value;
    }
    //method continues below...
```

When `modify()` is finished updating the domain object, we must let the viewer know to update the display. The viewer's `refresh()` method is used for this purpose. Calling `refresh()` with the domain object that changed causes the viewer to redraw the given row. If we skip this step, users will never see their changes once the edited cell loses focus:

```
    public void modify(Object element,
                       String property, Object value) {
      TableItem tableItem = (TableItem)element;
      EditableTableItem data =
                (EditableTableItem)tableItem.getData();
      if( NAME_PROPERTY.equals( property ) )
        data.name = value.toString();
      else
        data.value = (Integer)value;

      viewer.refresh(data);
    }
  });
```

The items given in the `CellEditor` array here are matched in order with the columns of the underlying table:

```
viewer.setCellEditors(new CellEditor[] {
      new TextCellEditor(parent),
```

```
           new ComboBoxCellEditor(parent, VALUE_SET )
       });
```

Next, the strings in setColumnProperties() are the names of the editable properties on our domain objects. They're also matched in order with the table's columns, so that in our example clicking column 0 will try to edit the name property,
and column 1 will edit the value property:

```
    viewer.setColumnProperties(new String[] {
            NAME_PROPERTY, VALUE_PROPERTY
        });
    }
}

class EditableTableItem
{
    ... //name and value properties
}
```

Using a ComboBoxCellEditor as we do here is tricky. The editor's constructor takes
an array of Strings that are the values presented for the user to choose from.
However, the editor expects Integers from getValue() and returns an Integer to
modify() when the edit is complete. These values should correspond to the index
of the selected value in the array of Strings passed to the ComboBoxCellEditor
constructor. In this simple example we save the Integer directly in the value field,
but in a real application you'll probably need utilities to easily convert back and
forth between indices and values.

Again, using CellEditors is an area where it's smart to pay attention to your
casting and error handling. Especially when different methods require you to cast
to different objects, as in the ICellModifier, it's easy to make a mistake the compiler can't catch for you. Due to JFace's exception handling, as we discussed earlier, these issues show up as cryptic "Application not initialized" runtime errors
that can be hard to track down if you don't know what you should be looking for.

9.2 *Creating menus*

Every graphical application uses a menu of some sort. You'll often find File, Edit,
and so on across the top of your application's window. These menus fill an
important role, because they provide a place for users to browse through the
functionality offered by your application.

We'll first discuss creating menus using SWT. We'll then revisit the JFace Action
classes that we mentioned in chapter 4, to discuss an alternate way to create
menus that allows for easy sharing of common code.

9.2.1 *Accelerator keys*

Before we get too deep into the specifics of menus, let's discuss how SWT handles accelerator keys. *Accelerator keys* are keyboard shortcuts that activate a widget without the user having to click it with the mouse. The best example is the ubiquitous Ctrl-C (or Open Apple-C if you're using a Mac) to copy text to the clipboard, the same as if you selected Copy from the Edit menu that's present in most applications. Offering accelerator keys for common tasks can greatly increase advanced users' productivity, because their hands don't have to continually switch between the keyboard and mouse. The accelerator keystroke for an item customarily appears next to the item's name in drop-down menus for the application, making it easier for users to learn the keystrokes as they use the application.

In both SWT and JFace, accelerator keys are expressed by using constants from the SWT class. The concept is the same as for styles: All the constants are bitwise ORed together to determine the final key combination. Additionally, chars are used to represent letters or numbers on the keyboard. Because a Java char can be automatically converted to an int, chars can be used just like the SWT style constants to build a bitmask. This bitmask is passed to the setAccelerator() method on a Menu to register the combination of keys that will activate that menu item. For example, a MenuItem whose accelerator is set to SWT.CONTROL | SWT.SHIFT | 't' will activate when the Ctrl, Shift, and T keys are pressed simultaneously.

9.2.2 *Creating menus in SWT*

When you're creating menus using SWT, you'll use only two classes: Menu and MenuItem. Although the classes themselves aren't complicated, several areas of complexity arise once you begin to use them.

Menu acts as a container for MenuItems. Menu extends Widget and contains methods for adding MenuItems and controlling the visibility and location of the menu. Menu also broadcasts events to implementors of the MenuListener interface, which receives notification when the menu is shown or hidden.

Menu supports three different styles, which go beyond controlling the visual appearance to determine the type of menu created:

- *SWT.POP_UP*—Creates a free-floating pop-up menu of the type that typically appears when you right-click in an application.

- *SWT.BAR*—Creates the menu bar at the top of an application window. A menu bar doesn't typically have selectable menu items; instead, it acts as a container for menu items that contain menus of type SWT.DROP_DOWN.

- *SWT.DROP_DOWN*—Creates the File, Edit, and other drop-down menus that we're all familiar with. These menus may contain a mix of MenuItems and submenus of their own.

A MenuItem is a widget that either can be selected by the end user or can display another menu. A MenuItem is always created as a child of a Menu. A variety of styles are available for MenuItems:

- *SWT.PUSH*—Creates a standard menu item with no frills.

- *SWT.CHECK, SWT.RADIO*—Add either a checkbox or radio button, as appropriate, which flips between on and off each time the item is selected.

- *SWT.SEPARATOR*—Visually separates groups of menu items. It displays the standard separator for your platform (usually a thin line) and may not be selected by the user.

- *SWT.CASCADE*—Creates a submenu. When a cascading menu item has a menu assigned to it, highlighting that item results in the submenu being displayed.

All MenuItems except separators broadcast SelectionEvents that can be listened for. Figure 9.2 shows the different menu styles.

Creating Menus is straightforward. Classes are instantiated and configured, and then assigned to the widgets on which they should be displayed. The following snippet shows how to create a File menu attached to the main window of your application:

```
Composite parent = ... //get parent
Menu menuBar = new Menu(parent.getShell(), SWT.BAR);

MenuItem fileItem = new MenuItem(menuBar, SWT.CASCADE);
fileItem.setText("&File");

Menu fileMenu = new Menu(fileItem);
fileItem.setMenu(fileMenu);

parent.getShell().setMenuBar(menuBar);
```

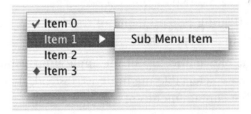

Figure 9.2
Menu types. From top to bottom, SWT.CHECK, SWT.CASCADE, SWT.PUSH, and SWT.RADIO.

Notice that you must first create the root menu bar and then add a menu item to hold each drop-down menu that will appear on it. At this point, we have a menu bar that displays File but is empty. Our next task is to populate this menu:

```
MenuItem open = new MenuItem(fileMenu, SWT.PUSH);
open.setText("Open...");
open.setAccelerator(SWT.CONTROL | 'o');
open.addSelectionListener(new SelectionListener() {
  public void widgetSelected(SelectionEvent event) {
    ... //handle selection
  }
};
```

Clicking File will now reveal a drop-down menu with an Open option. If Open is selected, the selection listener we've defined is invoked to display an Open File dialog or do whatever other action is appropriate to the application. We've also set the keyboard accelerator for this option to Ctrl-O by calling setAccelerator() with a bitmask of the keys we wish to assign. The result is that pressing Ctrl-O invokes the selection listener just as if it was selected with the mouse.

Creating a pop-up menu is similar to what we've done here, but there is a slight wrinkle. We don't need a menu bar, so we can start with the pop-up:

```
Composite parent = ... //get composite
final Menu popupMenu = new Menu(parent.getShell(), SWT.POP_UP);
```

Notice that we declare the Menu instance to be final. This is important, because we'll need to reference it in a listener later.

Creating the MenuItems is the same as for a drop-down menu. For variety, we'll show how to create a menu item that reveals a submenu when highlighted. The important point to notice in this process is that after the submenu is created, it must be assigned to its parent menu item using setMenu(), just as we did with the menu bar in our earlier example:

```
MenuItem menuItem = new MenuItem(popupMenu, SWT.CASCADE);
menuItem.setText("More options");

Menu subMenu = new Menu(menuItem);
menuItem.setMenu(subMenu);
MenuItem subItem = new MenuItem(subMenu, SWT.PUSH);
subItem.setText("Option 1");
subItem.addSelectionListener( ... );
```

Unlike a menu bar, a pop-up menu isn't displayed by default—you must decide when to display it. Typically this is done in response to a mouse right-click, so we'll use a MouseListener on the parent Composite. This is where we need the pop-up menu instance to be final, so we can reference it within our anonymous inner class:

```
parent.addMouseListener(new MouseListener() {
  public void mouseDown(MouseEvent event) {
    if(event.button == 2)
    {
      popupMenu.setVisible(true);
    }
  }
  ... //other MouseListener methods
});
```

MouseEvent contains information about the button that was clicked. The buttons are numbered: 1 is the left mouse button, and 2 is the right button. If this button was clicked, we make the pop-up menu visible; it's displayed at the location that was clicked. Pressing Esc or clicking anywhere other than on the menu automatically causes the pop-up to be hidden.

Now that you've seen how SWT handles menus, we'll turn our attention to the menu options offered by JFace.

9.2.3 *Using JFace actions to add to menus*

We've already discussed the design of JFace's Action classes in chapter 4. To review briefly, an action encapsulates the response to a single application level event, such as "Open a file" or "Update the status bar." This action can then be reused and triggered in different contexts, such as a toolbar button or a menu item. We'll discuss this last case here. By using actions to create your menus, instead of doing it by hand, you can simplify the design of your application and reuse common logic.

Using actions in a menu is similar to using them anywhere else. Remember that an IContributionManager is responsible for assembling individual Actions and transforming them into a form that can be displayed to the user. For menus, we'll use the MenuManager implementation of IContributionManager. After adding whatever actions are needed to the MenuManager, we can tell it to create a new menu or to add the actions to another menu. The code looks something like this:

```
Shell shell = ... //obtain a reference to the Shell
MenuManager fileMenuManager = new MenuManager("File");

IAction openAction = new OpenAction(...);
... //create other actions as appropriate

fileMenuManager.add(openAction);
... //add other actions

Menu menuBar = new Menu(shell, SWT.BAR);
fileMenuManager.fill(menuBar, -1);
shell.setMenuBar(menuBar);
```

Although we've still created the menu bar manually, we can add actions to the manager and let it worry about how the menu should be built. In this case, we end up with a File menu on the window's menu bar, because that is the name we gave the `MenuManager` when we instantiated it. The advantage of doing it this way instead of building menus by hand is that the action classes can be easily reused elsewhere. For example, if we have a toolbar that includes a button to let users open files, we can use the same `OpenAction` class there.

You must keep one caveat in mind when you're using menu managers: Once `fill()` or `createXXX()` has been called on a given instance, `Menu` and `MenuItem` instances are created and cached internally. This is necessary so that the manager can be used to update the menu. However, it also means that you shouldn't make further calls to `fill()` or `create()`, especially for a different type of menu. For example, suppose that after the previous code we called `createContextMenu()` on `fileMenuManager`. We would get exceptions when we tried to add the menu to a composite, because the menu would be the cached instance with type `SWT.CASCADE` instead of type `SWT.POP_UP` (which is required by context menus).

9.3 *Updating WidgetWindow*

Our pane for this chapter combines a table viewer, cell editors, and a context menu. We'll expand the snippets of a database editor that we discussed earlier and add a right-click menu that lets the user insert a new row. The final product looks like figure 9.3.

Listing 9.1 is longer than the code for most of our chapter panes, so we'll point out the most interesting bits before you begin reading it. The first thing to notice is the inner class `NewRowAction`. This class holds the logic to insert a new row into the table; it's added to the `MenuManager` we create in `createPane()`.

Next is the `createPane()` method, which is the entry point into the class. After delegating to methods to lay out the table and attach a label provider, content provider, and cell editor, we instantiate a `MenuManager` and use it to build a context

Figure 9.3   Our database table editor

menu that we then attach to the newly created Table. Finally, we pass the initial content to the viewer.

After createPane() come the private utility methods. The most important for our purposes is attachCellEditors(), which contains the logic to allow editing of individual table cells. Note that these modifications are performed directly on the domain objects.

At the end of the listing is the EditableTableItem class, which serves as a domain object for this example and is included in the same file for convenience.

Listing 9.1   Ch9TableEditorComposite.java

```java
package com.swtjface.Ch9;

import org.eclipse.jface.action.*;
import org.eclipse.jface.viewers.*;
import org.eclipse.swt.SWT;
import org.eclipse.swt.graphics.Image;
import org.eclipse.swt.layout.FillLayout;
import org.eclipse.swt.widgets.*;

public class Ch9TableEditorComposite extends Composite
{
  private static final Object[] CONTENT = new Object[] {        ❶ Initial content
        new EditableTableItem("item 1", new Integer(0)),
        new EditableTableItem("item 2", new Integer(1))
        };

  private static final String[] VALUE_SET = new String[] {
                                "xxx", "yyy", "zzz"
                                };
  private static final String NAME_PROPERTY = "name";
  private static final String VALUE_PROPERTY = "value";

  private TableViewer viewer;

  public Ch9TableEditorComposite(Composite parent)
  {
    super(parent, SWT.NULL);
    buildControls();
  }

  private class NewRowAction extends Action        ❷ NewRowAction class
  {
    public NewRowAction()
    {
      super("Insert New Row");
    }

    public void run()        ❸ run() method
    {
```

```
      EditableTableItem newItem =
            new EditableTableItem("new row", new Integer(2));
      viewer.add(newItem);
  }
}

protected void buildControls()
{
  FillLayout compositeLayout = new FillLayout();
  setLayout(compositeLayout);

  final Table table = new Table(this, SWT.FULL_SELECTION);
  viewer = buildAndLayoutTable(table);

  attachContentProvider(viewer);
  attachLabelProvider(viewer);
  attachCellEditors(viewer, table);

  MenuManager popupMenu = new MenuManager();          ❹ Build menu
  IAction newRowAction = new NewRowAction();
  popupMenu.add(newRowAction);
  Menu menu = popupMenu.createContextMenu(table);
  table.setMenu(menu);

  viewer.setInput(CONTENT);
}

private void attachLabelProvider(TableViewer viewer)
{
  viewer.setLabelProvider(new ITableLabelProvider() {
    public Image getColumnImage(Object element,
                                int columnIndex) {
      return null;
    }

    public String getColumnText(Object element,
                                int columnIndex) {       ❺ getColumnText()
      switch(columnIndex)                                  method
      {
        case 0:
          return ((EditableTableItem)element).name;
        case 1:
          Number index = ((EditableTableItem)element).value;
          return VALUE_SET[index.intValue()];
        default:
          return "Invalid column: " + columnIndex;
      }
    }

    public void addListener(ILabelProviderListener listener) {
    }

    public void dispose(){
    }
```

```
      public boolean isLabelProperty(Object element,
                                     String property){
        return false;
      }
      public void removeListener(ILabelProviderListener lpl) {
      }
    });
  }
  private void attachContentProvider(TableViewer viewer)
  {
    viewer.setContentProvider(new IStructuredContentProvider() {
      public Object[] getElements(Object inputElement) {
        return (Object[])inputElement;
      }

      public void dispose() {
      }

      public void inputChanged(Viewer viewer,
                               Object oldInput,
                               Object newInput) {

      }
    });
  }
  private TableViewer buildAndLayoutTable(final Table table)
  {
    TableViewer tableViewer = new TableViewer(table);

    TableLayout layout = new TableLayout();
    layout.addColumnData(new ColumnWeightData(50, 75, true));
    layout.addColumnData(new ColumnWeightData(50, 75, true));
    table.setLayout(layout);

    TableColumn nameColumn = new TableColumn(table, SWT.CENTER);
    nameColumn.setText("Name");
    TableColumn valColumn = new TableColumn(table, SWT.CENTER);
    valColumn.setText("Value");
    table.setHeaderVisible(true);
    return tableViewer;
  }
  private void attachCellEditors(final TableViewer viewer,
                                Composite parent)
  {
    viewer.setCellModifier(new ICellModifier() {
      public boolean canModify(Object element, String property){
        return true;
      }

      public Object getValue(Object element, String property) {
```

6 **getElements()**
method

buildAndLayoutTable() **7**
method

```
       if( NAME_PROPERTY.equals(property))
         return ((EditableTableItem)element).name;
       else
         return ((EditableTableItem)element).value;
     }

    public void modify(Object element,
                       String property,
                       Object value) {    ❽ modify() method
      TableItem tableItem = (TableItem)element;
      EditableTableItem data =
                  (EditableTableItem)tableItem.getData();
      if( NAME_PROPERTY.equals( property ) )
        data.name = value.toString();
      else
        data.value = (Integer)value;

      viewer.refresh(data);
     }
   });

   viewer.setCellEditors(new CellEditor[] {
          new TextCellEditor(parent),
          new ComboBoxCellEditor(parent, VALUE_SET )
        });

   viewer.setColumnProperties(new String[] {
          NAME_PROPERTY, VALUE_PROPERTY
        });
  }

}
class EditableTableItem      ❾ EditableTableItem class
{
  public String name;
  public Integer value;

  public EditableTableItem( String n, Integer v)
  {
    name = n;
    value = v;
  }
}
```

❶ These constants hold the data we'll use for our initial content. In a real application, this data would likely be read from a database or other external source.

❷ This class contains the logic to insert new rows into the data set. It extends Action so it can be used by a MenuManager.

③ To perform the necessary logic, we override the run() method defined in Action. The action framework ensures that this method is invoked at the appropriate time. Our implementation creates a new domain object and calls add() on the table viewer. Most real applications will need additional logic here to manage the collection of domain objects.

④ We build a simple context menu by creating a new MenuManager and adding the actions we want to use. In this case, we add the menu directly to the Table. If the tab contained more controls than just this table, then the menu would appear only when the user right-clicked on the table. If we wanted it to appear when the user clicked anywhere on the tab, we would need to add the menu to the parent Composite.

⑤ This is a standard LabelProvider implementation, similar to ones you've seen earlier. It returns the value of whichever property matches the requested column.

⑥ Our content provider assumes that whatever input it's given is an array of Objects. It performs the appropriate cast and returns the result.

⑦ Here we construct the table. We add two columns and set the header text.

⑧ The modify() method is the most important part of our CellModifier implementation. The element parameter contains the TableItem for the cell that was just changed. The domain object associated with this item is retrieved with the get-Data() method. We then check the propertyName parameter to determine what property was modified; we update the matching property on the domain object using the value parameter, which contains the date entered by the user.

⑨ This small class serves as the domain objects for our example.

Run this example by adding the following lines to WidgetWindow:

```
TabItem chap9TableEditor = new TabItem(tf, SWT.NONE);
chap9TableEditor.setText("Chapter 9");
chap9TableEditor.setControl(new Ch9TableEditorComposite(tf));
```

When you run this example, the initial window contains two rows with sample data. Right-clicking brings up a context menu that lets you insert a new row into the table. Double-clicking a cell allows you to edit the data, either by typing or by choosing from a drop-down menu.

9.4 Summary

Most of what you've seen with `Tables` and `TableViewers` should be familiar from chapter 8. The basic concepts of viewers and providers are identical to those we discussed earlier. Because tables impose a two-dimensional structure on data, they require more configuration than some of other widgets we've examined. The `TableLayout` and `TableColumn` classes create this structure for each table and control the details of how the table appears to the user.

After working through these two chapters, you should be well equipped to handle any requirement that calls for the use of one of these viewers, or any of the more esoteric classes such as `TableTreeViewer` that are included in JFace.

`CellEditors`, however, are a useful feature unique to `TableViewers`. `CellEditors` provide a framework for handling updates to specific cells in a table, and the predefined `CellEditor` classes provide an easy way to provide discrete options for the user to choose from.

Just about any application will need to provide a menu bar, and it's common to provide context menus that show only options that are relevant to what the user is currently doing. For example, right-clicking in a word processor typically brings up options related to formatting text. SWT makes creating these menus easy, and JFace adds the action framework to facilitate reusing logic easily regardless of the context from which it was invoked. We discussed the theory behind actions in chapter 4, and the examples we've shown here should give you a good feel for how they're used in practice.

10

Dialogs

If you want to be noticed, you must find a way to attract attention to yourself. Whether your goal is to woo a potential sweetheart or market a new invention, it's impossible to succeed if your target isn't aware of your efforts. The same principle holds for software. If your program needs something from the user, it must find a way to draw that user's attention to itself. There are a variety of ways to accomplish this, but the most common is to present the user with a dialog box. A *dialog box* is a window that is separate from your application's main window. When this window is placed in front of the application, the user is forced to pay attention to whatever you display there, whether it's a status message or a request for input, such as a filename to save to. Because displaying dialogs is such a common and necessary task, SWT and JFace provide support to make handling dialogs easy.

We need to discuss two independent `Dialog` classes: `org.eclipse.swt.widgets.Dialog` and `org.eclipse.jface.dialogs.Dialog`. As their package names suggest, the first class is part of SWT, whereas the second is from JFace. It would be possible to build an application using only the SWT dialogs, but doing so wouldn't be fun. Still, SWT provides several prebuilt dialogs that perform common tasks. We'll cover the use of the SWT dialogs first, followed by a comparison with JFace dialogs. We'll round out the chapter by creating a username/password prompt dialog to demonstrate how to write a custom dialog.

10.1 SWT dialogs

The abstract class `Dialog` provides the basis for all dialogs in SWT. By itself, this class is of little interest, because it doesn't provide much in the way of behavior. It's possible to derive your own SWT `Dialog` subclasses if you wish. However, deriving from the `Dialog` classes provided by JFace will make your job easier. Consequently, we'll discuss creating custom dialogs in the JFace section of this chapter.

SWT does provide prebuilt dialogs for common tasks that are convenient and easy to use. We'll discuss how and when to use each of these dialogs next.

10.1.1 ColorDialog

Suppose you're writing a text editor, and you want to let users specify the color of the text on the screen. You may be able to get away with letting them specify RGB values by hand if your target audience consists of hard-core programmers, but in general users want to see the available options and choose one by pointing and clicking. SWT does this for you with the class `ColorDialog`.

The grayscale nature of this book doesn't do the image justice, but figure 10.1 shows how the user can easily choose a color from a `Color-Dialog`.

Displaying this dialog is simple. Just instantiate it, and call `open()`:

```
ColorDialog dialog = new
   ColorDialog(shell);
RGB color = dialog.open();
```

If you wish to preselect a color, call `setRGB()` before opening the dialog.

The call to `open()` *blocks*, which means it won't return until the user clicks OK or Cancel. The selected color, if any, is returned from `open()` as an instance of `RGB`. `null` is returned if the user clicks Cancel. The selected color can also be retrieved later by using `getRGB()`.

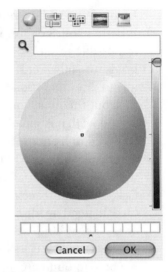

Figure 10.1
`ColorDialog` **allows the user to select from available colors.**

10.1.2 *DirectoryDialog*

`DirectoryDialog` chooses a target directory—for example, the location to which to save a group of files. The following snippet displays the directory chooser dialog along with a message explaining what the user is supposed to do:

```
DirectoryDialog dialog = new DirectoryDialog(shell);
dialog.setMessage("Choose a save directory");
String saveTarget = dialog.open();
if(saveTarget != null)
{
  java.io.File directory = new java.io.File(saveTarget);
  ...
}
```

The dialog looks something like figure 10.2.

Once the user has chosen a directory, the call to `open()` returns a `String` that holds the absolute path to the chosen directory. This `String` can be used to create a `java.io.File` and then manipulated accordingly. Should the user cancel, `open()` returns `null`.

Figure 10.2
`DirectoryDialog` **waiting for the user to choose a directory**

10.1.3 *FileDialog*

In many ways, `FileDialog` is similar to `DirectoryDialog`. The dialogs appear nearly identical, except that whereas `DirectoryDialog` displays only a list of directories, `FileDialog` adds the files present in each current directory to the display, as shown in figure 10.3.

The next snippet shows how to let the user select multiple files, as long as the filenames end in ".txt":

```
FileDialog dialog = new FileDialog(shell, SWT.MULTI);
dialog.setFilterExtensions(new String[] {"*.txt"});
dialog.open();
```

As usual, `open()` blocks and returns either the full path to the file as a `String`, or `null`. Unlike the dialogs you've seen before, `FileDialog` supports three different styles:

- *SWT.SAVE*—Treats the dialog as a save dialog, allowing the user to either select an existing file or type in the name of a new file to create.

- *SWT.OPEN*—Lets the user select a single existing file to be opened.

- *SWT.MULTI*—Lets the user select multiple files at once to be opened. Even if the user selects multiple files in a MULTI-style dialog, `open()` will return only

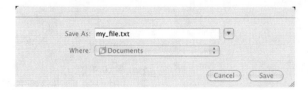

Figure 10.3
`FileDialog` **in Save mode allows the user to enter a filename to save to.**

one. `getFileNames()` must be used to retrieve the array of all filenames selected after `open()` returns.

Also of note in `FileDialog` are the methods `setFilterPath()`, `setFilterNames()`, and `setFilterExtensions()`. When they're called before the dialog opens, these methods can be used to restrict the list of files that are visible to the user. `setFilterPath()` takes a single `String` that's used as the path to the directory that should be displayed by default. The other two methods take arrays of `Strings`, which are used to assemble valid filenames and extensions. Our previous example filters out everything that doesn't end in "*.txt". Note that the filter is displayed to the user and is editable, so there is no guarantee that they won't select a file of a type other than what you expect.

10.1.4 *FontDialog*

Just as users of your text editor need to select a color for their text, they also need to select a font to display it in. For this purpose, we have `FontDialog`. Its use is nearly identical to that of the `ColorDialog` we discussed earlier:

```
FontDialog dialog = new FontDialog(shell);
FontData fontData = dialog.open();
```

`FontDialog` automatically picks up the fonts available to SWT on the user's system. This can result in a complex display, as figure 10.4 shows.

The returned `FontData` can be used to instantiate the correct font, as discussed in chapter 7.

10.1.5 *MessageBox*

If your application encounters an error it can't recover from, the typical response is to display a text message to the user and then exit. For this or any other purpose where you need to display a dialog with a message, SWT provides `MessageBox`. A

Figure 10.4
**FontDialog displays all fonts
installed on the user's system.**

Table 10.1 Valid button style combinations

Dialog button style combinations
SWT.OK
SWT.OK | SWT.CANCEL
SWT.YES | SWT.NO
SWT.YES | SWT.NO | SWT.CANCEL
SWT.RETRY | SWT.CANCEL
SWT.ABORT | SWT.RETRY | SWT.IGNORE

simple dialog that gives the user the option of continuing or not can be displayed with the following lines:

```
MessageBox dialog = new MessageBox(shell,
                    SWT.OK | SWT.CANCEL);
dialog.setMessage("Do you wish to continue?");
int returnVal = dialog.open();
```

There are two important steps when you're using MessageBox. The easy part is to set the text message to display using setMessage(). More complicated is setting the style. Using an icon style adds an appropriate icon next to your message. Styles can also be used to control what buttons the MessageBox displays. However, some styles are valid only in combination with certain other styles; the allowed combinations are presented in table 10.1. Any of these can also be freely combined with one of the icon styles, which are listed in table 10.2. If no button or an invalid button style is specified, SWT.OK is used, resulting in a single OK button. open() returns an integer matching the SWT constant of the button that was clicked.

Table 10.2 Dialog icons

Dialog icon	Indicates that...
SWT.ERROR_ICON	An error has occurred.
SWT.ICON_INFORMATION	The dialog is presenting noninteractive information to the user.
SWT.ICON_QUESTION	The dialog requires an answer (usually OK or Cancel) from the user.
SWT.ICON_WARNING	The user is about to perform a potentially harmful action.
SWT.ICON_WORKING	The program is in the middle of a task.

10.2 *JFace dialogs*

The standard JFace dialog classes are straightforward to use, because they work similarly to dialogs in other UI toolkits such as Swing. The main difference you need to be aware of is that whereas Swing provides `JOptionPane` with a variety of static methods to display message dialogs, error dialogs, and so on, JFace has a separate subclass for each of these dialog types that may be instantiated and displayed as is or subclassed to further customize appearance or behavior.

All JFace dialogs extend from the abstract class `org.eclipse.jface.dialogs.Dialog`, which itself extends `org.eclipse.jface.window.Window`. Figure 10.5 shows the relationship between the standard dialog classes. As you can see, the relationships are for the most part simple; the Error and Input dialogs rely upon interfaces outside the basic hierarchy.

A few design considerations are common to any subclass of `Dialog`. You change dialog behavior by overriding the `buttonPressed()` method. The default implementation closes the dialog immediately as soon as any button is clicked—even nonstandard buttons that you may have added yourself. If you wish to change this behavior or do processing of any kind before the dialog is closed, you must override

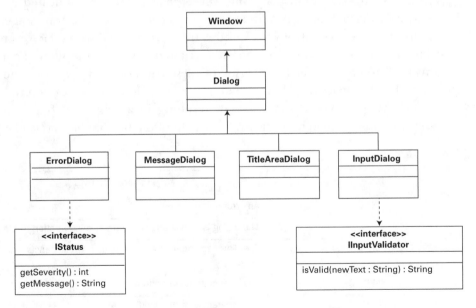

Figure 10.5   JFace dialog inheritance hierarchy

the method. Keep in mind that if you do override `buttonPressed()`, the dialog won't close unless you call `super.buttonPressed()` at the end of your implementation.

You can also get hooks into specific buttons by overriding `okPressed()` or `cancelPressed()` for any dialog that supports those buttons. Again, by default, these methods just close the dialog—if you're going to add behavior, be sure to call the parent method when you're done.

Finally, the `createButtonsForButtonBar()` method controls the buttons that are created for any given dialog. If you want to change the buttons for any dialog, this is the place to do it. The one exception is `MessageDialog`—because you'll much more frequently want to change the buttons in a message dialog, the constructor provides a convenient way to specify the buttons that should be displayed without having to create a subclass.

It's recommended that a dialog be *modal*, meaning that once it's opened, no other window can receive focus until the dialog is closed. Writing code that uses a modal dialog is generally simpler, because you can be sure that as long as the dialog is displayed, your user isn't interacting with the rest of your application. All the basic dialogs discussed in this section follow this recommendation. This impacts your code in two ways. First, it doesn't make sense to open a dialog without a parent window, so all our code examples include a parent `ApplicationWindow` for this purpose. Second, you must remember that in your code, the call to `open()` blocks, meaning that the method won't return until the dialog is dismissed in one way or another. `open()` returns an `int`, which is the zero-based index of the button that was clicked, or –1 if the dialog's window was closed by some means other than clicking a button (such as pressing the Esc key).

10.2.1 *Message dialogs*

A message dialog is used to display a message to the user. Little interaction is possible with a message dialog—the user is limited to dismissing the dialog by clicking one of the displayed buttons.

The following snippet shows how to display a message dialog—as you can see, displaying the dialog itself requires only two lines of code. This is roughly equivalent to calling `JOptionPane.showMessageDialog()` in Swing:

```
MessageDialog dialog =
  new MessageDialog(
    testWindow.getShell(),
    "Greeting Dialog", //the dialog title
    null,
    "Hello!  How are you today?",  //text to be displayed
    MessageDialog.QUESTION,        //dialog type
```

```
        new String[] { "Good",
                        "Been better",
                        "Excited about SWT!" },        //button labels
            0);
    dialog.open();
```

Message dialogs come in several different types, defined as static constants in the `MessageDialog` class. This type determines the image that's displayed; in our example, we get an image of a question mark, because we've declared this to be a dialog of type `QUESTION`. Other types include `ERROR`, `INFORMATION`, `WARNING`, and `NONE`. Each uses the standard image for that type on your operating system (except type `NONE`, which causes no image to be displayed).

You can also create buttons automatically by passing an array of `Strings` that are the button labels. For each label found, `MessageDialog` creates a corresponding button. By default, all buttons behave the same and close the dialog. In practice, it's unusual to find a message dialog with any button other than OK and perhaps Cancel.

The constructor also optionally accepts an image to be displayed.

10.2.2 *Error dialogs*

Error dialogs are in many ways similar to `MessageDialogs`, in that they display an error message to the user. You can mimic an `ErrorDialog` by creating a `MessageDialog` with type `ERROR`. However, the `ErrorDialog` allows you to display more in-depth error details by using the `IStatus` interface. `IStatus` holds a detailed message and information about the severity of each error that has occurred. The result can be seen in figure 10.6.

The error dialog shown in figure 10.6 is created with the following code. We create an instance of `ErrorDialog` and pass it an `IStatus` object that holds error information. The root `IStatus` holds several other instances of `IStatus` that provide increasingly granular details about the errors:

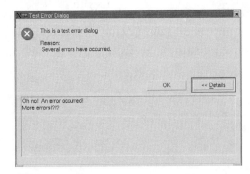

**Figure 10.6
An error dialog with multiple
instances of `IStatus`**

```
...
    ErrorDialog errorDialog = new ErrorDialog(testWindow.getShell(),
                            "Test Error Dialog",
                            "This is a test error dialog",
                            testWindow.createStatus(),
                IStatus.ERROR | IStatus.INFO );
...
    public IStatus createStatus()
    {
        final String dummyPlugin = "some plugin";

        IStatus[] statuses = new IStatus[2];

        statuses[0] = new Status(IStatus.ERROR,
                        dummyPlugin,
                        IStatus.OK,
                        "Oh no!  An error occurred!",
                        new Exception

        statuses[1] = new Status(IStatus.INFO,
                        dummyPlugin,
                        IStatus.OK,
                        "More errors!?!?",
                        new Exception() );

        MultiStatus multiStatus = new MultiStatus(dummyPlugin,
                        IStatus.OK
                        statuses,
                        "Several errors have occurred.",
                        new Exception() );
        return multiStatus;
    }
```

1 Severity mask

2 Status

3 Plug-in

4 Exception

5 MultiStatus

6 Severity

1 IStatus defines several severity-related constants. By bitwise ORing them together, we create a bitmask describing the severities we're interested in displaying. The severity set in each individual IStatus object is compared with this mask, and details of that object only are displayed in the case of a match. By changing INFO to WARNING in this example, the details of our second Status object are suppressed.

2 Here we create an instance of Status, which implements the IStatus interface. The idea is to encapsulate all the information about an error in this class and let the ErrorDialog or any other consumer decide what is appropriate to display based on the context.

3 IStatus requires a plug-in identifier, which is supposed to be a unique string. This identifier is never used for ErrorDialogs, so we give the object a dummy value.

4 The Status stores the exception it's given. The exception is included in the output of Status's toString() method and can also be retrieved using getException().

5 MultiStatus also implements the IStatus interface and groups together multiple instances of IStatus.

6 The severity set here is used to select an appropriate image to display in the dialog. The choices work the same as in a MessageDialog.

This code will display an error dialog with the message "Several errors have occurred", as you saw in figure 10.6. Clicking the Details button opens a panel at the bottom of the dialog with the messages from the two Status objects we've defined.

The Details button appears because the root IStatus object given to the dialog is a MultiStatus and returns true for the isMultiStatus() method. Upon seeing that it's dealing with a MultiStatus, the ErrorDialog calls getChildren() to retrieve the detailed status messages. If the root IStatus returns false for isMulti-Status(), a Details button won't appear. Children of a MultiStatus may be Multi-Statuses themselves, allowing you to build trees of arbitrary complexity, should the need arise. A MultiStatus's severity is equal to the greatest severity of its children. The Javadocs define a MultiStatus with no children as defaulting to a severity of OK.

As you can see, ErrorDialog provides a significantly more advanced error-reporting mechanism than using a MessageDialog of type ERROR. The primary drawback to using ErrorDialog, however, is that it's tied more closely to the Eclipse platform than we'd like, instead of being a purely JFace-based widget. Not only do the various IStatus-related classes come from org.eclipse.core.runtime, but they also ask for plug-in identifiers as parameters—a concept that's present in Eclipse but not in JFace. How serious a drawback this may be is open for debate; it's possible to use the classes in this case by passing dummy values, because the values aren't used. However, you can't pass null, because Status checks the plug-in value it's given and throws an internal assertion failure exception in case of null. Thus, using the classes is at minimum confusing, and in general creates an awkward design for any application not based on Eclipse. If you don't need to provide expanded details for your error messages, it's best to avoid ErrorDialog and stick to creating MessageDialogs with type ERROR. However, if you need the Details functionality, it may be worth making a small compromise in your application design to take advantage of these classes that have already been written and debugged.

10.2.3 *Input dialogs*

As the name suggests, an InputDialog is used to allow the user to enter text. These dialogs are primarily intended for relatively short amounts of text (one line at most). They fill the same role as Swing's JOptionPane.showInputDialog().

The key functionality provided by an `InputDialog` is the optional use of an `IInputValidator`, which is responsible for validating an input string. The following example prompts the user for a string that's from 5 to12 characters long:

```
IInputValidator validator = new IInputValidator() {
    public String isValid(String text) {  //return an error message,
            if(text.length() < 5)           //or null for no error
            return "You must enter at least 5 characters";
        else if(text.length() > 12)
            return "You may not enter more than 12 characters";
        else
            return null;
    }
};


        InputDialog inputDialog = new InputDialog( testWindow.getShell(),
                        "Please input a String", //dialog title
                        "Enter a String:",    //dialog prompt
                        "default text",       //default text
                        validator );          //validator to use
    inputDialog.open();
```

The `isValid()` method implements the validation check for the text entered by the user. The semantics of the method seem slightly odd at first glance, but they let you be flexible in communicating status back to the user. The method is passed the text to validate and returns null if the text is valid. If it's invalid, the method should return a `String` that's displayed to the user as an error message. It's permissible to return different error messages in different conditions, to help make it clear to the user exactly what you expect them to enter.

Note that this method is called frequently—each time the text is modified (every keystroke), it's checked for validity. This means your implementation should perform as little work here as possible in order to return quickly. Spending much time in this method will make your UI unbearably sluggish.

You may provide a default string to be entered into the dialog. You can pass null, in which case the text field is left empty. The validator passed may also be null, in which case any input is accepted.

The `InputDialog` is passed a title, a prompt, and optionally some default text and an instance of `IInputValidator`. The dialog is shown with OK and Cancel buttons. The OK button is enabled or disabled at any given time depending on the return value of `isValid()` from the supplied `IInputValidator`; if no validator is supplied, the button is always enabled. Once the dialog has been closed, you can retrieve the entered value using `getValue()`.

10.2.4 *Progress monitor dialogs*

Applications often perform tasks that take a long time to complete (in computer terms, at least). While your application is busy, it's important to let users know that you're working on fulfilling their request so they don't become frustrated. JFace makes doing so relatively easy by providing a framework for displaying the task status to the user. We'll start by discussing the ProgressMonitorDialog and how it fits into this framework.

You must understand several interfaces to effectively use a ProgressMonitor-Dialog. Figure 10.7 shows the relationship between these interfaces.

The most important things to note here are the IRunnableContext and IRunnableWithProgress interfaces. IRunnableContext provides a context for any long-running task, and ProgressMonitorDialog implements this interface. IRunnable-WithContext uses an instance of IRunnableWithProgress, which is meant to be implemented by a long-running task. IRunnableWithProgress is therefore the interface that your class must implement. Finally, IRunnableWithProgress is provided with an instance of IProgressMonitor, which it uses to report its progress as it executes.

When interacting with an IProgressMonitor, calls must take place in a certain sequence. The process starts by calling run() on an IRunnableContext, giving it an instance of IRunnableWithProgress. After doing whatever initialization might be necessary, IRunnableContext calls run() on IRunnableWithProgress, passing an IProgressMonitor. IRunnableWithProgress starts by calling beginWork() with the total amount of work it expects to do. It periodically calls worked() and subTask()

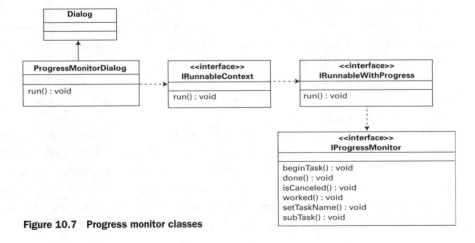

Figure 10.7   Progress monitor classes

to notify the progress monitor of its progress. It should also call isCanceled() to check whether it has been canceled. Finally, done() is called when the task is finished. After the call to done(), no more calls can be made on the IProgressMonitor.

IProgressMonitor assumes that your task can be broken into abstract *units of work*. It then provides a callback method to let you notify it that *x* units of work have been completed. Typically, this notification is called as the last step in a loop. However, if your task is a sequential series of slow operations, such as database or network accesses, you can assign a value to each operation as a percentage of the total work to be done. Doing so effectively decouples the implementation of the long-running task from the code that notifies the user how much work remains to be done. In our case, ProgressMonitorDialog implements IRunnableContext and provides the instance of IProgressMonitor; but because we deal only with the interfaces, the same code can be used with any implementation of IRunnableContext. In SWT/JFace, the only other implementation of IRunnableContext is ApplicationWindow, but it's conceivable that you could implement your own status notification for your specific application—for example, for truly long-running tasks, it may be appropriate to send an email as each stage is completed. In this case, you can use these same interfaces.

Our next code snippet provides an example of using a ProgressMonitorDialog. Note that the status text to display to the user is controlled by the IRunnableContext when it calls beginTask() and subTask(), whereas updating the progress bar on screen is handled by the IProgressMonitor as it receives calls through its worked() method:

```
ProgressMonitorDialog progressMonitor =
    new ProgressMonitorDialog(shell);
try
{
  IRunnableWithProgress runnable = new IRunnableWithProgress() {
    public void run( IProgressMonitor progressMonitor )
                throws InterruptedException
              {
              progressMonitor.beginTask("Doing hard work...",
                                    100);      ❶ Total work
              while(!taskCompleted())
              {
                progressMonitor.worked(10);    ❷ Amount worked
                progressMonitor.subTask("sub task: " +
                                        getCurrentTask());
                ... //Perform some long task
                if( progressMonitor.isCanceled() )   ❸ Canceled check
                {
                  throw new InterruptedException();
```

```
                      }
                   }
                   progressMonitor.done();        ④  Done
                }
           };
           progressMonitor.run(true,        ⑤  Fork
                               true,         ⑥  Cancellable
                               runnable );
      }
      catch (Exception e)
      {
         e.printStackTrace();
      }
```

❶ We must notify the ProgressMonitor that we're starting work on our task. Additionally, we must either tell it how many units of work we expect to perform or use the constant IProgressMonitor.UNKNOWN if we don't know. This value is a hint to the UI—if we end up performing more work than we specified, the progress bar will clear itself and start over until we tell it we're done.

❷ Here we notify the ProgressMonitor that we've performed some amount of work. This causes it to update the progress bar displayed to the user, if the increase is enough to be visible. In our case, each unit of work is 10% of the total, so every call to this method causes the bar to increase in length by a significant amount.

❸ If we allow the user the option of canceling our task, we must periodically check whether they have requested cancellation. IRunnableContext.run() specifies that when a task has canceled itself, it should throw an InterruptedException after doing whatever cleanup is necessary. This exception eventually propagates to the original caller of IRunnableContext.run().

❹ When we're finished, we must notify the IProgressMonitor.

❺ When starting a long-running task using an IRunnableContext, we're allowed to specify whether we should run the task in a separate thread. If you do run in a separate thread, you're responsible for ensuring that you access all resources in a thread-safe manner—see Chapter 4 for a discussion of threading and SWT.

❻ We can also specify whether this task may be canceled by the user. In the case of a ProgressMonitorDialog, this value decides whether a Cancel button is displayed. Generally, if your task takes long enough to require the use of a ProgressMonitor in the first place, you should allow the user to cancel it if at all possible. Note that clicking the Cancel button is only a recommendation to the running task; the task won't be forcibly stopped. It's up to the task to check for cancellation requests and handle them appropriately—it's free to ignore them, and by default it will do so if you forget to add the check to your code.

Using ProgressIndicator for more control

The `ProgressMonitorDialog` provides an easy way to keep the user informed of a task's progress. Sometimes, however, you'll want more control over the way in which a progress bar is presented. When necessary, SWT lets you instantiate and directly use widgets that control the progress bar, as we'll discuss next.

The `ProgressIndicator` widget allows you to display a progress bar without worrying about how to fill it. Like the `ProgressMonitorDialog`, it supports abstract units of work—you need only initialize the `ProgressIndicator` with the total amount of work you expect to do and notify it as work is completed:

```
ProgressIndicator indicator = new ProgressIndicator(parent);
...
indicator.beginTask(10);  //total work to be done. Control is
...                       //not displayed until this method is called
//use asyncExec() to update in the UI thread
Display.getCurrent()display.asyncExec(new Runnable() {
  public void run() {
    indicator.worked(1);       //inform the ProgressIndicator that
                             //some amount of work has completed

  }
});
```

As it receives notifications, the `ProgressIndicator` assumes responsibility for updating the appearance of the bar on the screen by calculating the percentage of the total work that has been completed.

The `ProgressIndicator` also provides an *animated* mode, where the total amount of work isn't known. In this mode, the bar continually fills and empties until `done()` is called. To use animated mode, you call `beginAnimatedTask()` instead of `beginTask()`; and there is no need to call the `worked()` method. Assuming your work is being correctly done in a non-UI thread, this implies that you don't need to worry about the `asyncExec()` call, either.

Occasionally, you may need more control than a `ProgressIndicator` allows. For times when you need to manipulate widgets at a low level, SWT provides the `ProgressBar`.

If you decide that you need to use a `ProgressBar` directly, you're taking responsibility for changing the display of the bar yourself. The following code snippet shows an example:

```
//styles are SMOOTH, HORIZONTAL, or VERTICAL
ProgressBar bar = new ProgressBar(parent, SWT.SMOOTH);
```

```
bar.setBounds(10, 10, 200, 32);
bar.setMaximum(100);
...
for(int i = 0; i < 10; i++) {
  //use asyncExec() to do updates in the UI thread
  Display.getCurrent()display.asyncExec(new Runnable() {
    public void run() {
      //update how much of the bar should be filled in
      bar.setSelection((int)(bar.getMaximum() * (i+1) / 10));
    }
  });
}
```

Note that in addition to needing to calculate the bar update amounts yourself, calling `setSelection()` causes the widget to be updated every time; this behavior is unlike that of `ProgressIndicator` or `ProgressMonitorDialog`, which will update the display only if it has changed by an amount that will be visible to the end user.

As you can see, there is more work involved with using `ProgressBars` than the other widgets we've discussed, and in general we recommend avoiding them unless you have no choice. However, you may occasionally need to use them—for example, if you need to unfill the bar, there is no way to do it with the higher-level controls.

10.2.5 *Custom dialogs*

Although the dialogs that we've discussed so far cover many common tasks, you'll frequently find that your application's requirements call for a unique dialog that the designers of JFace couldn't have anticipated. If you need to create a new type of dialog for your application, we recommend that you extend from the JFace `Dialog` class instead of using SWT's `Dialog`. The JFace framework provides more structure to make your job easier; using SWT, you would be taking on the job of writing most of this common functionality yourself.

Because JFace provides the framework necessary to manage opening and closing dialogs, your job primarily consists of defining the controls present on the page. `Dialog` provides several different hooks to use in defining the layout of your dialog, depending on the level of control you need. We'll discuss what methods are called in what order before we talk about when to override specific methods.

Because `Dialog` extends `Window`, everything starts with the `createContents()` method discussed in chapter 2. After it does some initialization, `createDialogArea()` is called. This method builds the top section of the dialog. After `createDialogArea()` returns, `createButtonBar()` is called and creates a new `Composite` and `Layout` for the bars at the bottom of the dialog. Finally, `createButtonBar()` calls `createButtonsForButtonBar()` to instantiate the buttons that appear on the dialog. By default, OK and Cancel buttons are created.

You're free to take control of this process at any point by overriding the appropriate methods. In general, however, you can limit yourself to implementing `createDialogArea()` or `createButtonsForButtonBar()`.

`createDialogArea()` takes a `Composite` that's used as the parent for any controls you create and must return a `Control` whose layout data is an instance of `GridData`. The easiest way to fulfill this contract is to call the default implementation before you do your own work:

```
Composite composite = (Composite)super.createDialogArea(parent);
...//add custom controls
return composite;
```

Other than these restrictions, you're free to add whatever controls are appropriate for your dialog.

Like `createDialogArea()`, `createButtonBar()` must return a `Control` with a `GridData` for its layout data. Rather than override `createButtonBar()`, however, it's simpler to implement `createButtonsForButtonBar()`, where you can focus on creating the buttons you need without worrying about layout issues. Buttons are created using the `createButton()` method. For example, the default implementation of `createButtonsForButtonBar()` uses the following code to create OK and Cancel buttons:

```
createButton( parent,
              IDialogConstants.OK_ID,
              IDialogConstants.OK_LABEL,
              true );        //make this button the default
createButton( parent,
              IDialogConstants.CANCEL_ID,
              IDialogConstants.CANCEL_LABEL,
              false );
```

`createButton()` takes the button's parent, an integer ID, the `String` to use as the label, and a flag indicating whether this button should be made the default. In addition to adding the button to its internal list and updating the layout data appropriately, by default `createButton()` also adds a `SelectionListener` to the button, which causes the dialog's `buttonPressed()` method to be called with the ID of the button that was clicked. You're free to override `createButton()` if you have requirements unique to your dialog, such as adding a specific style to all buttons created.

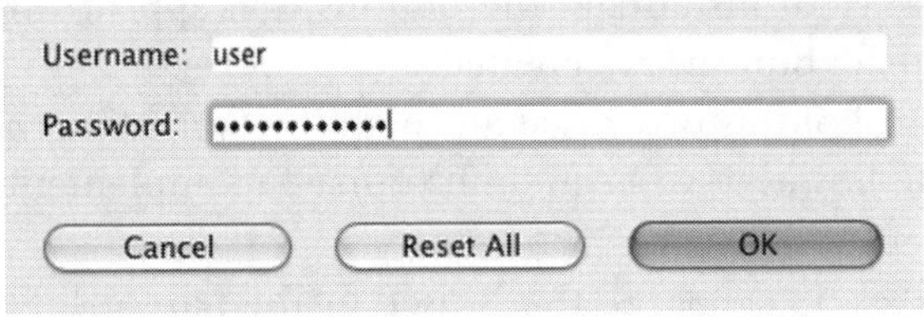

Figure 10.8
The custom password dialog

10.3 *Updating WidgetWindow*

You've already seen examples of invoking each of the dialogs provided by SWT and JFace, so our in-depth example for this chapter demonstrates creating a custom dialog. Listing 10.1 creates a subclass of Dialog that displays two text-entry fields, one for a username and one for a password. We've also added a third button that clears any text that has been entered. Figure 10.8 shows what this dialog will look like.

To accomplish this, we override the createDialogArea(), createButtonsFor-ButtonBar(), and buttonPressed() methods of Dialog. Notice that createDialog-Area() is the only one of these methods that is at all complex.

Listing 10.1   UsernamePasswordDialog.java

```java
package com.swtjface.Ch10;

import org.eclipse.jface.dialogs.Dialog;
import org.eclipse.jface.dialogs.IDialogConstants;
import org.eclipse.swt.SWT;
import org.eclipse.swt.layout.GridData;
import org.eclipse.swt.layout.GridLayout;
import org.eclipse.swt.widgets.*;

public class UsernamePasswordDialog extends Dialog
{
  private static final int RESET_ID =
              IDialogConstants.NO_TO_ALL_ID + 1;

  private Text usernameField;
  private Text passwordField;

  public UsernamePasswordDialog(Shell parentShell)
  {
    super(parentShell);                              super.createDialogArea() ❶
  }                                                             method

  protected Control createDialogArea(Composite parent)
  {
    Composite comp = (Composite)super.createDialogArea(parent);  ◄

    GridLayout layout = (GridLayout)comp.getLayout();
```

```
        layout.numColumns = 2;

        Label usernameLabel = new Label(comp, SWT.RIGHT);
        usernameLabel.setText("Username: ");

        usernameField = new Text(comp, SWT.SINGLE);
        GridData data = new GridData(GridData.FILL_HORIZONTAL);
        usernameField.setLayoutData(data);

        Label passwordLabel = new Label(comp, SWT.RIGHT);
        passwordLabel.setText("Password: ");

        passwordField = new Text(comp, SWT.SINGLE | SWT.PASSWORD);
        data = new GridData(GridData.FILL_HORIZONTAL);
        passwordField.setLayoutData(data);

        return comp;                          createButtonsForButtonBar()  ❷
    }                                         method

    protected void createButtonsForButtonBar(Composite parent)   ◁───────┘
    {
        super.createButtonsForButtonBar(parent);
        createButton(parent, RESET_ID, "Reset All", false);
    }

    protected void buttonPressed(int buttonId)    ❸  buttonPressed() method
    {
        if(buttonId == RESET_ID)
        {
            usernameField.setText("");
            passwordField.setText("");
        }
        else
        {
            super.buttonPressed(buttonId);
        }
    }
}
```

❶ We override `createDialogArea()` to instantiate the controls necessary for this dialog. First we call the method on the superclass to handle all the layout information. The superclass guarantees that it will return a Composite with a GridLayout, so it's safe to cast the object that is returned. After setting the layout to have two columns, we create a pair of labels and text fields to be displayed.

❷ Adding our Reset All button requires only a single line. We make sure to call super. `createButtonsForButtonBar()` so we get the standard OK and Cancel buttons.

❸ Finally, we want to react to the user's button clicks. When `createButton()` was called, it associated an appropriate listener with each button to ensure that `buttonPressed()` is called. We check the ID of the button to see if it matches the

ID we used to create the Reset All button earlier. If so, we reset the text on our text fields. Otherwise we can delegate to the superclass and let it handle the button click as normal.

Listing 10.2 presents the Composite, which isn't terribly interesting. Its only purpose is to launch our dialog. We can't display a dialog directly in the tab, so the Composite creates a button instead. When the button is clicked, the listener instantiates and displays the UsernamePasswordDialog we showed you earlier.

Listing 10.2   Ch10CustomDialogComposite.java

```java
package com.swtjface.Ch10;

import org.eclipse.swt.SWT;
import org.eclipse.swt.events.SelectionEvent;
import org.eclipse.swt.events.SelectionListener;
import org.eclipse.swt.layout.FillLayout;
import org.eclipse.swt.widgets.Button;
import org.eclipse.swt.widgets.Composite;

public class Ch10CustomDialogComposite extends Composite
{
  public Ch10CustomDialogComposite(Composite parent)
  {
    super(parent, SWT.NONE);
    buildControls();
  }

  protected void buildControls()
  {
    FillLayout layout = new FillLayout();
    setLayout(layout);

    Button dialogBtn = new Button(this, SWT.PUSH);
    dialogBtn.setText("Password Dialog...");
    dialogBtn.addSelectionListener(new SelectionListener() {

      public void widgetSelected(SelectionEvent e)
      {
        UsernamePasswordDialog dialog =
            new UsernamePasswordDialog(getShell());
        dialog.open();
      }

      public void widgetDefaultSelected(SelectionEvent e){}
    });
  }

}
```

After creating a button, we attach a `SelectionListener` to it. When the listener receives a widget-selected event, it creates a new `UsernamePasswordDialog` and opens it, just like any prebuilt dialog that comes with JFace.

You can run this example by adding the following lines to `WidgetWindow`:

```
TabItem chap10 = new TabItem(tf, SWT.NONE);
chap10.setText("Chapter 10");
chap10.setControl(new Ch10CustomDialogComposite(tf));
```

10.4 *Summary*

Using the dialog classes provided by JFace is generally straightforward, although you'll be well served by carefully considering the design of your application before you write any code.

`MessageDialog` and `InputDialog` provide powerful alternatives to the capabilities provided by the dialog support in Swing. Unlike `JOptionPane`'s static methods, the dialog classes in JFace may be subclassed and customized to meet your application's unique requirements, yet they provide easy-to-use options for handling the simple cases.

`ErrorDialog` provides more advanced error-reporting capabilities at the cost of introducing extra library dependencies into your application as well as parameters that you'll never use. You should give careful thought to these issues before you use `ErrorDialog`; but we think the class is valuable enough that it's sometimes worth using anyway, especially if you can effectively isolate knowledge of the `org.eclipse.core.runtime`-related classes and parameters from the rest of your application.

The `IProgressMonitor` framework, on the other hand, provides a clean, extensible set of classes ready to be used by your code. It's possible to manipulate the lower-level controls directly, but we recommend sticking to the framework classes and interfaces except in unusual circumstances. By writing to the `IRunnableWithProgress` and `IProgressMonitor` interfaces, you'll make it much easier to reuse your code in new situations as they arise.

Finally, when you're creating a custom dialog, you'll be better served by starting from the dialog class provided by JFace, as opposed to deriving from the basic SWT class. JFace's framework provides the structure needed to make creating a new dialog easy. All you need to do is override a couple of methods to define the specific components used by your dialog.

Wizards

11

Today, most people are familiar with the concept of an application providing a wizard for certain tasks. By separating a complex task into a series of steps, performed one at a time, it's possible to condense an otherwise intimidating set of options into a relatively pleasant end-user experience. A good example can be found in Eclipse when creating a new project. Eclipse supports development in a wide variety of languages, and each of those languages has many different options that can be configured for a new project. Rather than dump you straight into a dialog box filled with combo boxes, text-entry fields, and checkboxes, however, Eclipse guides you through the process of creating a new project one step at a time. You can choose the language for your new project, then a location, and then configure language-specific settings. Eclipse can infer sensible defaults for most of these options; any time after you've provided the bare minimum of information, you can click the Finish button to tell the program to go ahead with creating the project. If you choose to configure details yourself, you can freely move back and forth between steps, changing choices you made earlier. The whole experience is made enjoyable because you can see what effects your choices have before they're made permanent.

JFace provides a framework to help you create and use wizards in your own application. The framework is composed of a three-level hierarchy. Each level can contain multiple instances of the level below it—a container contains wizards, whereas wizards contain pages. Each level defines both an interface and a default implementation of that interface. It's generally easiest to subclass the default implementations, but for maximum flexibility the framework is designed to only reference objects by the interfaces. Any complete implementation of a wizard-related interface may be freely mixed with the existing classes with no problems.

Figure 11.1 provides an overview of the classes used to create a typical wizard. You should recognize some of these classes from our discussion of dialogs in the previous chapter.

Figure 11.1 shows how the classes and interfaces of the wizard framework fit together. The most important thing to take away is that the concrete classes at each level, WizardDialog and Wizard, depend only on the interface of the next level down, not the default implementation. This same property holds when traversing the other direction—although IWizardPage makes use of IWizard, it doesn't matter whether IWizard is implemented by Wizard or by some other class. We'll start at the bottom of the diagram and work our way upward through the hierarchy, discussing each of these classes in turn. We'll then show you how they work together.

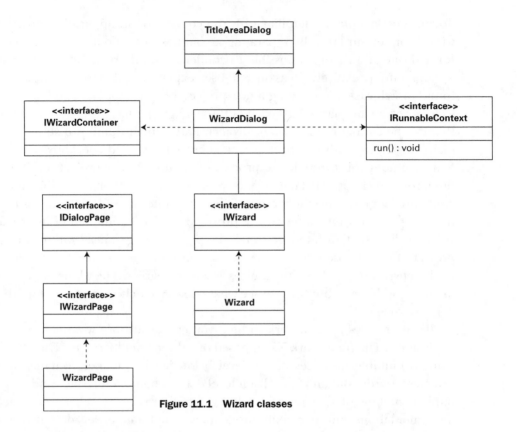

Figure 11.1   Wizard classes

11.1 *Multipage dialogs*

All the dialogs we discussed in the previous chapter consisted of a single page. All the available options were displayed at the same time, and the dialog could only open and close. However, a wizard needs to display more than one page in a single dialog. JFace provides a generic interface for use in multipage dialogs that serves as the parent of the wizard-specific interfaces. We'll briefly cover this generic interface before turning our attention to wizards.

11.1.1 *IDialogPage*

IDialogPage is the base interface for the pages in any multipage dialog. The interface provides methods to configure all the attributes for a given page, such as its title, a description, or an Image to display. The most important method is createControl(), which is called when it's time for the page to create its contents. JFace provides a default implementation of IDialogPage with the abstract

DialogPage class, which provides default implementations of all methods declared in the interface except createControl(). On its own, IDialogPage is neither very interesting nor useful, so we'll move on to discuss its most commonly used subinterface: IWizardPage.

11.1.2 *IWizardPage*

The basic element of the wizard is a page. A page should represent one step for the user in whatever process you're guiding them through. Key to creating a usable wizard is defining these steps well—too much information on the page is confusing, but too many separate steps are annoying for the user.

JFace uses the IWizardPage interface to represent a single page in a wizard. A variety of methods are defined in this interface; the most important ones are summarized in table 11.1.

Table 11.1 Important methods defined by IWizardPage

Method	Description
getName()	Each page must have a unique name. This method is often used to retrieve a particular page from the wizard.
getNextPage(), getPreviousPage()	These methods are called when the user clicks the Next or Previous button to move to another page. The proper page to move to (which may vary depending on selections the user has made) must be returned.
isPageComplete()	Indicates whether the user has filled out everything that is necessary on this page.
canFlipToNextpage()	Indicates whether the Next button should be available for use. This method typically returns true if the page is complete and at least one page is left in the wizard.

Several other straightforward getter and setter methods are also defined in IWizardPage. Implementing all of them could quickly become tedious. Luckily, JFace comes to your rescue with a default implementation—the WizardPage class.

11.1.3 *WizardPage*

WizardPage implements the IWizardPage interface and provides much of the basic logic for a page. You need only implement createControl() from IDialogPage to build the controls appropriate to your page, although a variety of other methods may be overridden if you wish to modify the page's behavior.

Listing 11.1 shows a sample implementation of `WizardPage`. The page presents a single checkbox, asking the user whether to use the default directory (perhaps for setting up a new Java project, or some similar task). Taken on its own, the class doesn't provide any interesting behavior. Later in the chapter, we'll show you how to combine multiple implementations of `IWizardPage` to build a complete wizard.

Listing 11.1   DirectoryPage.java

```java
package com.swtjface.Ch11;

import org.eclipse.jface.wizard.WizardPage;
import org.eclipse.swt.SWT;
import org.eclipse.swt.layout.GridLayout;
import org.eclipse.swt.widgets.*;

public class DirectoryPage extends WizardPage
{
  public static final String PAGE_NAME = "Directory";
  private Button button;

  public DirectoryPage()
  {
    super(PAGE_NAME, "Directory Page", null);    ❶ Constructor
  }

  public void createControl(Composite parent)    ❷ createControls() method
  {
    Composite topLevel = new Composite(parent, SWT.NONE);
    topLevel.setLayout(new GridLayout(2, false));

    Label l = new Label(topLevel, SWT.CENTER);
    l.setText("Use default directory?");

    button = new Button(topLevel, SWT.CHECK);

    setControl(topLevel);         ❸ setControl() method
    setPageComplete(true);        ❹ setPageComplete() method
  }

  public boolean useDefaultDirectory()      ❺ useDefaultDirectory() method
  {
    return button.getSelection();
  }
}
```

❶ The `WizardPage` constructor takes a page name (which must be unique in this wizard), the title for the page, and (optionally) an image descriptor for the image to display on this page.

② Your page must implement this method. Here you create all the controls that will be displayed on the page. For this example, we create a single label and a checkbox.

③ When you've finished creating your controls, you must call `setControl()` to let the superclass know about your new creations. Failing to do so results in internal JFace assertions failing at runtime.

④ This method is used to signal whether the page has sufficient information to allow the user to move on. For simplicity, we set it to `true` here. In most applications, you'll need to attach listeners to your controls and wait for events to signal that the user has entered all required data.

⑤ Here we make a public method available to allow the status of the checkbox to be queried. Other classes in the wizard can then query whether the user wants to use the default location, and act accordingly.

The page is responsible for maintaining its own state, but it doesn't need to worry about other pages in the wizard or where it fits into the overall flow. Its only job is to let the wizard framework know whether it's complete enough to move on.

11.2 *The wizard*

A wizard is a step up from an individual page. A wizard groups a collection of pages and represents the overall task that the user is trying to perform. In addition to grouping the pages, the wizard's primary responsibility is to keep track of whether the overall task has enough information to finish and to do whatever processing is necessary when the task is finished.

Like wizard pages, the wizard has both an interface and a default implementation.

11.2.1 *IWizard*

The `IWizard` interface has quite a few methods, most of which are straightforward accessors for configuration options. A few are worth mentioning in greater detail, however; we present them in table 11.2.

As with wizard pages, JFace saves you from the drudgery of implementing all the methods defined in `IWizard` by providing a default implementation in the form of the `Wizard` class.

Table 11.2 Important methods defined by the `IWizard` interface

Method	Description
`canFinish()`	Called periodically to check whether it's currently possible for this wizard to finish. The result is used to determine whether to enable the Finish button. Note that returning true doesn't imply that the wizard will immediately finish, only that if the user clicked the Finish button right now; any information he hasn't entered can be given reasonable defaults.
`createPageControls()`	Intended to allow the wizard to create the controls for all of its pages in advance, so that it can calculate the maximum size needed and avoid having to resize when switching from one page to another. The `Wizard` implementation of this method calls `createControl()` on all pages included in the wizard, which is generally what you want. However, this method can be overridden if you want to delay creation of some of the pages, especially if the creation is slow and may not be needed.
`performCancel()`	Provides notification that the user has asked to cancel the wizard. Any cleanup or other processing that should be done for a cancellation should be performed here. This method returns a boolean; returning false signals the framework that cancellation isn't allowed at the current time.
`performFinish()`	Provides notification that the user has successfully finished the wizard. All logic related to the wizard finishing should be performed here. Like `performCancel()`, this method returns a boolean, and returning false signals the framework that the finish request was refused.

11.2.2 *Wizard*

Continuing our example, we'll show the use of `Wizard`, JFace's default implementation of `IWizard`. Our subclass is simple, because `Wizard` does most of the work for us. Note that `Wizard` provides a variety of configuration options (such as setting images or colors) that we don't show here.

Our sample wizard continues the project setup that we discussed earlier, using the `DirectoryPage` class we developed. We'll discuss only the skeleton of the class here and present the full listing later in the chapter:

```
public class ProjectWizard extends Wizard
{
  public ProjectWizard()
  {
    super();
  }

  public void addPages()        ❶  addPages() method
  {
    addPage(new DirectoryPage());
    //... add other pages as needed
  }
```

```
    public boolean performFinish()    ❷  performFinish() method
    {
      DirectoryPage dirPage =
          (DirectoryPage)getPage(DirectoryPage.PAGE_NAME);
      if(dirPage.useDefaultDirectory())
      {
        ...
      }
      return true;
    }
    public boolean performCancel()    ❸  performCancel() method
    {
      //... perform cancel processing
      return true;
    }
  }
```

❶ This method is called to tell the wizard to add any pages it desires. Pages are normally displayed in the order they're added. To change this behavior, you must override getNextPage() and getPreviousPage().

❷ Here we go through the actual process of creating our project. The DirectoryPage we added earlier is retrieved using its page name, and it can then be queried for the data we're interested in. This also demonstrates why each page in a wizard must have a unique name—if there were duplicates, getPage() wouldn't be able to determine which page to return.

❸ If any cleanup must be done when the user cancels, we do it here.

As you can see, Wizard takes care of most of the work for you. Aside from setting configuration options, there is little to do other than implement performFinish() and, if you wish, performCancel().

11.3 *Putting it all together*

Finally, we come to the layer that controls the entire wizard: the wizard container. Although at first glance it may seem odd to have this separate from the wizard itself, it allows one container to group multiple wizards together and switch between them.

11.3.1 *Wizard containers*

A wizard container is meant to act as a host for one or more wizards. The IWizard-Container interface isn't interesting in itself—it provides methods to get the current page, several methods to update aspects of the container's window, and a method to programmatically change the currently displayed page. Most of the real action comes from WizardDialog, which implements IWizardContainer.

11.3.2 *WizardDialog*

Clients are free to provide their own implementations of IWizardContainer, but WizardDialog will be sufficient for most needs. Typically it isn't even necessary to subclass WizardDialog. We'll first show how to use WizardDialog as is, and then demonstrate creating a subclass that decides at runtime whether to display certain pages.

First, listing 11.2 shows the standard WizardDialog.

Listing 11.2   WizardDialogDemo.java

```java
package com.swtjface.Ch11;

import org.eclipse.jface.window.ApplicationWindow;
import org.eclipse.jface.wizard.WizardDialog;
import org.eclipse.swt.widgets.Display;

public class WizardDialogDemo
{
  public static void main(String[] args)
  {
    ApplicationWindow testWindow = new ApplicationWindow(null);

    testWindow.setBlockOnOpen(false);
    testWindow.open();

    ProjectWizard wizard = new ProjectWizard();
    WizardDialog wizardDialog = new WizardDialog(
                               testWindow.getShell(),
                               wizard);

    wizardDialog.create();
    wizardDialog.open();
  }
}
```

As our demo program shows, if all you wish to do is display a wizard's pages in order, using a WizardDialog is simple. Just pass the IWizard to the dialog's constructor and call open(), and your wizard's pages will be displayed in the order in which they were added.

A warning about initialization errors

The example code will run as we've presented it, but there is a gotcha to be aware of if you're testing wizard code on your own. When we were originally testing wizard functionality, we created a subclass of `WizardDialog` and added a `main()` method. Unfortunately, this doesn't work due to a subtle interaction between SWT and the java classloader. When you type `java TestWizardDialog`, the Java VM first loads and initializes the `TestWizardDialog` class; it then looks for and executes the `static void main()` method defined there. To initialize `TestWizardDialog`, the VM needs to initialize all of its superclasses, which include `org.eclipse.jface.dialogs.Dialog`. `Dialog`, however, has static initialization code that attempts to retrieve certain images from the `ImageRegistry`. Because the system hasn't been fully initialized at this point (remember, `main()` hasn't even started execution), retrieving the values from the registry fails, throwing a `NullPointerException` and causing the main thread to terminate. In a typical application this won't be an issue, because `main()` is usually located in a class by itself or in a subclass of `ApplicationWindow`. However, it's worth being aware of this potential issue here and in other SWT classes, in case you're ever bitten by it. The symptoms are strange, but the solution is simple—put your `main()` method in a class that doesn't extend an SWT class.

11.4 *Combining wizards*

Occasionally you may have a situation that requires the user to select from one of several possible wizards. A good example occurs in Eclipse when you select File->New->Other. You're shown a wizard with a variety of options to choose which new object you wish to create. Whichever one you choose launches a separate wizard as appropriate. JFace provides support for this use case with the `WizardSelectionPage` class and the `IWizardNode` interface.

11.4.1 *WizardSelectionPage*

`WizardSelectionPage` extends `WizardPage` and is in general intended to act like any other page in a wizard. One additional method is important for this class: `setSelectedNode()`, which takes an `IWizardNode` as a parameter. The subclass should call this method as appropriate when a node has been selected.

As is the case when you subclass `WizardPage` directly, you must implement `createControl()` in a subclass of `WizardSelectionPage`. The method should be implemented to present the available choices to the user—often it's in the form of a tree, but the JFace designers chose to not make any assumptions about what might be the best presentation for your situation. Each available selection should be tied to an instance of IWizardNode.

11.4.2 *IWizardNode*

An IWizardNode is intended to be a placeholder for an actual instance of a wizard. WizardSelectionPage passes these instances to setSelectedNode() and retrieves them from getSelectedNode() when the selection page has completed. This interface includes two important methods (see table 11.3).

Table 11.3   Important methods defined by the IWizardNode interface

Method	Description
getWizard()	Retrieves the wizard tied to this node. It's assumed that the wizard won't be created until this method is called for the first time, and that if this method is called multiple times, the same cached wizard instance will be returned rather than a new one being created every time.
isContentCreated()	Queries the status of an IWizardNode and checks whether it has already instantiated a wizard.

Generally, you'll use these classes by subclassing WizardDialog. After a WizardSelectionPage has finished, you'll call getSelectedNode() to retrieve the node the user chose. You can then call getWizard() on that node to retrieve the wizard and pass the wizard instance to setWizard() in WizardDialog.

11.5 *Persistent wizard data*

Sometimes you need to save a wizard's data between invocations. For example, the Create New Java Class wizard in Eclipse includes a series of checkboxes to generate code such as a public static void main() method or default implementations of abstract methods in the superclass. The state of these checkboxes is saved between uses of the wizard so that if you uncheck the box to generate a main() method once, you won't have to change it every time.

JFace provides a convenient way to manage these persistent settings with the DialogSettings class. Although theses techniques are often used with wizards, there is no reason the same classes can't be used by any other dialog that wishes to persist state.

11.5.1 *DialogSettings*

DialogSettings provides an implementation of the IDialogSettings interface using a hash table and backed by an XML file. This is sufficient for most needs; but you should generally reference objects in terms of the interface rather than the concrete implementation, in case you find it necessary to switch implementations at some point in the future.

Using IDialogSettings is simple:

```
IDialogSettings settings = new DialogSettings("mydialog");
settings.put("checkboxOneChecked", true);
settings.put("defaultName", "TestDialog");

settings.save("settings.xml");

IDialogSettings loadedSettings = new DialogSettings(null);
loadedSettings.load("settings.xml");

loadedSettings.getBoolean("checkboxOneChecked");
loadedSettings.get("defaultName");
```

When run, this code writes a simple XML file to the current directory that (once cleaned up for readability) looks something like this:

```
<?xml version="1.0" encoding="UTF-8"?>
<section name="mydialog">
  <item key="defaultName" value="TestDialog"/>
  <item key="checkboxOneChecked" value="true"/>
</section>
```

Storing values in XML this way has the advantage that it's easy to edit them by hand, either to test odd combinations of values or to make emergency repairs if invalid values are somehow stored.

Storing values

The values are put into the settings object. It may be saved either to a file by giving the save() method a filename (as shown) or to any java.io.Writer. Likewise, it's read from the file (or a java.io.Reader) using the load() method. Because DialogSettings loads and saves using XML, you'll need xercesImpl.jar and xmlParserAPIs.jar (from $ECLIPSE_HOME/plugins/org.apache.xerces_x.y.z) in your classpath.

The name you pass to the constructor of DialogSettings creates a *section*. Sections are ways to group related data in the overall dialog settings. You can retrieve a section by name using getSection(), which returns another instance of IDialogSettings. As you can see from the code that loads the settings, there is no need to specify section names when loading; they're picked up automatically from the file.

Retrieving values

Calling `get()` or `getArray()` returns null if no value has been set for the given key. However, the various numeric `get()`s throw `NumberFormatExceptions` if you attempt to retrieve a nonset value (or if the file has been edited by hand so it's no longer a valid number), so you must be prepared to handle these cases if there is a possibility that some values haven't been set.

How useful all this is depends on your target platform. In Java 1.4, similar functionality is provided by the classes in the `java.util.prefs` package. From a design standpoint, it's generally better to stick to the facilities provided by the base platform, but you don't have this luxury if you're supporting Java 1.3 or earlier in your application; in this case, `IDialogSettings` can make a convenient alternative.

11.6 *Updating WidgetWindow*

To create a functional wizard, we need a few more classes than are usually required for `WidgetWindow`. You saw `DirectoryPage` earlier in the chapter. In order to finish the example, we need to add a couple more pages, complete the implementation of `ProjectWizard`, and add a `Composite` subclass.

First, let's look at the `ChooseDirectoryPage`. This page is invoked when the user declines to use the default directory. The page presents a text input field for the user to enter a choice of directory. `ChooseDirectoryPage` is presented in listing 11.3.

> **NOTE** It's important to remember that this design is purely for the purpose of demonstrating how multiple wizard pages work. In a real application, you should let the user enter his choice of directory on the same page as the use default checkbox, and you'll probably use a `DirectoryDialog` as discussed in the previous chapter.

Listing 11.3   ChooseDirectoryPage.java

```
package com.swtjface.Ch11;

import org.eclipse.jface.wizard.WizardPage;
import org.eclipse.swt.SWT;
import org.eclipse.swt.layout.GridData;
import org.eclipse.swt.layout.GridLayout;
import org.eclipse.swt.widgets.*;

public class ChooseDirectoryPage extends WizardPage
```

```
{
  public static final String PAGE_NAME = "Choose Directory";

  private Text text;

  public ChooseDirectoryPage()
  {
    super(PAGE_NAME, "Choose Directory Page", null);
  }

  public void createControl(Composite parent)
  {
    Composite topLevel = new Composite(parent, SWT.NONE);
    topLevel.setLayout(new GridLayout(2, false));

    Label l = new Label(topLevel, SWT.CENTER);
    l.setText("Enter the directory to use:");

    text = new Text(topLevel, SWT.SINGLE);
    text.setLayoutData(new GridData(GridData.FILL_HORIZONTAL));

    setControl(topLevel);
    setPageComplete(true);
  }

  public String getDirectory()
  {
    return text.getText();
  }
}
```

This page is similar to `DirectoryPage`. The input field is presented to the user, and a public method is made available for the rest of the application to query the user's choice.

The final page in our example wizard is a summary of the user's choices. There is no user interaction on this page; it displays a text string indicating the choice made. `SummaryPage` appears in listing 11.4.

Listing 11.4 SummaryPage.java

```
package com.swtjface.Ch11;

import org.eclipse.jface.wizard.WizardPage;
import org.eclipse.swt.SWT;
import org.eclipse.swt.layout.FillLayout;
import org.eclipse.swt.widgets.Composite;
import org.eclipse.swt.widgets.Label;

public class SummaryPage extends WizardPage
{
  public static final String PAGE_NAME = "Summary";
```

```
      private Label textLabel;

      public SummaryPage()
      {
        super(PAGE_NAME, "Summary Page", null);
      }

      public void createControl(Composite parent)
      {
        Composite topLevel = new Composite(parent, SWT.NONE);
        topLevel.setLayout(new FillLayout());

        textLabel = new Label(topLevel, SWT.CENTER);
        textLabel.setText("");

        setControl(topLevel);
        setPageComplete(true);
      }

      public void updateText(String newText)
      {
        textLabel.setText(newText);
      }
    }
```

In some respects, this class is the opposite of the previous two. Instead of providing a method for clients to query the state of the page, the class offers a method to update the displayed text. As an alternative to forcing the state of the page to be explicitly updated, it would also be possible to let this class query some shared state when it needs to display itself, such as a Project object that represents the project that's in the process of being built. This approach would require overriding the setVisible() method defined in IDialogPage. When setVisible(true) is called, the textLabel and any other relevant widgets will be refreshed. In general, you should prefer this approach, because it localizes knowledge of how to display things to the SummaryPage. We implemented it as we did to avoid having to write a Project class and to keep the example short.

We next present the full implementation of ProjectWizard in listing 11.5. There are two enhancements over the snippet we showed earlier in the chapter. First, we've expanded the implementation of addPages() to add all the pages needed for the wizard. More importantly, we've expanded the logic in getNextPage().

Listing 11.5   ProjectWizard.java

```java
package com.swtjface.Ch11;

import org.eclipse.jface.wizard.IWizardPage;
import org.eclipse.jface.wizard.Wizard;

public class ProjectWizard extends Wizard
{
public void addPages()
   {
     addPage(new DirectoryPage());
     addPage(new ChooseDirectoryPage());
     addPage(new SummaryPage());
   }

   public boolean performFinish()
   {
     DirectoryPage dirPage = getDirectoryPage();
     if (dirPage.useDefaultDirectory())
     {
       System.out.println("Using default directory");
     }
     else
     {
       ChooseDirectoryPage choosePage = getChoosePage();
       System.out.println(
         "Using directory: " + choosePage.getDirectory());
     }
     return true;
   }

   private ChooseDirectoryPage getChoosePage()
   {
     return (ChooseDirectoryPage) getPage(
       ChooseDirectoryPage.PAGE_NAME);
   }

   private DirectoryPage getDirectoryPage()
   {
     return (DirectoryPage) getPage(DirectoryPage.PAGE_NAME);
   }

   public boolean performCancel()
   {
     System.out.println("Perform Cancel called");
     return true;
   }

   public IWizardPage getNextPage(IWizardPage page)
   {
     if (page instanceof DirectoryPage)
     {
```

```
      DirectoryPage dirPage = (DirectoryPage) page;
      if (dirPage.useDefaultDirectory())
      {
        SummaryPage summaryPage =
          (SummaryPage) getPage(SummaryPage.PAGE_NAME);
        summaryPage.updateText("Using default directory");
        return summaryPage;
      }
    }

    IWizardPage nextPage = super.getNextPage(page);
    if (nextPage instanceof SummaryPage)
    {
      SummaryPage summary = (SummaryPage) nextPage;
      DirectoryPage dirPage = getDirectoryPage();
      summary.updateText(
        dirPage.useDefaultDirectory()
         ? "Using default directory"
         : "Using directory:" + getChoosePage().getDirectory());
    }
    return nextPage;
  }
}
```

The meat of this class is contained in the getNextPage() method. It's here that we control the navigation between pages. We must handle two scenarios correctly.

First is the case when the user is leaving the DirectoryPage, which is where she can choose to use the default directory. The parameter passed to getNextPage() is the page the user is coming from, so we check whether it's the DirectoryPage. If so, after casting the parameter to the correct implementation of IWizardPage, we query the status of the checkbox. If it has been checked, we want to skip straight to the status page, so we retrieve it using getPage() and return it.

If the previous page wasn't DirectoryPage, or if the user unchecked the checkbox, we fall back on the default behavior for determining the next page by calling super.getNextPage(). However, if the next page will be the summary page, we need to make sure to update the text to reflect the user's current choice. In this case, we cast the IWizardPage to a SummaryPage and then retrieve the other pages as necessary to determine the correct text to display. As noted after our discussion of SummaryPage, this logic is caused by our not having a shared state available to SummaryPage; in general it should be avoided because the complexity can quickly become overwhelming in a wizard with more pages.

The final class to complete our example is the composite used by WidgetWindow, shown in listing 11.6. Like the composite used in the previous chapter, this one isn't very interesting. It presents a button that, when clicked, initializes and displays a `WizardDialog` with our `ProjectWizard`.

Listing 11.6   Ch11WizardComposite.java

```java
package com.swtjface.Ch11;

import org.eclipse.jface.wizard.WizardDialog;
import org.eclipse.swt.SWT;
import org.eclipse.swt.events.SelectionEvent;
import org.eclipse.swt.events.SelectionListener;
import org.eclipse.swt.layout.FillLayout;
import org.eclipse.swt.widgets.Button;
import org.eclipse.swt.widgets.Composite;

public class Ch11WizardComposite extends Composite
{
  public Ch11WizardComposite(Composite parent)
  {
    super(parent, SWT.NONE);
    buildControls();
  }

  protected void buildControls()
  {
    final Composite parent = this;
    FillLayout layout = new FillLayout();
    parent.setLayout(layout);

    Button dialogBtn = new Button(parent, SWT.PUSH);
    dialogBtn.setText("Wizard Dialog...");
    dialogBtn.addSelectionListener(new SelectionListener()
    {
      public void widgetSelected(SelectionEvent e)
      {
        WizardDialog dialog =
          new WizardDialog(
            parent.getShell(),
            new ProjectWizard());
        dialog.open();
      }

      public void widgetDefaultSelected(SelectionEvent e) {}
    });
  }

}
```

The part of this class to notice is in widgetSelected(), where we initialize the dialog. Notice that WizardDialog works exactly as we want with no modifications. We can pass a new instance of our ProjectWizard to it and let it do its thing.

11.7 *Summary*

The wizard framework builds on the dialog classes we've already discussed by adding support for multiple pages in a single dialog. There are three levels in the hierarchy of the wizard framework. IWizardContainer, which is implemented by WizardDialog, contains instances of IWizard, usually Wizard. An IWizard, in turn, contains multiple IWizardPages.

The life cycle of a wizard isn't complex. Each IWizardPage implements the createControl() method to build whatever controls are necessary to display. addPages() is called on IWizard, which instantiates and tracks the pages it intends to use. In the default Wizard implementation, this requires nothing more than calling addPage() for each one. As each page is displayed, isPageComplete() and canFlipToNextPage() are called to determine whether the Next and Previous buttons should be enabled. When the user clicks either Next or Previous, getNext-Page() or getPreviousPage() is called on the current page to determine which page should be displayed next. Finally, once the user clicks Finish or Cancel, performFinish() or performCancel() is called on the wizard itself to signal that the appropriate processing should be performed.

In addition to the standard three interfaces necessary to implement any wizard, JFace provides an additional level in the hierarchy that you can use to assemble multiple wizards. A WizardSelectionPage uses instances of IWizardNode to present multiple wizards to the user, allowing one to be selected. Each node is set up to instantiate the wizard only after it's selected, to avoid doing unnecessary work.

The IDialogSettings interface provides a way to easily store persistent settings data, as long as those settings can be represented by Java primitives. The default implementation, DialogSettings, serializes the objects to an XML file.

Advanced features

By now, you should be familiar with everything you need to build a working application using SWT and JFace. We've covered the essential widgets, shown you how to easily position them on the screen, and discussed the issues to keep in mind to ensure a well-designed piece of software. However, you'll want to become familiar with a few miscellaneous topics as your use of SWT increases.

This chapter covers a variety of issues. We'll start by discussing how to transfer data to and from the underlying operating system, and we'll show how to use this capability to implement drag-and-drop and copy-and-paste functionality in your applications. Next we'll discuss two frameworks provided by SWT for managing user preferences and enhancing how your labels are displayed by the viewer classes. Finally, we'll close with a brief look at a new widget provided in SWT 3.0, the Browser, which enables you to control the user's web browser from within your application.

Because some of these classes are designed around interacting directly with the underlying operating system, there are differences in how they function on different platforms. In addition, some widgets aren't fully supported on all platforms at the current time. We'll point out these platform-specific gotchas as we go along.

12.1 *Transferring data*

Although you may not notice it, almost any application you use is constantly shuffling data back and forth behind the scenes. Every time you cut and paste, the application must interact with the system *clipboard*, where data is stored temporarily. Dragging and dropping items requires similar communication, because the application needs to let the system know what kind of data formats it can provide as well as whether it will accept any given data type.

SWT handles many of the common cases automatically. For example, you saw in earlier chapters that it's possible to cut and paste text from a text control using the standard keyboard shortcuts for your operating system. However, you need to handle this work yourself if you wish to support drag-and-drop operations or cutting and pasting with application-specific formats. This section will cover how to do so, as we build a primitive file browser that supports dragging, dropping, and copy-and-paste operations both internally and interacting with the native operating system tools.

Before we get too deep into the technical details, look at figure 12.1, which shows what we're about to build. Two ListViewers are used, each displaying the

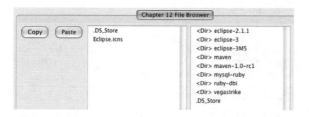

Figure 12.1
The File Browser, displaying the
contents of two different directories

contents of a certain directory. Dragging a file or files from one to the other will cause a corresponding file copy on disk. The Copy and Paste buttons copy the current selection in the left list to the system clipboard or paste files from the clipboard to the directory currently displayed in the left list, respectively.

12.1.1 *The Transfer class*

In order for data to be moved or copied between elements, there must be a way for those elements to agree on what format that data is in. If the application doesn't understand a given format, it won't make sense to try to import it—for example, there is no way for a text editor to handle an image that's dropped into it. SWT provides a relatively simple way for elements to negotiate what data formats are acceptable through the use of the `Transfer` class and its subclasses.

Each subclass of `Transfer` represents a certain type of data and knows how to convert that data between a Java representation and one that makes sense to the underlying operating system. SWT ships with `Transfer` subclasses to handle files, plain text, and text in Rich Text Format (RTF). If none of these meets your needs, you can write your own `Transfer` implementation, although doing so is beyond the scope of this book. Consult the Javadocs for `org.eclipse.swt.dnd.Transfer` and `org.eclipse.swt.dnd.ByteArrayTransfer` if you need a custom implementation.

For our purposes, we can treat the `Transfer` instances as black boxes that represent certain data types. Each subclass has a static factory method `getInstance()` to obtain an instance of the class. We can pass these instances around to designate what data types we're interested in, but we never need to call any methods on them ourselves. Under the hood, SWT calls `javaToNative()` and `nativeToJava()` when appropriate to transform data.

Table 12.1 shows the default general-purpose transfer agents that SWT provides.

Table 12.1   Default transfer agents provided by SWT

Transfer class name	Description
FileTransfer	Transfers one or more files. Data is an array of Strings, each of which is the path to a file or directory.
TextTransfer	Transfers plain text. Data is a String.
RTFTransfer	Transfers text in RTF. Data is a String with rich text formatting.

12.1.2   Drag-and-drop capability

Allowing a user to drag an item from its current location to wherever they wish it to be can help make your application's interface intuitive and easy to use. However, to accomplish this, a fair amount of work must go on behind the scenes. First, your application must make the system aware of the kinds of data it can provide or knows how to accept. These data types are configured separately for each widget—just because an object can accept objects dropped into it doesn't imply that it can provide data to be dragged out. Once the system is aware of the capabilities of the various widgets in your application, those widgets will receive events when a drag or drop occurs that it must use to implement appropriate logic.

Types of drag-and-drop operations

When a user drags an item from one place to another, there are typically multiple ways the action can be interpreted—for example, as either a copy or a move. Each operating system has different keyboard conventions that are used to toggle between these operations. However, your widgets also need to tell SWT what operations they support. A read-only display may support copying items by dragging them out but may not allow the user to move them. Support for these operations is designated by using constants from the org.eclipse.swt.dnd.DND class, summarized in table 12.2.

Table 12.2   Types of transfer operations

Operation constant	Description
DROP_COPY	The item is copied when dragged in or out of this control.
DROP_MOVE	The item is moved from its current location to wherever it's dropped.
DROP_LINK	Dropping the item creates a link back to the original.
DROP_NONE	Nothing happens when the item is dropped.

Dropping items into an application

You can register a control to be able to receive dropped data by using an instance of `DropTarget`. `DropTarget` stores both the type of data a widget can select and the operations that are legal to perform on that widget. The operating system uses this information to provide visual feedback as to whether an item may be dropped when it's dragged over the widget. Once the target has been registered, any `DropTargetListeners` will receive `DropTargetEvents` when the user attempts to drop something within the control.

Creating a `DropTarget` is simple. You instantiate it with a widget and a set of operations, and you set the allowed data types by calling `setTransfer()`. A listener is then attached, which contains the logic to execute when something is dropped. The following snippet demonstrates:

```
int operations = DND.DROP_MOVE | DND.DROP_COPY;
DropTarget target = new DropTarget(control, operations);
Transfer[] transfers = new Transfer[] {
   TextTransfer.getInstance(),
   RTFTransfer.getInstance() };
target.setTransfer(transfers);
target.addDropListener( new DropTargetListener(){...} );
```

If you're working with a viewer, you must call the method `addDropSupport()` on the viewer instance instead of attempting to manipulate the control directly. The next snippet, taken from our file browser example, shows how we add support for dropping files into a list viewer:

```
Transfer[] types = new Transfer[] {
  FileTransfer.getInstance()
};

viewer.addDropSupport(DND.DROP_COPY,
                      types,
                      new FileDropListener(this));
```

The registration process isn't complicated. The most important part is implementing the `DropTargetListener` interface. The methods in this interface are called in the following specific order as the user drags an item into a control:

1. *dragEnter()*—The cursor has entered the boundaries of the control while dragging an item.

2. *dragOver()*—The cursor is moving across the control, dragging an item.

3. *dragOperationChanged()*—This method may be called multiple times during the operation, whenever the user changes the type of operation to be

performed. This occurs most often when the user presses or releases a modifier key, such as Ctrl or Option.

4 *dropAccept ()*—The user has dropped an item in the control. This is the application's last chance to reject the drop or to change the type of operation being performed.

5 *drop ()*—The data has been dropped. The listener must implement the appropriate logic to handle the data it has been given.

Each method is given a `DropTargetEvent` containing information about the current operation. Most important, this event contains a list of data types that the data source can support, the current data type that will be dropped, the operations available to be performed, and the current operation to be performed. You can change the data type to be used and the operation to be performed by modifying the `currentDataType` and `detail` fields, respectively.

A sixth method, `dragLeave()`, may be called at any time before `dropAccept()`. This method lets the application know that the user has moved the cursor outside of the control and that no drop will occur.

Unless you need to dynamically change the data type or operation, the only method for which you need to implement logic is `drop()`. SWT and the operating system handle the other details; if a suitable agreement on data type and operation can't be reached, the drop won't be allowed, and your listener won't receive the events. Listing 12.1 shows how we implemented a `DropTargetListener` for the file browser example.

Listing 12.1   FileDropListener.java

```
package com.swtjface.Ch12;

import org.eclipse.swt.dnd.DropTargetEvent;
import org.eclipse.swt.dnd.DropTargetListener;

final class FileDropListener implements DropTargetListener
{
  private final FileBrowser browser;

  FileDropListener(FileBrowser browser)
  {
    this.browser = browser;
  }
  public void dragEnter(DropTargetEvent event) {}
  public void dragLeave(DropTargetEvent event) {}
  public void dragOperationChanged(DropTargetEvent event) {}
  public void dragOver(DropTargetEvent event) {}
  public void dropAccept(DropTargetEvent event) {}
```

```
public void drop(DropTargetEvent event)       ◁──── The drop method
{
   String[] sourceFileList = (String[])event.data;
   browser.copyFiles(sourceFileList);
}
}
```

The logic to implement the drop operation is simple. We only support the file transfer type, so when this method is called it's safe to assume that the data type is FileTransfer, which provides the data as an array of Strings. If we supported other data types, we would need to add conditional logic to react differently depending on the data type. Likewise, we can assume that the operation is a copy. Therefore, all our listener needs to do is extract the list of filenames and tell the FileBrowser component to copy them.

Dragging items from your application

Allowing data to be dragged from your application follows a process similar to what you just saw. A DragSource is created to register the control as a source of data. An implementation of DragSourceListener receives events when the user starts a drag operation and is responsible for implementing the logic once the item(s) have been dropped. The registration code looks almost identical. The first snippet shows how to create a DragSource by hand:

```
int operations = DND.DROP_MOVE | DND.DROP_COPY;
DragSource source =  new DragSource(control, operations);
Transfer[] transfers = new Transfer[] {
   TextTransfer.getInstance(),
   RTFTransfer.getInstance() };
source.setTransfer(transfers);
source.addDragListener( new DragSourceListener(){...} );
```

Just like for a DropTarget, when you're using a viewer a method on the viewer handles some of the work for you. The next excerpt shows the drag registration in the file browser example:

```
Transfer[] types = new Transfer[] {
  FileTransfer.getInstance()
};
...
viewer.addDragSupport(DND.DROP_COPY,
                      types,
                      new FileDragListener(this));
```

The DragSourceListener interface is much simpler than the one to handle drops; it consists of only three methods, called in the following order:

1 *dragStart()*—The user has started dragging data from this control. If the drag should be allowed to proceed, the doit field of the event must be set to true.

2 *dragSetData()*—A drop has been performed. This method must supply the data to be dropped by putting it in the event's data field.

3 *dragFinished()*—The drop has completed successfully. Any cleanup remaining to be done, such as deleting the original data for a move operation, should be performed here.

Each method receives a DragSourceEvent with data about the drag. Unlike the DropTargetEvent, this event may not be modified except as noted.

Listing 12.2 shows how we implement this listener in the filesystem browser.

Listing 12.2   FileDragListener.java

```java
package com.swtjface.Ch12;

import org.eclipse.swt.dnd.DragSourceEvent;
import org.eclipse.swt.dnd.DragSourceListener;

public class FileDragListener implements DragSourceListener
{
  private FileBrowser browser;

  public FileDragListener(FileBrowser browser)
  {
    this.browser = browser;
  }

  public void dragStart(DragSourceEvent event)
  {
    event.doit = true;        ❶ Drag has started
  }

  public void dragSetData(DragSourceEvent event)
  {
    event.data = browser.getSelectedFiles();    ❷ Provide data to be
  }                                                 transferred

  public void dragFinished(DragSourceEvent event) {}    ❸ Clean up
}
```

❶ This method is called when the user attempts to drag an item from the control. If this drag should be allowed, the doit field must be set to true. Our example always allows drags, so we always set this field to true.

❷ The item has been dropped in a receiver, and data must be provided. This data must match what is expected by the current data type, obtained from the dataType field. We only support FileTransfers, so our implementation gets the currently selected files from the browser and inserts them into the event.

❸ The operation has completed successfully. If the operation was a move, the original data should be deleted. Likewise, if any cleanup is associated with the other operation types, it should be performed in this method. Because our example only supports copying, our implementation is empty.

12.1.3 *Using the clipboard*

The process of copying data to or from the system clipboard has some similarities to dragging and dropping. It also uses Transfer subclasses to copy data to or from the operating system. The primary difference is that it isn't necessary to register in advance to use the system clipboard, as it is when you're dragging or dropping. Any time your application decides to cut, copy, or paste, usually in response to an Action of some sort, it can access the clipboard using the org.eclipse.swt.dnd.Clipboard class and do whatever it needs to do.

Each instance of Clipboard is created with a Display. Remember that on some platforms, accessing the clipboard may use native resources. It's therefore critical that you use dispose() to discard the Clipboard as soon as you've finished using it.

Putting data into the clipboard

Placing data on the system clipboard is a simple method call, setContents(). All it must do is pass the data, along with suitable Transfers to interpret it. This snippet shows how this is done for our filesystem browser:

```
Clipboard clipboard = new Clipboard(getDisplay());
FileTransfer transfer = FileTransfer.getInstance();
clipboard.setContents(
  new Object[] { browser.getSelectedFiles()},
  new Transfer[] { transfer });
clipboard.dispose();
```

Notice that we pass both an Object array and a Transfer array. These arrays must be the same size, and the Transfer instance at index i must be able to handle the Object at index i in the Object array. This way, all data in all supported formats is placed on the clipboard at once, and your application doesn't need to worry about when it's removed.

Although our example implements a copy operation, not a cut, the Clipboard doesn't care. It accepts the data; whether that data should be removed from its original source is up to the application and must be implemented separately.

Pasting data from the clipboard

Likewise, copying data from the clipboard is a simple process. When your application wishes to retrieve data that is currently stored in the clipboard, it can use two methods.

getAvailableTypeNames() returns an array of Strings with the names of all data types that the clipboard can currently provide. These values are operating-system dependent, and the String returned for a given data type will vary from platform to platform. Hence, this method is intended as a debugging aid and shouldn't be used in production code. However, when you're debugging and trying to figure out what data is currently on the clipboard, this method is invaluable.

getContents() takes a Transfer and returns the data from the clipboard in the format given by that Transfer, or null if no data can be provided in the given format. If your application supports multiple data formats, you'll typically call get-Contents() repeatedly, passing a different Transfer type each time, until you find data that you can handle.

This code implements a paste in the file browser example:

```
Clipboard clipboard = new Clipboard(getDisplay());
FileTransfer transfer = FileTransfer.getInstance();

Object data = clipboard.getContents(transfer);
if (data != null)
{
  browser.copyFiles((String[]) data);
}
clipboard.dispose();
```

You should always check for null after calling getContents(). It's always possible that the data currently on the clipboard can't be converted to a format your application understands, or that the clipboard is empty. Forgetting to check will eventually lead to NullPointerExceptions, which users never appreciate.

12.1.4 *The filesystem browser*

You've seen all the code our file browser uses to interact with the operating system. Some snippets have been presented out of context, however, and you haven't seen the `FileBrowser` class itself. For completeness, we'll present listings for the remaining code needed to compile and run this example.

First, listing 12.3 shows the `Composite` that builds the visual components. This class instantiates the visual controls and attaches listeners to the two buttons to handle the copy and paste logic when the buttons are clicked.

Listing 12.3   Ch12FileBrowserComposite.java

```java
package com.swtjface.Ch12;

import org.eclipse.swt.SWT;
import org.eclipse.swt.dnd.*;
import org.eclipse.swt.events.SelectionEvent;
import org.eclipse.swt.events.SelectionListener;
import org.eclipse.swt.layout.RowLayout;
import org.eclipse.swt.widgets.Button;
import org.eclipse.swt.widgets.Composite;

public class Ch12FileBrowserComposite extends Composite
{

  private FileBrowser browser;

  public Ch12FileBrowserComposite(Composite parent)
  {
    super(parent, SWT.NONE);

    RowLayout layout = new RowLayout(SWT.HORIZONTAL);
    setLayout(layout);

    Button copyButton = new Button(this, SWT.PUSH);
    copyButton.setText("Copy");
    copyButton.addSelectionListener(new SelectionListener()
    {

      public void widgetSelected(SelectionEvent e)
      {
        Clipboard clipboard = new Clipboard(getDisplay());

        FileTransfer transfer = FileTransfer.getInstance();
        clipboard.setContents(
          new Object[] { browser.getSelectedFiles()},
          new Transfer[] { transfer });
        clipboard.dispose();
      }

      public void widgetDefaultSelected(SelectionEvent e) {}
    });

    Button pasteButton = new Button(this, SWT.PUSH);
    pasteButton.setText("Paste");
    pasteButton.addSelectionListener(new SelectionListener()
    {
```

```
    public void widgetSelected(SelectionEvent e)
    {
      Clipboard clipboard = new Clipboard(getDisplay());
      FileTransfer transfer = FileTransfer.getInstance();

      Object data = clipboard.getContents(transfer);
      if (data != null)
      {
        browser.copyFiles((String[]) data);
      }
      clipboard.dispose();
    }

    public void widgetDefaultSelected(SelectionEvent e) {}
  });

  browser = new FileBrowser(this);
  new FileBrowser(this);
  }
}
```

Next, listing 12.4 shows the `FileBrowser` class. Each instance of `FileBrowser` creates and manages a `ListViewer`. A `ContentProvider` reads the contents of the current directory, and we add a sorter and a `LabelProvider` to make the display clearer. (We covered the use of these components in chapters 8 and 9, so we won't discuss them in detail here.) `FileBrowser` also contains public methods to retrieve the list of currently selected files and to copy a list of files into the current directory. This code isn't SWT related; if you're unfamiliar with what's going on, we recommend consulting the documentation for the `java.io` package.

Listing 12.4   FileBrowser.java

```
package com.swtjface.Ch12;

import java.io.*;
import java.util.*;

import org.eclipse.jface.viewers.*;
import org.eclipse.swt.dnd.*;
import org.eclipse.swt.widgets.Composite;

public class FileBrowser
{
  private ListViewer viewer;
  private File currentDirectory;

  public FileBrowser(Composite parent)
  {
    super();
```

```
    buildListViewer(parent);

    Transfer[] types = new Transfer[] {
      FileTransfer.getInstance()
    };

    viewer.addDropSupport(DND.DROP_COPY,
                          types,
                          new FileDropListener(this));
    viewer.addDragSupport(DND.DROP_COPY,
                          types,
                          new FileDragListener(this));
}

private void buildListViewer(Composite parent)
{
    viewer = new ListViewer(parent);
    viewer.setLabelProvider(new LabelProvider()
    {
      public String getText(Object element)
      {
        File file = (File) element;
        String name = file.getName();
        return file.isDirectory() ? "<Dir> " + name : name;
      }
    });

    viewer.setContentProvider(new IStructuredContentProvider()
    {

      public Object[] getElements(Object inputElement)
      {
        File file = (File) inputElement;
        if (file.isDirectory())
        {
          return file.listFiles();
        }
        else
        {
          return new Object[] { file.getName()};
        }
      }

      public void dispose()
      {
      }

      public void inputChanged(Viewer viewer,
                               Object oldInput,
                               Object newInput)
      {
      }
    });
```

```
      viewer.setSorter(new ViewerSorter()
      {

        public int category(Object element)
        {
          return ((File) element).isDirectory() ? 0 : 1;
        }

        public int compare(Viewer viewer, Object e1, Object e2)
        {
          int cat1 = category(e1);
          int cat2 = category(e2);
          if (cat1 != cat2)
            return cat1 - cat2;

          return ((File) e1).getName().compareTo(
                    ((File) e2).getName());
        }
      });

      viewer.addDoubleClickListener(new IDoubleClickListener()
      {

        public void doubleClick(DoubleClickEvent event)
        {
          IStructuredSelection selection =
            (IStructuredSelection) event.getSelection();
          setCurrentDirectory((File) selection.getFirstElement());
        }
      });

      setCurrentDirectory(File.listRoots()[0]);
    }

    private void setCurrentDirectory(File directory)
    {
      if (!directory.isDirectory())
        throw new RuntimeException(
          directory + " is not a directory!");

      currentDirectory = directory;
      viewer.setInput(directory);
    }

    String[] getSelectedFiles()
    {
      IStructuredSelection selection =
        (IStructuredSelection) viewer.getSelection();
      List fileNameList = new LinkedList();
      Iterator iterator = selection.iterator();
      while (iterator.hasNext())
      {
        File file = (File) iterator.next();
        fileNameList.add(file.getAbsoluteFile().toString());
```

```
    }
    return (String[]) fileNameList.toArray(
      new String[fileNameList.size()]);
}

void copyFiles(String[] sourceFileList)
{
  for (int i = 0; i < sourceFileList.length; i++)
  {
    File sourceFile = new File(sourceFileList[i]);
    if (sourceFile.canRead() && currentDirectory.canWrite())
    {
      File destFile =
        new File(currentDirectory, sourceFile.getName());
      if (!destFile.exists())
      {
        FileOutputStream out;
        FileInputStream in;
        try
        {
          out = new FileOutputStream(destFile);
          in = new FileInputStream(sourceFile);
          byte[] buffer = new byte[1024];
          while ((in.read(buffer)) != -1)
          {
            out.write(buffer);
          }
          out.flush();
          out.close();
          in.close();
          viewer.refresh();
        }
        catch (FileNotFoundException e)
        {
          e.printStackTrace();
        }
        catch (IOException e)
        {
          e.printStackTrace();
        }
      }
      else
      {
        System.out.println(
          destFile + " already exists, refusing to clobber");
      }
    }
    else
    {
      System.out.println(
        "Sorry, either your source file is not readable " +
```

```
                "or the target directory is not writable");
        }
      }
    }
  }
```

To run this code, add the following lines to `WidgetWindow`:

```
TabItem ch12Files = new TabItem(tf, SWT.NONE);
ch12Files.setText("Chapter 12 File Broswer");
ch12Files.setControl(new Ch12FileBrowserComposite(tf));
```

12.2 *Preferences*

Any nontrivial application has settings the user may configure. Although the specific options that may be modified are limitless and tightly tied to the specific application, the process of setting these options can generally be boiled down to a few interactions such as clicking a checkbox, choosing from a list, or choosing a target directory. JFace provides a framework to simplify storing a user's preferences, retrieving them, and presenting them to the user to be modified.

Like most areas of JFace, the preference framework is divided into a series of interfaces, each of which has a default implementation. You're free to use the provided concrete classes, or you may implement your own from scratch to meet your specific needs. We'll consider each interface, followed by the implementation provided by JFace.

The preferences framework is an extension of the JFace dialog framework. Only the `IPreferencePage` interface extends the interfaces from the dialogs package, but the assumption is that preferences will be displayed in a modal dialog. It's possible to change this behavior if you need to by writing your own implementation of `IPreferencePageContainer`, which we'll discuss later in the chapter.

12.2.1 *Preference pages*

Preferences are generally grouped into related sets, rather than strewn about randomly, in order to make it easier for a user to find the specific option he is looking for. In JFace, these sets are assigned to separate preference pages, which are displayed to the user one at a time. It isn't necessary to split up your settings, especially if there aren't many, but you must have at least one page.

IPreferencePage

The IPreferencePage interface extends IDialogPage. In addition to the IDialog-Page methods we discussed in chapter 11, seven new methods are defined (see table 12.3).

Table 12.3 Methods defined by the IPreferencePage interface

Method	Description
setContainer()	Associates an instance of IPreferencePageContainer with the page.
computeSize(), setSize()	Deal with the size of the control as it appears on screen. These methods are passed and return an instance of org.eclipse.swt.graphics.Point. Instead of representing an (x,y) coordinate, the fields of this Point object should be interpreted as the width and height, respectively, of the control.
okToLeave()	Called when the use wishes to flip to another page. Returning false prevents the user from leaving the page.
isValid()	Indicates whether the page is currently valid. Exactly what "valid" means is subjective, but it's generally an indicator of whether it's possible to leave the page or close the dialog in the current state.
performOk(), performCancel()	Indicate that the OK or Cancel button has been clicked, respectively. Any processing relevant to these events should be performed in these methods, both of which return a boolean indicating whether the event should be allowed to happen.

PreferencePage

The abstract class PreferencePage forms the basis of all implementations of IPreferencePage provided by JFace. Extending from DialogPage, PreferencePage provides much of the support needed to display preferences in a dialog, including a title and an optional image.

If you're subclassing PreferencePage directly, you must implement the abstract createControl() method to instantiate the controls necessary for the page. Again, this is the same as any other DialogPage. Two buttons, Apply and Defaults, are automatically added to the parent composite of your control unless the noDefaultAndApplyButton() method is called before the control is created. Typically this will be done in the constructor of your subclass if necessary.

By default, PreferencePage returns true for okToLeave() whenever isValid() returns true. Unless you change the validity of the page using setValid(), a PreferencePage will always consider itself to be valid. This also means that a user will be allowed to flip pages or close the dialog at any time.

The performOk(), performCancel(), performApply(), and performDefaults() methods may all be overridden to react to the occurrence of the appropriate event. By default, these methods do nothing, so you need to override them if you wish your page to do anything useful.

FieldEditorPreferencePage

The only subclass of PreferencePage provided by JFace, and the only one you'll need for the majority of cases, is FieldEditorPreferencePage. FieldEditorPreferencePage assumes that your preferences consist of a number of discrete fields that can be modified independently. The FieldEditorPreferencePage is meant to make it easy to collect all the FieldEditors necessary to edit the preferences for the page. As such, it implements and overrides all the methods from PreferencePage discussed in the previous section. Typically, you're left with only one method that you must implement.

createFieldEditors() is called once the page is ready to lay out the editors. All the method does is add the editors to be displayed using addField(). Editors are then laid out on the displayed control in the order in which they were added.

FieldEditorPreferencePage exposes only a few public methods beyond those present in PreferencePage, and clients generally have little need to call them.

12.2.2 Field editors

A field editor is responsible for displaying and editing a single preference value. The editor can range from displaying a text field and allowing the user to type, to opening a complex dialog and allowing the user to select a valid value. JFace includes nine concrete FieldEditor subclasses, which we'll discuss. These should cover most of your needs.

You must follow a few steps if you need to define your own FieldEditor subclass:

1   Think about the basic controls you'll need in order for your editor to function. Implement getNumberOfControls() to return the number of controls you'll be using. FieldEditor uses this value to figure out how to lay out your control.

2   In its implementation of createControl(), FieldEditor calls the abstract doFillIntoGrid() method. This should be implemented to instantiate your controls and add them to the Composite that's passed to the method.

3   If your editor includes a label, FieldEditor includes built-in support for storing the label text and the label control. You should use getLabelControl(Composite parent) in this case, rather than creating your own Label.

4 Implement the doLoad(), doLoadDefault(), and doStore() methods to load values from and persist them to the PreferenceStore associated with your editor. This store can be retrieved by using the getPreference-Store() method, which may return null if no persistent store has been configured for the editor.

In addition to implementing all the abstract methods, you can fire events when your editor's properties change. FieldEditor provides a fireValueChanged() method, which takes a property name, the old value, and the new value and automatically invokes any registered PropertyChangeListener. This isn't necessary if your control doesn't have any properties that are interesting to outside listeners—most of the FieldEditor subclasses included in JFace don't bother to fire these events, but the support is there if you need it.

Whether you're implementing a completely new editor or using a built-in one, it can be useful to add validation to your FieldEditor. You do so by overriding both the isValid() and refreshValidState() methods. By default, isValid() always returns true, and refreshValidState() does nothing. isValid() is simple: It returns true or false according to whether your editor currently contains a value that is valid to save. refreshValidState() is slightly more complicated. This method should query isValid() and, if the value has changed, fire a value-changed event for the property FieldEditor.IS_VALID. refreshValidState() is invoked at various times by the FieldEditor framework, particularly after loading and before attempting to save values.

Implementing your own FieldEditor may sound complicated, but you shouldn't need to do this very often. JFace provides nine types of FieldEditor (see table 12.4), and most of the time you should be able to use or subclass one of them.

Table 12.4   Field editors provided by JFace

Editor class	Description
BooleanFieldEditor	Displays its preference as checkboxes, which are checked to indicate true or unchecked to indicate false. By default, the checkbox appears to the left of any supplied label, but using the style BooleanFieldEditor.SEPARATE_LABEL creates the label on the left and the checkbox on the right.
ColorFieldEditor	Lets the user choose a color. A button is displayed; when it's clicked, another dialog is opened, allowing the user to see the available colors and choose one by pointing with the mouse. The chosen color is saved as an org.eclipse.swt.graphics.RGB value.

continued on next page

Table 12.4 **Field editors provided by JFace** *(continued)*

Editor class	Description
DirectoryFieldEditor	Lets the user choose any directory on the filesystem. A text field displays the current chosen directory. This value may be modified in place, or the displayed Browse button lets the user navigate the filesystem and choose a directory graphically.
FileFieldEditor	Lets the user choose a filename and location. You can filter the types of files displayed when browsing the filesystem by using the setFile-Extensions() method, which takes an array of Strings. Files must match one of the extensions in this array, or they won't be displayed.
FontFieldEditor	Lets the user choose a font, including size and bold or italic attributes. Clicking the Change button opens a dialog presenting all the available font options. Text demonstrating the chosen font is displayed; you can set the string to use for this text in FontFieldEditor's constructor. The value for this editor is returned as an org.eclipse.swt.graphics.FontData object.
IntegerFieldEditor	Ensures that any entered value is an integer. You can force the entered value to be in a certain range by using the setValidRange() method.
PathEditor	Lets the user choose multiple directory paths. The currently selected paths are displayed in a list on the left; buttons to add, remove, or change the order of the paths are on the right.

RadioGroupFieldEditor	Presents a set of mutually exclusive options, forcing the user to pick exactly one of them. Labels for the available options are specified in the constructor, along with the value to return if each one is selected. These are passed as a two-dimensional array of Strings, as shown here:
	`RadioGroupFieldEditor editor = new RadioGroupFieldEditor(`
	`        /*some other parameters*/,`
	`        new String[][] {`
	`          {"Option One", "Value1"},`
	`          {"Option Two", "Value2"} },`
	`        /*more parameters*/ );`

StringFieldEditor	Provides the user with a text field to enter a string of characters. This editor supports two options for validating the entered text: VALIDATE_ON_FOCUS_LOST and VALIDATE_ON_KEY_STROKE; you can toggle between them using setValidateStrategy(). By default, StringFieldEditor accepts any string as valid. To add your own validation, override the protected doCheckState() method. To limit the length of the entered text, use the setTextLimit() method.

12.2.3 *Preference page containers*

Just as wizard pages are hosted by a wizard container, preference pages are displayed by a preference page container.

IPreferencePageContainer

The `IPreferencePageContainer` interface must be implemented by any class that wishes to host preference pages. The interface is straightforward; it has only four methods (see table 12.5).

Table 12.5   Methods defined by the `IPreferencePageContainer` interface

Method	Description
`getPreferenceStore()`	Used by preference pages to retrieve a persistent store for their values
`updateButtons()`, `updateMessage()`, `updateTitle()`	Let pages request that the container update its display to match the currently active page

Although it's easy to implement `IPreferencePageContainer` if you need to, doing so generally isn't necessary. Preference pages are typically displayed in a dialog, and `PreferencePageDialog` provides a default implementation that handles this case well.

IPreferencePageNode

Whereas in a wizard dialog pages are typically displayed in a set order, preference pages may be filled out in any sequence the user desires. It would be unfriendly to force a user to click through several pages of options that she isn't interested in, just to modify one setting. However, avoiding this scenario necessitates a way to display a list of the pages to the user. A *preference node* fills this role.

A preference node combines a preference page with a unique ID and an optional title and image. The title and image are displayed to the user in a tree on the left side of a dialog; when one of them is clicked, the corresponding page is displayed on the right. This way, users can quickly navigate to the group of settings they're interested in. `IPreferenceNode` also adds support for making one node a subnode of another with the `add()` method; in this case, the children are shown when the parent is expanded in the tree. `PreferenceNode` provides a default implementation of `IPreferenceNode`, and you'll rarely need to implement the interface yourself.

Most of the methods on `PreferenceNode` are used by the framework. You can set a title and image when instantiating `PreferenceNode`. Typically the only other methods you'll ever need to call on it are `add()` and `remove()`, to manage the children associated with a given node.

PreferenceManager

`PreferenceManager` is a utility class that JFace uses to organize preference nodes. It introduces the concept of a *path*, which is used to identify nodes in the hierarchy. A path consists of a string made up of the IDs of one or more nodes, divided by a separator character. By default, the separator is a period (`.`), but you can change it by passing any other character to `PreferenceManager`'s constructor. The string is tokenized on the separator character, and each ID is used to search starting from the root, then the children of the first node found, then the next node's children, and so on, until the final node in the path has been found. You can add nodes at the root or as a child of any node currently in the structure, identified by its path.

PreferencePageDialog

`PreferencePageDialog` is JFace's implementation of `IPreferencePageContainer`. It extends `Dialog` and adds support for displaying preference pages. The pages available are displayed in a tree on the left, and the currently active page is displayed in the main area of the dialog. Once you have instantiated the dialog with an instance of `PreferenceManager` and associated a persistent store using `setPreferenceStore()`, you can call `open()`; `PreferencePageDialog` takes care of the rest.

12.2.4 Persistent preferences

Preferences aren't very useful if they must be reset each time an application is launched. JFace provides a way to make your preferences persistent using the `IPreferenceStore`.

IPreferenceStore

An `IPreferenceStore` maps preference names to values. Each named preference may have both a default value and a current value; if there is no current value, the default is returned. Preferences may be any of Java's primitive types (see also the discussion of `PreferenceConverter` for an easy way to store certain JFace objects in an `IPreferenceStore`). Each `get` and `set` method defined in this interface takes the name of the preference to operate on. Additionally, there are methods to set the default value for a given preference or reset a preference to the default, and a dirty indicator to check whether the store has been changed. A subinterface, `IPersistentPreferenceStore`, adds a `save()` method to persist the values.

PreferenceStore

JFace includes `PreferenceStore`, an implementation of `IPreferenceStore` that's based on the `java.util.Properties` class. `PreferenceStore` only saves properties that aren't equal to the default value, thereby minimizing the amount of data that must be written to disk. Values are persisted using the standard properties file format (name-value pairs separated by `=`). You have two options for loading and saving your data when using `PreferenceStore`. The simplest way is to specify a filename when instantiating a new instance:

```
PreferenceStore store = new PreferenceStore( "some_file_name" );
store.load();
```

Alternatively, you can give the store a stream to use when loading or saving:

```
PreferenceStore store = new PreferenceStore();
FileInputStream in = new FileInputStream( "some_file_name" );
store.load( in );
...
FileOutputStream out = new FileOutputStream( "some_file_name" );
store.save( out, "Custom Header" );
```

You must also remember to explicitly call `load()` before passing your `PreferenceStore` to a `PreferenceDialog`, because the dialog won't call the method on your behalf. It automatically calls `save()` when appropriate, however.

Note that calling the no-argument `load()` or `save()` method when no filename is specified in the `PreferenceStore` constructor results in an `IOException`. Because `PreferenceDialog` calls the no-argument method, you should always use the constructor that takes a filename; use the overloaded versions of `load()` and `save()` only if you need to copy the values to a backup stream.

PreferenceConverter

`PreferenceConverter` is another utility provided by JFace. It consists of a series of static methods used to set or retrieve common SWT objects that otherwise couldn't be used with an `IPreferenceStore`. Behind the scenes, `PreferenceConverter` serializes the object to or from a string format suitable for long-term storage. Values are set and retrieved like so:

```
IPreferenceStore store = ...
PreferenceConverter.setValue( store,
                              "color_pref",
                              new RGB(0, 255, 0) );

...
RGB color = PreferenceConverter.getColor( store,
                                          "color_pref" );
```

12.3 *Label decorators*

In our earlier discussion of ILabelProvider, we mentioned that there is an alternate implementation of IBaseLabelProvider. That implementation is in ILabel-Decorator, an interface designed to collaborate with basic label providers to provide additional information.

Label decorators are intended to "decorate" a given object's presentation with visual cues as to the object's current state. A good example can be found in the Package Explorer in Eclipse. The Package Explorer displays all the Java classes in the current project in a tree, organized by the package to which each belongs. A label provider displays each object's name along with an icon designating the object as either a class or package. Label decorations are added on top of the standard icons to designate abnormal conditions, such as the small red X that appears when there is a compilation error.

The main advantage of this design is the way it encourages decoupling. Continuing the Eclipse example, the standard label provider for a Java class only needs to know how to retrieve the name of a class and draw the basic icon. The logic to overlay the error icon (or warning icon, or any other variable status) is separated out into the decorator, where it can also be applied to packages or any other appropriate type of object. Likewise, because the Java class label provider isn't encumbered with code to display the status icons, it can easily be reused in another context where the status icons aren't desired.

12.3.1 *ILabelDecorator*

The main interface you'll use to implement decorator functionality is ILabelDec-orator. ILabelDecorator extends IBaseLabelProvider and is similar to ILabel-Provider. Two methods are defined: decorateText() and decorateImage(). Each is passed a domain object, along with the text or image that's currently being displayed. Each method returns the new text or image that should be displayed for the given domain object.

When you're implementing decorateImage(), keep in mind that each Image consumes relatively rare system resources. It's therefore important to avoid creating new `Images` if possible. Using the `ImageRegistry`, as we do in the example later in the chapter, is helpful to avoid instantiating unnecessary `Image` instances. Best practices for using `Images` are discussed further in chapter 7.

12.3.2 *DecoratingLabelProvider*

Once you've implemented the decorator, we need to make sure it gets a shot at performing its decorations. Rather than provide methods to explicitly add decorators to viewers, JFace supplies the `DecoratingLabelProvider` class. `DecoratingLabel-Provider` extends `LabelProvider` and thereby implements `ILabelProvider`. Instead of providing labels itself, `DecoratingLabelProvider` takes an instance of `ILabelPro-vider` and an `ILabelDecorator` in its constructor. Calls to `getText()` or `getImage()` are delegated first to the label provider and then to the label decorator. The `Dec-oratingLabelProvider` is then associated with the viewer, instead of calling `setLa-belProvider()` with the `ILabelProvider` directly.

Because `DecoratingLabelProvider` is an instance of `ILabelProvider`, you can easily chain decorators together by passing appropriate instances of `Decorat-ingLabelProvider` in the constructor instead of `LabelProviders`. Each decorator is then called in turn to build the final result. This technique is shown here:

```
DecoratingLabelProvider firstDecorator =
  new DecoratingLabelProvider( new MyLabelProvider(),
                               new FirstLabelDecorator() );
DecoratingLabelProvider secondDecorator =
  new DecoratingLabelProvider( firstDecorator,
                               new SecondLabelDecorator() );
viewer.setLabelProvider(secondDecorator);
```

12.3.3 *An example*

We'll now show an example of the decorator concepts we've discussed as they're used to build a tree showing the relationships between family members. Each person will be decorated with their family name and an icon indicating whether they are male or female. The infrastructure for this example is similar to the `TreeView-ers` we've discussed earlier. In the interest of conserving space, we won't reproduce the entire example; instead, we'll discussing only the sections that are relevant for label decorators.

The first step is to create the `TreeNode` class that represents each node in the tree. The member variables and constructor look like this:

```
public class TreeNode
{
  private String firstName;
```

```
private boolean isMale = false;
private String familyName;
private List children = new ArrayList();
private TreeNode parent;

public TreeNode(String firstName,
                String familyName,
                boolean male)
{
  this.firstName = firstName;
  this.familyName = familyName;
  isMale = male;
}
//accessor methods
...
}
```

Each of the attributes has an accessor, so that our decorator will be able to query the TreeNode for the data it needs.

Our implementation of ILabelDecorator is straightforward. Here we extend LabelProvider for the convenient implementations of the methods defined in IBaseLabelProvider:

```
public class FamilyDecorator
       extends LabelProvider
       implements ILabelDecorator
{
  private static final String MALE_IMAGE_KEY = "male";
  private static final String FEMALE_IMAGE_KEY = "female";
  private ImageRegistry imageRegistry;

  public FamilyDecorator(Shell s)
  {
    imageRegistry = new ImageRegistry(s.getDisplay());
    Image maleImage = new Image(s.getDisplay(), "male.gif");
    Image femaleImage = new Image(s.getDisplay(), "female.gif");
    imageRegistry.put(FEMALE_IMAGE_KEY, femaleImage);
    imageRegistry.put(MALE_IMAGE_KEY, maleImage);
  }


  public Image decorateImage(Image image, Object element)
  {
    if(element == null) return null;
    TreeNode node = (TreeNode)element;
    if(node.isMale())
    {
      return imageRegistry.get(MALE_IMAGE_KEY);
    }
    else
```

```
    {
      return imageRegistry.get(FEMALE_IMAGE_KEY);
    }
  }

  public String decorateText(String text, Object element)
  {
    if(element == null) return null;
    TreeNode node = (TreeNode)element;
    return text + " [" + node.getFamilyName() + "]";
  }

}
```

The constructor creates the `Images` we need and saves them in an `ImageRegistry` for future use. When `decorateImage()` is called, it checks the `isMale()` method of the `TreeNode` object and retrieves the appropriate image by name from the registry; this is then returned as the `Image` to display. (Note that this section has been simplified; in a real application, you'll typically need to draw your decoration on top of another image and return the combined result.)

`decorateText()` is also straightforward. Each node's family name is retrieved and appended to whatever text is already being displayed, and the result is returned as the text to display.

Finally, we create a `DecoratingLabelProvider` with an instance of our decorator and tell the viewer to use the new instance instead of the default label provider:

```
...
viewer.setLabelProvider(
      new DecoratingLabelProvider(
          (ILabelProvider)viewer.getLabelProvider(),
          new FamilyDecorator(getShell()))));
...
```

Note that here we retrieve the viewer's default label provider and pass it as the base for the `DecoratingLabelProvider` to use. In your own applications, this code may frequently be replaced with an instance of a custom label provider.

Running the demo results in a tree such as the one shown in figure 12.2.

The default label provider only added the text for each character's first name by calling

Figure 12.2
A decorated `TreeViewer`

`toString()` on each node. The icons and family names were added after the fact by our label decorator.

> **NOTE** *Using label decorators in Eclipse*—When you're using label decorators in an Eclipse plug-in, you must be aware of some additional gotchas, such as making sure you don't accidentally clobber the built-in decorators. Additional features are also available to you, such as configuring your decorators in the plugin.xml file. A detailed discussion of these issues is outside of the scope of this book; but the excellent article "Understanding Decorators in Eclipse" by Balaji Krish-Sampath, available online at www.eclipse.org/articles/Article-Decorators/decorators.html, will prove invaluable if you're working with decorators in Eclipse.

12.4 *The Browser widget*

With the rise of the World Wide Web, HTML has become one of the most important technologies for creating a user interface. It has the advantage of being simple to write, easy to understand, and quick to modify in order to try out different designs. When you're developing an application using a thick-client technology such as SWT or Swing, it's common to find yourself becoming envious of the quick development cycles afforded by an HTML-based interface. When you consider the vast amount of information that exists in HTML, sometimes it makes sense to design your application to be able to display HTML documents.

Thankfully, in the 3.0 release the SWT team has provided the `Browser` widget to make this easy to do. By using `Browser`, you can embed the user's web browser in your application and use it to display HTML without having to write a custom rendering engine. Additionally, because `Browser` uses the full-fledged native web browser for your platform, you gain the ability to handle JavaScript, XML, and any other format already understood by the browser.

Before we dive too deeply into our discussion of the `Browser` widget, a couple of caveats are in order:

- `Browser` isn't currently supported on all platforms. It works on Microsoft Windows without a problem, but using it on Linux requires Mozilla 1.5. OS X and other platforms don't support `Browser` at all; if you try to instantiate it, the result is an `SWTError`. This code is under active development, however, so if you're considering using `Browser` you should check the status under all platforms you plan to support.

- As of the time of this writing, the API for `Browser` is considered unstable. It will be finalized by the time the final version of SWT 3.0 is released, but it's possible that it will be different from the code samples we discuss here. In this case, you should consult the Javadocs for the version of the widget in your distribution to learn the differences.

The API for `Browser` is simple. It consists of methods to load the document found at a URL, to navigate backward and forward between pages, to refresh the current URL, and to stop the loading of the current page. Additionally, `Browser` broadcasts several unique events. At the current time, these events include opening, closing, and hiding windows; changing locations; and indicating progress as a page is loaded.

Using the `Browser` widget may also require additional native libraries, depending on your platform. There are no additional dependencies for Windows, but using `Browser` in the Linux/GTK distribution of SWT requires the libswt-mozilla-gtk library to be included in your `LD_LIBRARY_PATH`. On other supported platforms, you should check for the existence of a native library that includes the name of your platform's web browser.

We next provide a simple example of `Browser` in action. The code in listing 12.5 opens a browser window when you run it. A text box allows the user to type a URL, and when the Open button in the `WidgetWindow` is clicked, the corresponding location is opened in the browser. Forward and Back buttons let the user control navigation in the browser from within `WidgetViewer`. Running the example results in the screenshot shown in figure 12.3.

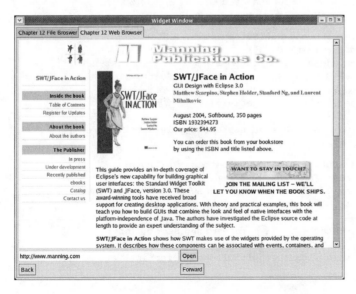

Figure 12.3
Mozilla embedded in
an SWT application

Listing 12.5   Ch12WebBrowserComposite.java

```
package com.swtjface.Ch12;

import org.eclipse.swt.SWT;
import org.eclipse.swt.browser.Browser;
import org.eclipse.swt.events.SelectionEvent;
import org.eclipse.swt.events.SelectionListener;
import org.eclipse.swt.layout.GridData;
import org.eclipse.swt.layout.GridLayout;
import org.eclipse.swt.widgets.*;

public class Ch12WebBrowserComposite extends Composite
{
  private Browser browser;

  public Ch12WebBrowserComposite(Composite parent)
  {
    super(parent, SWT.NONE);

    GridLayout layout = new GridLayout(2, true);
    setLayout(layout);

    browser = new Browser(this, SWT.NONE);        ❶ Create Browser instance
    GridData layoutData = new GridData(GridData.FILL_BOTH);
    layoutData.horizontalSpan = 2;
    layoutData.verticalSpan = 2;
    browser.setLayoutData(layoutData);
    browser.setUrl("http://www.manning.com/catalog/view.php?book=scarpino");

    final Text text = new Text(this, SWT.SINGLE);
    layoutData = new GridData(GridData.FILL_HORIZONTAL);
    text.setLayoutData(layoutData);

    Button openButton = new Button(this, SWT.PUSH);
    openButton.setText("Open");
    openButton.addSelectionListener(new SelectionListener() {
      public void widgetSelected(SelectionEvent e)
      {
        browser.setUrl(text.getText());        ❷ Open URL
      }
      public void widgetDefaultSelected(SelectionEvent e) {}
    });

    Button backButton = new Button(this, SWT.PUSH);
    backButton.setText("Back");
    backButton.addSelectionListener(new SelectionListener() {
      public void widgetSelected(SelectionEvent e)
      {
        browser.back();        ❸ Forward and Back buttons
      }
      public void widgetDefaultSelected(SelectionEvent e) {}
    });
```

```
        Button forwardButton = new Button(this, SWT.PUSH);
        forwardButton.setText("Forward");
        forwardButton.addSelectionListener(new SelectionListener() {
          public void widgetSelected(SelectionEvent e)
          {
            browser.forward();     ❸ Forward and Back buttons
          }
          public void widgetDefaultSelected(SelectionEvent e) {}
        });
      }
    }
```

❶ Browser is instantiated like any other control, with a parent Composite and a style parameter. Currently, Browser doesn't support any styles.

❷ Any valid URL can be opened by passing it to the setUrl() method. This will clear whatever page is currently loaded in the browser.

❸ The browser can be told to move forward and back through its history by calling the appropriate method.

If you're on a supported platform, you can run this example by adding these lines to WidgetWindow:

```
    TabItem ch12WebBrowser = new TabItem(tf, SWT.NONE);
    ch12WebBrowser.setText("Chapter 12 Web Browser");
    ch12WebBrowser.setControl(new Ch12WebBrowserComposite(tf));
```

12.5 *Summary*

We've covered several important topics in this chapter, and the volume of information can seem overwhelming. Don't worry about mastering it all at first glance; many of the concepts we've discussed aren't necessary for day-to-day programming with SWT and JFace. The important thing is to be aware of the capabilities that are present, so that when you find yourself needing to implement drag and drop or user preferences, you'll know where to turn.

You should also keep in mind that SWT is under constant development. Although at the time we're writing this, widgets such as Browser aren't fully supported on all platforms, the situation may have changed by the time you write your own SWT application. Check the articles available at www.eclipse.org to see what enhancements have been made since this book went to press.

13

Looking beyond SWT/JFace: the Rich Client Platform

This chapter covers

- The theory behind the Rich Client Platform (RCP)
- The classes that make RCP operation possible
- The Eclipse Forms toolset
- Building an example RCP application

So far, we've discussed how SWT serves as a general-purpose toolset for building GUI applications. We've also shown how JFace provides more specialized capabilities (`Actions`, `Contributions`, and `Viewers`) like those in the Eclipse platform. These aspects of JFace simplify the development process, as long as your GUI's operation resembles that of the Eclipse Workbench.

To conclude this book, we'd like to take this progression one step further. Instead of just using behavioral aspects of the Workbench, we'll now explore building complete, custom applications that look and function like Eclipse. We'll call them (lowercase) *workbenches*. Like JFace GUIs, they provide a great deal of functionality but remain simple to code.

This exciting capability is made possible by Eclipse's new Rich Client Platform (RCP). With RCP, not only can you create workbenches quickly, but you can also compile them into *standalone* applications. So, you won't need the entire Eclipse platform to run your GUIs.

In this chapter, we'll explain the underlying structure of RCP and progress through the stages of building a complete, standalone application. To make this even more interesting, we'll create this application using structures from Eclipse Forms. Eclipse Forms is more than a new package or plug-in: It's a complete toolkit for building powerful form-based applications.

Before you start coding, you need to understand how workbenches are structured.

13.1 Understanding RCP workbenches

We'll start our discussion by describing the building blocks that make up an RCP application. Figure 13.1 presents our favorite workbench—the Eclipse Workbench—with labels for its individual sections.

In previous chapters, we've discussed the title, menu, toolbar, and status line, and how to configure them inside user interfaces. A workbench is distinguished from these other GUIs by its editors and views. We'll discuss these now, along with the perspective that controls their placement.

13.1.1 Entering data with editors

Essentially, a workbench consists of an editor and a series of views that support the editing process. The Eclipse Workbench centers on a text editor whose view panes let you alter or examine the editor's environment. But in your RCP workbenches, you have many options beyond regular text editing. Figure 13.2 shows the full class hierarchy for workbench editors.

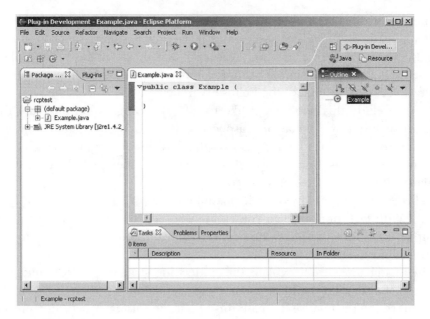

Figure 13.1 The structural elements of a workbench

Your editor doesn't need to be text-based or even single-paged. But it must be a subclass of `EditorPart`. This class contains the methods that communicate with the workbench.

At the far left of figure 13.2, the `GraphicalEditor` creates diagrams based on shapes and connections between them. (This is an involved topic and is the focus of appendix D.) In the center, the `TextEditor` and its superclasses contain only text. The `MultiEditor` contains a set of editors whose content can be communicated between them.

The `MultiPageEditorPart` is similar to the `MultiEditor` except that it holds a series of `Control`s that may or may not function as editors. Their only requirement is that they extend the `Control` class. The `FormEditor` is a particularly interesting and useful subclass of this editor; it creates a series of forms (`FormPages`) based on the content of a main editor.

You can build `TextEditors` and `MultiPageEditorParts` quickly by starting a Java plug-in project and selecting one of the editor-based templates. But if you want to create a `FormEditor`, you have to start from scratch.

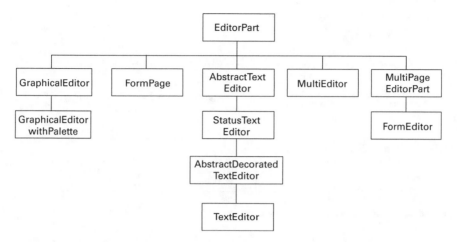

Figure 13.2 The EditorPart and its subclasses

13.1.2 *Displaying information with views*

Although a workbench's focal point is its editor, views are needed to organize the editor's content, examine its environment, and display its results. For example, the Eclipse Workbench contains views for navigating packages and directories, keeping track of tasks and errors, and displaying console output from the Java runtime. More than anything else, it's these views that have made Eclipse so popular as a development platform. Without them, it would be just a text editor with ties to the Java SDK.

It's simple to create views, particularly if you want panes that function like those in Eclipse. Figure 13.3 shows these different view types as ViewPart subclasses.

You can see what many of these classes look like by choosing the Window entry in the Eclipse menu and selecting Show View. The BookmarkNavigator looks like a specialized property view, and the ResourceNavigator view looks like the directory navigator that appears on the left-hand side of the Eclipse Workbench. The TaskList takes the same form as the corresponding window at the bottom of Eclipse. The PageBookView and its subclasses represent views with multiple pages.

You can also create views that look and behave completely differently than those in Eclipse. The ViewPart class is easy to extend; we'll create a complete view class as we progress through our RCP example.

Now that we've looked at the editors and views available, let's examine how these parts are integrated into the workbench. This capability is provided by perspectives.

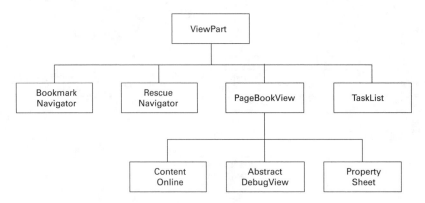

Figure 13.3 The ViewPart and its subclasses

13.1.3 Combining editors and views with perspectives

Just as SWT Composites use Layouts to arrange child components, workbenches select and organize editors and views with *perspectives*. For example, the Eclipse platform displays one set of editors and views in the Java perspective and another set when you choose the Debug perspective.

Although the majority of the work involved in RCP development deals with building and arranging editors and views, you also need to create a set of classes that provides the workbench's basic functionality. Next, we'll present these classes in the framework of building an RCP project.

13.2 RCP: Looking under the hood

The ability to create workbench editors and views isn't new. These classes have been around since Eclipse 2.1 and haven't changed significantly since the previous version. What makes the RCP so different is that, with very few classes, you can now create an entirely new, standalone application with these windows. In this section, we'll begin RCP development by creating an Eclipse project. Then, we'll create the three classes that make RCP operation possible.

13.2.1 Creating and configuring an RCP project

RCP development starts by creating an Eclipse plug-in project, but it's important to understand that the end result is *not* a plug-in. The ultimate goal is to build an application that functions independently from the Eclipse Workbench.

To make this point clear, we need to go into greater technical depth. The difference between a plug-in and an RCP application centers around a small kernel called the *platform runtime*. This is the first element of Eclipse to execute, and it functions by organizing plug-ins and controlling their operation. Unlike a plug-in, a workbench contains its own platform runtime, which means that it controls its own operation. You can execute a workbench like a regular Java application.

But even though a workbench operates differently than a plug-in, the process of creating one requires that you build a plug-in project. Let's get started.

> **NOTE** This chapter describes the process of building of a plug-in project, but doesn't provide the overall theory behind Eclipse plug-ins. For more information on the subject, we recommend *Eclipse in Action* by David Gallardo, Ed Burnette, and Rob McGovern (Manning, 2003).

Creating and configuring the RCPExample project

To begin, open Eclipse, select File->New->Plug-in Project, and click Next. Enter the name `com.swtjface.RCPExample`. Click Next to reach the Plug-in Content screen, and click Finish to create the project.

You don't need to modify the `RCPExamplePlugin` class that the wizard created, but the project's plugin.xml file must be updated to reflect the project's configuration. You can use the Plug-in Manifest Editor or change the file directly. Either way, listing 13.1 uses boldface to show the alterations you'll need to make.

Listing 13.1   plugin.xml

```xml
<?xml version="1.0" encoding="UTF-8"?>
<?eclipse version="3.0"?>
<plugin
  id="com.swtjface.RCPExample"
  name="RCPExample Plug-in"
  version="1.0.0"
  provider-name="SWTJFACE"
  class="com.swtjface.RCPExample.RCPExamplePlugin">

  <runtime>
    <library name="RCPExample.jar">
      <export name="*"/>
    </library>
  </runtime>

  <requires>
    <import plugin="org.eclipse.ui"/>
    <import plugin="org.eclipse.core.runtime"/>
    <import plugin="org.eclipse.ui.forms"/>
  </requires>
```

```
<extension point="org.eclipse.core.runtime.applications"
  id="ExampleApplication">
  <application>
    <run class="com.swtjface.RCPExample.ExampleApplication"/>
  </application>
</extension>
```
Tells workbench how to function as application

```
<extension point="org.eclipse.ui.views">
  <view
    id="com.swtjface.RCPExample.ExampleView"
    name="ExampleView"
    class="com.swtjface.RCPExample.ExampleView">
  </view>
</extension>
```
Matches view class with its identification information

```
<extension point="org.eclipse.ui.perspectives">
  <perspective
    id="com.swtjface.RCPExample.ExamplePerspective"
    name="ExamplePerspective"
    class="com.swtjface.RCPExample.ExamplePerspective"/>
  </extension>
</plugin>
```
Tells application what class will arrange its windows

13.2.2 *Building the application class*

The first extension in plugin.xml extends from org.eclipse.core.runtime.applications. This point makes it possible for workbenches to operate without Eclipse. Our example uses this extension to create a class called ExampleApplication. This class functions like the main() method of a regular Java application—it tells the runtime environment where it should begin processing.

Application classes need to implement the IPlatformRunnable interface in the org.eclipse.core.runtime package. This interface requires only one method, run(), which—like main()—may contain arguments that control the workbench's processing. In building an application class, you need to make sure that run() performs the application's top-level tasks. At the very least, it needs to create a Display object for the workbench and start the application's life cycle by invoking methods from PlatformUI.

Listing 13.2 shows the code for ExampleApplication; we recommend that you add it to the com.swtjface.RCPExample package. It won't compile yet, but the error will resolve once you add the ExampleAdvisor class.

Listing 13.2   ExampleApplication.java

```java
package com.swtjface.RCPExample;

import org.eclipse.core.runtime.IPlatformRunnable;
import org.eclipse.swt.widgets.Display;
import org.eclipse.ui.PlatformUI;
import org.eclipse.ui.application.WorkbenchAdvisor;

public class ExampleApplication implements IPlatformRunnable

{
  public Object run(Object args) throws Exception
  {
    WorkbenchAdvisor advisor = new ExampleAdvisor ();

    Display display = PlatformUI.createDisplay();


    int code = PlatformUI.createAndRunWorkbench(display, advisor);
    if (code == PlatformUI.RETURN_RESTART)
      return IPlatformRunnable.EXIT_RESTART;
    else
      return IPlatformRunnable.EXIT_OK;
  }
}
```

- **Associate WorkbenchAdvisor object with application** ← (points to `WorkbenchAdvisor advisor = new ExampleAdvisor ();`)
- **Create Display object for workbench** ← (points to `Display display = PlatformUI.createDisplay();`)
- **Start application** ← (points to `int code = PlatformUI.createAndRunWorkbench(display, advisor);`)

This application limits itself to the essentials—configuring a WorkbenchAdvisor, creating a Display, and starting the application. The createAndRunWorkbench() method continues functioning until you close the workbench. At that point, it returns a value that either restarts or exits the application. Beyond the methods shown here, the PlatformUI class also provides methods for obtaining IWorkbench and IPreferenceStore interfaces and lets you use isWorkbenchRunning() to check whether the workbench is running.

You might wonder how this small amount of code ties in with the editors, views, menus, and toolbars inside a workbench. This connection is provided by a very important class called WorkbenchAdvisor.

13.2.3 *Adding a WorkbenchAdvisor*

The WorkbenchAdvisor class is one of the RCP's main innovations. Despite its name, it performs a great deal of the work. This class concentrates the functions of controlling the workbench's operation and setting features of its appearance. To see how this works, let's examine the WorkbenchAdvisor class and the IWorkbenchWindowConfigurer interface that it accesses.

Controlling workbench operation with WorkbenchAdvisor methods

The WorkbenchAdvisor's methods let you perform processing tasks before each stage of your application's life cycle. For example, if you want to disable a feature during startup, you can do this in the preStartup() method. You can enable the feature afterward with postStartup(). The preWindowOpen() method is particularly important since it gives you a chance to configure the window's appearance before it's displayed in the workbench.

In addition to the life-cycle methods, the WorkbenchAdvisor also contains methods that let you configure aspects of the workbench. In our example, we'll invoke getInitialWindowPerspectiveId() to provide the ID of the perspective that we'll use. As you saw in plugin.xml, this is com.swtjface.RCPExample.ExamplePerspective.

Listing 13.3 shows how the WorkbenchAdvisor controls processing just before the window opens and how it lets you specify the workbench's perspective. We recommend that you add this class to the com.swtjface.RCPExample package.

> **Listing 13.3   ExampleAdvisor.java**

```java
package com.swtjface.RCPExample;

import org.eclipse.ui.application.WorkbenchAdvisor;
import org.eclipse.swt.graphics.Point;
import org.eclipse.ui.application.IWorkbenchWindowConfigurer;

public class ExampleAdvisor extends WorkbenchAdvisor
{
  public String getInitialWindowPerspectiveId()
  {
    return "com.swtjface.RCPExample.ExamplePerspective";
  }

  public void preWindowOpen(IWorkbenchWindowConfigurer configurer)
  {
    super.preWindowOpen(configurer);
    configurer.setTitle("RCPExample");
    configurer.setInitialSize(new Point(225, 250));
    configurer.setShowMenuBar(false);
    configurer.setShowStatusLine(false);
    configurer.setShowCoolBar(false);
  }
}
```

Set workbench's perspective according to its ID

Configure workbench's appearance

The WorkbenchAdvisor methods are simple, but controlling the workbench's appearance is performed with the IWorkbenchWindowConfigurer interface. In our example, the `WorkbenchAdvisor` obtains an instance of this with `preWindowOpen()` and uses its methods to set application parameters. This interface allows you to control the workbench's appearance; let's examine it more closely.

Configuring visuals with the IWorkbenchWindowConfigurer

Although your workbenches will necessarily look similar to Eclipse, the Rich Client Platform provides a great deal of design flexibility with the `IWorkbenchWindowConfigurer`. Our example `WorkbenchAdvisor` used a few of these to configure the application's title, size, menu bar, status line, and coolbar, but many more are available. Table 13.1 doesn't provide a complete account, but it lists those that directly affect the appearance of the workbench.

Table 13.1 Workbench configuration methods of the `IWorkbenchWindowConfigurer`

Method	Function
`addEditorAreaTransfer(Transfer)`	Provides a `Transfer` object for editor drag and drop
`configureEditorAreaDropListener` `(DropTargetListener)`	Sets the `DropTargetListener` needed to receive drag-and-drop events
`createCoolBarControl(Composite)`	Specifies the control to receive `CoolBar` entries
`createMenuBar()`	Creates a `Menu` within the workbench
`createPageComposite(Composite)`	Sets the container for the editors and views
`createStatusLineControl(Composite)`	Specifies the control to provide status-line information
`setInitialSize(Point)`	Provides the workbench's initial size
`setShellStyle(int)`	Specifies style bits for the workbench's `Shell` object
`setShowCoolBar(boolean)`	Tells the workbench if it should display a `CoolBar`
`setShowMenuBar(boolean)`	Tells the workbench if it should display a `Menu`
`setShowPerspectiveBar(boolean)`	Tells the workbench if it should display a bar to select different workbench perspectives
`setShowStatusLine(boolean show)`	Tells the workbench if it should display a status line
`setTitle(String title)`	Specifies a title for the workbench application

Many of these methods are similar to those found in SWT and JFace containers, but a few deserve additional attention. The first two, `addEditorAreaTransfer()` and `configureEditorAreaDropListener()`, provide drag-and-drop capability between editors and views, which enables you to cut and paste between windows. It's interesting that the `createXYZ(Composite)` methods let you create custom GUI components, but `setXYZ(true)` creates a default control provided by the application.

Now that we've discussed the workbench's fundamental classes and top-level appearance, we need to build a perspective to arrange its internal structure.

13.3 Adding views and perspectives

By default, workbenches contain editors to access, manipulate, and save file content. But the process of adding file handling to an RCP application is long and involved. To keep our example as simple as possible, we'll create a single view. In this section, we'll create the class for this view and the perspective needed to place it inside the workbench.

> **NOTE** If you want to see a full editor example involving file access and data persistence, skip ahead to appendix D.

13.3.1 Building views

Essentially, a view is an editor without data-entry or file operations. Views provide user interaction, but none of the user's actions need to be saved. Further, views activate immediately, without waiting for the user to select an appropriate file.

Rather than use a preconfigured class like `ResourceNavigator`, our custom view extends from `ViewPart`. You need only one method to configure its appearance and operation: `createPartControl(Composite)`. The `Composite` argument of this method serves as the view's top-level container. Later, when we discuss the child components provided by Eclipse Forms, we'll add a series of widgets to this parent `Composite`.

For now, the `ExampleView` class provides empty methods for `createPartControl(Composite)` and `setFocus()`. The workbench invokes this second method when the user clicks on the view; you can add code to customize how the view operates when it receives focus.

Our example, shown in listing 13.4, performs only the view's default operation. We recommend that you add this class to the `com.swtjface.RCPExample` package.

Listing 13.4   ExampleView.java

```
package com.swtjface.RCPExample;

import org.eclipse.swt.widgets.Composite;
import org.eclipse.ui.part.ViewPart;

public class ExampleView extends ViewPart
{
```

```
    public void createPartControl(Composite parent)
    {
    }

    public void setFocus()
    {
    }
}
```

Now that we have a basic shell for our view, we need to place it inside the workbench. For this, we'll need to create a perspective.

13.3.2 *Arranging workbench windows with a perspective*

The plugin.xml file holds a separate extension for the perspective. This tells the workbench what editors and views will be used and where they should be placed. It also specifies the interface that our class will implement: IPerspectiveFactory.

By itself, the IPerspectiveFactory interface is easy to understand. It obtains an IPageLayout object and configures this to provide the workbench's appearance. Its only method is createInitialLayout(IPageLayout), which makes it simple to code.

Configuring the IPageLayout is more involved. By default, the layout assumes the presence of a single editor with no views. In our example, we need to make the editor invisible and add our ExampleView to the IPageLayout.

Table 13.2 lists a number of IPageLayout methods that make this possible. Other methods add folders, placeholders, and wizard shortcuts, but those in the table are sufficient for most workbenches.

Table 13.2 Configuration methods of the IPageLayout class

Method	Function
addShowViewShortcut(String)	Creates a Window->Show View option in the menu
addView(String, int, float, String)	Adds a view to the workbench with the given ID at the specified position and dimensional ratio
GetEditorArea()	Returns the ID of the workbench's editor
isFixed()	Returns whether the layout is changeable
setEditorAreaVisible(boolean)	Specifies whether the editor will be displayed
setFixed()	Specifies whether the layout is fixed in form

The addView() method is the most crucial method in the IPageLayout interface, and it's important to understand how it works. Its four arguments are as follows:

- *viewID*—A String (specified in plugin.xml) that identifies the view.

- *relationship*—An int that specifies where the view should be placed relative to a reference. This can be IPageLayout.TOP, IPageLayout.BOTTOM, IPageLayout.RIGHT, or IPageLayout.LEFT.

- *ratio*—A float that describes what percentage of the reference should be taken up by the view.

- *refID*—A String that identifies the reference window.

An editor is automatically created in a workbench, so we'll use that as our reference. But because we haven't mentioned an editor in plugin.xml, we'll use getEditorArea() to obtain our refID. Further, to ensure that the view takes up the entire workbench area, our example invokes setEditorAreaVisible(false).

Listing 13.5 presents the code for the example perspective. We recommend that you add it to the com.swtjface.RCPExample package.

Listing 13.5 ExamplePerspective.java

```
package com.swtjface.RCPExample;

import org.eclipse.ui.*;

public class ExamplePerspective implements IPerspectiveFactory
{
  public void createInitialLayout(IPageLayout layout)
  {
    String editor = layout.getEditorArea();
    layout.addView("RCPExample.ExampleView",
      IPageLayout.RIGHT, 0f, editor);
    layout.setEditorAreaVisible(false);
    layout.setFixed(true);
  }
}
```

Since the perspective makes the editor invisible, the relationship and ratio arguments in addView() aren't important. The view occupies the entire workbench. To see this, you need to execute the example; but because our example is an application (not a plug-in), we need to look into a separate process.

13.3.3 *Executing an RCP application*

Once we're finished with the example, you'll see how to compile it into a standalone Java application. But if you only want to check to make sure that it works, you can run it inside of Eclipse. This process consists of these steps:

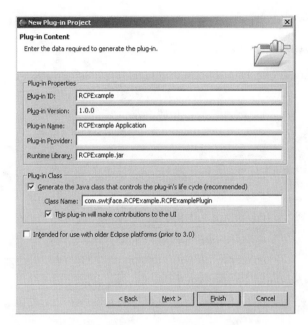

Figure 13.4
Eclipse dialog to configure
application execution

1 In the Eclipse main menu, choose the Run option under the Run menu item.

2 In the left pane, select the Run-time Workbench option, and click the New button. A New_Configuration option appears; the window looks like that in figure 13.4.

3 At the top, enter **RCPExample** as the workbench name. You can leave the Workspace Location alone, but you need to select `com.swtjface.RCPExample.ExampleApplication` in the Program To Run group.

4 Click the Plug-ins tab, and select the Choose Plug-ins And Fragments To Launch From The List radio button. Click Deselect All.

5 Select *only* the com.swtjface.RCPExample checkbox under Workspace Plug-ins. Click Add Required Plug-ins, click Apply, and then click Run.

The resulting workbench should look like that shown in figure 13.5. At present, it doesn't look exciting. But that will change once we add the new containers and components provided by the Eclipse Forms toolset.

13.3.4 *Reviewing the RCP process*

Before you learn about the new and exciting components provided by Eclipse Forms, it will be helpful to look at the classes you've created and how they

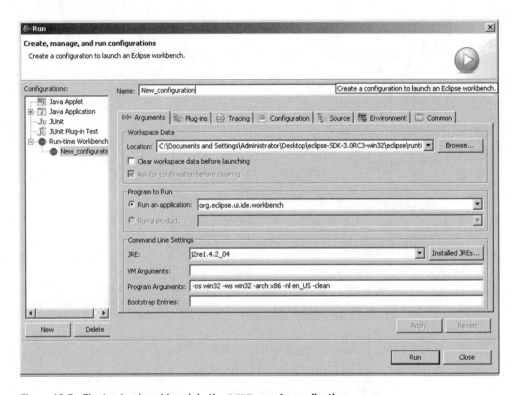

Figure 13.5   The top-level workbench in the RCPExample application

interact. This will clarify the structure of the RCP and make its development process clearer.

So far, we've provided the code for five important files:

- *ExampleApplication.java*—Starts initial execution, and points to the ID of
  the application's WorkbenchAdvisor
- *ExampleAdvisor.java*—Provides overall visual configuration of the workbench, and identifies its perspective according to its ID
- *ExamplePerspective.java*—Arranges the panes within the workbench, and
  identifies each (in our case, only the view) by its ID
- *ExampleView.java*—Provides the behavior and appearance of the window
  that makes up the workbench
- *plugin.xml*—Matches each of the classes mentioned here to a specific ID

As you can see, these files progress from the top-level application execution to the low-level configuration of an individual window. By understanding each step of the development process, you'll be better able to improve and debug your future RCP applications. But to finish the ExampleRCP project, we need to present the new components contained in the Eclipse Forms toolset.

13.4 Populating forms with Eclipse Forms widgets

Eclipse's Plug-in Manifest Editor used to bother us. It has hyperlinks, expandable sections, and a cleaner, more professional appearance than anything we could build with SWT/JFace. But after discovering the Eclipse Forms toolset, we can add these features to our applications and make them look just as sharp. The goal of this section is to show you how to do this.

We'll start by examining the FormToolkit class that creates new GUI components. Then, we'll see what Composites the Eclipse Forms toolset has to offer and add a number of them to the ExampleView class. Finally, we'll examine the Hyperlink class and the capability of adding text-based events.

13.4.1 Using FormToolkit and the Eclipse Forms containers

In SWT/JFace, you create widgets and add them to a parent Composite. Using Eclipse Forms, you start with a FormToolkit object and create components by invoking its methods. To show you what components are available, we'll divide these methods into two categories: those that create regular SWT widgets and those that create Eclipse Forms widgets.

Adding SWT components with the FormToolkit

Table 13.3 lists the FormToolkit methods that create SWT widgets inside a form. In each case, the method returns an instance of the desired component. (Refer to chapters 3 and 5 if any of these look unfamiliar.)

Table 13.3 FormToolkit methods for creating SWT widgets

Method	Function
createButton(Composite, String, int)	Returns a Button with the given text and style
createComposite(Composite)	Returns a Composite object
createComposite(Composite, int)	Returns a Composite object with the given style
createLabel(Composite, String)	Returns a Label with the given text

continued on next page

Table 13.3   `FormToolkit` methods for creating SWT widgets *(continued)*

Method	Function
`createLabel(Composite, String, int)`	Returns a `Label` with the given text and style
`createSeparator(Composite, int)`	Returns a `Separator` with the given style
`createTable(Composite, int)`	Returns a `Table` with the given style
`createText(Composite, String)`	Returns a `Text` object with the given text
`createText(Composite, String, int)`	Returns a `Text` object with the given text and style
`createTree(Composite, int)`	Returns a `Tree` with the given style

It's important to remember that many of these `Controls` need to be adapted for insertion into the form. This limits the component's colors to those used in the form and provides keyboard access and tracking. The `FormToolkit`'s `adapt()` method makes this possible.

Alternatively, you can use the `Controls` provided by the Eclipse Forms toolkit. First we'll present the new `Composite` classes provided by Eclipse Forms, and then we'll update the `ExampleView` class with them.

Understanding Eclipse Forms Composites

When you're building form-based applications, you need more capabilities than those provided by regular SWT `Composites`. For this reason, Eclipse Forms provides a series of container classes that simplify form development. These are listed in table 13.4.

Table 13.4   `FormToolkit` methods for creating Eclipse Forms `composites`

Method	Function
`createCompositeSeparator(Composite)`	Returns a `Composite` to serve as a separator
`createExpandableComposite(Composite, int)`	Creates an `ExplandableComposite` object
`createForm(Composite)`	Creates a `Form` object in the `Composite`
`createFormText(Composite, boolean)`	Returns a `FormText`, and sets HTML reading
`createPageBook(Composite, int)`	Returns a `ScrolledPageBook` `Composite`
`createScrolledForm(Composite)`	Returns a `ScrolledForm` `Composite`
`createSection(Composite, int)`	Returns a `Section` `Composite`

We'll discuss the `Form`, `FormText`, and `ExpandableComposite` classes here. `Forms` serve as the top-level containers in a form-based application, but `FormText` `Composites` are more interesting. Not only can you can configure them for word wrapping, but they also can display text marked with HTML.

`ExpandableComposites` make it possible to expand and collapse regions of a GUI by clicking on toggle signs called `Twisties`. These regions are represented by `Composites` that are added to the `ExpandableComposite` with its `setClient()` method. This is useful for forms with optional sections that need to save space.

Listing 13.6 creates these components inside the `createPartControl()` method of the `ExampleView` class. We recommend that you update the `Example-View` with this code.

Listing 13.6   ExampleView.java (updated)

```
package com.swtjface.RCPExample;

import org.eclipse.swt.widgets.*;
import org.eclipse.ui.forms.widgets.*;
import org.eclipse.ui.part.ViewPart;

public class ExampleView extends ViewPart
{
  public void createPartControl(Composite parent)
  {
   FormToolkit kit = new FormToolkit(parent.getDisplay());
    Form form = kit.createForm(parent);
    ColumnLayout layout = new ColumnLayout();
    form.getBody().setLayout(layout);

    ExpandableComposite exComp = kit.createExpandableComposite
      (form.getBody(), ExpandableComposite.TWISTIE);
    exComp.setText("The Eclipse Forms toolset is:");
    exComp.setExpanded(true);

    FormText ft = kit.createFormText(exComp, true);
    exComp.setClient(ft);
    String html = "<form><li>Useful</li><li>Powerful</li>" +
      "<li>Simple</li></form>";
    ft.setText(html, true, false);
  }

  public void setFocus()
  {
  }
}
```

❶ Use FormToolkit to create form containers

Configure ExpandableComposite for display ❷

❸ Configure FormText for display

❶ You need to call the `Form.setBody()` method to associate a layout with the container. This method provides the `Form`'s underlying `Composite`.

❷ The `ExpandableContainer.TWISTIE` style creates a triangle component that controls the state of the container. The `setClient(ft)` method tells it to expand and collapse the `FormText`, and `setExpanded(true)` tells the container that its initial state should be expanded.

❸ When you're using `FormText` objects to display HTML, you need to set the second argument of `setText()` to `true`. Also, make sure the HTML starts with `<form>` and ends with `</form>`.

Figure 13.6 shows how these containers work together. It's important to note that, because we chose a `Form` container, the background is white and the text takes the font and size shown.

Figure 13.6
The `ExampleView` with an expandable container and HTML display

Just as with SWT `Composites`, you can control how child components are arranged with layouts. You can still use the `Layout` classes from chapter 6, and you can also use two subclasses provided by Eclipse Forms: `ColumnLayout` and `TableWrapLayout`. The first organizes widgets into vertical columns and tries to keep children at their preferred size. The second produces a table format similar to that used in HTML, where cells expand to provide word-wrapping of text.

Now that we've discussed Eclipse Forms `Composites` and how they arrange children, let's look into the newest child component available for use: the `Hyperlink`.

13.4.2 *Firing text-based events with Hyperlinks*

Regular hyperlinks function by causing a web browser to jump to a new URL, but Eclipse Forms `Hyperlinks` provide more flexibility. In essence, they are `Labels` that generate new events called `HyperlinkEvents`. By creating appropriate event-handling routines, you can use these events to perform whatever processing you choose.

Components can respond to HyperlinkEvents with addHyperlinkListener().
Table 13.5 lists the methods needed to implement the HyperlinkListener interface and those contained in the HyperlinkEvent class.

**Table 13.5 Methods to implement the HyperlinkListener interface and contained in the Hyper-
linkEvent class**

Method	Function
IHyperlinkListener.linkActivated()	Performs processing if the link is clicked
IHyperlinkListener.linkEntered()	Performs processing if the mouse hovers over the link
IHyperlinkListener.linkExited()	Performs processing if the mouse leaves the link
HyperlinkEvent.getHref()	Returns the Object specified with setHref()
HyperlinkEvent.getLabel()	Returns the text of the Hyperlink that fired the event
HyperlinkEvent.getStateMask()	Returns the modifier keys pressed during activation

When you click the link, the LinkActivated() method fires. The other event-
handling methods, LinkEntered() and LinkExited(), work similarly to the Mouse-
Entered() and MouseExited() methods discussed in chapter 4. Since most forms
only require LinkActivated(), we recommend creating a HyperlinkAdapter.

HTML hyperlinks use an HREF attribute to tell the web browser which URL to
locate upon activation. Eclipse Forms Hyperlinks have setHref() and getHref()
methods, but they serve a different purpose. In this case, setHref() stores an
Object for use during processing.

As shown, you can access this Object with the HyperlinkEvent's getHref()
method. You can also access the Hyperlink's text with getLabel() and determine
which modifier keys were pressed with getStateMask().

The following snippet shows how to create a Hyperlink with a FormToolkit
object (ft), and the process of setting and retrieving data using setHref() and
getHref(). In this case, clicking the Hyperlink changes its text to the String
assigned with setHref():

```
final Hyperlink hl = ft.createHyperlink(form.getBody(), "Click",
  SWT.NULL);
hl.setHref("http://www.eclipse.org/");
hl.addHyperlinkListener(new HyperlinkAdapter()
{
  public void linkActivated(HyperlinkEvent e)
  {
```

```
    hl.setText((String)e.getHref());
    }
  });
```

By default, `Hyperlinks` are displayed in black without an underline. You can change these parameters with the `Hyperlink`'s `setUnderline(boolean)` method and the `Control`'s `setForeground(Color)` method. You can also standardize your `Hyperlinks`' appearance throughout your form by obtaining a `HyperlinkGroup` with the `FormToolkit`'s `getHyperlinkGroup()` method and adding each link to the group.

The `HyperlinkGroup` object's methods are listed in table 13.6.

Table 13.6 `HyperlinkGroup` methods for controlling `Hyperlink` appearance

Method	Function
`add(Hyperlink)`	Performs processing if the link is clicked
`getLastActivated()`	Returns the most recently clicked `Hyperlink`
`setBackground(Color)`	Sets the foreground color of the group's `Hyperlinks`
`setForeground(Color)`	Sets the foreground color of the group's `Hyperlinks`
`setHyperlinkUnderlineMode(int)`	Determines whether the links should be underlined

The code in bold in listing 13.7 updates the `ExampleView`'s `createPartControl()` method to provide a `Button` and a series of `Hyperlinks`. When activated, these links update the `Button` to display the text stored by their `setHref()` methods.

Listing 13.7   ExampleView.java (completed)

```java
package com.swtjface.RCPExample;

import org.eclipse.swt.SWT;
import org.eclipse.swt.widgets.*;
import org.eclipse.ui.forms.*;
import org.eclipse.ui.forms.events.HyperlinkAdapter;
import org.eclipse.ui.forms.events.HyperlinkEvent;
import org.eclipse.ui.forms.widgets.*;
import org.eclipse.ui.part.ViewPart;

public class ExampleView extends ViewPart
{
  public void createPartControl(Composite parent)
  {
    FormToolkit kit = new FormToolkit(parent.getDisplay());
    Form form = kit.createForm(parent);
    ColumnLayout layout = new ColumnLayout();
    form.getBody().setLayout(layout);
```

```
ExpandableComposite exComp = kit.createExpandableComposite
   (form.getBody(), ExpandableComposite.TWISTIE);
exComp.setText("The Eclipse Forms toolset is:");
exComp.setExpanded(true);

FormText ft = kit.createFormText(exComp, true);                      Add
exComp.setClient(ft);                                             separator
String html = "<form><li>Useful</li><li>Powerful</li>" +         and button
   "<li>Simple</li></form>";
ft.setText(html, true, false);

Label sep = kit.createSeparator(form.getBody(), SWT.HORIZONTAL);
final Button button = kit.createButton(form.getBody(),
   "Favorite color?", SWT.NULL);

HyperlinkGroup hg = kit.getHyperlinkGroup();
hg.setHyperlinkUnderlineMode(HyperlinkSettings.UNDERLINE_HOVER);
hg.setForeground(parent.getDisplay().getSystemColor
   (SWT.COLOR_RED));

String[] cnames = {"red", "green", "yellow", "blue"};
Hyperlink[] hl = new Hyperlink[4];
String name;                                       Create HyperlinkGroup;
for (int i=0; i<4; i++)                              standardize links'
{                                                       appearance
   name = "My favorite color is "+cnames[i]+".";
   hl[i] = kit.createHyperlink(form.getBody(), name, SWT.NULL);
   hg.add(hl[i]);

                                                   Add Hyperlinks to form
                                                   and HyperlinkGroups


   hl[i].setHref(cnames[i]);                       Store color name
   hl[i].addHyperlinkListener(new HyperlinkAdapter()   to Hyperlink
   {
      public void linkActivated(HyperlinkEvent e)
      {
         button.setText("My favorite color is "       Retrieve color
            + (String)e.getHref() + ".");              name; update
         button.redraw();                             button text
      }
   });
   }
}

public void setFocus()
{
}
}
```

Figure 13.7
The completed `ExampleView`, with
expandable containers and hyperlinks

Figure 13.7 shows the result of the completed `ExampleView`.

Now that we've completed our discussion of creating workbenches with the Rich Client Platform, let's take advantage of its main benefit: standalone application development. So far, we've created an Eclipse plug-in that can be executed as an application, but we need to compile it into a form that can be run with a regular Java compiler.

13.5 *Building a standalone RCP application*

Having finished the workbench plug-in, it's time to turn it into a regular Java application. This straightforward process requires three steps:

1   Export the RCPExample project to a directory.

2   Add the necessary plug-ins to the exported directory.

3   Enter the command to launch the application.

We'll start with step 1, which involves creating a separate directory to hold the workbench application and its support files.

13.5.1 *Exporting RCPExample to an application directory*

Because Eclipse does most of the work, the first task is simple. Follow these steps:

1   To create the directory, go to the Eclipse Workbench and right-click the project name, `com.swtjface.RCPExample`. Choose the Export option in the context menu.

2   Select the Deployable plug-ins and fragments option, and click Next.

3   When the Export Plug-ins and Fragments dialog appears, make sure that the `com.swtjface.RCPExample` checkbox is the only one selected.

4 Under Export Options, choose to deploy the plug-in as a directory structure.

5 Enter a path name for the directory. In the dialog shown in figure 13.8, we've chosen to export the plug-in to C:\RCPExample. Click Finish.

Figure 13.8
The dialog settings for exporting `com.swtjface.RCPExample` **to a directory**

Look through the directory that you've created. You should see a folder called plugins and, immediately inside that, one called RCPExample_1.0.0. There, you should find plugin.xml and RCPExample.jar. You may not think these two files are sufficient for the application, and you're right. Next, we'll add plug-ins to provide the workbench's complete functionality.

13.5.2 *Adding plug-ins to the application directory*

Just as you have to add classpath variables to make an Eclipse-based application run, you need to add plug-ins to execute a workbench application. Unfortunately, Eclipse won't do this for you. So, you need to go through your $ECLIPSE/ plugins folder and copy the following directories to the plugins folder in your application directory:

- org.eclipse.core.expressions_x.y.z
- org.eclipse.core.runtime_x.y.z
- org.eclipse.jface_x.y.z
- org.eclipse.help_x.y.z
- org.eclipse.osgi_x.y.z
- org.eclipse.swt_x.y.z
- org.eclipse.ui.forms_x.y.z
- org.eclipse.ui.workbench_x.y.z
- org.eclipse.ui_x.y.z
- org.eclipse.update.configurator_x.y.z

In addition, you need to add the specific SWT plug-in(s) needed for your operating system and windowing system. In Windows, this is org.eclipse.swt.win32_x.y.z; for Linux GTK, the plug-in is org.eclipse.swt.gtk_x.y.z. Just to be safe, we recommend copying every plug-in that contains *org.eclipse.swt* in its title.

Finally, you need to add the file that lets you execute the application. Find startup.jar in the top-level Eclipse directory ($ECLIPSE), and copy it to your top-level application directory. On our Windows system, this directory is C:\RCPExample.

Once you're finished with this step, you're ready to execute the workbench. In the next section, we'll show you how this is done.

13.5.3 *Executing the application*

In the application directory, execute the following command:

```
java -cp startup.jar org.eclipse.core.launcher.Main –application
RCPExample.ExampleApplication
```

This should launch the view. If it doesn't, find the log file in the configuration directory in your application directory; this file will describe any errors that arose in processing the application.

But if the form appears, congratulations! You've successfully used the Rich Client Platform to build a standalone workbench. This capability will enable you to build powerful, extensible applications based on the Eclipse framework. And who knows? Maybe future developers will devote their time to building plug-ins for your workbench.

13.6 *Summary*

The Rich Client Platform builds on what we've discussed in SWT and JFace and provides a simple means of building workbenches with editors and views. As you've seen, these can be exported as standalone applications. Similarly, the Eclipse Forms toolset augments the widgets and containers from SWT/JFace to enable rapid development of form-based interfaces.

It seems that each passing month brings a new and incredible capability involving SWT/JFace. Eclipse.org has just released a new version of its Visual Editor that lets you build SWT GUIs in a graphical development environment (think MS Visual Studio). The open-source GCJ tool can turn SWT/JFace code into native executables, and Sun's Java Web Start can deploy SWT/JFace applications across the Internet.

Learning SWT/JFace can be an exciting process, but the new applications are more exciting still. What will happen when the 3-D programming language, OpenGL, merges with the rest of the SWT toolset? Will SWT/JFace become executable in browsers and revolutionize applets in the same way that it's revolutionized desktop development? What about J2EE?

One thing's for certain: The SWT/JFace toolkit is becoming more important as Eclipse gains in capability and popularity. Those familiar with its development will have an advantage as new technologies become available. We hope that this book has provided you with a firm foundation on which to build new and more exciting graphical applications.

We, the authors, would like to thank you for sharing your time with us. If you'd like to contact us for any reason, you can reach us through our publisher at www.manning.com.

Creating projects with SWT/JFace

Before you can begin coding with SWT and JFace, you need to prepare the Eclipse development environment to include the two libraries. This appendix focuses on the steps needed to ensure that your GUI code will compile and execute properly.

We hold Eclipse in the highest esteem, but if you intend to market your own SWT/JFace applications, you'll need to know how to build GUIs that can run without the Workbench. Therefore, this appendix is divided into two parts. The first outlines the steps needed to set up an SWT/JFace project in Eclipse. The second shows how to accomplish the same purpose using the Java SDK (Java, Javac, and so on).

A.1 *Eclipse-based SWT/JFace development*

All the code samples in this book are part of one large project, `WidgetWindow`, and each chapter adds classes in a separate package. Therefore, for this book, you need to perform the process outlined here only *once*.

A.1.1 *SWT and JFace projects in Windows*

In writing this book, we have assumed that you're already familiar with Eclipse. But a brief review of creating projects will be helpful if you are out of practice. In particular, this section outlines the process of setting up the `WidgetWindow` project in Eclipse. For a full description of Eclipse projects, we recommend *Eclipse in Action* by David Gallardo, Ed Burnette, and Robert McGovern (Manning, 2003).

The steps for setting up an SWT/JFace Eclipse project in Windows are listed in table A.1.

Table A.1 Preparing an SWT/JFace application in Eclipse for Windows

	Goal	Procedure
1	Acquire the necessary software tools.	1. If it isn't already available, download the Java SDK (ver. 1.2.2 or later) from http://java.sun.com. Install the SDK in your operating system. 2. Download the Eclipse SDK (ver. 2.0 or later) from Eclipse.org at www.eclipse.org/downloads/index.php. No installation is necessary. 3. If you're interested, download the source code for SWT from Eclipse.org by scrolling down the same page in the Eclipse.org site.

continued on next page

Table A.1   Preparing an SWT/JFace application in Eclipse for Windows *(continued)*

	Goal	Procedure
2	Create the WidgetWindow project.	1. Start the Eclipse IDE, click the File option in the main menu, and select New->Project from the drop-down menus that appear. 2. In the first page of the New Project Wizard, click Java in the left pane and Java Project in the right pane. Click Next. 3. Enter WidgetWindow as the project name and leave the default option checked. Click Finish. Doing so creates a WidgetWindow project and places it in the WidgetWindow directory. 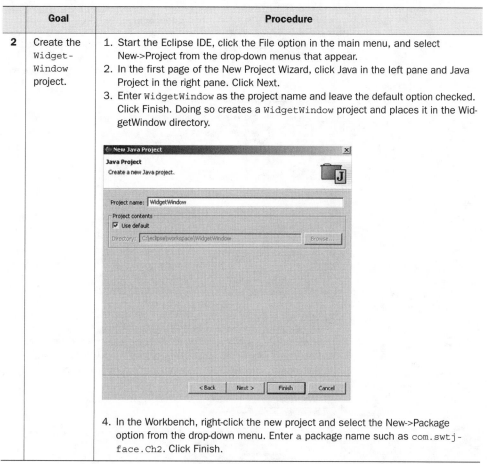 4. In the Workbench, right-click the new project and select the New->Package option from the drop-down menu. Enter a package name such as com.swtj-face.Ch2. Click Finish.

continued on next page

Table A.1 Preparing an SWT/JFace application in Eclipse for Windows *(continued)*

	Goal	Procedure
3	Start the process of creating classpath variables for the SWT/JFace libraries.	1. Right-click the `WidgetWindow` project and choose Properties, the final option in the pull-down menu. Click the Java Build Path option at left on the screen. You'll now tell the Java compiler where to find the necessary SWT/JFace files. 2. Click the Libraries tab just below the Java Build Path title. Click the Add Variable button. These variables will represent the libraries (*.jar) you need for compilation. In the New Variable Classpath Entry dialog, click the Configure Variables button. 3. When the Preferences window appears, click New. Enter `SWT_LIB` as the variable name, and click File to search for its corresponding library. 4. In the dialog that appears, search the directory to find $ECLIPSE/plugins/ org.eclipse.swt.win32_x.y.z/ws/win32/swt.jar. Select this file and click Open. Click OK in the New Variable Entry dialog, and the SWT_LIB variable will join the list of classpath variables.

continued on next page

Table A.1 Preparing an SWT/JFace application in Eclipse for Windows *(continued)*

	Goal	Procedure
4	Create variables for the libraries needed for JFace.	1. Use the procedure described previously to create a variable named JFACE_LIB for the jface.jar (or jface_new.jar) file at $ECLIPSE/plugins/ org.eclipse.jface_x.y.z/. 2. Create a variable named BOOT_LIB for the runtime.jar file located at $ECLIPSE/ plugins/org.eclipse.core.boot_x.y.z/. 3. Create a variable named RUNTIME_LIB for the runtime.jar file located at $ECLIPSE/plugins/org.eclipse.core.runtime_x.y.z/. 4. Create a variable named WORKBENCH_LIB for the workbench.jar (or workbench_new.jar) file at $ECLIPSE/plugins/org.eclipse.ui.workbench_x.y.z/. 5. Click OK in the Preferences window.

5	Add these variables to the Widget-Window project.	1. In the Workbench, right-click on the WidgetWindow project, and select the Properties option.
		2. Select the Java Build Path option in the left pane, and click the Libraries tab on the right pane.
		3. Click the Add Variable button. In the New Variable Classpath Entry box, select the JFACE_LIB, BOOT_LIB, RUNTIME_LIB, and WORKBENCH_LIB variables. Click OK after each.
		4. Use the procedure described previously to create a variable named JFACE_LIB for the jface.jar (or jface_new.jar) file at $ECLIPSE\plugin\org.eclipse.jface_x.y.z\.
		5. Create a variable named BOOT_LIB for the runtime.jar file located at $ECLIPSE\plugins\org.eclipse.core.boot_x.y.z\.
		6. Create a variable named RUNTIME_LIB for the runtime.jar file located at $ECLIPSE\plugins\org.eclipse.core.runtime_x.y.z\.
		7. Create a variable named WORKBENCH_LIB for the workbench.jar (or workbench_new.jar) file at $ECLIPSE\plugins\org.eclipse.ui.workbench_x.y.z\.
		8. Click OK in the Preferences window.
		
		Package Explorer
		WidgetWindow
		  JRE System Library [j2re1.4.2_0...
		  JFACE_LIB - C:\newestEclipse\ec...
		  RUNTIME_LIB - C:\newestEclipse...
		  SWT_LIB - C:\newestEclipse\eclip...
		  WORKBENCH_LIB - C:\newestEcl...
		  BOOT_LIB - C:\newestEclipse\ecl...

continued on next page

Table A.1   Preparing an SWT/JFace application in Eclipse for Windows *(continued)*

	Goal	Procedure
6	Add the native graphics library to the project.	1. To enable communication between SWT/JFace commands and the operating system calls, you need to make the SWT native graphics file available. It's called swt-win-*nnnn*.dll, and it's located at $ECLIPSE/plugins/ org.eclipse.swt.win32_x.y.z/os/win32/x86. 2. Once you've found the graphics library, you need to make sure the application launcher can use it. The documentation lists a number of ways to do this, but we've found that adding a copy to the $JAVA/jre/bin directory works best. Other methods, which can be less reliable, include the following: Option 1: Copy and paste these files directly in the `WidgetWindow` project. Option 2: Include the native library in any directory pointed to by the `java.library.path` variable. This variable, among others, can be seen by clicking Help->About Eclipse Platform->Configuration Details. Option 3: Go to Control Panel->System->Advanced->Environmental Variables and update the `PATH` variable with the directory containing the library file.

A.1.2   *SWT and JFace projects in *nix*

Table A.2 shows the steps needed to prepare a project to use the SWT/JFace toolset. Although they're geared for Linux and GTK, the procedures should be similar for any *nix platform and windowing system.

Table A.2   Preparing an SWT/JFace application in Eclipse for *nix

	Goal	Procedure
1	Acquire the necessary software tools.	1. If it isn't already available, download the Java SDK (ver. 1.2.2 or later) from http://java.sun.com. Install the SDK in your operating system. 2. Download the Eclipse SDK (ver. 2.0 or later) from Eclipse.org at www.eclipse.org/downloads/index.php. 3. Unzip the file. The resulting directory will be called $ECLIPSE. 4. If you're interested, download the source code for SWT from Eclipse.org by scrolling down the same page in the Eclipse.org site.

continued on next page

Table A.2   Preparing an SWT/JFace application in Eclipse for *nix *(continued)*

	Goal	Procedure
2	Create the `WidgetWind ow` project.	1. Start the Eclipse IDE, click the File option in the main menu, and select New->Project from the drop-down menus that appear. 2. In the first page of the New Project Wizard, click Java in the left pane and Java Project in the right pane. Click Next. 3. Enter `WidgetWindow` as the project name and leave the default options checked. Click Finish. Eclipse will create a `WidgetWindow` project and add it to the WidgetWindow directory. 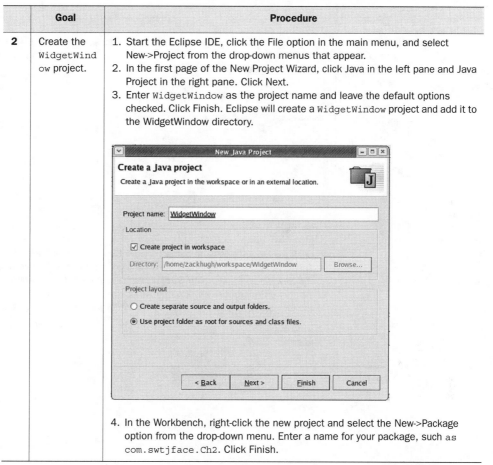 4. In the Workbench, right-click the new project and select the New->Package option from the drop-down menu. Enter a name for your package, such as `com.swtjface.Ch2`. Click Finish.

continued on next page

Table A.2   Preparing an SWT/JFace application in Eclipse for *nix *(continued)*

	Goal	Procedure
3	Start the process of creating classpath variables for the SWT/JFace libraries.	1. Right-click the `WidgetWindow` project and choose Properties. Click the Java Build Path option at the left of the screen. You'll now tell the Java compiler where to find the necessary SWT/JFace files. 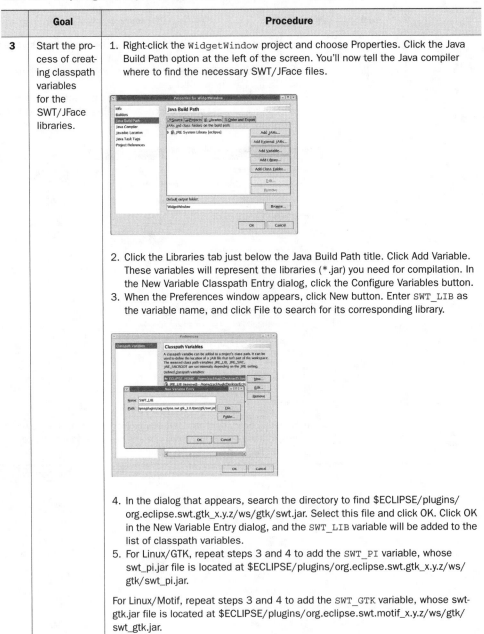 2. Click the Libraries tab just below the Java Build Path title. Click Add Variable. These variables will represent the libraries (*.jar) you need for compilation. In the New Variable Classpath Entry dialog, click the Configure Variables button. 3. When the Preferences window appears, click New button. Enter `SWT_LIB` as the variable name, and click File to search for its corresponding library. 4. In the dialog that appears, search the directory to find $ECLIPSE/plugins/ org.eclipse.swt.gtk_x.y.z/ws/gtk/swt.jar. Select this file and click OK. Click OK in the New Variable Entry dialog, and the `SWT_LIB` variable will be added to the list of classpath variables. 5. For Linux/GTK, repeat steps 3 and 4 to add the `SWT_PI` variable, whose swt_pi.jar file is located at $ECLIPSE/plugins/org.eclipse.swt.gtk_x.y.z/ws/ gtk/swt_pi.jar. For Linux/Motif, repeat steps 3 and 4 to add the `SWT_GTK` variable, whose swt-gtk.jar file is located at $ECLIPSE/plugins/org.eclipse.swt.motif_x.y.z/ws/gtk/ swt_gtk.jar.

continued on next page

Table A.2 Preparing an SWT/JFace application in Eclipse for *nix *(continued)*

	Goal	Procedure
4	Create additional variables for the libraries needed for JFace.	1. Use the procedure described earlier to create a variable named JFACE_LIB for the jface.jar (or jface_new.jar) file at $ECLIPSE/plugins/org.eclipse.jface_x.y.z/. 2. Create a variable named BOOT_LIB for the runtime.jar file located at$ECLIPSE/plugins/org.eclipse.core.boot_x.y.z/. 3. Create a variable named RUNTIME_LIB for the runtime.jar file located at $ECLIPSE/plugins/org.eclipse.core.runtime_x.y.z/. 4. Create a variable named WORKBENCH_LIB for the workbench.jar (or workbench_new.jar) file at $ECLIPSE/plugins/org.eclipse.ui.workbench_x.y.z/. 5. Once finished, click OK in the Preferences window.
5	Add these variables to the Widget-Window project.	1. In the New Variable Classpath Entry dialog, select each of the variables you've created—SWT_LIB, SWT_PI_LIB (or SWT_GTK), JFACE_LIB, BOOT_LIB, RUNTIME_LIB, and WORKBENCH_LIB—and click OK. 2. Click OK to return to the Workbench.

continued on next page

Table A.2   **Preparing an SWT/JFace application in Eclipse for *nix** *(continued)*

	Goal	Procedure
6	Add the native graphics file (files) to the project.	1. To provide communication between the SWT/JFace commands and the operating system calls, you need to make the SWT native graphics files available. The first step involves finding them. The locations for these files are as follows:

Platform
Native library file
Library pathname

Linux GTK
libswt-gtk-*nnnn*.so
libswt-gtk-pi.*nnnn*.so
libswt-gnome-gtk-*nnnn*.so
org.eclipse.swt.gtk_x.y.z/os/linux/x86

Linux Motif
libswt-motif-*nnnn*.so
libswt-gtk-motif.*nnnn*.so
libswt-gnome-gtk-*nnnn*.so
libswt-motif-*nnnn*.so
libswt-kde-motif.*nnnn*.so
org.eclipse.swt.motif_x.y.z/os/linux/x86

Solaris
libswt-cde-motif-*nnnn*.so
org.eclipse.swt.photon_x.y.z/os/qnx/x86

AIX Motif
libswt-motif-*nnnn*.so
org.eclipse.swt.motif_x.y.z/os/ppc

PhotonQNX
libswt-photon-*nnnn*.so
org.eclipse.swt.photon_x.y.z/os/qnx/x86

2. Once you've found the necessary file or files, you need to make sure the application launcher can find them. The documentation lists a number of ways to do this, but we've found that adding the files to the /usr/lib directory works best. This isn't the safest thing to do, but it's reliable.

Other methods, which can be less reliable, include the following:

Option 1: Copy and paste these files directly in the `WidgetWindow` project.
Option 2: Include the native library in any directory pointed to by the `java.library.path` variable. This variable, among others, can be seen by clicking Help->About Eclipse Platform->Configuration Details.
Option 3: Make sure the `LD_LIBRARY_PATH` environmental variable contains the directory in which these library files are located.

A.1.3 *SWT in OS X*

Since the advent of OS X, the Macintosh has become popular as a platform for Java development. In fact, much of this book and many of the examples were originally developed on OS X. However, due to SWT's use of native libraries, running an SWT application on OS X is more complicated than the instructions for Windows and Linux described in the previous sections. This section addresses the steps necessary to get an SWT application running on OS X; the rest of this section assumes that you're using a Mac.

If you examine your Eclipse installation, you'll notice that instead of the single executable file that is found on Windows or Linux, there is a directory called Eclipse.app. Naming the directory with an .app extension and conforming to a certain specification causes the operating system to treat the directory as an application to be launched when double-clicked. To run your own SWT application, you'll need to set up the same directory structure. We recommend using Ant or some other tool to perform this step as part of your standard build process.

Although OS X supports launching Java applications by double-clicking a .jar file, in order to properly hook an SWT application into the native event queue you need to launch your code through a small wrapper program. This executable file is called java_swt, and it can be found at $ECLIPSE_HOME/Eclipse.app/Contents/ MacOS/java_swt. This program will launch first and will load your application's .class files after it has set things up for you.

We'll assume you're assembling an application named Foo. Follow these steps:

1. Create a directory called Foo.app, which will eventually hold your complete application.

2. After you've built a .jar containing your application's files as usual, copy it, along with the SWT/JFace .jar files and any other necessary third-party libraries, to Foo.app/Contents/Resources/Java. The SWT native libraries (files ending in .jnilib) should be put in Foo.app/Contents/Resources/Java/dll. Finally, copy the java_swt executable to Foo.app/Contents/MacOS.

3. Once the file is copied, you must also make sure the executable permission is set on the file. If you're using Ant, remember that the copy task doesn't preserve file permissions. If your application doesn't launch when clicked, and there are no error messages, check that the permissions are set correctly.

4   Once you've placed your application's files, you need to create couple of additional files describing your application to the operating system. Both files belong in Foo.app/Contents:

- The file PkgInfo should contain a single line of text. If you've registered as an Apple developer and received a creator code for your application, use it.
- A bit more complicated is the Info.plist file, which contains XML describing various aspects of your application. We don't have space to discuss the format of this file in detail here; a working version is available from this book's website, and you can easily customize it for your needs. Of particular note are the `CFBundleExecutable` entry, which tells the OS to execute java_swt when the application is clicked, and an entry allowing you to specify a file containing the icon that should be displayed for your application. At the bottom of the file is an entry that describes the environment to be used when the JVM is launched. Change the `ClassPath` attribute to name the .jar files used by your own application, and change the `MainClass` attribute so it names the class containing your application's `main()` method.

These instructions seem complicated, but it's fairly simple to get things up and running, especially if you look at a working example. Additionally, these tasks are all easily scriptable using Ant, so they can be automated.

A.2 *SWT/JFace in standalone applications*

Even without the Eclipse platform, the process of building an SWT/JFace project is straightforward. The only real work involves telling the Java compiler where to find the libraries. The steps are listed in table A.3.

Table A.3   Preparing an SWT/JFace application for standalone development

	Goal	Procedure

1	Add the necessary SWT/JFace library files to the Java classpath.	1. Add the SWT library or libraries (described earlier) to your compilation path. Then, add the library files needed for JFace.
		2. Add the `-Djava.library.path=` option to the compiler command followed by the directory containing the native graphics library. The path to this library was described earlier.
		3. As a Windows example, the compiler command would have the following option: `-Djava.library.path=`
		
		`C:\eclipse\plugins\org.eclipse.swt.win32`
		`3.0.0\os\win32\x86.`

With the `WidgetWindow` project set up, you can begin building classes and displaying their GUIs. Fortunately, programming with the SWT and JFace libraries is simpler than preparing the Workbench to compile their applications.

OLE and ActiveX
in SWT/JFace

In earlier chapters, we explored how SWT is built in layers: a small library of C code built with Java Native Interface (JNI) interacts with the underlying operating system to provide the necessary building blocks for more elaborate capabilities. One of the design goals of the native layer was for it to be very small, often providing simple wrappers around native APIs. Using this novel approach, the OTI/IBM team has been able to give programmers unprecedented access to the native capabilities of all supported platforms. In so doing, the team chose not limit itself to the features common to all platforms. Among these platforms, Microsoft Windows offers a unique capability that has appealed to Visual Basic programmers for many years: reusable binary objects, otherwise known as COM objects.

SWT/JFace programmers haven't been left out; this appendix covers the nature and depth of COM support in SWT. Specifically, you'll see how you can include ActiveX controls and OLE documents inside your applications in just a few SWT method calls. So that you can fully take advantage of this feature, we'll first review some basic COM features and general principles.

B.1 COM simplified

Microsoft designed the Component Object Model (COM) to try to solve a simple problem: how to reuse binary objects. Previous solutions based solely on shared libraries (Dynamic Link Libraries [DLLs]) showed that they weren't practical for C++ programming and that managing their proliferation on a given system was in itself a major cause of application problems. In the process of designing a replacement solution, Microsoft felt it should also address a new class of problems for the time: location transparency.

In the end, the new technology was built to provide a unique solution for situations using three distinct types of objects:

- *In-process objects* share the same address space as the client code using them (the code is inside DLLs).

- *Local out-of-process objects* are located on the same computer as the client code but reside in a separate address space (inside a separate EXE file).

- *Remote objects* are located inside an EXE or DLL on a different machine and are accessible via remote procedure calls.

These are important concepts for anyone interested in doing COM with SWT/JFace.

B.1.1 *IUnknown/IDispatch*

COM is based on the notion of *interfaces*. Interfaces allow the logical grouping of functionalities as well as their discovery at runtime by querying the objects themselves. Each interface has an identifier (IID) that uniquely defines both the methods available and their physical placement relative to one another in memory. Physically, interfaces are organized into *vtables* (arrays of function pointers). The notion of physical ordering of these functions is crucial, as you'll see when we investigate the details of SWT programming. COM makes widespread usage of *Globally Unique Identifiers (GUIDs)*. Specific GUID uses include object identifiers, type library identifiers, and interface identifiers. The algorithm for generating these IDs is beyond the scope of this book, but it's described on the Microsoft Developers Library web site (msdn.microsoft.com).

The way COM interfaces are versioned may surprise Java programmers: An interface that has been published can't be modified. Instead, it must be extended via an entirely new interface. According to Microsoft's best practices, the new interface should have the same base name followed by a version number that increases for each new version. For example, when Microsoft needed to give users more control over the web browser ActiveX control, it extended the original IWebBrowser interface with a richer IWebBrowser2.

Unlike the Java model, where class files contain enough metadata to allow the reflection API to return a complete description of objects and methods, the COM runtime discovery model is based on the existence of IUnknown, a core interface that all others extend. Given a specific GUID, QueryInterface returns a pointer to the interface implementation. The two other IUnknown functions, AddRef and Release, are responsible for tracking the number of references to the interface and returning all allocated resources to the operating system. Reference counting is an important aspect of COM programming and is the cause of many bugs that are difficult to identify.

SWT fully adheres to Microsoft's guidelines for reference counting, but sometimes you'll need to remember these simple rules: Clients are responsible for calling AddRef and Release on every interface they query; and both calls must be made on the same interface reference, to allow an object to track the references on a per-interface basis rather than for the whole object. These important functions are listed in table B.1.

Table B.1   Functions of the `IUnknown` COM interface

IUnknown function	Description
AddRef	Increases the reference count for this interface
QueryInterface	Returns pointers to supported interfaces
Release	Decreases the reference count for this interface

Using this simple design, and with the aid of a small runtime library that provides support for registering, discovering, and instantiating objects, it's possible to start creating powerful reusable binary entities using a language like C or C++. Objects can then be segregated into families based on their implementing predefined sets of interfaces, all deriving from the core `IUnknown`. Over the years, Microsoft has defined several such families: scriptable objects, ActiveX controls, active documents, and so on. Some of these definitions have gradually evolved toward fewer mandatory interfaces and more optional behaviors.

Although a powerful concept, this interface proved too complicated for high-level languages like VBScript, JScript, and the first versions of Visual Basic. To allow these interpreter-based languages (and other scripting languages) to access COM objects, Microsoft defined another key COM interface. `IDispatch` allows object capabilities to be queried by name rather than by interface identifier. Like all the other COM interfaces, `IDispatch` extends `IUnknown`. Each method that needs to be publicized is given a unique dispatch identifier that can be used to invoke it. *COM automation* (or just *automation*) is the process of letting client code interface with a COM object using the `IDispatch`-based discovery and invocation mechanism. The flexibility it provides comes at a price: the automation querying and invocation process is significantly slower that the default binary binding used for non-automation calls. The functions provided by this interface are shown in table B.2.

Table B.2   Functions of the `IDispatch` COM interface

IDispatch function	Description
AddRef	Increases the reference count for this interface
GetIDsOfNames	Maps a single member and an optional set of argument names to a corresponding set of integer dispatch IDs (DISPIDs)
GetTypeInfo	Gets the type information for an object

continued on next page

Table B.2 Functions of the `IDispatch` COM interface *(continued)*

IDispatch function	Description
GetTypeInfoCount	Retrieves the number of type information interfaces that an object provides (either 0 or 1)
Invoke	Provides access to properties and methods exposed by an object
QueryInterface	Returns pointers to supported interfaces
Release	Decreases the reference count for this interface

SWT provides methods for two of these functions. Provided with an optional list of method names, `GetIDsOfNames()` returns a list of matching dispatch IDs (DISPIDs). These can be used in subsequent calls to the `Invoke()` method to trigger their execution. Using this simple mechanism, objects can expose both methods and properties. COM recognizes four reasons to call `Invoke()`:

- To call a method (`DISPATCH_METHOD`)
- To retrieve the value of a property (`DISPATCH_PROPERTYGET`)
- To modify the value of a property (`DISPATCH_PROPERTYPUT`)
- To modify the value of a property that is a reference to another object (`DISPATCH_PROPERTYPUTREF`)

NOTE You may wonder why there's no way to get the value of a property that is a reference to an object. This situation is covered by `DISPATCH_PROPERTYGET` via the fact that all automation methods manipulate a universal data type called `Variant`. A variant is a unique way to represent all the possible data types supported by automation-capable languages. You can find the nature of the content of a given variant by ORing predefined constants. Possible contents include a simple string (BSTR in COM parlance), a primitive type, or a reference to an object. Object references come in two flavors: a reference to an `IUnknown` and a reference to an `IDispatch` instance. Variants are a rich data type, and at this point SWT supports only a portion of the complete specification. Notably absent is support for `Safe-Arrays` (the Visual Basic way of dealing with arrays) and user-defined types (the Visual Basic types).

B.1.2 *Object hosting*

The ability to reuse the capabilities of an external object by embedding the object directly inside your application lies at the heart of client-side COM programming. COM provides two types of user experiences for interacting with embedded objects. In the first scenario, the embedded object retains its own interface that users see in a window that's separate from the main application window. In the second scenario, known as *in-place activation*, the user can interact with the embedded object without leaving the container document or application. In this scenario, the container and the embedded object collaborate to provide a composite menu bar where commands and features from both applications are available at the same time. The richer of the two scenarios, in-process activation is also more complicated to program, because it requires (among other things) that mouse and keyboard events be routed properly. COM allows both local servers (standalone EXEs like Microsoft Word) and in-process servers (DLLs) to be in-place-activated.

In both scenarios, the container must implement a number of predefined COM interfaces in order for the embedded object to communicate with it. Microsoft refers to these mandatory interfaces as *sites*. The complete description of all the site interfaces and the features they provide is beyond the scope of this book. In most cases, the interfaces implemented by the SWT programmers are enough; however, in some situations you'll need to extend one of the default site classes and implement additional site interfaces. Hosting an ActiveX control versus an OLE document requires the implementation of two sets of COM interfaces, described in tables B.3 and B.4. One of the examples later in this appendix shows how to create a custom container by extending an existing one.

Table B.3 Document site interfaces

Interface	Description
IAdviseSink	Receives general notifications from the embedded object
IOleClientSite	Manages general communication with the container
IOleInPlaceSite	Manages in-place activation of the hosted control
IOleDocumentSite	Provides a means to activate a hosted document
IUnknown	The fundamental COM interface

Table B.4 Control site interfaces

Interface	Description
IAdviseSink	Receives general notifications from the embedded object
IOleControlSite	Manages general communication with the container
IOleInPlaceSite	Manages in-place activation of the hosted control
IUnknown	The fundamental COM interface

B.1.3 Object instantiation

For the most part, instantiating a COM object is a straightforward task. The simplest case involves a single call to `CoCreateInstance()`. However, more complex object-instantiation strategies involve calling `OleCreate()` and passing it an instance of `IStorage` that represents either a new document or one that you intend to edit; or calling `CoGetClassObject()` to obtain an instance of an ActiveX `IObjectFactory` or `IObjectFactory2`, and then calling their respective `CreateInstance()` or `CreateInstanceLic()` method to obtain the new object's `IUnknown` instance.

You use the latter approach to instantiate ActiveX controls that need a license key to operate. Microsoft added licensing to ActiveX controls in order to prevent programmers from creating their own applications by reusing the controls redistributed with other applications; you had to purchase the development version of the controls to use them. SWT contains a default implementation of these instantiation strategies, but you may need to replicate them inside your code to address current limitations or bugs in SWT. The beauty of the SWT COM library layering is that you'll be able to do so easily.

B.1.4 Event handling

The COM object embedding model includes a rich mechanism for dispatching and handling events. It's based on several simple notions. A *sink* interface is an interface exposed by a COM client; it's called by a COM server as a *callback* for the purpose of *sinking* (handling) event notifications. In order for a server to dispatch events to a client's sink interface, the client code needs a process to pass a sink reference to the server. This is done via server *connection points*. A connection point is the server-based mechanism that handles notification to the client's sink interface. A server exposes all of its connection points by implementing the `IConnectionPointContainer` interface. Clients call `FindConnectionPoint()`, passing it the GUID of an interface to get a reference to the `IConnectionPoint` exposed by the server for this sink interface. `IConnectionPoint` contains the `Advise()` and `Unadvise()` methods to start and stop the flow of incoming events on the sink interface, respectively.

B.1.5 Threading model

The COM threading model is based on the notion of *apartments*. An apartment is an arbitrary construct meant to help the COM runtime library make the right decisions about how to route method calls to a COM object. The simplest of all scenarios is the *single-threaded apartment* (STA) model where the runtime takes care of all concurrency problems (which happens when multiple threads in the client code call the same method on the same object at the same time) transparently. This is done by creating a hidden window and using Windows' default message-passing mechanism to ensure that all the method calls are serialized.

In the *multithreaded apartment* (MTA) model, each COM object must be multi-thread-aware to ensure that no data corruption can arise as the result of two simultaneous calls from two distinct client threads. In recent versions of Windows, Microsoft has added more threading models that are beyond the scope of this book.

Like Swing, SWT doesn't contain any synchronization code to guard against resource corruption due to concurrency. The rationale behind this decision is that in most cases, the performance trade-off is too great to be justifiable. Consequently, synchronization is entirely your responsibility. To avoid introducing synchronization code, the SWT team chose to support only the STA threading model where no special code is required; all synchronization issues are handled by the COM runtime.

B.2 *The SWT COM library*

True to the general philosophy adopted for SWT, support for COM comes in the form of a minimal amount of C code coupled with a series of Java classes building on these foundations. The interesting side effect is that SWT COM programming is very similar to C++ COM programming. This can be a double-edged sword. The bonus is that whenever you're in doubt about how to use a specific SWT feature, you can look for help in the Microsoft documentation. The trade-off is that you'll sometimes be looking at unusual and nonintuitive Java code. As you get more familiar with code from both languages, you'll come to enjoy the outcome and forget about the means.

In the following sections, we'll cover the parts of the SWT COM library shown in figure B.1. We'll begin with a tour of the native language part of the library and then look at the user-oriented Java classes that use it. The `OleEventTable`, `OleEventSink`, and `OlePropertyChangeSink` classes are only visible inside the `org.eclipse.swt.ole.win32` package.

B.2.1 *The native language support library*

When you look at figure B.1, don't be fooled by the names of the packages. The code inside `org.eclipse.swt.internal.ole.win32` isn't just for SWT developers, and you'll often find yourself referring to it for advanced SWT COM applications.

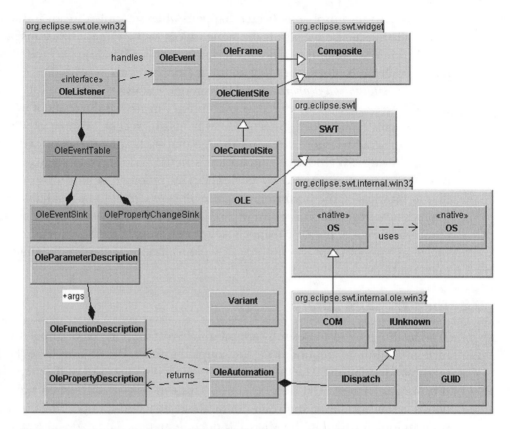

Figure B.1   Core components of the SWT COM library

The org.eclipse.swt.internal.ole.win32.COM class

As we discussed, the COM threading model supports several options. The COM specification mandates that every thread that wants to use COM must first call the runtime to specify a threading model. SWT performs this mandatory initialization for you inside a static block located in the COM class. The default threading model is apartment-threaded; therefore you don't have to do anything special to ensure that all calls to embedded COM objects are serialized.

The class has no constructor or instance members, but it contains a long series of constants and static methods. The static methods are mostly native methods named after their C equivalents. Their role is to expose the COM runtime to Java. The method signature is often identical to the original Windows

API. So, when in doubt, look at the original Microsoft documentation for explanations and examples.

Half the constants are instances of another class from the same package. SWT stores objects and interfaces unique identifiers using the GUID class For the most part you need not concern yourself with GUID because it contains no methods. However, it has an interesting public static final field named sizeof that contains the size of the structure in bytes. The COM SWT code uses this pattern in all classes that map to a native structure (more on this in section B.2.2).

Chances are, all the interfaces you'll ever need to access are defined in COM as public constants. The following examples were taken from the source code and show how you should define any interface not already included:

```
public static final GUID IIDIUnknown =
        IIDFromString("{00000000-0000-0000-C000-000000000046}");
public static final GUID IIDIDispatch =
        IIDFromString("{00020400-0000-0000-C000-000000000046}");
```

IIDFromString() returns an instance of GUID based on the string representation of an interface identifier. Similarly, CLSIDFromProgID() and CLSIDFromString() let you find an object's GUID from the same string representation or from the object's program identifier. To instantiate a COM object, you need to find either of these two values. The IsEqualGUID() method lets you compare two GUIDs for identity, which you need to do to implement the QueryInterface() when creating custom COM interfaces.

The COM class also contains the low-level SWT code to access native drag and drop: the RegisterDragDrop(), RevokeDragDrop(), and DoDragDrop() methods. The latest version of SWT introduced a new cross-platform level of abstraction that uses this code. More interestingly, the class lets you manipulate OLE storage files. StgCreateDocfile() allows you to create a new file; StgIsStorageFile() lets you test if a file is an OLE storage file; a call to ReleaseStgMediums() is necessary to release the memory allocated by COM to an open storage file; and StgOpenStorage() is used to open a storage file.

If you're familiar with Visual Basic, you know how simple it is to deal with strings. This simplicity comes at a price for people programming with lower-level languages. OLE strings, otherwise known as BSTR, can be manipulated using the SysAllocString(), SysFreeString(), and SysStringByteLen() methods. Sometimes COM requires that newly allocated memory be placed under the control of its runtime (often the case when dealing with automation) to allow sharing of that memory between different process address spaces. You can use CoTaskMemAlloc()

and `CoTaskMemFree()`, respectively, to allocate or free blocks of memory compatible with COM.

Several of the methods from the `COM` class come with multiple prototypes, due to the strongly typed nature of Java. For example, the `MoveMemory()` method comes in 16 different flavors, one for each of the main types of COM structures you may have to manipulate. Keep in mind that using them takes you one step closer to function pointers (and therefore dangerously closer to memory leaks) than the makers of Java intended.

The most unconventional part of the `COM` class is a series of `VtblCall()` native static methods with different parameter combinations. These cover the method signatures for all the COM interfaces supported by SWT. The first two parameters are the index of the method that needs to be called in the vtable followed by the address of the table. The native code uses the index to find the address of the method to call inside the vtable and calls it with the remaining parameters. In the following example, `int COM.VtblCall(int fnNumber, int ppVtbl, GUID arg0, int[] arg1)` is called to implement the `QueryInterface()` method from `IUnknown`:

```
public int QueryInterface(GUID riid, int ppvObject[]) {
  return COM.VtblCall(0, address, riid, ppvObject);
}
```

The org.eclipse.swt.internal.ole.win32.COMObject class

Although it isn't composed of native methods, the `COMObject` class belongs to the lower level of the COM library. Its purpose is to provide a Java representation of the vtable at the heart of every COM object. The class contains 80 public methods with the same signature—`public int methodXX(int[] args)`—and an equal number of matching callbacks prototyped `static int callbackXX(int[] callbackArgs)`. Each method is a placeholder for the matching method inside the vtable of the COM interface.

By default, the 80 `methodXX()` methods return a constant called `COM.E_NOTIMPL` that tells the caller that the method isn't implemented. This avoids COM errors and gives you room to implement complex COM interfaces. All COM interfaces extend one another to form a hierarchy, and each level of inheritance translates into an extension of the methods in the vtable. Provided that some of the standard COM interfaces are two or three levels down from `IUnknown`, the creators of SWT have tried to anticipate future growth.

The class constructor is an array of `int`. Its size is the number of methods in the vtable, and its content is the number of parameters each vtable method takes. Be sure you don't make any mistakes when you create this array, or you'll be in for difficult debugging and crashes. Internally, the constructor uses this information to create an array of callbacks, one for each of the methods in the vtable. The native layer uses these callbacks to invoke Java code when COM needs to invoke a method from your interface.

Program identifiers revisited

Table B.5 contains the program identifiers for several common applications you may encounter in your exploration of the SWT COM library.

Table B.5 Common program identifiers

Program identifier	Description
Shell.Explorer	Internet Explorer
Word.Application	Microsoft Office Word application (as an out-of-process server)
Word.Document	Microsoft Office Word document
Excel.Application	Microsoft Office Excel application (as an out-of-process server)
Excel.Sheet	Microsoft Office Excel document
Excel.Chart	Microsoft Office Excel chart
PowerPoint.Show	Microsoft Office PowerPoint presentation
Visio.Drawing	Visio document
PDF.PdfCtrl.5	Adobe Acrobat PDF Reader 5.0
MediaPlayer.MediaPlayer	Windows Media Player
Agent.Control	Microsoft Agent control
DHTMLEdit.DHTMLEdit	DHTML Edit control for IE5
InternetShortcut	Internet shortcut

If you don't find the application you're looking for, open the standard Microsoft Registry Editor that comes with Windows and look under the key `My Computer\ HKEY_CLASSES_ROOT`. It contains a list of IDs for all the applications installed on your machine. Figure B.2 shows the program ID for the Web Browser control (the reusable part of Internet Explorer). Unless you have a specific reason not to do so, it's good practice to leave the terminating version number out of the name. COM uses the `CurVer` key to find out which version is current and uses it automatically.

Microsoft created this mechanism to allow the transparent migration of applications. However, some vendors don't follow this guideline; in this case you'll have

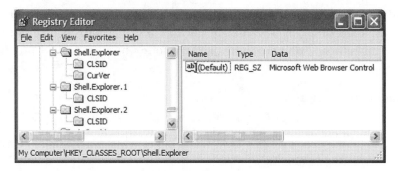

Figure B.2   The program ID for the reusable Web Browser control

to keep the version number as an integral part of the name (see Adobe Acrobat in the table B.5).

B.2.2   *The Java COM library*

The `org.eclipse.swt.internal.ole.win32` and `org.eclipse.swt.ole.win32` packages sit directly above the native library. The second package contains all the high-level code necessary to write COM client code with SWT. As shown in figure B.1, three classes consist of implementation details that aren't exposed outside of the package boundaries. `OleEventTable()` is a lookup mechanism that maps an event type to a specific listener, and `OleEventSink()` is the heart of SWT's ability to receive and dispatch COM events to your code; it contains a partial `IDispatch` implementation that can be a source of ideas for how to implement one yourself. Note that the `OLE` class contains mostly constants and a utility method to convert COM errors into SWT exceptions.

The org.eclipse.swt.internal.ole.win32.IUnknown class

By now you're familiar with the role played by the `IUnknown` COM interface in the discovery process of COM features. Even though it's described as a COM interface, the SWT team chose to implement it as a Java class. Its constructor takes one parameter: `int address`. Its value is the address of the vtable containing the implementation of the interface. All the methods of the COM `IUnknown` interface are implemented as normal Java methods with parameters similar to those of the native COM counterpart. These methods are implemented by calling `COM.Vtbl-Call()` with all the parameters and the index of the native method in the vtable. The following snippets show the implementation of `QueryInterface()` and `AddRef()`, which are the first two physical methods in the `IUnknown` COM interface:

```
public int QueryInterface(GUID riid, int ppvObject[]) {
  return COM.VtblCall(0, address, riid, ppvObject);
}
public int AddRef() {
  return COM.VtblCall(1, address);
}
```

Figure B.3 is a class diagram showing all the COM interfaces declared in the SWT COM library. In section B.3.3, we explain how to add new interface declarations when these aren't enough.

The org.eclipse.swt.ole.win32.OleFrame class

To embed a COM object (ActiveX control or OLE document) in your SWT application, you need to create a container window. As you've seen, COM mandates that this container implement certain interfaces in order for the embedded object to dialog with it. SWT provides the OleFrame class for that purpose. Although the

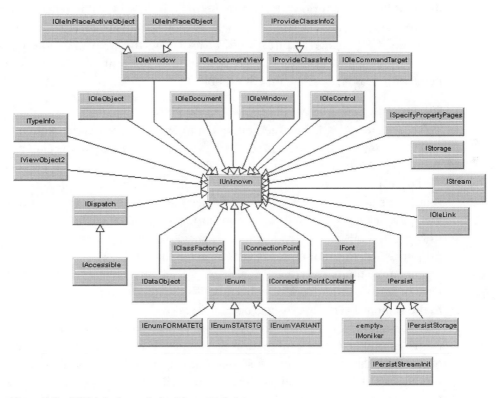

Figure B.3 COM interfaces derived from IUnknown

class is derived from `Composite`, it makes no sense to assign it a layout or try to add `Control` children. The only reason for inheriting from `Composite` is to access the window-management capabilities offered by `Composite`, in order to implement the `IOleInPlaceFrame` COM interfaces.

Internally, `OleFrame` handles sizing, menu management, and window placement. Looking at figure B.3, you'll notice that `IOleInPlaceFrame` isn't on the diagram. SWT doesn't require that you declare a COM interface (create a class derived from `IUnknown` that lists all its methods) in order to implement it. All that is required is that you create an instance of `COMObject` with public methods mapping the methods exposed by the COM interface.

When activated, OLE documents negotiate with the container to display their menu bar. Using public methods from `OleFrame`, your application can contribute menu items to the final menu bar. When adding menu items, you can choose between three locations on the menu bar—File (on the far left), Container (in the middle), or Window (far right, before Help)—by calling `SetFileMenus()`, `SetContainerMenus()`, and `SetWindowMenus()`, respectively. All three methods take an array of SWT `MenuItem`. Just before displaying the menu bar, the embedded object calls `IOleInPlaceFrame.InsertMenus()`; at that point `OleFrame` merges your items with those from the embedded object.

The org.eclipse.swt.ole.win32.OleClientSite class

The `OleClientSite` class implements a complete COM site. Aside from implementing the mandatory `IUnknown`, `IOleClientSite`, and `IAdviseSink`, the class also implements in-place activation via the optional `IOleInPlaceSite` and `IOleDocumentSite`.

This class contains several useful public methods. `doVerb()` plays an important role in the activation process, as you'll see later. `SaveFile()` can be used to save the current OLE document to a normal file (`includeOleInfo = false`) or to a storage file (`includeOleInfo = true`). `showProperties()` lets you display all the properties of the embedded COM object in a separate window, provided the object implements the `ISpecifyPropertyPages` interface. The only control you have over the window is its title, because it's created by the COM runtime via a call to the standard `COM.OleCreatePropertyFrame()`.

`queryStatus()` is a helper method that accepts the ID of a command and returns a bitwise OR'd combination of `OLECMDF_SUPPORTED`, `OLECMDF_ENABLED`, and `OLECMDF_LATCHED` indicating the status of the specified command. This method is usually called before a call to `exec()` to verify that the command is available before executing it. Both functionalities are based on querying the embedded object for its `IOleCommandTarget` interface and subsequently calling the `QuerySta-tus()` or `Exec()` method on this interface.

You may be faced with situations where the site doesn't implement some interfaces that are necessary to provide more control over the embedded COM object. Fortunately, the SWT team structured the code in a way that makes it easy to extend. You need to follow three rules:

1 The constructor of your derived class must call the parent constructor before anything else.

2 You need to override the protected `createCOMInterfaces` (where you create one `COMObject` instance for each COM interface you want your site to support) and `disposeCOMInterfaces` (where you call the `dispose()` method for each of the `COMObject` instances previously created).

3 You must ensure that your new `QueryInterface()` method properly delegates to its parent (we present a complete example in section B.3.3).

The org.eclipse.swt.ole.win32.OleControlSite class

The `OleControlSite` class inherits from `OleClientSite` and provides the extended capabilities necessary to host an ActiveX control. The visible differences from the parent class are full support for events and property change notifications from the ActiveX control, simplified access to well-known control properties (straight method calls instead of COM automation calls), and direct access to ambient properties.

You can access the container's ambient properties via calls to the `setSiteProp-erty()` and `getSiteProperty()` methods. For example, the Web Browser control has properties that determine whether the browser should support embedded ActiveX controls or JavaScript scripts. The font as well as color of the ActiveX control are accessible via `setFont()`, `getFont()`, `setBackground()`, `getBackground()`, `setForeground()`, and `getForeground()`.

`addEventListener()` allows you to register instances of `OleListener` in order to receive specific events. You can register a single listener instance for several event types, in which case your handler will probably contain an `if` statement based on the value of `OleEvent.type`. Alternatively, you can register different listeners for the various events your application needs to handle. When you're no longer interested in receiving an event, don't forget to call the `removeEventListener()` method. Similar methods exist for receiving notifications about changes in the value of a property.

The org.eclipse.swt.ole.win32.OleAutomation class

Dealing with dispatch interfaces (COM interfaces that extend `IDispatch`) can lead to code that's hard to read, involving many `Variant` instances copied to and from arrays. `OleAutomation` provides a wrapper to manipulate the functionality delivered by the `IDispatch` COM interface. Two constructors are available. The first takes an instance of `OleClientSite` (remember that `OleControlSite` extends `OleClientSite`, which guarantees that the class works for both ActiveX controls and OLE documents) and uses package-level methods to obtain the client's private instance of the `org.eclipse.swt.internal.ole.win32.IDispatch` class. The second constructor directly takes an instance of `IDispatch` as its unique parameter. Both constructors acquire an `ITypeInfo` reference via a call to `QueryInterface()` on the object.

Internally, this reference is used in the implementation of all the public methods involved in describing the dispatch interface. This gives you access to the complete type library for the interface. The first method, `getTypeInfoAttributes()`, returns a structure of type `TYPEATTR` that contains a high-level description of the interface. The description includes such information as the interface GUID, the number of variables it exposes, and its total number of methods. The following code snippet shows how to access all the variables of an automation interface:

```
OleControlSite site = new OleControlSite(frame, SWT.NONE, progID);   ❶ Acquire
OleAutomation auto = new OleAutomation(site);                           TYPEATTR
TYPEATTR typeattr = auto.getTypeInfoAttributes();
if (typeattr != null && typeattr.cVars > 0) {
  System.out.println("\n\nVariables for " + progID + " :\n");
  for (int i = 0; i < typeattr.cVars; i++) {                         ❷ Loop over
    OlePropertyDescription data = auto.getPropertyDescription(i);       properties
    System.out.println("PROPERTY (id = " + data.id + ") :"
      + "\n\tName : " + data.name + "\n\tType : "
      + getTypeName(data.type) + "\n");
  }
}
```

❶ Based on a program ID similar to those listed in table B.5, we create a control site and then use it to create an `OleAutomation` wrapper.

❷ The `cVars` field contains the number of variables exposed by the interface. Successive calls to `getPropertyDescription()` return `OlePropertyDescription` instances. The class contains the description for an `Automation` property. Its type field contains an OR'ed combination of the different variant types described in OLE.java (`OLE.VT_XXXX`). Similarly, we could enumerate all the public methods of an interface by calling the `getFunctionDescription()` method with successive integer values, provided this index remains inferior to `typeattr.cFuncs`.

Besides providing a description of the interface, OleAutomation also contains methods to simplify accessing the properties of the COM object (setProperty() and getProperty()). As you may recall from the general discussion on COM and automation, properties are exposed via public getters and setters rather than data. Consequently, setProperty() and getProperty() are convenience wrappers around the more general invoke() method. All automation calls into the object ultimately translate into a call to IDispatch.Invoke() using one of the four standard dispatch codes (DISPATCH_XXXX constants from COM) as the fourth parameter. Finally, getIDsOfNames() is a thin wrapper that simplifies calling GetIDsOfNames() from the underlying IDispatch interface.

B.3 Doing COM with SWT

You should now have an idea about how to embed a COM object in an SWT-based application. In this section, we'll put this understanding to the test and write some examples, as well as explore patterns that will help you write more complex code.

B.3.1 A simple example

Before we dive further into the full life cycle of a COM object embedded inside an SWT container, we'll write the simplest possible example. Despite its simplicity, listing B.1 shows several important aspects of SWT COM programming. Its purpose is to embed an instance of Internet Explorer inside a SWT frame and display the home page of the Manning Publications web site.

Listing B.1   SimpleBrowser.java

```
package com.swtjface.AppB;
import org.eclipse.swt.widgets.*;
import org.eclipse.swt.*;
import org.eclipse.swt.events.*;
import org.eclipse.swt.layout.*;
import org.eclipse.swt.ole.win32.*;
public class SimpleBrowser {
  private Shell shell;
  private OleAutomation automation;
  public Shell open(Display display) {
    this.shell = new Shell(display);
    shell.setLayout(new FillLayout());
    OleFrame frame = new OleFrame(shell, SWT.NONE);
    OleControlSite controlSite =
        new OleControlSite(frame, SWT.NONE, "Shell.Explorer");
    automation = new OleAutomation(controlSite);
    boolean activated =
```

```
                (controlSite.doVerb(OLE.OLEIVERB_INPLACEACTIVATE) == OLE.S_OK);
        this.openURL("html://www.manning.com/");
        shell.open();
        return shell;
    }
    public void openURL(String url) {
        int[] rgdispid =
            automation.getIDsOfNames(new String[]{"Navigate", "URL"});
        int dispIdMember = rgdispid[0];
        Variant[] rgvarg = new Variant[1];
        rgvarg[0] = new Variant(url);
        int[] rgdispidNamedArgs = new int[1];
        rgdispidNamedArgs[0] = rgdispid[1];
        Variant pVarResult =
            automation.invoke(dispIdMember, rgvarg, rgdispidNamedArgs);
    }
    public static void main(String[] args) {
        Display display = new Display();
        Shell shell = (new SimpleBrowser()).open(display);
        while (!shell.isDisposed()) {
            if (!display.readAndDispatch()) {
                display.sleep();
            }
        }
        display.dispose();
    }
}
```

Creating a COM object

The first step creates the container where the COM object (ActiveX control or OLE document) will be embedded. For that we instantiate an `OleFrame`, as follows:

```
Display display = new Display();
Shell shell = new Shell(display);
OleFrame frame = new OleFrame(shell, SWT.NONE);
```

SWT provides two site implementations, one for OLE documents (`OleClientSite`) and one for ActiveX controls (`OleControlSite`). When in doubt about which to use for a COM object you want to embed, look at its type library to see if it implements either the `IOleDocument` or `IOleControl` interface. To do so, you can use Microsoft's OLE View, which is distributed with all major development tools and presented by msdn.microsoft.com (see figure B.4).

The constructor for `OleClientSite` lets you create a site based on a program ID (see table B.5 for a list of program IDs for known applications) or a filename. In the latter case, the shell does all the work of matching it to the corresponding

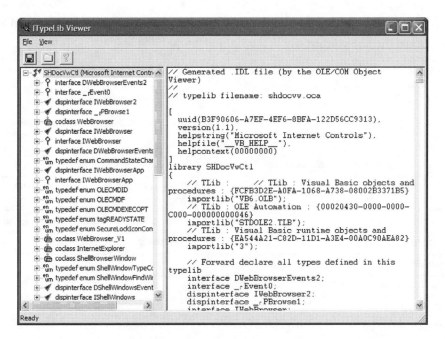

Figure B.4   The type library for Internet Explorer displayed in Microsoft OLE View

program ID based on the file extension. Behind the scenes, OleClientSite transparently creates an instance of IStorage that it then passes to the object:

```
OleClientSite clientSite =
    new OleClientSite(frame, SWT.NONE, "Word.Document");

File file = new File ("C:\\file1.doc");
OleClientSite clientSite =
    new OleClientSite(frame, SWT.NONE, file);
```

Embedding an ActiveX control is much simpler and only involves creating an instance of OleControlSite by passing its constructor the control's program ID:

```
OleControlSite controlSite =
    new OleControlSite(frame, SWT.NONE, "Shell.Explorer");
```

Activating an object

Creating an object isn't enough to make it become visible inside its container. It needs to be activated by the container. Activation is controlled by the doVerb() method. Table B.6 lists all the possible values for the method's unique parameter. In most cases, you'll us OLE.OLEIVERB_INPLACEACTIVATE to activate an ActiveX control in place. OLE documents work differently; the COM runtime must first start the associated application and ask it on behalf of your container to open the document in the site you supply.

Table B.6 Standard verbs for manipulating OLE objects

ProgID	Description
`OLE.OLEIVERB_DISCARDUNDOSTATE`	Closes the OLE object and discards the undo state
`OLE.OLEIVERB_HIDE`	Hides the OLE object
`OLE.OLEIVERB_INPLACEACTIVATE`	Opens the OLE object for editing in place
`OLE.OLEIVERB_OPEN`	Opens the OLE object for editing in a separate window
`OLE.OLEIVERB_PRIMARY`	Opens the OLE object for editing (the action that occurs when a user double-clicks on the object inside the container)
`OLE.OLEIVERB_PROPERTIES`	Requests the OLE object properties dialog
`OLE.OLEIVERB_SHOW`	Shows the OLE object
`OLE.OLEIVERB_UIACTIVATE`	Activates the UI for the OLE object

People have reported trouble activating certain documents, particularly Microsoft Office documents. In these cases, better results have been reported using `OLE.OLEIVERB_SHOW` as the activation verb.

Also remember that OLE documents are complete applications hosted inside your container. It's a common mistake to activate an OLE document in a container that doesn't have a menu bar—some applications will forgive you, others won't. Remember: always create your application's menu bar before activating an OLE document, as in the following snippet.

```
Display display = new Display();
Shell shell = new Shell(display);
shell.setLayout(new FillLayout());
Menu bar = new Menu(shell, SWT.BAR);        Before activating
shell.setMenuBar(bar);                      OLE document
OleFrame frame = new OleFrame(shell, SWT.NONE);
OleClientSite clientsite;
try {
    clientsite = new OleClientSite(frame, SWT.NONE, "PowerPoint.Slide");
    shell.layout();                              Activation of Microsoft
    clientsite.doVerb(OLE.OLEIVERB_SHOW);    ◄┘  Office OLE document
} catch (SWTException ex) {
    System.out.println("Failed to create <<PowerPoint Document>> : " +
                    ex.getMessage());
    return;
}
shell.open();
```

```
while (shell != null && !shell.isDisposed()) {
  if (!display.readAndDispatch())
    display.sleep();
```

Saving changes to an OLE document

At this point, we've successfully activated an OLE document inside an SWT container, and the user would like to save her changes. The first step is to call isDirty() from the OleClientSite to test that the file needs saving. When it is the case, we can proceed to call the save() method, passing it a standard java.io.File instance and a boolean indicating whether to save the file as a standard file (includeOleInfo = false) or a storage file (includeOleInfo = true). It's a good practice to save the document to a temporary file and replace the original file only if the operation is successful. The following snippet illustrates the process:

```
if (clientSite.isDirty()) {
  File tempFile = new File(file.getAbsolutePath() + ".tmp");
  file.renameTo(tempFile);
  if (clientSite.save(file, true)){
    // save was successful so discard the backup
    tempFile.delete();
  } else {
    // save failed so restore the backup
    tempFile.renameTo(file);
  }
}
```

Disposing of an object

The examples we've looked at so far have been simple in the sense that the container was only dealing with a single embedded object. However, nothing prevents your container from embedding several objects. OLE documents negotiate with their container about the content of the main menu toolbar. Consequently, your container must implement a strict control over the activation process. You should activate each COM object individually when doing so makes the most sense—for example, upon receiving a mouse double-click event—and deactivate them before activating the next one. To deactivate an object, call the deactivateIn-PlaceClient() method from its OleClientSite.

When you're done working with an embedded COM object, you must remember to perform one last task. The class diagram in figure B.1 showed that OleFrame, OleClientSite, and OleControlSite are all subclasses of org.eclipse.swt.widgets.Composite. As such, it's imperative that you dispose of them by calling dispose(). Unless you've saved all changes made to an OLE document prior to calling dispose(), they will be lost.

Handling properties

To access automation properties, you must first get their dispatch identifier (dispid) by calling getIDsOfNames() on the OleAutomation wrapper. You can use the resulting int in subsequent calls to getProperty() or setProperty(). Also keep in mind that all property values have the Variant type, which is the standard automation data type. A common source of mistakes is improperly initializing a variant by selecting the wrong type attributes, especially when dealing with variants that are references rather than contain data. The following snippet reads the Document property from an automation server:

```
OleAutomation server = new OleAutomation(…);
int[]documentID = server.getIDsOfNames(new String[]{"Document"});
if (documentID == null) return null;
Variant pVarResult = server.getProperty(documentID[0]);
```

Interacting with an object

One of the compelling reasons for embedding COM objects (ActiveX controls or OLE documents) in your application is the ability to inherit portions of the object's native user interface inside your own. However, this is only a small part of the possible interactions.

Using the invoke() method from OleAutomation gives you access to the entire object model of a COM component. Using it is a simple extension of what we did to access a property. A call to getIDsOfNames() with the name of a command returns its dispid, and once again all values have the Variant type. (Note that dealing with Microsoft Word presents some unique problems: When you're invoking a command that doesn't return a value, it's preferable to use the invokeNoReply() method.)

SWT also gives you access to the event model of an embedded COM object by registering instances of OleListener with an OleControlSite. You'll have to dig inside each type library to find the specific int value for the event you wish to subscribe to. As we've discussed, you can either register the same listener for multiple events or use distinct listeners for each event.

All handlers implement one unique method: void handleEvent(OleEvent event). By reading the type library, you'll find the number and type of parameters associated with the event. SWT copies them into an array that's publicly accessible from the event as public Variant[] arguments. The parameters are ordered from left to right in the prototype from the type library. For example, the following information is from the Excel 10.0 type library. In this scenario, SeriesIndex would be arguments[0] and PointIndex would be stored in arguments[1]:

```
dispinterface ChartEvents {
    ...
    [id(0x00000602), helpcontext(0x00010602)]
        void SeriesChange(
                        [in] long SeriesIndex,
                        [in] long PointIndex);
    ...
}
```

B.3.2 *SWT COM programming patterns*

What seems at first like a disconcerting way of writing Java code has identifiable patterns that are repeated throughout. Understanding them is the key to writing more serious COM-related code with SWT. Let's review some of these patterns.

Null-terminated strings

In some instances, you'll be forced to deal with the fact that C/C++ strings are terminated by the null-end-of-string character (\0). This code snippet shows how to create a null-terminated string from a Java String:

```
String lpsz = "This is a string";
char[] buffer = (lpsz +"\0").toCharArray();
```

The next snippet shows a way to turn a null-terminated string back into a Java String. We hope that future versions of SWT will include a way to find the length of a native string directly:

```
public static String getString(int addr) {
    String str = null;
    TCHAR buffer = new TCHAR (0, 256);        │ Assume String is shorter
    OS.MoveMemory (buffer, addr, 256);         │ than 256 characters
    str = buffer.toString(0, buffer.strlen());  ◁── Trim excess characters
    return str;
}
```

Pointer to structure

A common situation in SWT Windows/COM programming has to do with handling pointers. Typically you'll deal with a pointer to a native Windows structure, a pointer to a string, or a pointer to a native type. Many of the Windows APIs manipulate 32-bit quantities that are pointers to complex data structures. The creators of SWT mapped these structures to Java classes with public data members and no methods. The many versions of MoveMemory() contain the necessary JNI code to initialize the public data members of all the supported structures one field at a time. As we previously discussed, each structure includes the following line of code, where XXX is the size of the structure in bytes:

```
public static final int sizeof = XXX;
```

The pointers are mapped to Java int. In the following snippet, we use an int as a pointer to a GUID and copy the data into an already allocated GUID object:

```
GUID guid = new GUID();
COM.MoveMemory(guid, riid, GUID.sizeof);
```

A typical misconception could lead you to declare only the guid variable and not allocate the memory for the structure, which would cause a memory violation error.

Pointer to pointer to an interface

Another recognizable pattern in COM programming with SWT has to do with the notion of pointers to pointers. Many COM methods take one or more parameters that are pointers to interface pointers. In the following code snippet, we're looking at this coding pattern in the context of obtaining a temporary instance of IStorage (similar code is invoked every time you create a new automation document with SWT):

```
int[] tempStg = new int[1];        ❶ Allocate int array
int grfMode = COM.STGM_READWRITE |
              COM.STGM_SHARE_EXCLUSIVE |
              COM.STGM_DELETEONRELEASE;
int result = CO .StgCreateDocfile(null, grfMode, 0, tmpStg);   ❷ Method call

if (result != COM.S_OK)    ❸ Status check
   OLE.error(OLE.ERROR_CANNOT_CREATE_FILE, result);
IStorage st = new IStorage(tmpStg [0])    ❹ Create reference
```

❶ An int array with a size of 1 is created. This is a pointer (the reference to the array) to a pointer (the first value of the array).

❷ The array is passed to a method that expects a pointer to a pointer to a COM interface.

❸ All COM methods return an HRESULT: a 4-byte value where the sign bit is used to communicate the presence/absence of an error. Errors are reported using the static method error() defined in the org.eclipse.swt.internal.win32.OS class. The method builds an error message based on the error code and throws an SWTException. Note that SWTException extends RuntimeException; consequently, the exception isn't declared in any method signature, and handling it is left to your discretion.

❹ If there are no errors, the method initializes the first value of the array with the address of the reference. All that's left is to instantiate the proper IUnknown derived class, which we do by passing the address to the constructor.

B.3.3 Advanced topics

Now that we've discussed the standard methods for incorporating COM inside SWT code, it's time to go further. This section will explain how to customize applications with your own OLE/COM interfaces and `QueryInterfaces`. Then, we'll investigate more advanced data structures such as `IDispatch` parameters and `SafeArrays`.

Adding new interfaces to the org.eclipse.swt.internal.ole.win32 package

Despite the long list of interfaces supplied in the `org.eclipse.swt.internal.ole.win32` package, you may need an interface that isn't defined. Listing B.2 shows how to create a Java class that describes a COM interface. In the simpler cases, your interface will inherit directly from `IUnknown` and add one or more methods; our next example will show a slightly more complicated scenario.

Listing B.2 IPersistFile.java

```java
package org.eclipse.swt.internal.ole.win32;
public class IPersistFile extends IPersist {
  public IPersistFile(int address) {
    super(address);
  }
  public int IsDirty() {
    return COM.VtblCall(4, address);
  }
  public int Load(String szFileName, int dwMode) {
    char[] fileName = (szFileName + "\0").toCharArray();
    int pszFileName = 0;
    COM.MoveMemory(pszFileName, fileName, 4);
    return COM.VtblCall(5, address, pszFileName, dwMode);
  }
  public int Save(String szFileName, boolean fRemember) {
    char[] fileName = (szFileName + "\0").toCharArray();
    int pszFileName = 0;
    COM.MoveMemory(pszFileName, fileName, 4);
    return COM.VtblCall(6, address, pszFileName, fRemember);
  }
  public int SaveCompleted(int pszFileName) {
    return COM.VtblCall(7, address, pszFileName);
  }
  public int GetCurFile() {
    return COM.VtblCall(8, address);
  }
}
```

According to the Microsoft documentation, `IPersistFile` extends `IPersist`, which inherits from `IUnknown`. Before starting the implementation, we must count the number of methods already implemented by the complete chain of parent interfaces. The index of the first new method is the total plus one: in this case, 4. `IUnknown` contains three methods (index 0 to 2), and `IPersist` contains a single method (index 3). For the sake of simplifying the code, it directly accesses the `address` field from the `IUnknown` class. Unfortunately at this point `address` has package-only visibility, which is the reason for the package declaration on the first line of the listing. Alternatively, we could have replaced every reference to `address` with a call to the public method `getAddress()`. Finally, notice that the body of the `Save()` and `Load()` methods uses the null-terminated strings pattern we just described.

Implementing a known COM interface

Let's walk through the steps of the complete implementation of a standard COM interface. We'll implement `IDocHostUIHandler`; the reason for this choice will become evident at the end of this appendix.

`COMObject` contains a long list of empty methods. This is our first stop: We need to create an instance that maps to the methods of `IDocHostUIHandler`. The following snippet shows how to do this. Each of the interface's methods is mapped to a locally defined method of the Java class taking the same number of parameters as its COM counterpart:

```
iDocHostUIHandler = new COMObject(new int[]{2, 0, 0, 4, 1, 5, 0,
                        0, 1, 1, 1, 3, 3, 2, 2, 1, 3, 2}) {
    public int method0(int[] args)
        {return QueryInterface(args[0], args[1]);}
    public int method1(int[] args)
        {return AddRef();}
    public int method2(int[] args)
        {return Release();}
    public int method3(int[] args)
        {return ShowContextMenu(args[0], args[1], args[2], args[3]);}
    public int method4(int[] args)
        {return GetHostInfo(args[0]);}
    public int method5(int[] args)
        {return ShowUI(args[0], args[1], args[2], args[3], args[4]);}
    public int method6(int[] args)
        {return HideUI();}
    public int method7(int[] args)
        {return UpdateUI();}
    public int method8(int[] args)
        {return EnableModeless(args[0]);}
    public int method9(int[] args)
        {return OnDocWindowActivate(args[0]);}
    public int method10(int[] args)
        {return OnFrameWindowActivate(args[0]);}
    public int method11(int[] args)
```

❶ Interface signature

❷ Method implementations

```
            {return ResizeBorder(args[0], args[1], args[2]);}
        public int method12(int[] args)
            {return TranslateAccelerator(args[0], args[1], args[2]);}
        public int method13(int[] args)
            {return GetOptionKeyPath(args[0], args[1]);}
        public int method14(int[] args)
            {return GetDropTarget(args[0], args[1]);}
        public int method15(int[] args)
            {return GetExternal(args[0]);}
        public int method16(int[] args)
            {return TranslateUrl(args[0], args[1], args[2]);}
        public int method17(int[] args)
            {return FilterDataObject(args[0], args[1]);}
    };
```

❶ The Microsoft specification shows that `IDocHostUIHandler` contains 18 methods. The array contains the number of input parameters for each of these 18 methods.

❷ `Method0()` is mapped to a privately defined `QueryInterface` method that takes two parameters. The rest of the code maps the other methods to other private methods while preserving the same ordering as in the COM interface definition.

Rolling your own QueryInterface

Of all the methods that you'll implement when designing custom interface implementations, `QueryInterface()` presents the most difficulties. The following code demonstrates several useful patterns for implementing your own:

```
protected int QueryInterface(int riid, int ppvObject) {     ❶ Signature
    int result = super.QueryInterface(riid, ppvObject);      ❷ Delegation
    if (result == COM.S_OK)
        return result;
    if (riid == 0 || ppvObject == 0)
        return COM.E_INVALIDARG;
    GUID guid = new GUID();
    COM.MoveMemory(guid, riid, GUID.sizeof);
    if (COM.IsEqualGUID(guid, COM.IIDIDocHostUIHandler)) {   ❸
        COM.MoveMemory(ppvObject,                             Check
                    new int[]{iDocHostUIHandler.getAddress()}, requested
                    4);                                       interface



                    QueryInterface must increment reference
    AddRef();      ⮪ count before returning interface
    return COM.S_OK;    ← Return error-free status code
    }
    COM.MoveMemory(ppvObject, new int[] {0}, 4);  ← Clear pointer
    return COM.E_NOINTERFACE;
}
```

❶ In general, it's a good idea to make all your COM interface implementation methods protected or with limited visibility, because these methods exist only so you can call them in the context of your COM object. `QueryInterface` takes only two parameters. In C++, `riid` is a reference to an interface ID that translates into a Java `int`.

❷ This implementation of `QueryInterface` was taken from a class extending `OleClientSite`, for the purpose of creating an extended client site. This new site implements one more interface than the default `OleClientSite`. First, the code attempts to delegate to the parent `QueryInterface`. If the parent returns `S_OK`, then the interface was found and its address is already inside `ppvObject`. All that's left is to return the status code.

❸ Next we must check that the GUID of the requested interface matches an interface supported by this object. In this case, the new client site adds support for `COM.IIDIDocHostUIHandler`. If the two GUIDs are identical, then we need to copy the address of the private instance of the class that implements `IDocHostUIHandler` to the result pointer.

Passing IDispatch references as parameters

A common situation may require that you pass a reference to an `IDispatch` as a parameter to a method exposed by the COM object you host inside your application. The following is the Interface Definition Language (IDL) description for a method from the Microsoft Excel object model. The `_Chart` interface contains the `SetSourceData()` method, which takes a `Range` pointer as its first parameter. Looking at the object model also shows that the `Range` interface is derived from `IDispatch`:

```
[id(0x00000585), helpcontext(0x00010585)]
void SetSourceData(
               [in] Range* Source,
               [in, optional] VARIANT PlotBy);
```

The proper way to invoke `SetSourceData()` consists of passing the range reference as a `byRef Variant`, as follows:

```
{
  Variant rangeVar = //execute some method on another automation object
  IDispatch rangeDisp = rangeVar.getDispatch();
  OleAutomation range = rangeVar.getAutomation();

  rgdispid = chart.getIDsOfNames(new String[]{"SetSourceData",
    "Source"});
  int hGlobal = OS.GlobalAlloc(OS.GMEM_FIXED, 4);
  OS.Memmove(hGlobal, new int[] {rangeDisp.getAddress()}, 4);
```

❶ Obtain reference to method

❷ Check requested interface

```
    int ptr = OS.GlobalLock(hGlobal);
    Variant rangeRefVar =
        new Variant(ptr, OLE.VT_BYREF | OLE.VT_DISPATCH);
    chart.invoke(rgdispid[0],
            new Variant[]{rangeVar},
            new int[]{rgdispid[1]});
}
```

❸ **Create variant**

❶ As usual, we must get the method's `dispid` from its name.

❷ We create a pointer to the `Range` reference by allocating 4 bytes of memory and copying the address of `Range` to it.

❸ Using our new pointer to the `Range`, we can create a new `Variant` using the `OLE.VT_BYREF` | `OLE.VT_DISPATCH` style. `VT_BYREF` indicates that the variant contains a pointer to something, and `VT_DISPATCH` indicates that the something is an `IDispatch` reference.

Anatomy of a storage file

The example in listing B.3 shows how to explore the content of a storage file. The code also shows how to use a class derived from `IEnum` to perform an enumeration.

Listing B.3   Storage.java

```
package com.swtjface.AppB;
import java.io.File;
import org.eclipse.swt.internal.ole.win32.*;
import org.eclipse.swt.internal.win32.*;
import org.eclipse.swt.ole.win32.*;
public class Storage {
  public static void main(String[] args) {
    if (args.length == 0) {
      System.out.println("Usage: java Storage <file name>");
      return;
    }
    String fileName = args[0];
    parseFile(new File(fileName));
  }
  public static void parseFile(File file) {
    char[] fileName = (file.getAbsolutePath() + "\0").toCharArray();
    IStorage storage = null;
    if (COM.StgIsStorageFile(fileName) == COM.S_OK) {
      int mode = COM.STGM_READ | COM.STGM_TRANSACTED |
              COM.STGM_SHARE_EXCLUSIVE;

      int[] address = new int[1];
      int result = COM.StgOpenStorage(fileName, 0, mode, 0, 0, address;
      if (result != COM.S_OK)
```

Method takes null-terminated string

Get IStorage reference (pointer in address[0])

```
        OLE.error(OLE.ERROR_CANNOT_OPEN_FILE, result);
      storage = new
   IStorage(address[0]);    ←─ Dereference pointer; get IStorage
   int[] ppEnum = new int[1];
      result = storage.EnumElements(0, 0, 0, ppEnum);
      if (result != COM.S_OK)
        OLE.error(OLE.ERROR_ACTION_NOT_PERFORMED, result);
      IEnumSTATSTG enum = new IEnumSTATSTG(ppEnum[0]);  ←

      // loop over the file content
      int rgelt = OS.GlobalAlloc(OS.GMEM_FIXED | OS.GMEM_ZEROINIT,
                           STATSTG.sizeof);
      int[] pceltFetched = new int[1];
      enum.Reset();
     while (enum.Next(1, rgelt, pceltFetched) == COM.S_OK
         && pceltFetched[0] == 1) {
        STATSTG statstg = new STATSTG();
        COM.MoveMemory(statstg, rgelt, STATSTG.sizeof);
        System.out.println(getString(statstg.pwcsName));
      }
      OS.GlobalFree(rgelt);
      enum.Release();
      storage.Release();
    }
  }
  public static String getString(int addr) {
    String str = null;
    TCHAR buffer = new TCHAR (0, 256);
    OS.MoveMemory (buffer, addr, 256);
    str = buffer.toString(0, buffer.strlen());
    return str;
  }
}
```

Annotations in the code:
- **Get IEnumSTATSTG**
- **Access STATSTG structure one at a time**
- **Release interfaces**

Looking inside a SafeArray

When Microsoft needed to add support for arrays to automation, it created the notion of SafeArray: a structure that describes the characteristics of an array and holds its data. Dealing with SafeArrays was deemed complicated enough that Microsoft created a specific API for that purpose. For memory, the anatomy of a SafeArray is as follows (the offset and size information will help you understand the code that follows):

```
typedef struct  tagSAFEARRAYBOUND {
    ULONG cElements;                      // offset 0, size 4
    LONG lLbound;                         // offset 4, size 4
} SAFEARRAYBOUND;

typedef struct  tagSAFEARRAY {
```

```
    USHORT cDims;                       // offset 0,  size 2
    USHORT fFeatures;                   // offset 2,  size 2
    ULONG  cbElements;                  // offset 4,  size 4
    ULONG  cLocks;                      // offset 8,  size 4
    PVOID  pvData;                      // offset 12, size 4
    SAFEARRAYBOUND rgsabound[ ... ];    // offset 16
} SAFEARRAY;
```

Unfortunately there is currently no special support for `SafeArray` in SWT. However, based on the C definition of the `SafeArray` structure, it's possible to display their content. The following is an extract from the type library for the Web Browser ActiveX control:

```
interface DWebBrowserEvents : IUnknown {
    ...
    [helpstring("Fired when a new hyperlink is being navigated to.")]
    HRESULT _stdcall BeforeNavigate(
                [in] BSTR URL, long Flags, BSTR TargetFrameName,
                VARIANT* PostData,
                BSTR Headers, [in, out] VARIANT_BOOL* Cancel);
    ...
}
```

The Microsoft web site states that `PostData` (parameter number 4) is a `Variant` that contains a reference to a `Variant` that is itself a `SafeArray`. The following code uses some of the simpler patterns we reviewed to parse the content of an array:

```
public void handleEvent(OleEvent event) {
  Variant varPostData = event.arguments[4];
  int pPostData = varPostData.getByRef();
  short[] vt_type = new short[1];
  OS.MoveMemory(vt_type, pPostData, 2);
  if (vt_type[0] == (short)(OLE.VT_BYREF | OLE.VT_VARIANT)) {    Check second
    int[] pVariant = new int[1];                                Variant type:
    OS.MoveMemory(pVariant, pPostData + 8, 4);                  SafeArray of
    vt_type = new short[1];                                     unsigned char
    OS.MoveMemory(vt_type, pVariant[0], 2);
    if (vt_type[0] == (short)(OLE.VT_ARRAY | OLE.VT_UI1)) {
      int[] pSafearray = new int[1];                          Establish pointer
      OS.MoveMemory(pSafearray, pVariant[0] + 8, 4);          to SafeArray
      short[] cDims = new short[1];
      OS.MoveMemory(cDims, pSafearray[0], 2);
      System.out.println("total dimensions= "+cDims[0]);
      int[] pvData = new int[1];
      OS.MoveMemory(pvData, pSafearray[0] + 12, 4);
      int offset = 0; int arrayboundOffset = 0;
      for (int i = 0; i < cDims[0]; i++) {    ◄— Iterate through dimensions
        int[] cElements = new int[1];
```

First 4 bytes of SafeArrayBound: number of elements ⌐

```
OS.MoveMemory(cElements,pSafearray[0]+16+arrayboundOffset,4);  ◄─┘
```

Jump to next SafeArrayBound ⌐

```
arrayboundOffset += 8;   ◄────────┘
System.out.println("dim "+i+" has "+cElements[0]+"elements");
for (int j = 0; j < cElements[0]; j++) {
   char[] ui1_data = new char[1];
   OS.MoveMemory(ui1_data, pvData[0]+offset, 1);
   System.out.println("data at "+j+" is "+ui1_data[0]);
   offset += 1;
  }
 }
    }
  }
}
```

B.3.4 *A final example*

Let's work on something more elaborate that brings together everything we've covered so far. The enhanced version of our `SimpleBrowser` from listing B.1, shown in listing B.4, is now capable of displaying a personalized context menu as well as saving the content of the page to a file.

Listing B.4   BetterBrowser.java

```java
package com.swtjface.AppB;
import org.eclipse.swt.SWT;
import org.eclipse.swt.internal.ole.win32.*;
import org.eclipse.swt.internal.win32.*;
import org.eclipse.swt.layout.*;
import org.eclipse.swt.ole.win32.*;
import org.eclipse.swt.widgets.*;

public class BetterBrowser {
  private Shell shell;
  private OleAutomation automation;
  static final int DocumentComplete = 104;
  static final int NavigateComplete = 101;
  private int globalDispatch;

  public Shell open(Display display) {
    this.shell = new Shell(display);
    shell.setLayout(new FillLayout());
    OleFrame frame = new OleFrame(shell, SWT.NONE);
    OleControlSite controlSite = new ExtWebBrowser(frame, SWT.NONE,
                                          "Shell.Explorer");

    automation = new OleAutomation(controlSite);
    boolean activated =
```

```
              (controlSite.doVerb(OLE.OLEIVERB_INPLACEACTIVATE) == OLE.S_OK);

   OleListener listener = new OleListener() {
     public void handleEvent(OleEvent event) {
       switch (event.type) {
         case DocumentComplete : {
                 Variant varResult = event.arguments[0];
                 IDispatch dispatch = varResult.getDispatch();
                 Variant variant = new Variant(automation);
                 IDispatch top = variant.getDispatch();
                 varResult = event.arguments[1];
                 String url = varResult.getString();
           if (globalDispatch != 0 && dispatch.getAddress()
             == globalDispatch) {
             /* final document complete */
             globalDispatch = 0;
           }
           System.out.println("DocComplete");
           break;
         }
         case NavigateComplete : {
           Variant varResult = event.arguments[0];
           IDispatch dispatch = varResult.getDispatch();
           if (globalDispatch == 0)
             globalDispatch = dispatch.getAddress();
           System.out.println("NavComplete");
           break;
         }
       }
       Variant[] arguments = event.arguments;
       for (int i = 0; i < arguments.length; i++)
         arguments[i].dispose();
     }
   };
   controlSite.addEventListener(DocumentComplete, listener);
   controlSite.addEventListener(NavigateComplete, listener);

   this.openURL("http://www.manning.com");
   shell.open();
   return shell;
}
public void openURL(String url) {
   int[] rgdispid = automation.getIDsOfNames
     (new String[]{"Navigate", "URL"});
   int dispIdMember = rgdispid[0];
   Variant[] rgvarg = new Variant[1];
   rgvarg[0] = new Variant(url);
   int[] rgdispidNamedArgs = new int[1];
   rgdispidNamedArgs[0] = rgdispid[1];
   Variant pVarResult = automation.invoke(dispIdMember, rgvarg,
       rgdispidNamedArgs);
}
```

```java
public static void main(String[] args) {
    Display display = new Display();
    Shell shell = (new BetterBrowser()).open(display);
    while (!shell.isDisposed()) {
        if (!display.readAndDispatch()) {
            display.sleep();
        }
    }
    display.dispose();
}

public OleAutomation getHtmlDocument(OleAutomation browser) {
    int[] htmlDocumentID =
        browser.getIDsOfNames(new String[]{"Document"});
    if (htmlDocumentID == null) return null;
    Variant pVarResult = browser.getProperty(htmlDocumentID[0]);
    if (pVarResult == null || pVarResult.getType() == 0) return null;
    //IHTMLDocument2
    OleAutomation htmlDocument = pVarResult.getAutomation();
    return htmlDocument;
}

class ExtWebBrowser extends OleControlSite {

    COMObject iDocHostUIHandler;

    public ExtWebBrowser(Composite parent, int style, String progId) {
        super(parent, style, progId);
    }

    protected void createCOMInterfaces () {

        super.createCOMInterfaces();
        iDocHostUIHandler =
            new COMObject(new int[]{2, 0, 0, 4, 1, 5, 0, 0, 1,
                                    1, 1, 3, 3, 2, 2, 1, 3, 2}){
                public int method0(int[] args)
                    {return QueryInterface(args[0], args[1]);}
                public int method1(int[] args) {return AddRef();}
                public int method2(int[] args) {return Release();}
                public int method3(int[] args)
                    {return ShowContextMenu(args[0], args[1], args[2],
                        args[3]);}
                public int method4(int[] args)
                    {return GetHostInfo(args[0]);}
                public int method5(int[] args)
                    {return ShowUI(args[0], args[1], args[2], args[3],
                        args[4]);}
                public int method6(int[] args) {return HideUI();}
                public int method7(int[] args) {return UpdateUI();}
                public int method8(int[] args)
                    {return EnableModeless(args[0]);}
                public int method9(int[] args)
```

```
                {return OnDocWindowActivate(args[0]);}
            public int method10(int[] args)
                {return OnFrameWindowActivate(args[0]);}
            public int method11(int[] args)
                {return ResizeBorder(args[0], args[1], args[2]);}
            public int method12(int[] args)
                {return TranslateAccelerator(args[0], args[1], args[2]);}
            public int method13(int[] args)
                {return GetOptionKeyPath(args[0], args[1]);}
            public int method14(int[] args)
                {return GetDropTarget(args[0], args[1]);}
            public int method15(int[] args)
                {return GetExternal(args[0]);}
            public int method16(int[] args)
                {return TranslateUrl(args[0], args[1], args[2]);}
            public int method17(int[] args)
                {return FilterDataObject(args[0], args[1]);}
        };
}
protected void disposeCOMInterfaces() {
  super.disposeCOMInterfaces();
  if (iDocHostUIHandler != null)
    iDocHostUIHandler.dispose();
  iDocHostUIHandler = null;
}
protected int QueryInterface(int riid, int ppvObject) {
  int result = super.QueryInterface(riid, ppvObject);
  if (result == COM.S_OK)
    return result;
  if (riid == 0 || ppvObject == 0)
    return COM.E_INVALIDARG;
  GUID guid = new GUID();
  COM.MoveMemory(guid, riid, GUID.sizeof);
  if (COM.IsEqualGUID(guid, COM.IIDIDocHostUIHandler)) {
    COM.MoveMemory(ppvObject, new int[]
     {iDocHostUIHandler.getAddress()}, 4);
    AddRef();
    return COM.S_OK;
  }
  COM.MoveMemory(ppvObject, new int[]{0}, 4);
  return COM.E_NOINTERFACE;
}

//~- IDocHostUIHandler ----------------------------
int EnableModeless(int EnableModeless) {
  return COM.E_NOTIMPL;
}
int FilterDataObject(int pDO, int ppDORet) {
  return COM.E_NOTIMPL;
}
int GetDropTarget(int pDropTarget, int ppDropTarget) {
```

```java
    return COM.E_NOTIMPL;
}
int GetExternal(int ppDispatch) {
  return COM.E_NOTIMPL;
}
int GetHostInfo(int pInfo) {
  return COM.E_NOTIMPL;
}
int GetOptionKeyPath(int pchKey, int dw) {
  return COM.E_NOTIMPL;
}
int HideUI() {
  return COM.E_NOTIMPL;
}
int OnDocWindowActivate(int fActivate) {
  return COM.E_NOTIMPL;
}
int OnFrameWindowActivate(int fActivate) {
  return COM.E_NOTIMPL;
}
int ResizeBorder(int prcBorder, int pUIWindow, int fFrameWindow) {
  return COM.E_NOTIMPL;
}
int ShowContextMenu(int dwID, int ppt,
  int pcmdtReserved, int pdispReserved) {
  int [] pts = new int[2];
  OS.MoveMemory(pts, ppt, 8);

  System.out.println(dwID);
    Menu menu = new Menu (shell, SWT.POP_UP);
    MenuItem item = new MenuItem (menu, SWT.PUSH);
    item.setText ("Save Source");
    item.addListener (SWT.Selection, new Listener () {
      public void handleEvent (Event e) {
          System.out.println ("Save Selected");
          if (globalDispatch != 0) {
            IUnknown iuk = new IUnknown(globalDispatch);
          int[] ppvObject = new int[1];
          if (iuk.QueryInterface(COM.IIDIPersistFile, ppvObject)
            == COM.S_OK) {
            IPersistFile pf = new IPersistFile(ppvObject[0]);
            pf.Save("c:\\test.html", false);
            pf.Release();
          }
          }
      }
    });
    item = new MenuItem (menu, SWT.PUSH);
    item.setText ("View Source");
    item.addListener (SWT.Selection, new Listener () {
      public void handleEvent (Event e) {
```

```
            System.out.println ("View Selected");
          }
        });
        menu.setLocation (pts[0], pts[1]);
        menu.setVisible (true);
        Display display = getShell().getDisplay();
        while (!menu.isDisposed () && menu.isVisible ()) {
          if (!display.readAndDispatch ()) display.sleep ();
        }
        menu.dispose ();
      return COM.S_OK;
  }

  int ShowUI(int dwID, int pActiveObject, int pCommandTarget,
    int pFrame,int pDoc) {
    return COM.E_NOTIMPL;
  }
  int TranslateAccelerator(int lpMsg, int pguidCmdGroup,
    int nCmdID) {
    Menu menubar = getShell().getMenuBar();
    if (menubar != null && !menubar.isDisposed()
      && menubar.isEnabled()) {
      Shell shell = menubar.getShell();
      int hwnd = shell.handle;
      int hAccel = OS.SendMessage(hwnd, OS.WM_APP + 1, 0, 0);
      if (hAccel != 0) {
        MSG msg = new MSG();
        OS.MoveMemory(msg, lpMsg, MSG.sizeof);
        if (OS.TranslateAccelerator(hwnd, hAccel, msg) != 0)
          return COM.S_OK;
      }
    }
    return COM.S_FALSE;
  }
  int TranslateUrl(int dwTranslate, int pchURLIn, int ppchURLOut) {
    return COM.E_NOTIMPL;
  }
  int UpdateUI() {
    return COM.E_NOTIMPL;
  }
  }
}
```

Changeable GUIs
with Draw2D

The SWT/JFace toolset has two shortcomings that we haven't addressed. The first involves building truly *custom* widgets. Because it relies on native widgets, SWT/JFace makes it difficult to extend the `Control` class. So, you can't create your own components.

SWT/JFace's second deficiency involves building *graphical editors*. These applications are similar to normal GUIs, but they allow you to manipulate diagrams and save their models to a file. Generally, these diagrams represent large systems, like those found in Computer-Aided Design (CAD), Unified Modeling Language (UML) software, and graphical software development tools such as Microsoft's Visual Studio. With great pains, SWT/JFace can be used to build a graphical editor, but the toolset wasn't designed for this purpose. We need a tool that specifically addresses the requirements of building graphical editors.

In response to these concerns, the Eclipse designers created the Draw2D and Graphical Editing Framework (GEF) libraries. The Draw2D tool lets you render GUI components with whatever appearance and functionality you prefer. It provides this capability by creating a high-level drawing region that operates independently from the native platform. The GEF library combines these Draw2D figures into a framework suitable for graphical editing.

This appendix presents Draw2D, and appendix D covers GEF. Because GEF requires Draw2D to provide its graphics, these two appendices can be taken as a whole. Old-fashioned at heart, we'll present these toolsets in the context of building a flowchart editor. Our first step involves creating the graphical region and the shapes needed to represent different types of operation. This is a job for Draw2D.

C.1 Understanding Draw2D

The Draw2D library provides a great deal of freedom in generating custom components, but you pay a price in the amount of code needed to implement them. Draw2D relies on many constructs from SWT (*not* JFace), but you must draw and design most of the graphical components within it. You also need to specify their event responses and any drag-and-drop capability. Essentially, the Draw2D library serves as a complete graphics package, with the additional feature that these graphics can be moved and associated with events.

This section begins the discussion by providing an overview of Draw2D's central classes and their functions. Then, we'll intersperse theoretical discussion with the development of the flowchart's graphics. We'll cover the drag-and-drop capability as well as the process of adding `Connector` objects between shapes. Let's start with the basics.

C.1.1   *Using Draw2D's primary classes*

If you've understood our discussion of SWT so far, then Draw2D won't present much difficulty. As shown in table C.1, the two libraries use related classes and provide similar structures for drawing, event handling, and component layout. In fact, all Draw2D GUIs must be added to an SWT `Canvas`. The first difference is that whereas a normal `Canvas` adds a `GC` object to provide graphics, a `Canvas` in a Draw2D application uses an instance of a `LightweightSystem`.

Table C.1   Three primary classes of the Draw2D library

Class	Function	Similar SWT class
`LightweightSystem`	High-level environment for rendering images	`Display`
`Figure`	Component or container within a `LightweightSystem` object	`Shell`, `Control`, `Composite`
`Graphics`	Provides a graphical region within a `Figure`	`GC`

`LightweightSystems` function similarly to `Display` objects in SWT. They have no visual representation but provide event handling and interaction with the external environment. As the name implies, `LightweightSystems` operate at a level removed from the operating system. This means you lose the advantages of SWT/JFace's heavyweight rendering, such as its rapid execution and native look and feel. However, now you can truly customize the appearance and operation of your components.

Without question, the most important class in Draw2D is the `Figure`, and the majority of our Draw2D discussion will focus on its methods and subclasses. Like an SWT `Shell`, it must be added to a `LightweightSystem` in order to provide a basis for the GUI's appearance. Like an SWT `Control`, it provides for resizing and relocating, adding `Listeners` and `LayoutManagers`, and setting colors and fonts. It also functions like a `Composite` in SWT, providing methods for adding and removing other `Figure` objects—children—within its frame. This is shown in figure C.1.

However, unlike `Widget` and `Control` objects, you can easily subclass `Figures`. Their graphical aspects can be represented by a drawing or image. Not only can

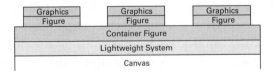

**Figure C.1
Class relationships within
Draw2D user interfaces**

Figures use separate Listener interfaces, they can also perform the majority of their event handling by themselves. Figures can even initiate specific kinds of events to alert other objects in the GUI.

To add images and drawings to Figures, you need to use instances of the Graphics class. It functions similar to SWT's GC (graphics context) class, and it provides methods for incorporating graphics in a given area. It also contains many of the same methods as GC, particularly for drawing lines and shapes, displaying images, and working with fonts. However, the Graphics class provides one very different capability: Its objects can be moved, or *translated*, within the Lightweight-System. This means that when you want to change the position of a graphical component, Draw2D provides its own drag-and-drop capability to translate a Figure to the desired location.

C.1.2 *The Flowchart application*

UML has long been preeminent in modeling software, but flowcharts are still helpful in depicting sequential operations within a program. Our Draw2D example focuses on drawing a simple flowchart, as shown in figure C.2.

This appendix provides the code needed to create this figure in Draw2D. Appendix D will show you how to build a full flowchart editor based on the Figures we build here.

At the time of this writing, the Draw2D/GEF plug-ins aren't included in Eclipse and must be downloaded separately. Currently, you can acquire the GEF Software Development Kit (SDK) from www.eclipse.org/gef. This file, which contains the GEF and the Draw2D libraries, can be quickly integrated by placing it in the $ECLIPSE directory and decompressing its contents. Doing so will place the Draw2D/GEF plug-ins in the $ECLIPSE/plugins directory and their features in the $ECLIPSE/features directory.

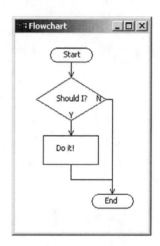

Figure C.2
A simple flowchart. Not much help for complex projects, but always good for nostalgia.

Because the code in this appendix is lengthy, we recommend that you download our files from the Manning web site (www.manning.com/scarpino). However, if you intend to build your own application, start by adding a com.swtjface.AppB package to the WidgetWindow project. Then, create a classpath variable,

Draw2D_LIB, pointing to $ECLIPSE/plugins/org.eclipse.draw2d_x.y.z/draw2d.jar. Add this variable to the project.

The Draw2D library incorporates many classes and capabilities, and this appendix can't cover every facet of its operation. Therefore, we'll concentrate on those classes that perform the main work of the toolset. This means investigating the Figure class and its subclasses in greater depth.

C.2 *Draw2D Figures*

As you'll see, it takes a fair amount of code to build a Draw2D GUI. However, unlike those in an SWT/JFace GUI, Draw2D elements can be moved and manipulated. These components, including the overall container, are descendents of Draw2D's main class, Figure. This class contains a number of subclasses that produce the visual aspects of the toolset's GUI. Figure C.3 shows a small but important subset.

These subclasses will be used extensively in the flowchart editor, particularly those involving Connections and Layers. But first, we need to explore Figures in general.

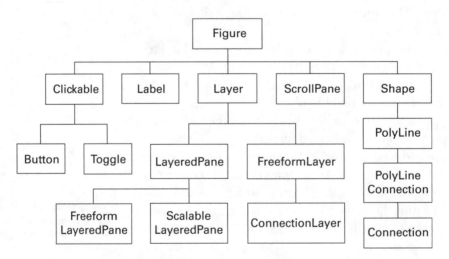

Figure C.3   The Draw2D Figure class and a portion of its subclasses. Many of these play an important role in the flowchart editor presented in appendix D.

C.2.1 Figure methods

Like the SWT `Control` class, the `Figure` class contains many methods for manipulating its properties. We can't describe all 137 of them, but we can divide them into four main categories:

- Working with the `Figure`'s visual aspects
- Event handling
- Keeping track of parents and children
- Managing graphics

If you've come this far, then you can probably figure out all you need to know from the Draw2D Javadocs. However, we'll provide a brief description of these categories here.

Working with a Figure's visual aspects

The methods in the first category are exactly like those in SWT. These include getting and setting the `Figure`'s bounds, location, and size. The `Figure`'s maximum and minimum size can be controlled as well as its border size and visible area. This category also provides methods for changing the `Figure`'s foreground and background color and getting/setting its focus and visibility parameters.

Event handling in Draw2D

The process of handling events in Draw2D is also similar to SWT, but it provides a few new `events` and `listeners`. Unlike SWT, `Figures` can handle many of their own events. The entire list of `listeners` and their handling methods is shown in table C.2.

Table C.2 Figure methods for `event` listening and handling

Draw2D listener	Event-handling method(s)
addFocusListener()	handleFocusGained() handleFocusLost()
addKeyListener()	handleKeyPressed() handleKeyReleased()
addMouseListener()	handleMouseDoubleClicked() handleMousePressed() handleMouseReleased()

continued on next page

Table C.2 Figure methods for event listening and handling *(continued)*

Draw2D listener	Event-handling method(s)
addMouseMotionListener()	handleMouseDragged() handleMouseEntered() handleMouseExited() handleMouseHovered() handleMouseMoved()
addListener()	N/A
addAncestorListener()	N/A
addFigureListener()	N/A
addPropertyChangeListener()	N/A

The first five methods look and act just like those in SWT, with addListener() receiving untyped Events. But the last three methods are unique to Draw2D.

The addAncestorListener() method responds to any changes to the Figure's ancestors and functions like the Swing implementation. Similarly, the FigureListener responds whenever the Figure is moved.

The last method, addPropertyChangeListener(), lets you create your own events. This process starts by associating a property, such as a Figure's location, with a String descriptor. Then, when firePropertyChange() is invoked with this String, any PropertyChangeListeners listening for this property change respond. We'll revisit this subject in greater depth when we discuss the GEF and its model classes.

Parent and child Figures

SWT and JFace allow components to be included in other components by providing a Composite class. But in Draw2D, any Figure can be a container, and any Figure can be contained. Therefore, Draw2D uses the term *parent* to refer to the outer graphic and *child* to refer to the graphic contained within. You create and manipulate these relationships with the methods listed in table C.3.

Table C.3 Parent/child methods of the Figure class

Method	Function
add(Figure, Object, int)	Adds a child Figure with the given constraint and List index
getChildren()	Returns a List of child Figures

continued on next page

Table C.3 **Parent/child methods of the** `Figure` **class** *(continued)*

Method	Function
`getParent()`	Returns the `Figure`'s parent `Figure`
`setChildrenEnabled(boolean)`	Enables or disables the `Figure`'s children
`setConstraint(Figure, Object)`	Sets a constraint for the given child `Figure`

In SWT, `Buttons` and `Labels` add themselves to `Composites` by identifying parents in their constructors. In Draw2D, a parent `Figure` uses its `add()` method to include `Figures` in its `List` of children. This method can include an optional constraint (such as the child's size or location) and/or an index in the parent's `List`. Parent `Figures` can obtain this `List` with the `getChildren()` method, and children can access their parent with `getParent()`. Parents can also enable or disable children with `setChildrenEnabled()` or alter an aspect of the child with `setConstraint()`.

Managing graphics

Although Draw2D provides a `Graphics` class that performs most of the duties of SWT's `GC`, `Figures` have a few graphical methods of their own. Not only can they control their display with `paint()`, they can also use `paintBorder()` and `paintClientArea()` to select which section to show. `Figures` can display their children with `paintChildren()` or use `paintFigure()` to only show themselves. There are also a number of `repaint()` methods available, which work similarly to those in SWT.

Draw2D contains methods for finding information about the user's selection location. This is different from SWT because Draw2D is particularly concerned with precise mouse movements, whereas an SWT GUI is only concerned about the selected `Control`. These methods include `FindMouseEventAt()`, `FindFigureAt()`, and `FindFigureAt()`.

C.2.2 Using Labels and Clickables

The first `Figure` subclasses for our investigation are the simplest: `Labels` and `Clickables`. These objects look and act similarly to their SWT counterparts, but there are a few interesting concerns that you need to keep in mind.

Labels

Draw2D `Labels` resemble those of SWT but contain more methods for text measurement and image location. You can measure the parameters of the `Label`'s `String` through `getTextBounds()` and `getTextLocation()`. Similarly, if the `Label` is associated with an `Image`, then `getIconBounds()` and `getIconAlignment()` will provide information about the `Image`.

Clickables

This class, which includes `Buttons` and `Toggles`, provides binary information concerning the user's preferences. Like SWT `Buttons`, they can be configured with style bits to appear like toggle buttons, checkboxes, or regular pushbuttons. You can also control their selection and add images or text. But there are two main differences between Draw2D `Clickables` and SWT `Buttons`. The first is that `Clickables` can take the appearance of any Draw2D `Figure`. The second has to do with `Clickable` event handling.

Draw2D user interfaces are generally more complex than those created with SWT and JFace. Therefore, a `Clickable`'s state information is managed by a `ButtonModel` or `ToggleModel` object. This separates the component's appearance from its behavior and enables you to develop the two aspects independently. You can also contain these `Model` objects in a `ButtonGroup`, which manages multiple `Clickables` at once.

`Clickables` update their `Model` objects by calling `fireChangeEvent()`, which works like the `Figure`'s `firePropertyChangeEvent()`. `Clickable` properties, such as `MOUSEOVER_PROPERTY` and `PRESSED_PROPERTY`, are represented by constants in the `Model` class. When they change, the `Model` may fire a number of Draw2D events or inform its `ButtonGroup` by default.

Example application

The code in listing C.1 won't be used in our flowchart editor, but it shows how Draw2D `Clickables`, `Models`, and `ButtonGroups` work together. In this case, we use the `CheckBox` subclass of `Clickable` and associate it with a `ToggleModel`.

Listing C.1   Draw2D_Example.java

```java
package com.swtjface.AppC;

import org.eclipse.swt.widgets.*;
import org.eclipse.draw2d.*;
import org.eclipse.draw2d.Label;
import org.eclipse.draw2d.geometry.*;

public class Draw2D_Example
{
  public static void main(String args[])
  {
    final Label label = new Label("Press a button!");
    Shell shell = new Shell();
```

```java
LightweightSystem lws = new LightweightSystem(shell);
Figure parent = new Figure();
parent.setLayoutManager(new XYLayout());
lws.setContents(parent);

Clickable above = new CheckBox("I'm above!");
parent.add(above, new Rectangle(10,10,80,20));
ButtonModel aModel = new ToggleModel();
aModel.addChangeListener(new ChangeListener()
{
  public void handleStateChanged(ChangeEvent e)
  {
    label.setText("Above");
  }
});
above.setModel(aModel);

Clickable below = new CheckBox("I'm below!");
parent.add(below, new Rectangle(10,40,80,20));
ButtonModel bModel = new ToggleModel();
bModel.addChangeListener(new ChangeListener()
{
  public void handleStateChanged(ChangeEvent e)
  {
    label.setText("Below");
  }
});
below.setModel(bModel);

ButtonGroup bGroup = new ButtonGroup();
bGroup.add(aModel);
bGroup.add(bModel);
bGroup.setDefault(bModel);

parent.add(label, new Rectangle(10,70,80,20));
shell.setSize(130,120);
shell.open();
shell.setText("Example");
Display display = Display.getDefault();
while (!shell.isDisposed())
{
  if (!display.readAndDispatch())
    display.sleep ();
}
  }
}
```

As you can see, a Draw2D application is just an SWT Shell with a LightweightSystem and Figures. It's important to understand that the ChangeListener is created by the button's Model and responds to any mouse action, including clicks and hovering. Also, because the two Models are added to the ButtonGroup, only one of them can be selected at a time.

In order for the parent Figure to understand the Rectangle constraints of its children, you must configure it with a LayoutManager called XYLayout. We'll now focus on LayoutManagers and how they enable you to determine how children are arranged within Figures.

C.3 *Using LayoutManagers and panes*

LayoutManagers, like SWT's Layout classes, specify how child components should be positioned and sized in a container. This section describes LayoutManager's subclasses and how you can use them.

In addition, we'll go over Draw2D's *panes*: ScrollPanes, LayerPanes, and their subclasses. Draw2D has no Composite class, but these panes generally serve as background containers for its GUIs. As you'll see, these window-like classes provide a number of capabilities that make it simple to build graphical editors. We'll finish this section by creating the first flowchart Figure by extending the FreeformLayeredPane class.

C.3.1 *Understanding LayoutManager subclasses*

In SWT, containers rely on a default layout policy for their children; but Draw2D demands that you choose a LayoutManager subclass. Two of these, FlowFigureLayout and ScrollBarLayout, are only useful for specific Figures, so we'll concentrate on three (see table C.4).

Table C.4   LayoutManager subclasses

Subclass	Description
AbstractHintLayout	Uses *hint* constraints to determine the size of the child Figures, calculating one dimension based on a specified value for the other
DelegatingLayout	Allows children to set their own size according to a Locator constraint
XYLayout	Gives the parent the responsibility for sizing and positioning its children according to a Rectangle constraint

It's important to understand that when a parent Figure uses its add() method with a position constraint, its LayoutManager is responsible for interpreting the constraint and setting the child's location as needed.

We'll choose the XYLayout for our editor. Now we need a suitable container class: We'll choose the LayeredPane.

C.3.2 LayeredPanes

Since Draw2D applications can become very complex, a LayeredPane provides many levels for displaying Figures. Using transparent Layers, you can separate the graphical aspects of your GUIs. Different Layers can have different properties, including separate LayoutManagers. This will be important for our editor, because we add not only Figures but also Connections and feedback.

The first step in understanding how LayeredPanes work is learning about Layers. These transparent objects can be manipulated as individual Figures, and the Layer class contains two methods of its own: containsPoint() and findFigureAt(). These objects have fixed boundaries, but the FreeformLayer subclass can be extended in all directions. This is necessary for a graphical editing application whose drawings are larger than the window's visible region.

A LayeredPane adds new Layers with its add() method, which specifies the Layer object, a key to identify it, and an index representing its position. It can also remove Layers or change their positions in its stack.

By choosing subclasses of LayeredPane, you can increase its capabilities. If you'd like to be able to zoom in on sections of the pane, choose ScalableLayeredPane. Use FreeformLayeredPane if you'd like to extend the window in all directions. If you want both capabilities, use ScalableFreeformLayeredPane. In our case, we're only interested in extensibility; listing C.2 shows the FreeformLayeredPane that we'll use as the basis of our editor.

Listing C.2   ChartFigure.java

```java
package com.swtjface.AppC;

import org.eclipse.draw2d.*;

public class ChartFigure extends FreeformLayeredPane
{
  public ChartFigure()
  {
    setLayoutManager(new FreeformLayout());
    setBorder(new MarginBorder(5));
    setBackgroundColor(ColorConstants.white);
    setOpaque(true);
  }
}
```

We configure the FreeformLayeredPane with its appearance constraints, but we don't add any Layers yet. That will happen later in the editor's development.

C.3.3 ScrollPanes and Viewports

Before ending our discussion of Draw2D's panes, we need to briefly mention ScrollPanes. These classes are easy to understand and function by creating Scrollbars on top of another Figure. The bars' visibility can be configured so that they are always showing, never showing, or shown only when needed.

At any given time, only a section of the ScrollPane can be seen. This visible region is called a Viewport. These work similarly to Layers but provide more methods for controlling size and shape. There is also a FreeformViewport for panes that can be extended in all directions.

Now that we've built the primary container for our application, we need to create the shapes that will be added to its diagram. For this, we need to investigate Draw2D's Graphics class and its drawing capability.

C.4 Using the Graphics class to create Shapes

In SWT, graphic contexts (GCs) can either be created as separate objects or obtained as part of a PaintEvent. But in Draw2D, a Figure can acquire a Graphics object by one of the paint methods described in section C.2.1. The vast majority of the Graphics methods are exactly the same as those in GC; the only important difference is that Draw2D allows a Graphics object to move through its translate() method.

However, Draw2D provides more powerful capabilities for creating and manipulating Shapes. As you'll see, it has packages of helpful classes for working with geometry and graphs.

C.4.1 Using the Graphics class

As we've mentioned, the Graphics methods are nearly identical to those of SWT's GC. Therefore, in this subsection we'll create the classes that represent the components shown in figure C.2. To clarify, these three Figures function as follows:

- *DecisionFigure*—Contains a question. One input, two outputs (Yes or No).
- *ProcessFigure*—Contains an action to be followed. One input, one output.
- *TerminatorFigure*—Represents the start or end of the flowchart. If it's used as a start, only the output should be connected. If it's used as an end, only the input should be connected.

In each case, the Figure's size is controlled by a variable called bounds. Its text is set with a message String. These constraints are controlled outside of their Figure classes, so you won't be able to view them yet.

The code for these classes, including the paintFigure() method that creates the Graphics object, is shown in listings C.3 through C.5.

Listing C.3   DecisionFigure.java

```java
package com.swtjface.AppC;
import org.eclipse.draw2d.*;
import org.eclipse.draw2d.geometry.*;

public class DecisionFigure extends ActivityFigure
{
  FixedAnchor inAnchor, yesAnchor, noAnchor;

  public DecisionFigure()
  {
    inAnchor = new FixedAnchor(this);
    inAnchor.place = new Point(1, 0);
    targetAnchors.put("in_dec",inAnchor);

    noAnchor = new FixedAnchor(this);
    noAnchor.place = new Point(2, 1);
    sourceAnchors.put("no",noAnchor);

    yesAnchor = new FixedAnchor(this);
    yesAnchor.place = new Point(1, 2);
    sourceAnchors.put("yes",yesAnchor);
  }

  public void paintFigure(Graphics g)
  {
    Rectangle r = bounds;
    PointList pl = new PointList(4);
    pl.addPoint(r.x + r.width/2, r.y);
    pl.addPoint(r.x, r.y + r.height/2);
    pl.addPoint(r.x + r.width/2, r.y + r.height-1);
    pl.addPoint(r.x + r.width, r.y + r.height/2);
    g.drawPolygon(pl);
    g.drawText(message, r.x+r.width/4+5, r.y+3*r.height/8);
    g.drawText("N", r.x+7*r.width/8, r.y+3*r.height/8);
    g.drawText("Y", r.x+r.width/2-2, r.y+3*r.height/4);
  }
}
```

Because of the `DecisionFigure`'s irregular diamond shape, we need to create a separate `Polygon` by specifying a series of `Points`. Thankfully, the `ProcessFigure` is a `Rectangle` and is much easier to code.

Listing C.4   ProcessFigure.java

```java
package com.swtjface.AppC;
import org.eclipse.draw2d.*;
import org.eclipse.draw2d.geometry.*;

public class ProcessFigure extends ActivityFigure
{
  FixedAnchor inAnchor, outAnchor;

  public ProcessFigure()
  {
    inAnchor = new FixedAnchor(this);
    inAnchor.place = new Point(1, 0);
    targetAnchors.put("in_proc", inAnchor);

    outAnchor = new FixedAnchor(this);
    outAnchor.place = new Point(1, 2);
    sourceAnchors.put("out_proc", outAnchor);
  }

  public void paintFigure(Graphics g)
  {
    Rectangle r = bounds;
    g.drawText(message, r.x + r.width/4, r.y + r.height/4);
    g.drawRectangle(r.x, r.y, r.width-1, r.height-1);
  }
}
```

Since the `TerminatorFigure` contains two arcs on either side, it isn't nearly as easy to draw as the `ProcessFigure`. However, its code is easy to understand.

Listing C.5   TerminatorFigure.java

```java
package com.swtjface.AppC;

import org.eclipse.draw2d.*;
import org.eclipse.draw2d.geometry.*;

public class TerminatorFigure extends ActivityFigure
{
  FixedAnchor inAnchor, outAnchor;

  public TerminatorFigure()
  {
    inAnchor = new FixedAnchor(this);
```

```
      inAnchor.place = new Point(1, 0);
      targetAnchors.put("in_term",inAnchor);

      outAnchor = new FixedAnchor(this);
      outAnchor.place = new Point(1, 2);
      sourceAnchors.put("out_term",outAnchor);
   }
   public void paintFigure(Graphics g)
   {
      Rectangle r = bounds;
      g.drawArc(r.x + r.width/8, r.y, r.width/4, r.height-1, 90, 180);
      g.drawLine(r.x + r.width/4, r.y, r.x + 3*r.width/4, r.y);
      g.drawLine(r.x + r.width/4, r.y + r.height-1, r.x + 3*r.width/4,
                 r.y + r.height-1);
      g.drawArc(r.x + 5*r.width/8, r.y, r.width/4, r.height-1, 270, 180);
      g.drawText(message, r.x+3*r.width/8, r.y+r.height/8);
   }
}
```

Clearly, there's a great deal more to these classes than just drawings. The added complexity is present for two reasons. First, these Figures need to be connected to other Figures, which means they need ConnectionAnchors (called FixedAnchors). Second, these Figures will play an important role in the full flowchart editor that we'll create in appendix D. Many of their methods can't be explained until then (but they're worth waiting for!).

Since all these Figures extend from an ActivityFigure, it would be a good idea to show what that is. This superclass contains all the methods common to our DecisionFigure, ProcessFigure, and TerminatorFigure. As you can see from listing C.6, most of its methods keep track of Connections and their anchors.

Listing C.6 ActivityFigure.java

```
package com.swtjface.AppC;

import org.eclipse.draw2d.*;
import org.eclipse.draw2d.geometry.*;

import java.util.*;

abstract public class ActivityFigure
   extends Figure
{
   Rectangle r = new Rectangle();
   Hashtable targetAnchors = new Hashtable();
   Hashtable sourceAnchors = new Hashtable();
   String message = new String();
```

```java
public void setName(String msg)
{
  message = msg;
  repaint();
}

public ConnectionAnchor ConnectionAnchorAt(Point p)
{
  ConnectionAnchor closest = null;
  long min = Long.MAX_VALUE;
  Hashtable conn = getSourceConnectionAnchors();
  conn.putAll(getTargetConnectionAnchors());
  Enumeration e = conn.elements();
  while (e.hasMoreElements())
  {
    ConnectionAnchor c = (ConnectionAnchor) e.nextElement();
    Point p2 = c.getLocation(null);
    long d = p.getDistance2(p2);
    if (d < min)
    {
      min = d;
      closest = c;
    }
  }
  return closest;
}

public ConnectionAnchor getSourceConnectionAnchor(String name)
{
  return (ConnectionAnchor)sourceAnchors.get(name);
}

public ConnectionAnchor getTargetConnectionAnchor(String name)
{
  return (ConnectionAnchor)targetAnchors.get(name);
}

public String getSourceAnchorName(ConnectionAnchor c)
{
  Enumeration enum = sourceAnchors.keys();
  String name;
  while (enum.hasMoreElements())
  {
    name = (String)enum.nextElement();
    if (sourceAnchors.get(name).equals(c))
      return name;
  }
  return null;
}

public String getTargetAnchorName(ConnectionAnchor c)
{
  Enumeration enum = targetAnchors.keys();
```

```
  String name;
  while (enum.hasMoreElements())
  {
    name = (String)enum.nextElement();
    if (targetAnchors.get(name).equals(c))
      return name;
  }
  return null;
}

public ConnectionAnchor getSourceConnectionAnchorAt(Point p)
{
  ConnectionAnchor closest = null;
  long min = Long.MAX_VALUE;
  Enumeration e = getSourceConnectionAnchors().elements();
  while (e.hasMoreElements())
  {
    ConnectionAnchor c = (ConnectionAnchor) e.nextElement();
    Point p2 = c.getLocation(null);
    long d = p.getDistance2(p2);
    if (d < min)
    {
      min = d;
      closest = c;
    }
  }
  return closest;
}

public Hashtable getSourceConnectionAnchors()
{
  return sourceAnchors;
}

public ConnectionAnchor getTargetConnectionAnchorAt(Point p)
{
  ConnectionAnchor closest = null;
  long min = Long.MAX_VALUE;
  Enumeration e = getTargetConnectionAnchors().elements();
  while (e.hasMoreElements())
  {
    ConnectionAnchor c = (ConnectionAnchor) e.nextElement();
    Point p2 = c.getLocation(null);
    long d = p.getDistance2(p2);
    if (d < min)
    {
      min = d;
      closest = c;
    }
  }
  return closest;
```

```
      }

    public Hashtable getTargetConnectionAnchors()
    {
      return targetAnchors;
    }
  }
```

We'll describe these ConnectionAnchors and Connections shortly. But first, we need to address Draw2D's package for geometry and shapes.

C.4.2 Draw2D geometry and graphs

You've seen how Points and Rectangles are used, but Draw2D provides many more classes for incorporating shapes in GUIs. For higher-precision measurements, Draw2D provides PrecisionPoints, PrecisionRectangles, and Precision-Dimensions. It contains Ray objects that function like mathematical vectors and a Transform class to translate, rotate, and scale graphical Points and dimensions.

The org.eclipse.draw2d.graph package contains a number of useful classes for creating and analyzing directed graphs. Along with basic Nodes and Edges, this package also provides a DirectedGraphLayout for arranging them. Graph theory is far beyond the scope of this appendix, but if it interests you, this package should prove helpful.

Draw2D's Figures aren't connected by Edges, but by Connection objects. To finish our flowchart diagram, we need to show you how this class operates.

C.5 Understanding Connections

The FixedAnchor class has figured prominently in our code listings so far. These objects (subclasses of AbstractConnectionAnchor) enable you to add lines, or Connections, between two Figures. Because Connections create relationships between components, they're fundamental in system models and diagrams. However, managing Connections and their ConnectionAnchors can be complicated, so it's important that you understand how they function.

C.5.1 Working with ConnectionAnchors

ConnectionAnchors don't have a visual representation. Instead, they specify a point on a Figure that can receive Connections. You add them by identifying the Figure in the ConnectionAnchor's constructor method. This Figure is called the anchor's *owner*, not its parent.

The difficulty in working with anchors isn't adding them, but placing them appropriately. For this reason, the only method required by the ConnectionAnchor interface is getLocation() (see listing C.7).

Listing C.7 FixedAnchor.java

```java
package com.swtjface.AppC;

import org.eclipse.draw2d.*;
import org.eclipse.draw2d.geometry.*;

public class FixedAnchor
   extends AbstractConnectionAnchor
{
  Point place;

  public FixedAnchor(IFigure owner)
  {
    super(owner);
  }

  public Point getLocation(Point loc)
  {
    Rectangle r = getOwner().getBounds();
    int x = r.x + place.x * r.width/2;
    int y = r.y + place.y * r.height/2;
    Point p = new PrecisionPoint(x,y);
    getOwner().translateToAbsolute(p);
    return p;
  }
}
```

The getLocation() method is called whenever the owner's location changes. The Point returned by the method tells the GUI where the anchor should be positioned. In our case, we use getOwner() to obtain the owner's bounds and a constraint called place. This variable specifies the anchor's location as a proportion of the owner's dimensions. This way, if the Figure's size changes, the anchor will still be positioned properly.

For example, we want the input connection into our DecisionFigure to be located at the top of its bounds and halfway across its width. We set this in our class as follows:

```
inAnchor = new FixedAnchor(this);
inAnchor.place = new Point(1, 0);
targetAnchors.put("in_dec",inAnchor);
```

Here, place is set to (1,0) to tell the anchor to be located at 1/2 its width and 0/2 its height, as measured from the top, leftmost corner of the Figure's enclosing Rectangle. The anchor is then placed in a Hashtable with a String key. This doesn't mean anything in Draw2D, but it will be important when we use this Figure in the GEF editor.

C.5.2 Adding Connections to the GUI

Working with Connections is easier than dealing with their anchors, because Draw2D takes care of drawing the line. Draw2D's implementation of the Connection interface is PolylineConnection, which is a connected line. Our subclass of PolylineConnection is PathFigure (see listing C.8).

Listing C.8   LiPathFigure.java

```
package com.swtjface.AppC;

import org.eclipse.draw2d.*;

public class PathFigure extends PolylineConnection
{
  public PathFigure()
  {
    setTargetDecoration(new PolylineDecoration());
    setConnectionRouter(new ManhattanConnectionRouter());
  }
}
```

Of course, Connections are more than connected lines. We need to set their source and target Figures, and we can configure their appearance and routing. With regard to appearance, you can add decorations to the start and end of the Connection by calling setSourceDecoration() or setTargetDecoration(). In our case, we create a new PolylineDecoration for the end of the Connection, which looks like a triangle tip.

In addition to decorators, you can add Labels or other Figures to Connections by using a ConnectionEndpointLocator. These objects are created with a Connection object and a boolean value representing whether the Figure should be added at the start or end. Then, setVDistance() tells the new Figure how far away it should be from the Connection, and setUDistance() specifies the distance to the Connection's source or target.

The Connection's router refers to the path it takes from one anchor to the next. The four subclasses of AbstractConnectionRouter are listed in table C.5.

Table C.5 AbstractConnectionRouter **subclasses**

Subclass	Description
AutomaticRouter	Positions Connections so that they never intersect, or intersect as little as possible
ManhattanConnectionRouter	Positions Connections so that all bends are made with right angles
ConnectionRouter.NullConnectionRouter	Positions Connections in a straight line from the source anchor to the target
BendpointConnectionRouter	Creates moveable points (Bendpoints) for each bend in the Connection

As you can see in figure C.2, our PathFigures always bend at right angles; this is because we chose to use the ManhattanConnectionRouter. It's important to note, though, that if your LayeredPane contains a ConnectionLayer, you can also use it to set the routing.

Now that you understand Draw2D's Figures and Connections, we'll combine the two in our final section.

C.6 Putting it all together

We're nearly ready to add the main class of the diagram. But to allow users to reposition Figures, you need to understand how drag-and-drop works in Draw2D. We'll also present the FigureFactory class so that you can centralize Figure allocation.

C.6.1 Drag-and-drop in Draw2D

We've already mentioned a number of important listeners and events in Draw2D, but none of them involved DragSources, DropTargets, or anything resembling the drag-and-drop capability of SWT. This is because at the time of this writing, Draw2D has yet to incorporate this feature. Therefore, our Dnd class, shown in listing C.9, relies on the Figure's ability to translate itself according to the distance between its present and future locations.

Listing C.9   Dnd.java

```java
package com.swtjface.AppC;

import org.eclipse.draw2d.*;
import org.eclipse.draw2d.geometry.*;

public class Dnd extends MouseMotionListener.Stub
  implements MouseListener
{
  public Dnd(IFigure figure)
  {
    figure.addMouseMotionListener(this);
    figure.addMouseListener(this);
  }
  Point start;
  public void mouseReleased(MouseEvent e){}
  public void mouseClicked(MouseEvent e){}
  public void mouseDoubleClicked(MouseEvent e){}
  public void mousePressed(MouseEvent e)
  {
    start = e.getLocation();
  }
  public void mouseDragged(MouseEvent e)
  {
    Point p = e.getLocation();
    Dimension d = p.getDifference(start);
    start = p;
    Figure f = ((Figure)e.getSource());
    f.setBounds(f.getBounds().getTranslated(d.width, d.height));
  }
};
```

Because this class extends MouseMotionListener.Stub, it doesn't need to add all the methods for a MouseMotionListener. But because it needs to respond to mouse clicks, it implements MouseListener and needs to add all the methods for this interface.

C.6.2   *Creating Figures with a FigureFactory*

To prevent outside methods from directly invoking constructor methods, the editor uses the *factory pattern* for its Figures. This is a single class whose static methods create new Figures for insertion into the GUI. The code for the FigureFactory is shown in listing C.10.

```
Listing C.10   FigureFactory.java
```

```java
package com.swtjface.AppC;

import org.eclipse.draw2d.IFigure;

public class FigureFactory
{

  public static IFigure createTerminatorFigure()
  {
    return new TerminatorFigure();
  }

public static IFigure createDecisionFigure()
  {
    return new DecisionFigure();
  }

  public static IFigure createProcessFigure()
  {
    return new ProcessFigure();
  }

  public static PathFigure createPathFigure()
  {
    return new PathFigure();
  }

  public static ChartFigure createChartFigure()
  {
    return new ChartFigure();
  }
}
```

We've created all the Figures needed for the flowchart and the factory class that creates them. Now we can add the final executable that combines them.

C.6.3 *The Flowchart class*

To finish the application, listing C.11 presents the Flowchart class.

```
Listing C.11   Flowchart.java
```

```java
package com.swtjface.AppC;

import org.eclipse.swt.widgets.*;
import org.eclipse.draw2d.*;
import org.eclipse.draw2d.geometry.*;

public class Flowchart
{
```

```
public static void main(String args[])
{
    Shell shell = new Shell();
    shell.setSize(200,300);
    shell.open();
    shell.setText("Flowchart");
    LightweightSystem lws = new LightweightSystem(shell);
    ChartFigure flowchart = new ChartFigure();
    lws.setContents(flowchart);

    TerminatorFigure start = new TerminatorFigure();
    start.setName("Start");
    start.setBounds(new Rectangle(40,20,80,20));
    DecisionFigure dec = new DecisionFigure();
    dec.setName("Should I?");
    dec.setBounds(new Rectangle(30,60,100,60));
    ProcessFigure proc = new ProcessFigure();
    proc.setName("Do it!");
    proc.setBounds(new Rectangle(40,140,80,40));
    TerminatorFigure stop = new TerminatorFigure();
    stop.setName("End");
    stop.setBounds(new Rectangle(40,200,80,20));

    PathFigure path1 = new PathFigure();
    path1.setSourceAnchor(start.outAnchor);
    path1.setTargetAnchor(dec.inAnchor);
    PathFigure path2 = new PathFigure();
    path2.setSourceAnchor(dec.yesAnchor);
    path2.setTargetAnchor(proc.inAnchor);
    PathFigure path3 = new PathFigure();
    path3.setSourceAnchor(dec.noAnchor);
    path3.setTargetAnchor(stop.inAnchor);
    PathFigure path4 = new PathFigure();
    path4.setSourceAnchor(proc.outAnchor);
    path4.setTargetAnchor(stop.inAnchor);

    flowchart.add(start);
    flowchart.add(dec);
    flowchart.add(proc);
    flowchart.add(stop);
    flowchart.add(path1);
    flowchart.add(path2);
    flowchart.add(path3);
    flowchart.add(path4);

    new Dnd(start);
    new Dnd(proc);
    new Dnd(dec);
    new Dnd(stop);

    Display display = Display.getDefault();
    while (!shell.isDisposed())
    {
```

```
      if (!display.readAndDispatch())
        display.sleep();
    }
  }
}
```

Although the code for this class is long, its operation is easy to understand. After the ChartFigure is added to the LightweightSystem, four component Figures are created and initialized. These components are connected with four PathFigures. After all the Figures are added to the diagram, the code associates a Dnd object with each component.

The diagram we've created is more interesting than many of our SWT GUIs, but it leaves much to be desired. We'd like to add and remove Figures and the Connections between them. We want to resize them and set their messages during operation. Finally, we'd like to persist our flowcharts in a file so we don't have to rebuild them every time we close the application.

All of this is possible, but it's not easy. If you thought the code in this appendix was involved, you haven't seen anything yet. In appendix D, we'll introduce the Graphical Editing Framework.

The Graphical Editing Framework (GEF)

GEF development is, without question, the most complex topic thus far—it would take an entire book to examine the GEF toolset in full. So, this appendix will only describe the structure and function of a simple (*but complete*) graphical editor.

Building a graphical editor involves much more than Draw2D Figures: It requires a sound knowledge of plug-ins, Model-View-Controller (MVC) architecture, JavaBean components, JFace Viewers, JFace Actions, JFace properties, and many of the classes that make up the Eclipse Workbench. Although this appendix won't attempt to explain any of these concepts in depth, we'll clarify how they work together in the GEF. Learning to build a graphical editor isn't easy, but with sufficient experience, you can create powerful applications with reusable, interchangeable code.

GEF development is complicated but not impossible. How do you eat a two-ton elephant? One bite at a time.

D.1 A GEF overview

Before we go into the nuts and bolts of GEF development, it will be helpful to discuss how the machine works as a whole. A graphical editor functions by allowing a user to create a visual representation of a complex system. The editing process is performed by adding graphical elements to a container, setting their properties, and creating relationships between them. Once these elements and relationships are set, the editor must be able to persist the editor's state in a file. Of course, this file doesn't keep track of every color, dimension, and pixel in the editor. Instead, it contains the diagram's information—its *meaning*—which has been separated from its appearance.

D.1.1 Separation of concerns theory

Not only does GEF development split information and appearance, it also requires classes for every separable aspect of the editor. That is, a GEF editor isn't a single, monolithic application, but a combination of many small objects that communicate using standard interfaces. This modular structure makes editor code easy to replace and maintain. However, the multiplicity of parts makes the learning curve steep.

Figure D.1 shows how the MVC architecture provides a separation of concerns. The View is the easiest to understand, since it provides the component's display. The Model aspect is more subtle; put simply, it holds the properties of the editor that can be modified by the user. These could include the size and location of the

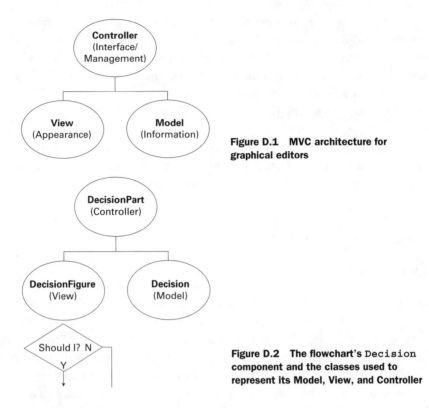

Figure D.1   MVC architecture for graphical editors

Figure D.2   The flowchart's Decision **component and the classes used to represent its Model, View, and Controller**

editor's components and the presence and placement of the connections between them.

The Controller manages the component's interaction with the rest of the GUI. It receives notice of user input and directs changes to its Model and View objects. It keeps track of connections between components and any message communication. In essence, the Controller aspect takes care of everything that isn't related to the Model or View.

D.1.2   *Separation of concerns: GEF implementation*

Every editable component in a GEF editor consists of three objects that provide its MVC structure. The View aspect is generally implemented as a Figure or Image. The Controller is a subclass of AbstractGraphicalEditPart. A Model class extends only Object. Figure D.2 shows the classes that will be used to create our Decision component and the naming conventions for each.

Thankfully, we created the View aspects of the editor's components in appendix C. We can now show how these aspects work together during editing.

NOTE   Although the EditPart object makes up the Controller aspect of a GEF component, the *entire* MVC combination is generally referred to as an EditPart, or *component*, or just *part*. Therefore, we'll refer to the aspects described in figure D.2 collectively as a DecisionPart.

D.1.3 MVC interaction

It isn't difficult to see how the Model, View, and Controller classes function individually. The main obstacle to understanding the GEF is dealing with their interactions, both between themselves and with the rest of the application. Even the simplest editing modification requires a complex data exchange involving Tools, Requests, EditPolicys, Commands, and PropertyChangeEvents. We'll cover these topics in staggering detail to enable you to customize your GEF editor. But since you're still in the first section, a quick analogy will be helpful.

Think about how your nervous system works. Your senses perceive a stimulus and send their impression to the nervous system. The nervous system, functioning like a switchboard, updates the brain with the new information. The brain sends a response, and the nervous system extends or retracts muscles to move the skeleton. This interaction is shown in figure D.3.

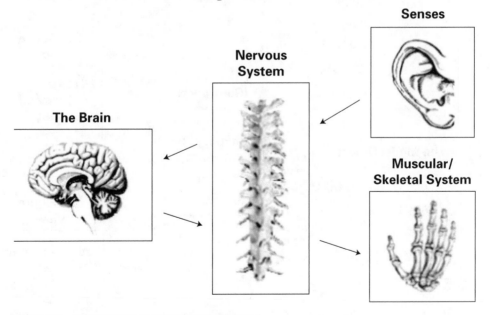

Figure D.3   The GEF/nervous system analogy, part 1

When you examine the interaction between the classes that make up GEF's MVC architecture, the process may seem similar. When the user causes an event, a `Tool` object sends a `Request` to the selected `EditPart`. This `EditPart` uses a `List` of `EditPolicys` to create a `Command` that updates the Model class. When the Model changes, it fires a `PropertyChangeEvent`. After receiving this event, the `EditPart` modifies the component's `Figure` (View) by invoking one of its `refresh()` methods. This process is shown in figure D.4.

This comparison isn't perfect, but it provides a framework for understanding the many interfaces and objects that take part in the editing process. As we progress into greater detail, it's easy to lose sight of the big picture; we hope you'll keep this analogy in mind.

D.1.4 *Building the flowchart editor*

A graphical editor requires classes for the Model, View, and Controller aspects of each component. For the flowchart editor, the top-level (parent) component will be the `Chart`, which serves as the main container for the rest of the GUI elements. We've already created the View (`ChartFigure`), so we need to build a Controller (`ChartPart`) and a Model (`Chart`).

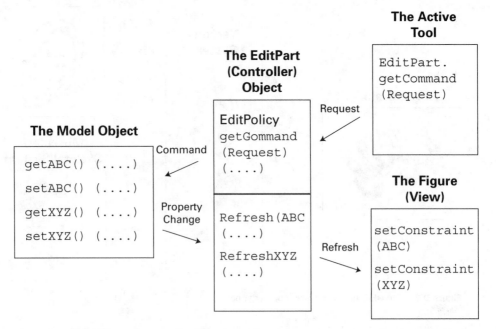

Figure D.4   The GEF/nervous system analogy, part 2

The three shapes in the editor, corresponding to the `Decision`, `Terminator`, and `Process` components, also require MVC triples. This means building `Edit-Parts` and Model classes in addition to the `Figures` created in appendix C. Because these three components have so much in common, we'll show how to create an abstract class called an `Activity`; then, each concrete class will extend the `ActivityPart`, `ActivityFigure`, or `Activity` class. In addition, we'll show how to build an MVC triple for connections: `Path`, `PathPart`, and `PathFigure`.

Once we've finished with the individual components, we'll explain how they communicate. This will require `Commands`, `Requests`, and `EditPolicys`. In addition, we'll show how a palette adds components to the editor and how an `EditorPart` keeps track of the entire application.

This may seem confusing, but figure D.5, which depicts the full class hierarchy of the `FlowchartProject`, should help.

Table D.1 shows our plan of attack for building the graphical editor. Since the editing process begins with adding components from the editor's palette, that's where we'll start.

Table D.1 Creating the flowchart editor using the GEF

	Goal	Procedure
1	Create `Figure` objects to represent elements of the flowchart (already accomplished).	1. Create a container to serve as the application's top-level `Figure`. 2. Build child `Figures` to be placed in the container. 3. Extend the `ConnectionAnchor` and `PolylineConnection` classes to provide connections between `Figures`.
2	Create the project, `FlowchartProject`.	1. Create a blank Java plug-in project for the flowchart. 2. Configure plugin.xml to reflect the editor's configuration. 3. Add the class libraries needed for Draw2D, GEF, and Workbench integration. 4. Build an organized package structure to hold the project's classes. 5. Add the `Figure` classes to the appropriate package.
3	Build the palette for the flowchart editor and the drag-and-drop ability.	1. Create a subclass of `PaletteViewer`. 2. Add the tool entries needed for selection, marquee selection, and connections to a `PaletteGroup`. 3. Add the template entries needed to add components to the `GraphicalViewer` to a secondary group. 4. Create a class to provide drag-and-drop between the palette and the main viewer.

continued on next page

Table D.1   Creating the flowchart editor using the GEF *(continued)*

	Goal	Procedure
4	Add Model classes for the `Figure`s.	1. Build a top-level Model class (`AbstractChartElement`) incorporating the methods needed for firing `PropertyChangeEvent`s. 2. Create an abstract class (`Activity`) that will be extended by the components. 3. Add Model classes for the components: `Decision`, `Process`, and `Terminator`. 4. Create a Model class for the container (`Chart`), with methods for handling children. 5. Create a Model class for the connections (`Path`). 6. Build a factory class (`ModelFactory`) that will convert templates into Models.
5	Add `Command`s to provide interfaces to the Model classes.	1. Build `Command`s for creating and deleting components from the editor. 2. Build `Command`s for making connections and changing component shapes.
6	Create `EditPart`s to combine the Model and `Figure` classes.	1. Create an `EditPart` (`ChartPart`) for the container. 2. Create an abstract `EditPart` for `Process`, `Terminator`, and `Decision` components. 3. Build individual concrete `EditPart`s for the components. 4. Add an `EditPart` (`PathPart`) for the component connections.
7	Create `EditPolicy`s to provide manipulation of the `EditPart` objects.	1. Create an `EditPolicy` for the container (`LayoutPolicy`). 2. Create an `EditPolicy` for general components (`ComponentPolicy`). 3. Create an `EditPolicy` for the node components (`NodePolicy`).
8	Enable `Action`s to provide multiple methods of editing.	1. Create a `ContextMenuProvider` for immediate Undo, Redo, Delete, and Save. 2. Create `RetargetAction`s to enable users to edit with the Eclipse Workbench. 3. Add these `RetargetAction`s to an `ActionBarContributor`.
9	Create the overall `FlowchartEditor` class.	Create a `FlowchartEditor` class that will 1. Save a `Chart` object to a file and retrieve `Chart` objects from files. 2. Configure and initialize a `GraphicalViewer` and a `PaletteViewer`. 3. Use a `KeyHandler` and a `CommandStack` to keep track of user activity.

Since this section has summarized the entire GEF development, you may feel overwhelmed. Don't worry! All of this will be become clearer as you start programming. Let's begin by creating the project, aptly named `FlowchartProject`.

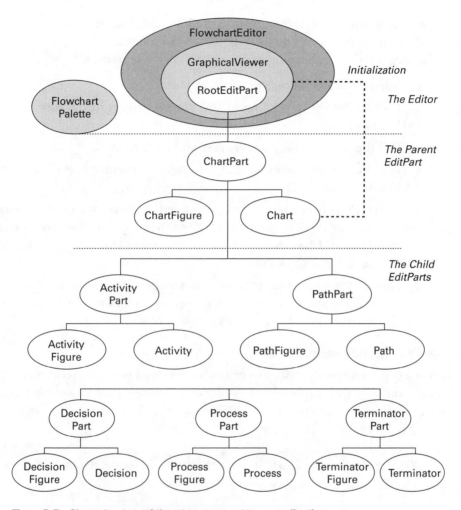

Figure D.5 Class structure of the FlowchartEditor application

D.2 Creating the FlowchartProject

Although much of this book was written for both Eclipse-based and standalone Java development, this section assumes you're building this project using Eclipse. A user can run normal Java applications whenever he pleases, but Eclipse editors are activated only when an appropriate file is selected for editing. This means Eclipse needs to know in advance which editor should be used for a given file type. In our case, the Workbench needs to know that the flowchart editor should be activated whenever the user edits a flowchart file, designated by *.fcf. A Draw2D application won't do the job: We need a plug-in.

To begin building this plug-in project, follow these steps:

1   Select File->New->Project.

2   Choose Plug-in Development and Plug-in Project in the New Project dialog. Click Next.

3   Call the project `FlowchartProject` and click Next.

4   Use the default values for Plug-in Project Structure and click Next once more.

5   In the Plug-in Content dialog, you need to make two changes. First, use `swtjface` as the provider name. Then, leaving the checkboxes checked, change the Class Name field to `com.swtjface.flowchart.Flowchart-ProjectPlugin`. Click Finish.

6   Now that you've created the project, you need to tell the Workbench what the editor is and what resources it needs to function. You do this by setting the parameters in the project's plugin.xml file.

D.2.1 Configuring the Plugin.xml file

Every Eclipse plug-in describes its characteristics and resource requirements in its plugin.xml file. You can modify this file with Eclipse's Plug-in Manifest Editor or code it directly. The plugin.xml code for our flowchart editor is shown in listing D.1.

Listing D.1   The plugin.xml file

```
<?xml version="1.0" encoding="UTF-8"?>
<?eclipse version="3.0"?>
<plugin
  id="FlowchartProject"
  name="Flowchart Plug-in"
  version="1.0.0"
  provider-name="swtjface"
  class="com.swtjface.flowchart.FlowchartProjectPlugin">

  <runtime>
    <library name="flowchart.jar">
    <export name="*"/>
    </library>
  </runtime>
  <requires>
```

Identifies project's plug-in information

```
    <import plugin="org.eclipse.core.runtime"/>
    <import plugin="org.eclipse.core.runtime.compatibility"
      optional="true"/>
    <import plugin="org.eclipse.core.resources"/>
    <import plugin="org.eclipse.ui.views"/>
    <import plugin="org.eclipse.ui.workbench"/>
    <import plugin="org.eclipse.jface"/>
    <import plugin="org.eclipse.ui.ide"/>
    <import plugin="org.eclipse.draw2d"/>
    <import plugin="org.eclipse.gef"/>
  </requires>

  <extension
    point="org.eclipse.ui.editors">
    <editor
     default="true"
     name="Flowchart Editor"
     extensions="fcf"
     icon="eclipse.gif"
     class="com.swtjface.flowchart.FlowchartEditor"
     contributorClass=
       "com.swtjface.flowchart.actions.
         FlowchartActionBarContributor"
     id="GEF Flowchart Editor">
    </editor>
  </extension>
</plugin>
```

Lists plug-ins needed for project

Provides information about editor

NOTE   Since every editor requires an icon, we've chosen to use the eclipse32.gif image from `org.eclipse.platform_x.y.z`. This file must be added to the project in order for the plug-in to function.

The first sections of this file specify the identification information about the plug-in and the libraries it needs to operate. The plug-in class, FlowchartProject-Plugin, has already been created and added to the `com.swtjface.flowchart` package; this file shouldn't be modified.

The important configuration information for our editor is contained in the <extension></extension> tags, including the main class for the editor and the contribution class needed to incorporate Workbench Actions into our editor. The line extensions="fcf" ensures that the editor will be activated whenever the user creates a file with the *fcf* suffix.

Along with the extension for the editor, many GEF projects incorporate a wizard to build an initial *.fcf file for the editor. Doing so is straightforward but beyond the scope of this appendix. For further information about plug-ins, wizard extensions, and XML configuration, we recommend *Eclipse in Action*, by David Gallardo, Ed Burnette, and Robert McGovern (Manning, 2003).

D.2.2 Adding class libraries

Depending on which version of Eclipse you use, the necessary plug-ins may have already been added to the project. If you open the Plug-in Dependencies in the Package Explorer, you may already see a list of jar files; if so, you can skip this subsection. If not, you need to include a number of class libraries. Since the boot.jar and runtime.jar files were automatically added during project creation, add the JFACE_LIB and WORKBENCH_LIB variables created in appendix A and the DRAW2D_LIB variable created in appendix C. You also need to add the OSGI_LIB variable created in chapter 4.

Unlike the other graphical applications in this book, GEF editors need to be integrated in the Eclipse Workbench. This means you need to add even more libraries. Table D.2 lists the jar files required to work with Workbench parts and recommended names for their classpath variables.

Table D.2   Additional libraries needed for GEF applications

Classpath variable	Library file
GEF_LIB	$ECLIPSE/plugins/org.eclipse.gef_x.y.z/gef.jar
UI_EDITORS_LIB	$ECLIPSE/plugins/org.eclipse.ui.editors_x.y.z/editors.jar
UI_IDE_LIB	$ECLIPSE/plugins/org.eclipse.ui.ide_x.y.z/ide.jar
UI_LIB	$ECLIPSE/plugins/org.eclipse.ui_x.y.z/ui.jar
UI_VIEWS_LIB	$ECLIPSE/plugins/org.eclipse.ui.views_x.y.z/views.jar

Once we've created these classpath variables and added them to Flowchart-Project, we can begin adding packages and classes.

D.2.3 Adding packages and classes

GEF projects keep their code organized with a series of packages that represent different aspects of the editor. Package names may differ from one application to the next, but table D.3 lists those used in the flowchart editor. We recommend that you add them to the FlowchartProject inside the src directory.

Table D.3 Class packages in the flowchart editor

Package	Function
com.swtjface.flowchart	Editor's EditorPart and plug-in
com.swtjface.flowchart.actions	Classes that create and manage Actions
com.swtjface.flowchart.commands	Classes used to modify the Model properties
com.swtjface.flowchart.dnd	Classes that provide the drag-and-drop capability
com.swtjface.flowchart.editpart	Editor's EditParts
com.swtjface.flowchart.figures	Graphics used to create EditPart visuals
com.swtjface.flowchart.model	Information contained in the EditParts
com.swtjface.flowchart.palette	GUI element used to instantiate EditParts
com.swtjface.flowchart.policies	Policies available for the EditParts

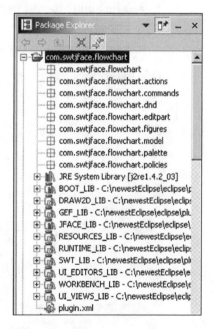

Since the Figure objects for this project have already been written, we can add them to the project. To do this, we move Activity-Figure.java, ChartFigure.java, DecisionFigure.java, FigureFactory.java, FixedAnchor .java, PathFigure.java, ProcessFigure.java, and TerminatorFigure.java to the com.swtj-face.flowchart.figures package. The end result of this process is shown in figure D.6.

Now that we've added these files, we've completed the View aspect of the editor. However, these Figures aren't much use unless users can add them to the editor. Toward this end, our next goal is to discuss GEF palettes.

Figure D.6
The package structure for
FlowchartProject

D.3   *Creating the editor's PaletteViewer*

Look at figure D.7. In the simplest terms, it shows a Canvas with a LightweightSystem object—just like any Draw2D application. What differentiates a GEF editor from a Draw2D application or text editor is its Viewer. Viewer classes, as described earlier, rest on top of a component and control its appearance and event handling. In this case, we have two of them: a Viewer that represents the main editor and one that contains the palette. Since the palette is the first object a user will come in contact with, we'll start our GEF discussion by examining the PaletteViewer.

The PaletteViewer class builds components and handles events for the left-hand section of the Canvas, whose default width is 125 pixels. Like the viewer on the right-hand side, it implements the GraphicalViewer interface. But PaletteViewer has a number of distinguishing features:

- The ability to add buttons that provide editing functions, called ToolEntrys
- The ability to add buttons that create new components, called TemplateEntrys
- Configuration information contained in a single object, the PaletteRoot

This PaletteRoot is important for a PaletteViewer because it provides the entries that will be available to the user. Like a Model class, it contains the palette's

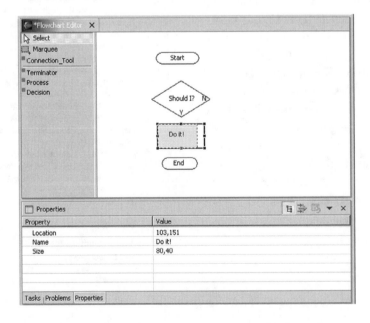

Figure D.7
The flowchart editor in its dazzling glory

information. The `getPaletteRoot()` method configures one of these objects by creating and populating a `List` of `PaletteGroups`. In `FlowchartPalette`, the first `PaletteGroup`, `toolGroup`, contains a `List` of tool-related entries. The second, `templateGroup`, contains a `List` of template-related entries. The code is shown in listing D.2, and we recommend that you add this to the `com.swtjface.flowchart.palette` package.

Listing D.2   FlowchartPalette.java

```java
package com.swtjface.flowchart.palette;

import java.util.*;
import com.swtjface.flowchart.model.*;
import org.eclipse.gef.palette.*;
import org.eclipse.jface.resource.*;

public class FlowchartPalette
{
  public static final String
    TERMINATOR_TEMPLATE = "TERM_TEMP",
    DECISION_TEMPLATE = "DEC_TEMP",
    PROCESS_TEMPLATE = "PROC_TEMP";

  public static PaletteRoot getPaletteRoot()
  {
    PaletteRoot root = new PaletteRoot();

    PaletteGroup toolGroup = new PaletteGroup("Chart Tools");
    List toolList = new ArrayList();

    ToolEntry tool = new SelectionToolEntry();        ◄──────┐
    toolList.add(tool);
    root.setDefaultEntry(tool);                              Create palette
                                                             entries that
    tool = new MarqueeToolEntry();                    ◄──    activate tools
    toolList.add(tool);

    tool = new ConnectionCreationToolEntry(           ◄──────┘
      "Connection_Tool", "Used to connect multiple components", null,
      ImageDescriptor.getMissingImageDescriptor(),
      ImageDescriptor.getMissingImageDescriptor() );
    toolList.add(tool);
    toolGroup.addAll(toolList);        ◄── Add tool entry list to group
```

```
PaletteGroup templateGroup =
  new PaletteGroup("Chart Templates");
List templateList = new ArrayList();

CombinedTemplateCreationEntry entry = new
  CombinedTemplateCreationEntry(
    "Terminator", "Start or End Component", TERMINATOR_TEMPLATE,
    new ModelFactory(TERMINATOR_TEMPLATE),
    ImageDescriptor.getMissingImageDescriptor(),
    ImageDescriptor.getMissingImageDescriptor());
templateList.add(entry);

entry = new CombinedTemplateCreationEntry(
  "Process", "Action within a flowchart", PROCESS_TEMPLATE,
  new ModelFactory(PROCESS_TEMPLATE),
  ImageDescriptor.getMissingImageDescriptor(),
  ImageDescriptor.getMissingImageDescriptor());
templateList.add(entry);

entry = new CombinedTemplateCreationEntry(
  "Decision", "Choosing between 'Yes' and 'No'", DECISION_TEMPLATE,
  new ModelFactory(DECISION_TEMPLATE),
  ImageDescriptor.getMissingImageDescriptor(),
  ImageDescriptor.getMissingImageDescriptor());
templateList.add(entry);

templateGroup.addAll(templateList);

List rootList = new ArrayList();
rootList.add(toolGroup);
rootList.add(templateGroup);

root.addAll(rootList);
return root;
  }
}
```

Create palette entries that activate tools

⟵ **Add template entry list to group**

⟵ **Add both groups to palette**

As you can see, a `PaletteRoot` is a collection of `PaletteGroups`, which are collections of entries. These entries, represented by the `ToolEntry` and `CombinedTemplateCreationEntry` classes, create buttons that will be added to the palette. Except for the `SelectionTool` and the `MarqueeSelectionTool`, these entries are initialized with descriptors, images, and classes that implement the `CreationFactory` interface. But before we can discuss their constructor methods, we need to explain how `Tools` and templates work.

D.3.1 *Handling events with the ToolEntry and Tool classes*

The first three entries in our palette are `ToolEntrys`, which provide the ability to select and connect existing components. Whenever any of these entries are clicked, they create a new `Tool` object. The top tool entry, labeled Select, creates a `SelectionTool`; the Marquee entry creates a `MarqueeSelectionTool`; and the Connection_Tool entry creates a `ConnectionCreationTool`.

The entries are simple to understand, but what exactly is a `Tool`? A `Tool` provides a distinctive means of interpreting keyboard and mouse events. For example, when you click a component with the `SelectionTool` activated, there will be a different result than if the `ConnectionCreationTool` had been activated. This is because the two `Tools` have different handlers for `MouseEvents`; they also interact differently with components and their `EditParts`. These `Tool/EditPart` interactions are accomplished through `Requests`.

Table D.4 lists a group of important `Tools` provided in GEF, their functions, and the `Requests` they send to `EditParts` during activation.

Table D.4 Class packages in the `FlowchartProject` project

Tool	Tool description	Requests
ConnectionBendpoint Tracker	Creates or moves `Bendpoints` within a `Connection`	BendpointRequest
ConnectionCreationTool	Tells the `EditPart` that it will be the start of a new connection	ConnectionCreation Request
CreationTool	Creates new `EditParts` (components)	CreateRequest
MarqueeSelectionTool	Selects all the `EditParts` within the marquee	SelectionRequest
ResizeTracker	Tells the `EditPart` to change its size	ChangeBounds Request
SelectionTool	Tells an `EditPart` that it has been selected or that the mouse cursor has come in contact with the component	SelectionRequest LocationRequest

It's important to note that `DragTrackers` such as `ResizeTracker` and `Connection-BendpointTracker` are also GEF `Tools`. They determine how `DragEvents` affect an `EditPart`. Whereas a `Tool`'s activation is independent of the components in the editor, `DragTrackers` are specified in `EditParts`. In many cases, a high-level `Tool` transfers its event-handling authority to the `DragTracker` associated with the `EditPart`.

For example, when a user clicks a `Decision` component, the `SelectionTool` will activate. But if the user presses the button and moves the mouse, then the `SelectionTool` delegates authority to the `DecisionPart`'s `DragTracker`.

Requests

Requests are the means by which Tools perform editing. When a component is clicked with the SelectionTool activated, the Tool sends a SelectionRequest or a LocationRequest to the EditPart. Similarly, when the ConnectionCreationTool is activated, the tool sends a CreateConnectionRequest. In each case, the Request provides the EditPart with information about the event, such as which key was pressed or which button was clicked.

When an EditPart receives a Request, it responds with a Command object if one is available. This Command tells the Tool how the EditPart should be altered when the event occurs. Once the Tool receives a Command, it takes responsibility for modifying the EditPart by invoking the Command's execute() method. We'll discuss Commands in depth shortly.

We need to mention two points about Requests. First, there is no subpackage (such as com.swtjface.flowchart.requests) for Requests because GEF already provides all the classes that will be needed in most editors. However, users can create their own Tools and Requests as needed.

Second, although Requests are generally categorized according to their class, they're further distinguished by a TYPE field. This integer makes the Request's function more specific. For example, when the mouse hovers over an EditPart, the SelectionTool sends a LocationRequest to the component. Because this LocationRequest's TYPE field is REQ_SELECTION_HOVER, the part knows that the mouse is hovering above it.

EditDomains and Tools

Although EditDomain objects operate behind the scenes, it's important to know what they are and how they relate to palettes and palette entries. EditDomains keep track of an editor's state information, and part of this information consists of which Tool is currently active. The EditDomain sets the editor's default Tool, which is usually the SelectionTool, and manages the process of switching from one Tool to the next. It ensures that only one Tool is active at any time and directs events to it.

This object also plays a role in creating an editor's palette. The EditDomain ensures that the PaletteViewer receives the PaletteRoot containing the List of ToolEntrys and TemplateEntrys. Then, it determines which Tool in the List is the default tool and activates this Tool when the editor initializes.

D.3.2 Creating components with templates

At the time of this writing, the GEF documentation describes many classes that create and handle templates, but it never explains exactly what a template is. An examination of the code tells us that a template is *any object that can be matched to a component*. If you'd like to number your components, then you can use ints or chars as your templates. For our editor, we'll use Strings. That is, TERM_TEMP is the template that corresponds to the Terminator component, PROC_TEMP represents the Process, and DEC_TEMP represents the Decision.

TemplateEntry objects

Just as a ToolEntry creates Tool objects, TemplateEntrys create templates. After clicking a TemplateEntry in the palette, the user can either drag the template to the editor or click an area in the editor. Once the drop location is determined, the editor's TemplateTransferDropTargetListener determines how the component will be created.

In our example, the entry list consists of CombinedTemplateCreationEntrys, which create both a template and a CreationEntryTool to create the template's matching component. The constructor for these entries requires a number of fields to specify its appearance and operation:

- *label (a String)*—The entry's name
- *shortDesc (a String)*—Description when the mouse hovers over the entry
- *template (an Object; a String, in our case)*—The component to be created
- *factory (a CreationFactory)*—The class that builds the component
- *iconSmall (an ImageDescriptor)*—The image shown near the label
- *iconLarge (an ImageDescriptor)*—The image shown during the drag

For our flowchart editor, we'll use getMissingImageDescriptor() to provide the icons. These are the small, red squares provided by the JFace library.

So far, we've discussed every aspect of palette entry constructors except the CreationFactory.

Converting templates to Model classes with a CreationFactory

Components are created when the user drags a template from the palette and drops it in a container. The CreationTool tells the editor which component to build by identifying a class that implements the CreationFactory interface.

This important interface contains only two methods: getNewObject() receives a template object and returns a newly created Model object for the requested component, and getObjectType() returns the template created by the palette tool. The code in listing D.3 shows how these methods are used in the flowchart

editor's `ModelFactory` class. We recommend that you place this class in the
`com.swtjface.flowchart.model` package.

Listing D.3   ModelFactory.java

```java
package com.swtjface.flowchart.model;

import org.eclipse.gef.requests.CreationFactory;
import com.swtjface.flowchart.palette.*;

public class ModelFactory
  implements CreationFactory
{

  private String template;

  public ModelFactory(Object str)
  {
    template = (String) str;
  }
  public Object getNewObject()              ⟵ Create Model objects according
  {                                              to their templates root
    if (FlowchartPalette.TERMINATOR_TEMPLATE.equals(template))
      return new Terminator();
    if (FlowchartPalette.DECISION_TEMPLATE.equals(template))
      return new Decision();
    if (FlowchartPalette.PROCESS_TEMPLATE.equals(template))
      return new Process();
    return null;
  }

  public Object getObjectType()
  {
      return template;
  }
  public static Chart getChart()            ⟵ Create Model objects
  {                                              without templates
      return new Chart();
  }

  public Path getPath()
  {
      return new Path();
  }
}
```

In this case, `getNewObject()` checks to see if it recognizes the template. If it does, then
the method returns a constructed Model object that contains the component's information. In addition, this class contains two methods, `getChart()` and `getPath()`,

which return Model objects for the `Chart` and `Path` components. These objects require separate methods because they aren't directly created with templates.

TemplateTransferDropTargetListeners

Like any drag-and-drop operation, a `DropTargetListener` must be present in order to respond to a `DropTargetEvent`. GEF provides a class specifically for responding to template drops: `TemplateTransferDropTargetListener`. This class must be extended to identify the `CreationFactory` that will construct the Model.

For our flowchart editor, this subclass is `FlowchartDropTargetListener`; its code is presented in listing D.4. We recommend that you add this class to the `com.swtjface.flowchart.dnd` package.

Listing D.4 FlowchartDropTargetListener.java

```
package com.swtjface.flowchart.dnd;

import org.eclipse.gef.EditPartViewer;
import org.eclipse.gef.dnd.TemplateTransferDropTargetListener;
import org.eclipse.gef.requests.CreationFactory;

import com.swtjface.flowchart.model.ModelFactory;

public class FlowchartDropTargetListener
  extends TemplateTransferDropTargetListener
{

  public FlowchartDropTargetListener(EditPartViewer viewer)
  {
    super(viewer);
  }

  protected CreationFactory getFactory(Object template)
  {
    return new ModelFactory(template);     ←⏤ Identifies class needed to
  }                                              create Model objects
}
```

As you can see, the only difference between the `FlowchartDropTargetListener` and the `TemplateTransferDropTargetListener` is the `ModelFactory` class. Now that you know how these Model objects are created, you need to learn how they work.

D.4 The Model aspect: Model classes

The fundamental question in building Model classes is this: What information should be saved to a file? You don't need to persist each pixel in the main window.

A good rule of thumb is that every editable aspect of a component should be saved and incorporated in its Model class. This section will show how these classes are formed and how their structures are used in the flowchart editor.

D.4.1 *Model classes and JavaBeans*

The role of a Model class is to keep track of a component's editable characteristics, called *properties*. Each property has a mutator method (setXYZ()) to specify its value and an accessor method (getXYZ()) to acquire it. The Model class also fires events when these properties change. Both the event and listener classes needed for this are provided by the java.beans package.

This relationship between Model classes and the JavaBean library is deliberate. For those unfamiliar with component-based (JavaBean) software development, the goal is to construct applications with simple, reusable objects that keep track of information. Java doesn't provide a specific class for JavaBeans, but instead gives rules for their interfaces and methods. Because GEF Model classes follow these rules, they're considered JavaBeans.

In addition to the accessor and mutator methods, Sun's JavaBean specification also describes the event model needed for dealing with PropertyChangeEvents. The GEF implementation of this model is shown in figure D.8. It's important to note that although the methods are contained in the Model class, the EditPart invokes them.

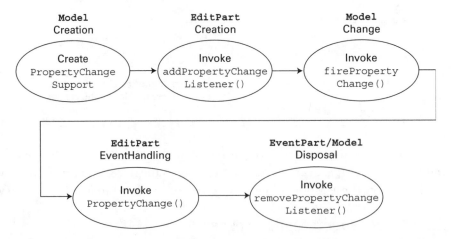

Figure D.8 The PropertyChangeEvent model for GEF Model classes

First, a Model object creates a `PropertyChangeSupport` instance during its creation. This enables an `EditPart` to listen to its `PropertyChangeEvents`. Then, when the `EditPart` is created, it calls the Model's `addPropertyChangeListener()` method to be able to respond to these events. Whenever a property changes, the Model calls its `firePropertyChange()` method, and the `EditPart` handles the Event with its `propertyChange()` method. When the component is deallocated, the `EditPart` calls the Model's `removePropertyChangeListener()` method.

These methods must be available in each Model class you build. Therefore, you can save yourself effort by creating an abstract class for your Models.

D.4.2 *The AbstractChartElement class*

Since all Model classes must contain these event-handling methods, it makes sense to incorporate them in an abstract class. For our project, this class is called `AbstractChartElement`. Listing D.5 presents the code for this class; we recommend that you add it to the `com.swtjface.flowchart.model` package.

NOTE   This class provides listeners for receiving events and methods to fire them, but it doesn't implement `propertyChange(PropertyChangeEvent)`, which is the only event-handling method in the `PropertyChangeListener` interface. This method is invoked by the `EditPart`, which controls the Model and View.

Listing D.5   AbstractChartElement.java

```java
package com.swtjface.flowchart.model;
import java.io.*;
import java.beans.*;

abstract public class AbstractChartElement
  implements Cloneable, Serializable
{
  public static final String
    SIZE = "size", LOC = "location", NAME = "name",
    CHILD = "children", TARGETS = "targets", SOURCES = "sources";

  transient protected PropertyChangeSupport listeners = new
    PropertyChangeSupport(this);

  public void addPropertyChangeListener(PropertyChangeListener pcl)
  {
    listeners.addPropertyChangeListener(pcl);
  }
  public void removePropertyChangeListener
    (PropertyChangeListener pcl)
```

Properties to be monitored ◁

◁

Provide property monitoring

```
  {
    listeners.removePropertyChangeListener(pcl);       <─┘  Provide property
  }                                                          monitoring

  protected void firePropertyChange(String propName,
    Object old, Object newValue        <── Send alert if property changes
  {
    listeners.firePropertyChange(propName, old, newValue);
  }

  private void readObject(ObjectInputStream in) throws IOException,
    ClassNotFoundException
  {
    in.defaultReadObject();
    listeners = new PropertyChangeSupport(this);
  }
}
```

Each of the property changes has a String as a label. The first three, SIZE, LOC, and NAME, refer to changes in a component's size, location, and message, respectively. A CHILD property change is fired whenever a new part is added to the container (Chart). Similarly, TARGETS and SOURCES events are fired whenever a new source or target connection is made or removed.

Another important point about this class is that it implements the Serializable interface. This means concrete subclasses can be converted into bytes and persisted in a file. The transient keyword preceding the PropertyChangeSupport declaration means that this class *cannot* be serialized. Therefore, when the top-level Model is saved to a file, it won't include these objects. For this reason, the readObject() method at the end of the code creates a new PropertyChangeSupport object when the Model is deserialized.

By making our Model classes descendants of AbstractChartElement, we ensure that each of these methods will be available. The first concrete Model class that we'll discuss is Chart, which holds the information concerning the editor's container.

D.4.3 *The Chart class*

Despite its importance, a Chart object doesn't hold a great deal of data. Its function is to keep track of child Model classes by adding and removing them from an ArrayList. The code for this class is shown in listing D.6; add it to com.swtjface.flowchart.model.

Listing D.6   Chart.java

```java
package com.swtjface.flowchart.model;

import java.util.*;

public class Chart
  extends AbstractChartElement
{
  protected List children = new ArrayList();

  public List getChildren()
  {
    return children;
  }

  public void addChild(Activity child)
  {
    children.add(child);
    firePropertyChange(CHILD, null, child);
  }

  public void removeChild(Activity child)
  {
    children.remove(child);
    firePropertyChange(CHILD, null, child);
  }
}
```

These methods are straightforward: addChild() and removeChild() perform the essential job of mutator methods, whereas getChildren() provides access to the object's properties. If any properties change, then a PropertyChangeEvent is created and fired.

The Chart class may not be exciting, but as you'll see later, it's vital in saving the editor's contents to a file. Now that you've seen how these children are arranged, let's look at their abstract superclass, Activity.

D.4.4 *The Activity class*

For the flowchart editor's Decision, Process, and Terminator components, five fields need to be stored:

- *size*—The part's x and y dimensions, represented by a Dimension
- *location*—The part's position, represented by a Point
- *name*—The part's message, represented by a String
- *sources*—The part's SourceConnections, contained in a Vector
- *targets*—The part's TargetConnections, contained in a Vector

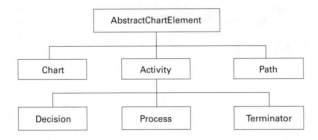

Figure D.9
The Model classes of the
flowchart editor

Since this list is the same for each Model, we'll use the same class, `Activity`, to hold the information for the components. This class will contain mutator and accessor methods for each of the above properties.

Now that we have the `Activity` class, we can see the entire Model class hierarchy, shown in figure D.9.

The full code for the `Activity` class is shown in listing D.7.

Listing D.7 Activity.java

```java
package com.swtjface.flowchart.model;

import java.util.*;
import org.eclipse.draw2d.geometry.*;
import org.eclipse.ui.views.properties.*;

public class Activity
   extends AbstractChartElement implements IPropertySource
{
   // Information content of the Model class
   private String name;
   private Point location = new Point(0,0);
   private Dimension size = new Dimension(-1,-1);
   protected Vector targets = new Vector(2);
   protected Vector sources = new Vector(2);

   public Dimension getSize()
   {return size;}

   public void setSize(Dimension dim)
   {
      if (size.equals(dim)) return;
      size = dim;
      firePropertyChange(SIZE, null, size);
   }

   public Point getLocation() {return location;}

   public void setLocation(Point place)
   {
```

Accessor/mutator
method for
Model class

```
    if (location.equals(place)) return;
    location = place;
    firePropertyChange(LOC, null, place);
}

public String getName()
{return name;}

public void setName(String str)
{
  if (str.equals(name)) return;
  name = str;
  firePropertyChange(NAME, null, str);
}

public Vector getConnections()
{
  Vector v = getSourceConnections();
  v.addAll(getTargetConnections());
  return v;
}

public Vector getSourceConnections()
{
  return (Vector)sources.clone();
}

public void addSourceConnection(Path p)
{
  sources.add(p);
  firePropertyChange(SOURCES, null, p);
}

public void removeSourceConnection(Path p)
{
  sources.remove(p);
  firePropertyChange(SOURCES, null, p);
}

public Vector getTargetConnections()
{
  return (Vector)targets.clone();
}

public void addTargetConnection(Path p)
{
  targets.add(p);
  firePropertyChange(TARGETS, null, p);
}

public void removeTargetConnection(Path p)
{
  targets.remove(p);
  firePropertyChange(TARGETS, null, p);
```

Accessor/mutator method for Model class

```
  }
  public Object getEditableValue()
  {return null;}
  public IPropertyDescriptor[] getPropertyDescriptors()
  {
    return new IPropertyDescriptor[]
    {
      new TextPropertyDescriptor(NAME, "Name"),
      new TextPropertyDescriptor(SIZE, "Size"),
      new TextPropertyDescriptor(LOC, "Location")
    };
  }
  public Object getPropertyValue(Object propName)
  {
    if (propName.equals(SIZE))
      return getSize().width + "," + getSize().height;
    else if(propName.equals(LOC))
      return getLocation().x + "," + getLocation().y;
    else if(propName.equals(NAME))
      return getName();
    return null;
  }
  public void setPropertyValue(Object propName, Object value)
  {
    String str = (String)value;
    int comma = str.indexOf(",");
    if (propName.equals(SIZE))
      setSize(new Dimension(Integer.parseInt
        (str.substring(0,comma)),
        Integer.parseInt(str.substring(comma+1))));
    else if (propName.equals(LOC))
      setLocation(new Point(Integer.parseInt
        (str.substring(0,comma)),
        Integer.parseInt(str.substring(comma+1))));
    else if (propName.equals(NAME))
      setName(str);
  }
  public boolean isPropertySet(Object id)
  {return true;}
  public void resetPropertyValue(Object id)
  {}
}
```

Interface with Eclipse Property View

Interface with Eclipse Property View

A bit longer than the Chart Model, isn't it? As you can see, keeping track of many properties can be complicated, especially Connections. But in addition, we've

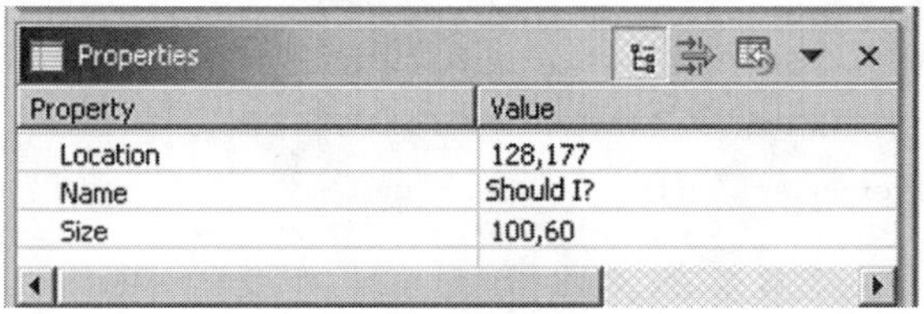

Figure D.10
Example property view for the flowchart editor

added six methods needed to implement the IPropertySource interface. By doing so, users can change the size, location, and name of an Activity component using a Property View. This window is provided by the Eclipse Workbench; an example is shown in figure D.10.

The IPropertySource methods make it possible to transfer property values between the Model and Eclipse's Property View: The first method, getProperty-Descriptors(), tells the View what properties it needs to display and that input should be provided through a textbox. The next two methods get and set the EditPart's property values; the fourth, resetPropertyValue(), returns the default property. isPropertySet() returns whether the property value is equal to its default, and getEditableValue() returns the object responsible for keeping track of the EditPart's property.

Now that we've taken care of the abstract superclass, we need to create the concrete subclasses. The code for these Model classes—Decision, Process, and Terminator—is shown in listings D.8, D.9, and D.10.

Listing D.8   Decision.java

```java
package com.swtjface.flowchart.model;

import org.eclipse.draw2d.geometry.Dimension;

public class Decision extends Activity
{
  public Decision()
  {
    setName("Decision");
    setSize(new Dimension(100,60));
  }
}
```

Listing D.9   Process.java

```java
import org.eclipse.draw2d.geometry.Dimension;

public class Process extends Activity
{
  public Process()
  {
    setName("Process");
    setSize(new Dimension(80,40));
  }
}
```

Listing D.10   Terminator.java

```java
package com.swtjface.flowchart.model;

import org.eclipse.draw2d.geometry.Dimension;

public class Terminator extends Activity
{
  public Terminator()
  {
    setName("Term");
    setSize(new Dimension(80,20));
  }
}
```

These classes do nothing more than set their message and size during construction. It's easy to remove them and use only the `Activity` Model class. However, for the purposes of teaching the GEF, we've made sure that each MVC triple has its own Model class.

D.4.5 *The Path class*

In addition to creating classes for the `Activity` components, we need to create Model classes for their `Connections`. This `Path` class doesn't fire `PropertyChangeEvents` or display information in the Property View, but it keeps track of which `Activity` objects it connects (`source` and `target`) and the names of its anchors (`sourceName` and `targetName`). The code for this class is provided in listing D.11.

Listing D.11   Path.java

```java
package com.swtjface.flowchart.model;

public class Path
  extends AbstractChartElement
{
```

```
protected Activity source, target;
protected String sourceName, targetName;

public void attachSource()
{
  if (getSource() == null ||
    getSource().getSourceConnections().contains(this))
    return;
  getSource().addSourceConnection(this);
}

public void detachSource()
{
  if (getSource() == null)
    return;
  getSource().removeSourceConnection(this);
}

public void attachTarget()
{
  if (getTarget() == null ||
    getTarget().getTargetConnections().contains(this))
    return;
  getTarget().addTargetConnection(this);
}

public void detachTarget()
{
  if (getTarget() == null)
    return;
  getTarget().removeTargetConnection(this);
}

public Activity getSource()
{
  return source;
}

public void setSource(Activity e)
{
    source = e;
}

public Activity getTarget()
{
  return target;
}

public void setTarget(Activity e)
{
  target = e;
}

public String getSourceName()
```

```
  {
    return sourceName;
  }
  public void setSourceName(String s)
  {
    sourceName = s;
  }
  public String getTargetName()
  {
    return targetName;
  }
  public void setTargetName(String s)
  {
    targetName = s;
  }
}
```

Again, these methods are easy to understand. The only new concepts involve attaching and detaching Connections. These functions tell their source and target Activity Models that a new Connection has been added or removed. This is one of the few instances where one Model class interacts with another.

The process of modifying components begins with the mutator methods of the Model classes and the PropertyChangeEvents that they fire. However, these methods are only invoked by Command objects. Therefore, to continue discussing the editing process, our next step must involve investigating Commands.

D.5 Changing Model properties with Commands

When we briefly discussed Commands in the last section, we mentioned how they're created in response to Requests. We can't discuss the full process by which a Request becomes a Command just yet. But in this section, we'll describe the Command's purpose and structure and then build customized classes for our editor.

D.5.1 Commands and CommandStacks

It's possible to extend the Request class, but doing so is generally unnecessary since GEF provides so many subclasses of its own. However, you'll have to build all your own Command classes; you must do so because Commands interact with Model objects, which have no standard structure beyond accessor/mutator methods. But GEF does provide an abstract Command class, and it's important that you understand how it works.

The execute() method performs the real work of the Command by invoking the mutator methods (setXYZ()) of the Model class. This execute() method is called by the active Tool after it receives the Command in response to its Request. Commands can also have other methods and fields associated with them, and these are generally used to provide information for the execute() method.

Two other important Command methods are undo() and redo(). As expected, these methods are used to reverse the results of execute() or reinvoke it. For these methods to work, the editor must keep track of which Commands have been executed. The data structure used for this task is the CommandStack, which is initialized during the editor's construction. This object pushes executed Commands onto its Undo stack and pushes undone Commands onto its Redo stack. The Redo stack is cleared whenever a new Command is executed.

Our flowchart editor needs four concrete Command classes. We'll start with the first Command that will be executed in a normal GEF editor: the CreateCommand.

D.5.2 *The CreateCommand class*

The CreateCommand is used to update the Chart container with a new component. It also initializes the properties of the new component by setting its size and location. The execute() method of the CreateCommand is simple and requires only the Model class of the parent (parent), the added child (child), and the child's bounds (rect). The code is provided in listing D.12.

Listing D.12   CreateCommand.java

```
package com.swtjface.flowchart.commands;

import org.eclipse.draw2d.geometry.Rectangle;
import org.eclipse.gef.commands.Command;
import com.swtjface.flowchart.model.*;

public class CreateCommand extends Command
{
  private Chart parent;
  private Activity child;
  private Rectangle rect;

  public void execute()
  {
    if (rect != null)
    {
      child.setLocation(rect.getLocation());
      if (!rect.isEmpty())
        child.setSize(rect.getSize());
    }
    parent.addChild(child);
```

```
    }

    public void setParent(Chart sa)
    {parent = sa;}

    public void setChild(Activity activity)
    {child = activity;}

    public void setConstraint(Rectangle bounds)
    {rect = bounds;}

    public void redo()
    {execute();}

    public void undo()
    {parent.removeChild(child);}
}
```

The `execute()` method calls the `setLocation()` and `setSize()` methods of the `Activity` object and adds the new child to the `Chart` with its `addChild()` method. The `redo()` method reinvokes `execute()`, and `undo()` calls the `removeChild()` method. The `setParent()`, `setChild()`, and `setConstraint()` methods provide initialization parameters to the `Command` during its formation.

The `CreateCommand` class is simple to understand. However, because the `PathCommand` deals with `Path` objects, it's slightly more complicated.

D.5.3   *The PathCommand class*

The process of creating a `Connection` presents greater complications than building a child Model class in a parent. With connections, or `Paths` in our case, the Model must keep track of both of the components to which it's attached and the names of the anchors in each component. Also, just as the `CreateCommand` adds an `Activity` to a `Chart`, this command tells both the source and target `Activity` objects to add this `Path` to their `ArrayLists` (see listing D.13).

Listing D.13   PathCommand.java

```
package com.swtjface.flowchart.commands;

import org.eclipse.gef.commands.Command;
import com.swtjface.flowchart.model.*;

public class PathCommand
     extends Command
{
    protected Activity oldSource, source;
    protected Activity oldTarget, target;
```

```
    protected String oldSourceName, sourceName;
    protected String oldTargetName, targetName;
    protected Path path;

    public PathCommand()
    {}

    public boolean canExecute()
    {
      return true;
    }

    public void execute()
    {
      if (source != null)
      {
        path.detachSource();
        path.setSource(source);
        path.setSourceName(sourceName);
        path.attachSource();
      }
      if (target != null)
      {
        path.detachTarget();
        path.setTarget(target);
        path.setTargetName(targetName);
        path.attachTarget();
      }
    }

    public void redo()
    {
      execute();
    }

    public void undo()
    {
      source = path.getSource();
      target = path.getTarget();
      sourceName = path.getSourceName();
      targetName = path.getTargetName();

      path.detachSource();
      path.detachTarget();
      path.setSource(oldSource);
      path.setTarget(oldTarget);
      path.setSourceName(oldSourceName);
      path.setTargetName(oldTargetName);

      path.attachSource();
      path.attachTarget();
    }

    public void setSource(Activity newSource)
```

```
    {
      source = newSource;
    }

    public void setSourceName(String newSourceName)
    {
      sourceName = newSourceName;
    }

    public void setTarget(Activity newTarget)
    {
      target = newTarget;
    }

    public void setTargetName(String newTargetName)
    {
      targetName = newTargetName;
    }

    public void setPath(Path p)
    {
      path = p;
      oldSource = p.getSource();
      oldTarget = p.getTarget();
      oldSourceName = p.getSourceName();
      oldTargetName = p.getTargetName();
    }
  }
```

This Command changes the properties of the Path and its source and target Activity objects, but not the Chart. It's important to understand that Connection objects aren't considered children of other components; they're part of an internal Vector in each EditPart.

Now that you know how new Model classes are created, the next class describes how they're removed from the Chart and deallocated.

D.5.4 The DeleteCommand class

The DeleteCommand reverses the actions of both the CreateCommand and the Path-Command and is performed in two steps. First, it deletes the Path objects associated with the selected component. This process involves detaching the Path from both the deleted component and the one to which it was attached. The second step removes the child Activity from the parent Chart. This is shown in listing D.14.

```java
package com.swtjface.flowchart.commands;

import java.util.*;

import org.eclipse.gef.commands.Command;
import com.swtjface.flowchart.model.*;

public class DeleteCommand extends Command
{
  private Chart parent;
  private Activity child;
  private List sourceConnections = new ArrayList();
  private List targetConnections = new ArrayList();

  private void deleteConnections(AbstractChartElement a)
  {
    if (a instanceof Chart)
    {
      List children = ((Chart)a).getChildren();
      for (int i = 0; i < children.size(); i++)
        deleteConnections((Activity)children.get(i));
    }
    else
    {
      sourceConnections.addAll
        (((Activity)a).getSourceConnections());
      for (int i = 0; i < sourceConnections.size(); i++)
      {
        Path path = (Path)sourceConnections.get(i);
        path.detachSource();
        path.detachTarget();
      }
      targetConnections.addAll
        (((Activity)a).getTargetConnections());
      for (int i = 0; i < targetConnections.size(); i++)
      {
        Path path = (Path)targetConnections.get(i);
        path.detachSource();
        path.detachTarget();
      }
    }
  }

  public void execute()
  {
    deleteConnections(child);
    parent.removeChild(child);
  }

  private void restoreConnections()
  {
```

```
      for (int i = 0; i < sourceConnections.size(); i++)
      {
        Path path = (Path)sourceConnections.get(i);
        path.getTarget().addTargetConnection(path);
        path.getSource().addSourceConnection(path);
      }
      sourceConnections.clear();
      for (int i = 0; i < targetConnections.size(); i++)
      {
        Path path = (Path)targetConnections.get(i);
        path.getSource().addSourceConnection(path);
        path.getTarget().addTargetConnection(path);
      }
      targetConnections.clear();
    }

  public void setChild (Activity a)
  {child = a;}

  public void setParent(Chart c)
  {parent = c;}

  public void redo()
  {execute();}

  public void undo()
  {
    parent.addChild(child);
    restoreConnections();
  }
}
```

The code is somewhat involved, but the theory of operation is straightforward. The execute() method removes the Path objects from both the source and target Activity objects, and then it removes the deleted Activity objects from the Chart. The undo() method restores the component's connections and adds it to the Chart.

D.5.5   *The SetConstraintCommand class*

So far, we've created Commands that modify every aspect of the editor's Model except the appearance of the individual components. Since we want the user to be able to change the size and shape of Activity objects, we need to create a Command that invokes their appropriate mutator methods. This is the purpose of the SetConstraintCommand, which is one of the simplest of the Commands in our project. Its code is presented in listing D.15.

Listing D.15 SetConstraintCommand.java

```java
package com.swtjface.flowchart.commands;

import org.eclipse.draw2d.geometry.*;
import com.swtjface.flowchart.model.*;

public class SetConstraintCommand
  extends org.eclipse.gef.commands.Command
{
  private Point oldPos, newPos;
  private Dimension oldSize, newSize;
  private Activity act;

  public void execute()
  {
    oldSize = act.getSize();
    oldPos  = act.getLocation();
    act.setLocation(newPos);
    act.setSize(newSize);
  }

  public void setLocation(Rectangle r)
  {
    setLocation(r.getLocation());
    setSize(r.getSize());
  }

  public void setLocation(Point p)
  {newPos = p;}

  public void setPart(Activity part)
  {this.act = part;}

  public void setSize(Dimension p)
  {newSize = p;}

  public void redo()
  {
    act.setSize(newSize);
      act.setLocation(newPos);
  }

  public void undo()
  {
    act.setSize(oldSize);
    act.setLocation(oldPos);
  }
}
```

This `Command` changes the `Activity`'s `size` and `location` parameters, but not its name. For this, we'll use a direct statement from the `Activity`'s `EditPart`, which we'll discuss next.

D.6 *The Controller aspect: EditPart classes*

Now that we've handled the View and Model aspects of the application's components, we need to start building their Controllers, represented by `EditPart` objects. Previously, we described the function of a Controller as "everything else," but now we need to be more specific. An `EditPart`'s activity may be divided into three main functions:

- Respond to Model changes and update the component's View
- Keep track of the component's `Connections` and `ConnectionAnchors`
- Activate `EditPolicys` and associate them with their editing roles

The first function is important to understand. An `EditPart`'s `activate()` method is called during its creation. This invokes the Model's `addPropertyChangeListener()` method and enables the `EditPart` to respond to property changes in the Model. This response is performed with the `propertyChange()` method, which updates the View with the new information from the Model.

For example, when a `SetConstraintCommand` is executed, it calls the Model's `setSize()` and `setLocation()` methods. When these properties change, the two `PropertyChangeEvents` are received by the `EditPart`, which modifies the `Figure`'s size and location.

In addition to updating size and location, many `EditParts` must manage `Connection` objects. These `EditParts` need to implement the `NodeEditPart` interface, which provides methods for matching `Connections` with `ConnectionAnchors`. When a `PathCommand` needs to know where to attach a new `Connection`, it communicates with a `NodeEditPart`.

The last `EditPart` function deals with `EditPolicys`, which determine the different ways the component can be edited. These policies function by creating `Command` objects in response to `Requests`. An `EditPart` specifies its applicable policies with the `createEditPolicies()` method and contains them in a `List`. We'll discuss these objects further in the next section.

Although we refer to these objects as `EditParts`, all of the GEF Controllers are really extensions of the `AbstractGraphicalEditPart` class. This class provides many of the methods needed for `Connection` management and child/parent interaction. It also creates a default `DragTracker` object to handle `DragEvents`.

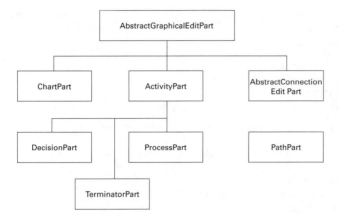

Figure D.11
The `EditPart` hierarchy
for the flowchart editor

The `EditPart` class hierarchy for our flowchart editor is shown in figure D.11. Just as we had an abstract class for `Activity` models, we now have an abstract `ActivityPart` for our `Process`, `Decision`, and `Terminator` `EditParts`. The editor also includes `ChartParts` for the container and `PathParts` that extend the `ConnectionEditPart` class.

Before we can discuss the individual classes, we need to show how these objects are created. Therefore, our next subject is the `EditPartFactory` class.

D.6.1 *Creating new EditParts with EditPartFactory objects*

Earlier, we showed how palettes add Model classes to the parent container, but we didn't mention how new `EditParts` are formed. When a new child Model is created from its template, the parent Model fires a `PropertyChangeEvent`. In response, the parent `EditPart` invokes its `refreshChildren()` method. If any child Models exist without matching `EditParts`, then this method calls the `createChild()` method.

`createChild()` accesses the editor's `EditPartFactory` object. Just as our `ModelFactory` created Model classes according to templates, our `PartFactory` creates `EditParts` according to their Models. The interface specifies only one method, `createEditPart()`; as listing D.16 shows, this is the only method we need. If you're coding these classes, we recommend that you add this class (and all the classes in this section) to the `com.swtjface.flowchart.editpart` package.

Listing D.16   PartFactory.java

```java
package com.swtjface.flowchart.editpart;

import org.eclipse.gef.EditPart;
import org.eclipse.gef.EditPartFactory;
import com.swtjface.flowchart.model.*;
import com.swtjface.flowchart.model.Process;

public class PartFactory implements EditPartFactory
{
  public EditPart createEditPart(EditPart context, Object model)
  {
    EditPart part = null;
    if (model instanceof Decision)
      part = new DecisionPart();
    else if (model instanceof Process)
      part = new ProcessPart();
    else if (model instanceof Terminator)
      part = new TerminatorPart();
    else if (model instanceof Path)
      part = new PathPart();
    else if (model instanceof Chart)
      part = new ChartPart();
    part.setModel(model);
    return part;
  }
}
```

Like the `ModelFactory` class, the `PartFactory` is simple. However, the operation of the individual `EditParts` is more involved. We'll begin with the parent `EditPart` of the flowchart editor, the `ChartPart`.

D.6.2 *The ChartPart class*

A `GraphicalViewer` object is initialized by specifying the highest-level Model class in the editor. In our case, this is the `Chart` class. Afterward, it calls its `setContents()` method, which tells the `PartFactory` to create a new `ChartPart`. The viewer's `RootEditPart` uses this object to create, activate, and remove child components from the editor. The code for this class is presented in listing D.17.

Listing D.17   ChartPart.java

```java
package com.swtjface.flowchart.editpart;

import java.beans.PropertyChangeEvent;
import java.beans.PropertyChangeListener;
import java.util.List;

import org.eclipse.draw2d.IFigure;
```

```java
import org.eclipse.gef.EditPolicy;
import org.eclipse.gef.editparts.*;

import com.swtjface.flowchart.figures.FigureFactory;
import com.swtjface.flowchart.model.Chart;
import com.swtjface.flowchart.policies.*;

public class ChartPart extends AbstractGraphicalEditPart
  implements PropertyChangeListener
{
  public void propertyChange(PropertyChangeEvent evt)
  {
    String prop = evt.getPropertyName();
    if (Chart.CHILD.equals(prop))
      refreshChildren();
  }

  protected IFigure createFigure()
  {
    return FigureFactory.createChartFigure();
  }

  protected void createEditPolicies()
  {
    installEditPolicy(EditPolicy.LAYOUT_ROLE, new LayoutPolicy());
  }

  public void activate()
  {
    if (isActive())
      return;
    super.activate();
    getChart().addPropertyChangeListener(this);
  }

  public void deactivate()
  {
    if (!isActive())
      return;
    super.deactivate();
    getChart().removePropertyChangeListener(this);
  }

  protected Chart getChart()
  {
    return (Chart)getModel();
  }

  protected List getModelChildren()
  {
    return getChart().getChildren();
  }
}
```

◁⌐ **Update children if CHILD property**

◁⌐ **Start monitoring property changes**

◁⌐ **Stop monitoring property changes**

The first method handles the `PropertyChangeEvents` created by the `Chart` object. When invoked, it calls `refreshChildren()`, which activates child `EditParts` and removes deleted children. The next method, `createFigure()`, builds a `ChartFigure` using the `FigureFactory`. The `createEditPolicies()` method sets two policies for the part and the roles they will perform. The next two methods take care of activation and deactivation, and the last two methods access the Model object of the `EditPart` and its children.

D.6.3 *The ActivityPart class*

Because of its connections and properties, the `ActivityPart` contains more methods than any other `EditPart` in our project. But, as shown in listing D.18, the structure remains similar to that of `ChartPart`.

It begins with the event-handling method, `propertyChange()`, and continues with the methods needed to alter the View. It contains `activate()` and `deactivate()` methods, and it adds `EditPolicys` to its internal `List`. But after its Model-accessing methods, the `ActivityPart` contains four methods related to `ConnectionAnchor` objects. These are the methods that the class must provide as part of the `NodeEditPart` interface, which makes the process of adding and removing `Connections` possible.

Listing D.18 ActivityPart.java

```
package com.swtjface.flowchart.editpart;

import java.beans.*;
import java.util.*;

import org.eclipse.draw2d.ConnectionAnchor;
import org.eclipse.draw2d.geometry.*;
import org.eclipse.gef.*;
import org.eclipse.gef.requests.DropRequest;

import com.swtjface.flowchart.figures.*;
import com.swtjface.flowchart.model.*;
import com.swtjface.flowchart.policies.*;

abstract public class ActivityPart
  extends org.eclipse.gef.editparts.AbstractGraphicalEditPart
  implements NodeEditPart, PropertyChangeListener
{
  public void propertyChange(PropertyChangeEvent evt)
```

```
{
  String prop = evt.getPropertyName();
  if (Activity.CHILD.equals(prop))
    refreshChildren();
  else if (Activity.TARGETS.equals(prop))
    refreshTargetConnections();
  else if (Activity.SOURCES.equals(prop))
    refreshSourceConnections();
  else if (Activity.SIZE.equals(prop) ||
    Activity.LOC.equals(prop) ||
    Activity.NAME.equals(prop))
    refreshVisuals();
}
```

Update feature according to property name

```
protected void refreshVisuals()
{
  getActivityFigure().setName(getActivity().getName());
  Point loc = getActivity().getLocation();
  Dimension size = getActivity().getSize();
  Rectangle r = new Rectangle(loc ,size);
  ((GraphicalEditPart) getParent()).setLayoutConstraint
    (this, getFigure(), r);
}
```

Update name and bounds for Figure and Model

```
public void activate()
{
  if (isActive())
    return;
  super.activate();
  getActivity().addPropertyChangeListener(this);
}

public void deactivate()
{
  if (!isActive())
    return;
  super.deactivate();
  getActivity().removePropertyChangeListener(this);
}

protected void createEditPolicies()
{
  installEditPolicy(EditPolicy.COMPONENT_ROLE,
    new ComponentPolicy());
  installEditPolicy(EditPolicy.GRAPHICAL_NODE_ROLE,
    new NodePolicy());
}
```

```
public ConnectionAnchor getSourceConnectionAnchor          ◄─┐
  (ConnectionEditPart connEditPart)                          │
{                                                            │
  Path Path = (Path) connEditPart.getModel();               │
  return getActivityFigure().                                │
    getSourceConnectionAnchor(Path.getSourceName());         │
}                                                            │
                                                             │
public ConnectionAnchor getSourceConnectionAnchor          ◄─┤
  (Request request)                                          │
{                                                            │
  Point pt = new Point(((DropRequest)request).getLocation()); │
  return getActivityFigure().getSourceConnectionAnchorAt(pt); │
}                                                            │
                                                             │
public ConnectionAnchor getTargetConnectionAnchor          ◄─┤
  (ConnectionEditPart connEditPart)                          │   NodeEdit-
{                                                            │   Part
  Path Path = (Path) connEditPart.getModel();               │   interface
  return getActivityFigure().                                │   methods
    getTargetConnectionAnchor(Path.getTargetName());         │
}                                                            │
                                                             │
public ConnectionAnchor getTargetConnectionAnchor          ◄─┤
  (Request request)                                          │
{                                                            │
  Point pt = new Point(((DropRequest)request).getLocation()); │
  return getActivityFigure().getTargetConnectionAnchorAt(pt); │
}                                                            │
                                                             │
public String mapSourceConnectionAnchorToName              ◄─┤
  (ConnectionAnchor c)                                       │
{                                                            │
  return getActivityFigure().getSourceAnchorName(c);         │
}                                                            │
                                                             │
public String mapTargetConnectionAnchorToName              ◄─┘
  (ConnectionAnchor c)
{
  return getActivityFigure().getTargetAnchorName(c);
}

protected ActivityFigure getActivityFigure()
{
  return (ActivityFigure) getFigure();
}

protected Activity getActivity()
{
  return (Activity)getModel();
}

protected List getModelSourceConnections()
{
```

```
      return getActivity().getSourceConnections();
   }

   protected List getModelTargetConnections()
   {
      return getActivity().getTargetConnections();
   }
}
```

The one method not included in the ActivityPart is createFigure(), which is needed to initialize the component's View aspect. Because this is the only distinguishing factor between the ActivityPart's subclasses, it must be specified in the ProcessPart, DecisionPart, and TerminatorPart classes. The code for these classes is shown in listings D.19, D.20, and D.21.

Listing D.19   ProcessPart.java

```
package com.swtjface.flowchart.editpart;

import org.eclipse.draw2d.IFigure;
import com.swtjface.flowchart.figures.FigureFactory;

public class ProcessPart extends ActivityPart
{
   protected IFigure createFigure()
   {
      return FigureFactory.createProcessFigure();
   }
}
```

Listing D.20   DecisionPart.java

```
package com.swtjface.flowchart.editpart;

import org.eclipse.draw2d.IFigure;
import com.swtjface.flowchart.figures.FigureFactory;

public class DecisionPart extends ActivityPart
{
   protected IFigure createFigure()
   {
      return FigureFactory.createDecisionFigure();
   }
}
```

Listing D.21   TerminatorPart.java

```
package com.swtjface.flowchart.editpart;

import org.eclipse.draw2d.IFigure;
```

```
import com.swtjface.flowchart.figures.FigureFactory;

public class TerminatorPart extends ActivityPart
{
  protected IFigure createFigure()
  {
    return FigureFactory.createTerminatorFigure();
  }
}
```

It's important to note that the ActivityPart object responds to events related to new and deleted Connections, but the PathPart doesn't. This is the case because these events are triggered only once the source and target Connections are added to the Activity's Model.

D.6.4 *The PathPart class*

Since the PathPart doesn't respond to Connection changes, and its activation and deactivation are handled by the ConnectionEditPart superclass, all our class needs to do is specify its applicable policies and the Figure that should be constructed upon its creation. The code is shown in listing D.22.

Listing D.22   PathPart.java

```
package com.swtjface.flowchart.editpart;

import org.eclipse.draw2d.*;

import org.eclipse.gef.editparts.AbstractConnectionEditPart;
import com.swtjface.flowchart.figures.FigureFactory;

public class PathPart extends AbstractConnectionEditPart
{
  protected void createEditPolicies()
  { }

  protected IFigure createFigure()
  {
    return FigureFactory.createPathFigure();
  }
}
```

Now that we've completed building the EditParts for the flowchart editor, we need to examine their policies. This will enable us to finally show the entire process of how a Tool's Request becomes a Model's Command.

D.7 Creating Commands with EditPolicy objects

Let's say that your editing project has a ChangeColorCommand, and you want this Command to execute whenever the component receives a DirectEditRequest. For another component, you want the ChangeShapeCommand to be executed for this Request. Clearly, you need to modify the EditPart classes of these components, since these are the objects that receive Requests. But how do you make this distinction?

The answer involves EditPolicys, which make it possible for EditParts to control how Commands are created in response to Requests. This section discusses how EditPolicy objects operate, the policies provided by the GEF, and how they're implemented in our editor.

D.7.1 The getCommand() method

Just as execute() makes Command operation possible, the getCommand() method performs the work for EditPolicys. Once a Tool determines which EditPart should receive a given Request, it calls the part's getCommand() method with the Request object as its parameter. Then, the EditPart iterates through its list of EditPolicy objects and invokes each of their getCommand() methods. In each case, if the policy can respond to the Request, it returns a Command object to the Tool, which executes it.

In addition, EditPolicys provide information to the Command that specify how its execution should be performed. That is, they tell the Command which Model properties should be modified and provide any parameters associated with the Request.

D.7.2 GEF policies in the flowchart editor

Although you can create customized EditPolicys from scratch, the GEF toolset provides a number of helpful abstract classes. To build concrete EditPolicys, you only need to specify which Model objects and properties should be changed when the Command executes. This section describes the main abstract policies we'll need for our editor and how you can extend them.

The flowchart editor needs three policies in order to function:

- *ComponentPolicy*—Removes Activity objects from the Chart
- *NodePolicy*—Manages the process of adding new Paths
- *LayoutPolicy*—Creates and arranges Activity objects in the Chart

Each of these classes extends an existing GEF policy class. Their inheritance structure is shown in figure D.12.

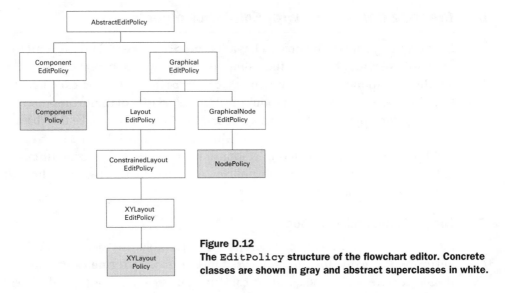

Figure D.12
The `EditPolicy` structure of the flowchart editor. Concrete classes are shown in gray and abstract superclasses in white.

The `ComponentEditPolicy` creates `Commands` when an `EditPart` is deleted or orphaned from a container. The `GraphicalEditPolicy` contains a number of subclasses for creating, deleting, and adding children to a `LayoutManager`. The `GraphicalNodeEditPolicy` subclass creates `Commands` for creating connections to and from a component. The GEF library provides many more policies than those shown in figure D.12, particularly subclasses of `GraphicalEditPolicy`; the library's documentation summarizes their functions.

Although our naming convention may seem lazy, there is a good reason. As we add new components and more functionality to the editor, we need to keep track of component behaviors. If we use names like `ChartPolicy` and `ActivityPolicy`, then it will be difficult to see which capabilities are present and which need to be added. Therefore, our policy names closely resemble those of their superclasses.

The LayoutPolicy class

The top-level policy in our project is the `LayoutPolicy`, which handles creating, deleting, and reshaping components in the `ChartPart`. This policy places children according to a `Rectangle` constraint, which specifies the component's dimensions and size. In addition, it lets the user resize children by creating a `ResizableEditPolicy` for each of its children.

The code for this class is shown in listing D.23. This, and all classes in this section, should be added to the `com.swtjface.flowchart.policies` package.

Listing D.23 LayoutPolicy.java

```java
package com.swtjface.flowchart.policies;

import org.eclipse.draw2d.PositionConstants;
import org.eclipse.draw2d.geometry.Rectangle;

import org.eclipse.gef.*;
import org.eclipse.gef.commands.Command;
import org.eclipse.gef.editpolicies.*;
import org.eclipse.gef.requests.*;

import com.swtjface.flowchart.model.*;
import com.swtjface.flowchart.commands.*;

public class LayoutPolicy extends XYLayoutEditPolicy
{
  protected Command createAddCommand(EditPart childEditPart,
    Object constraint)
  {
    Activity part = (Activity) childEditPart.getModel();
    Rectangle rect = (Rectangle)constraint;

    CreateCommand create = new CreateCommand();
    create.setParent((Chart)(getHost().getModel())); 
    create.setChild(part);                             // Set parameters of
    create.setConstraint(rect);                        // Command
    return create;
  }

  protected Command createChangeConstraintCommand
    (EditPart child, Object constraint)
  {
    SetConstraintCommand locationCommand =
      new SetConstraintCommand();
    locationCommand.setPart((Activity)child.getModel());
    locationCommand.setLocation((Rectangle)constraint);
    return locationCommand;
  }

  protected Command createChangeConstraintCommand
  (ChangeBoundsRequest request, EditPart child, Object constraint)
  {
    SetConstraintCommand cmd = (SetConstraintCommand)
      createChangeConstraintCommand(child, constraint);
      return cmd;
  }

  protected Command getCreateCommand(CreateRequest request)
  {
```

```
    CreateCommand create = new CreateCommand();
    create.setParent((Chart)(getHost().getModel()));
    create.setChild((Activity)(request.getNewObject()));
    Rectangle constraint = (Rectangle)getConstraintFor(request);
    create.setConstraint(constraint);
    return create;
  }

  protected Command getDeleteDependantCommand(Request request)
  {return null;}

  protected EditPolicy createChildEditPolicy(EditPart child)
  {
    ResizableEditPolicy policy = new ResizableEditPolicy();
    policy.setResizeDirections(PositionConstants.EAST |        ◄─┐  Specify how
      PositionConstants.WEST | PositionConstants.NORTH |          figure can be
      PositionConstants.SOUTH);                                   resized
    return policy;
  }
}
```

The `createAddCommand()` and `getDeleteDependantCommand()` methods return `null` because their functions are already accomplished: `getCreateCommand()` takes care of building new components, and `getDeleteCommand()` deletes them. This second method is part of our next policy, the `ComponentPolicy`.

The ComponentPolicy class

The `ComponentEditPolicy` superclass provides `Commands` when the user wants to remove a component from its container (make it an orphan) or delete it altogether. Since our only container in the flowchart is the `ChartPart`, there is no difference between becoming an orphan and being deleted. So, the only method in listing D.24 creates a `DeleteCommand`.

Listing D.24   ComponentPolicy.java

```
package com.swtjface.flowchart.policies;

import org.eclipse.gef.commands.Command;
import org.eclipse.gef.editpolicies.*;
import org.eclipse.gef.requests.*;

import com.swtjface.flowchart.model.*;
import com.swtjface.flowchart.commands.*;

public class ComponentPolicy extends ComponentEditPolicy
{
  protected Command createDeleteCommand(GroupRequest request)
  {
```

```
      Object parent = getHost().getParent().getModel();
      DeleteCommand deleteCmd = new DeleteCommand();
      deleteCmd.setParent((Chart)parent);
      deleteCmd.setChild((Activity)getHost().getModel());
      return deleteCmd;
   }
}
```

Because our `ActivityParts` have so much work to do, they require two policies. The `ComponentPolicy` shown in listing D.24 lets them handle their responsibilities as child components. But in order to manage `Connection` objects, they need a `NodePolicy`.

The NodePolicy class

The abstract `GraphicalNodeEditPolicy` class creates and initializes the parameters of a `PathCommand`. The subclass in our editor is called `NodePolicy`, and its code is shown in listing D.25. The `createDummyConnection()` serves an interesting purpose: It doesn't create a real `Connection`, but instead displays a new connection to the user before they choose a target component.

Listing D.25   NodePolicy.java

```
package com.swtjface.flowchart.policies;

import org.eclipse.draw2d.*;
import org.eclipse.gef.GraphicalEditPart;
import org.eclipse.gef.Request;
import org.eclipse.gef.commands.Command;
import org.eclipse.gef.requests.*;

import com.swtjface.flowchart.commands.*;
import com.swtjface.flowchart.model.*;
import com.swtjface.flowchart.figures.*;
import com.swtjface.flowchart.editpart.*;

public class NodePolicy
   extends org.eclipse.gef.editpolicies.GraphicalNodeEditPolicy
{
   protected Connection createDummyConnection(Request req)
   {
      PolylineConnection conn = FigureFactory.createPathFigure();
      return conn;
   }
   protecded Command getConnectionCompleteCommand      <—  Finish connection
      (CreateConnectionRequest request)
   {
      PathCommand command = (PathCommand)request.getStartCommand();
```

```
    command.setTarget(getActivity());
    ConnectionAnchor ctor = getActivityPart().
      getTargetConnectionAnchor(request);
    if (ctor == null)
      return null;
    command.setTargetName(getActivityPart().
      mapTargetConnectionAnchorToName(ctor));
    return command;
}

protected Command getConnectionCreateCommand        ◁— Start connection
(CreateConnectionRequest request)
{
    PathCommand command = new PathCommand();
    command.setPath(new Path());
    command.setSource(getActivity());
    ConnectionAnchor ctor = getActivityPart().
      getSourceConnectionAnchor(request);
    command.setSourceName(getActivityPart().
      mapSourceConnectionAnchorToName(ctor));
    request.setStartCommand(command);
    return command;
}

protected ActivityPart getActivityPart()
{return (ActivityPart) getHost();}

protected Activity getActivity()
{return (Activity) getHost().getModel();}

protected Command getReconnectTargetCommand         ◁— Reconnect target
    (ReconnectRequest request)
{
    PathCommand cmd = new PathCommand();
    cmd.setPath((Path)request.getConnectionEditPart().getModel());
    ConnectionAnchor ctor = getActivityPart().
      getTargetConnectionAnchor(request);
    cmd.setTarget(getActivity());
    cmd.setTargetName(getActivityPart().
      mapTargetConnectionAnchorToName(ctor));
    return cmd;
}

protected Command getReconnectSourceCommand         ◁— Reconnect source
    (ReconnectRequest request)
{
    PathCommand cmd = new PathCommand();
    cmd.setPath((Path)request.getConnectionEditPart().getModel());
    ConnectionAnchor ctor = getActivityPart().
      getSourceConnectionAnchor(request);
    cmd.setSource(getActivity());
    cmd.setSourceName(getActivityPart().
      mapSourceConnectionAnchorToName(ctor));
```

```
      return cmd;
   }

   protected ActivityFigure getActivityFigure()
   {
      return (ActivityFigure)((GraphicalEditPart)getHost()).getFigure();
   }
}
```

We've presented `Tools`, `Requests`, `Commands`, and `EditPolicys`. But one class of GEF objects demands our attention: `Actions` make it possible for menu items and tool-bar options to perform the same kind of functionality as `Tools`, and they're the subject of the next section.

D.8 *Adding Actions to the editor*

Users expect multiple ways to accomplish an editing task. For example, the Eclipse Workbench lets users copy GUI elements with a keystroke (Ctrl-C), a menu item (Edit->Copy), or an option in a context menu. GEF enables you to provide these capabilities through `Actions`.

These are essentially the same JFace `Actions` as those discussed in Chapter 4. They can be associated with text, images, and accelerator keys; and they can appear as buttons, toolbar items, or options in a menu. However, GEF's `Actions` have two important differences.

First, they're subclasses of `WorkbenchPartAction`, whose hierarchy is shown in figure D.13. Second, although they invoke `run()` when activated, their operation varies from class to class. A `SelectionAction` functions like a `Tool` by sending the selected component a `Request`. `StackActions` function by accessing the `Command Stack`, and `EditorPartActions` work by accessing the `EditorPart` itself.

Figure D.13
A context menu in a GEF editor

In order to function, `WorkbenchPartActions` need to notify the editor of their presence. This is accomplished by adding them to the editor's `ActionRegistry`.

D.8.1 *The ActionRegistry and ContextMenus*

Every `GraphicalEditor` creates an `ActionRegistry` as part of its initialization and populates it by calling `createActions()`. The code is shown here:

```
action = new UndoAction(this);
registry.registerAction(action);
getStackActions().add(action.getId());

action = new RedoAction(this);
registry.registerAction(action);
getStackActions().add(action.getId());

action = new SelectAllAction(this);
registry.registerAction(action);

action = new DeleteAction((IWorkbenchPart)this);
registry.registerAction(action);
getSelectionActions().add(action.getId());

action = new SaveAction(this);
registry.registerAction(action);
getPropertyActions().add(action.getId());

action = new PrintAction(this);
registry.registerAction(action);
```

We mention this code for two reasons. First, it's helpful to know which Actions have already been added to your GraphicalEditor by default. It also shows that, in addition to the ActionRegistry, the editor keeps track of certain groups of Action classes.

These groups include PropertyActions, which deal with changes to the editor's state; StackActions, which manipulate the CommandStack; and SelectionActions, which communicate with selected components. If you intend to add custom Actions to your editor, you need to register them in the ActionRegistry and add them to any groups to which they belong. You do so by implementing the create-Actions() method in your editor.

After you add your Actions to the editor, you need to make them available to the user. One of the simpler ways to do this involves a ContextMenu, shown in figure D.14. This menu is easily accessible by right-clicking in the editor's main window.

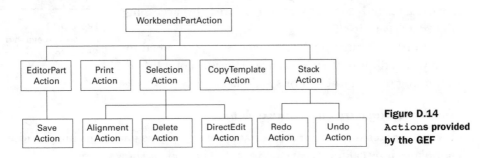

Figure D.14
Actions provided by the GEF

For our flowchart editor, we'll only use the Actions that are added by default, so we won't need to create any new classes. Instead, we'll create a ContextMenuProvider and add our desired Actions to it (see listing D.26). We recommend that you add this class to the com.swtjface.flowchart.actions package.

Listing D.26   FlowchartContextMenuProvider.java

```java
package com.swtjface.flowchart.actions;

import org.eclipse.jface.action.*;
import org.eclipse.ui.actions.ActionFactory;
import org.eclipse.gef.*;
import org.eclipse.gef.ui.actions.*;

public class FlowchartContextMenuProvider
      extends ContextMenuProvider
{
  private ActionRegistry actionRegistry;

  public FlowchartContextMenuProvider(EditPartViewer viewer,
    ActionRegistry registry)
  {
    super(viewer);   ◄──── Add menu to editor's Viewer
    setActionRegistry(registry);
  }

  private ActionRegistry getActionRegistry()
  {
    return actionRegistry;
  }

  public void setActionRegistry(ActionRegistry registry)
  {
    actionRegistry = registry;
  }

  public void buildContextMenu(IMenuManager menu)
  {
    GEFActionConstants.addStandardActionGroups(menu);

    IAction action;
    action = getActionRegistry().getAction
      (ActionFactory.UNDO.getId());
    menu.appendToGroup(GEFActionConstants.GROUP_UNDO, action);   ◄─────

    action = getActionRegistry().getAction
      (ActionFactory.REDO.getId());
    menu.appendToGroup(GEFActionConstants.GROUP_UNDO, action);   ◄─────

    action = getActionRegistry().getAction
      (ActionFactory.DELETE.getId());
    if (action.isEnabled())
      menu.appendToGroup(GEFActionConstants.GROUP_EDIT, action);   ◄─────
```

Add GEF Action to ContextMenu

Add GEF Action to ContextMenu

```
        action = getActionRegistry().getAction        ◄────┐ Add GEF Action to
          (ActionFactory.SAVE.getId());                     │ ContextMenu
        if (action.isEnabled())
          menu.appendToGroup(GEFActionConstants.GROUP_SAVE, action);
      }
    }
```

The buildContextMenu() method acquires a MenuManager and searches through the ActionRegistry to find desired Actions. Then, it calls the appendToGroup() method to include them in the context menu.

Context menus are helpful, but it would be more interesting to include our Actions in the Eclipse Workbench. To accomplish this, we need to use a new kind of Action.

D.8.2 Redirecting Workbench actions with RetargetAction

The Eclipse Workbench contains a number of global Actions that can be triggered through its main menu and toolbar. We'd like to redirect them to allow users to perform editing in our editor and use Actions such as Undo, Redo, and Delete.

The process is simple. First, we need to create a set of RetargetActions and add them to the editor's ActionRegistry. Then, these Actions must be made available to the user. All of this can be accomplished with one class: ActionBarContributor.

RetargetActions

RetargetActions function by directing the effects of the Workbench's internal Actions to an application. When we use one of these Actions, its corresponding menu option is available for our editor. For example, when we add the DeleteRetargetAction, the Workbench's Edit->Delete can be used to delete an EditPart.

Table D.5 shows the RetargetActions provided by the GEF. Our editor uses the DeleteRetargetAction, the CopyRetargetAction, and the UndoTargetAction. There is no SaveRetargetAction because saving an editor's contents is always directed to the editor being used.

Table D.5   GEF retargetable actions

Action	Function	Label
`AlignmentRetargetAction`	Aligns `EditParts`	No
`CopyRetargetAction`	Copies and pastes components	No
`DeleteRetargetAction`	Removes `EditParts` from the editor	No
`RedoRetargetAction`	Reexecutes the given `Command`	Yes
`UndoRetargetAction`	Negates the effect of the last `Command` execution	Yes
`ZoomInRetargetAction`	Focuses on a smaller area within the editor	No
`ZoomOutRetargetAction`	Views a greater area of editor space	No

The Label column in the table refers to whether the `RetargetAction` can be given a custom label, which works like a tooltip. Only `UndoRetargetAction` and `RedoRetargetAction` are subclasses of `LabelRetargetAction`; the rest of the `RetargetActions` retain the label specified by the Workbench.

Because GEF makes `RetargetActions` so easy to use, we don't need to create separate classes for them. Instead, we only need a single `ActionBarContributor`.

The ActionBarContributor class

`FlowchartProject`'s plugin.xml file specifies its `contributorClass` field as `com.swtjface.Actions.FlowchartActionBarContributor`. This tells the Workbench that this class will access and modify its resources. In particular, this class functions by specifying which global `Actions` should be redirected and how they should be made available to the user.

An `ActionBarContributor` adds `Actions` to an application's main menu or `ToolBar/CoolBar`. For the flowchart editor, we need to add `RetargetActions` to the Workbench's toolbar. The code for the `FlowchartActionBarContributor` is presented in listing D.27. If you're coding these classes, we recommend that you add this to the `com.swtjface.flowchart.actions` package.

Listing D.27   FlowchartActionBarContributor.java

```
package com.swtjface.flowchart.actions;

import org.eclipse.jface.action.IToolBarManager;
import org.eclipse.ui.actions.ActionFactory;
import org.eclipse.gef.ui.actions.*;

public class FlowchartActionBarContributor
```

```
    extends ActionBarContributor
{
  protected void buildActions()
  {
    addRetargetAction(new UndoRetargetAction());       Retarget
    addRetargetAction(new RedoRetargetAction());       Workbench Actions
    addRetargetAction(new DeleteRetargetAction());     to editor
  }
  public void contributeToToolBar(IToolBarManager toolBarManager)
  {
    toolBarManager.add(getAction(ActionFactory.UNDO.getId()));
    toolBarManager.add(getAction(ActionFactory.REDO.getId()));
    toolBarManager.add(getAction(ActionFactory.DELETE.getId()));
  }
  protected void declareGlobalActionKeys()      Use Actions from
  {}                                            Workbench's toolbar
}                                                         to editor
```

These methods are easy to understand. The `buildActions()` method updates the `ActionRegistry` with `RetargetActions`. Then `declareGlobalActionKeys()` can be used to match them with keystrokes. The `contributeToToolBar()` method adds them to the Workbench's `ToolBarManager`.

Although the `Actions` in the flowchart editor are fairly simple, multifunctional editors require many more capabilities. To add them, you need a sound understanding of how the `Request-EditPolicy-Command` process works. Therefore, instead of discussing a new facet of the GEF, we'll like to present two detailed, complete examples of how the GEF performs component and connection editing.

D.9 Editing with GEF: two examples

We've discussed the GEF's basic objects and their functions, but you haven't seen the full editing process from start to finish. Therefore, this section presents two examples that show how a user-generated `Event` results in a modification to an `EditPart`'s Model and View aspects. We hope these examples clarify how `Tools`, `EditParts`, and Model classes function, and the relationships between them.

D.9.1 Example 1: deleting a component with a keystroke

Users expect that when they click a component and press the Delete key, the component and its connections will disappear. This process is is simple and obvious to the user, but it takes some time to understand what's going on under the hood.

1: EditorPart sends user-initiated event to Tool

The process of deleting a component has two Events. First, the component needs to be selected. This could result from a number of actions, but we'll assume the user pressed and lifted her mouse button on the component. Next is a KeyEvent fired by the Delete key.

The editor's LightWeightSystem forwards the MouseEvent to the editor's Edit-Domain. The EditDomain determines which Tool should receive the Event and invokes the Tool's mouseDown() method. In our example, the EditDomain transfers the MouseEvent to the SelectionTool. When the SelectionTool receives it, it determines whether the cursor was over an EditPart. If so, it sends the EditPart a SelectionRequest by invoking the part's getCommand(Request) method.

2: KeyHandler receives Delete keystroke and responds

Once the EditPart is selected, the SelectionTool receives the Delete keystroke and calls its KeyDown() method. However, this tool can't recognize the Delete key, so its method returns false.

But when the user releases the Delete key, the SelectionTool calls its KeyUp() method, which sends the key to the editor's KeyHandler. This object has already been initialized with a HashMap containing pairs of keys and Action objects. Therefore, it understands that the Delete key corresponds to a DeleteAction. Once the KeyHandler matches the two, it invokes the DeleteAction's run() method to execute the Action.

3: DeleteAction sends DeleteRequest to part

The DeleteAction's run() method invokes its createRequest() method to generate a DeleteRequest. It sends the Request object to the selected EditPart by invoking the part's getCommand(Request) method with a DeleteRequest. If multiple EditParts have been selected for deletion, then a DeleteRequest is sent to each.

4: EditPart determines which EditPolicy to use

When its getCommand() method is invoked, the EditPart accesses its List of Edit-Policys, which was populated with createEditPolicies(). The EditPart then calls the getCommand() method contained in each of its EditPolicy classes, and if any can accept the DeleteRequest, it returns a Command object. Those that can't do so return null. If multiple EditPolicys return a Command, the EditPart combines them using the chain() method contained in the Command class.

5: Policy returns DeleteCommand to delete EditPart

When the EditPart has finished cycling through its available policies, its getCommand() method completes; it returns a DeleteCommand object if any of these policies were able to interpret the DeleteRequest. If so, the execute() method of the DeleteCommand is called. In our code, this method removes the Connection objects associated with the EditPart. Then, it invokes the parent's removeChild() method.

6: EditPart's parent deactivates part

When its removeChild() method is called, the parent Model object removes the child EditPart from its list of children and fires a PropertyChangeEvent. The parent's EditPart responds by calling propertyChange(). In our editor, this method invokes refreshChildren().

This method searches through the parent's List of child Models and their EditParts. Since the deleted part's Model has been removed, the parent invokes removeChild(), which calls the part's deactivate() and removeNotify() methods. These methods tell the part to remove its ConnectionEditParts and children. Finally, the parent's removeChildVisual() method removes the child's Figure from the editor.

D.9.2   Example 2: how connections are created

To further describe GEF's Event-Request-Policy-Command-PropertyChangeEvent methodology, this subsection will present a second example involving connections between EditParts. So far, we've created a great deal of code that creates and manipulates these objects, but we haven't described their interrelated activity.

1: User's palette selection creates Tool

Users start the process by clicking the ConnectionCreationToolEntry in the FlowchartPalette. Doing so creates a ConnectionCreationTool object, which now handles all external events.

2: User chooses an EditPart as connection source

If the user clicks an EditPart, the ConnectionCreationTool creates a CreateConnectionRequest and initializes it with the location of the mouse click. The tool then determines which part has been targeted and sends the request by invoking the part's getCommand() method.

3: CreateConnectionRequest becomes a Command

When the `Editpart` receives the request from the tool, it searches its policies in the `EditPolicyIterator` to see if any can respond. In the case of our flowchart editor, the `NodePolicy`, a subclass of `GraphicalNodeEditPolicy`, starts the response by creating a `PathCommand` and initializing its parameters. These four parameters are as follows:

- The `Path` object, which holds the connection information
- The `Activity` object from which the connection starts (source)
- The `ActivityPart`'s `ConnectionAnchor`
- The `String` name used to represent the `ConnectionAnchor`

To initialize the first two fields, the tool creates a new `Path` object and uses the selected `ActivityPart` as the source. Getting the third and fourth fields is more involved.

This process starts by invoking the part's `getConnectionAnchor()` method with the location of the selection. This method calls `getConnectionAnchorAt()` method in the `Activity` class, which returns the anchor object. To match the anchor to the terminal name, the policy calls the `ActivityPart`'s `mapConnectionAnchorTo-Terminal()` method, which finds the terminal by calling the `ActivityFigure`'s `getConnectionAnchorName()` method. Once the command is fully initialized with the anchor and terminal, it's sent to the `ConnectionCreationTool` as the return value of the `getCommand()` method.

It's important to understand that this `Command` won't be executed immediately. Instead, it's stored in the `startCommand` field of the request and is executed after the second `EditPart` has been selected.

4: Tool creates new Path object

When the `ConnectionCreationTool` receives the command, it sets the editor's state to `STATE_CONNECTION_STARTED`. Then, it uses its `handleMove()` method to update the editor's appearance. This means creating a `Path` object between the source's anchor and the current mouse position. The process of providing this graphical update, or *feedback*, begins with invoking the source `ActivityPart`'s `showSource-Feedback()` method with a new `CreateConnectionRequest`. The part passes this request to its policies and, by default, invokes the `showSourceFeedback()` method of the `GraphicalNodeEditPolicy`. This method calls the `createDummyConnection()` method of our `NodePolicy`, which returns the new `Path` object.

5: User moves mouse and chooses second EditPart

As the user moves the pointer, the ConnectionCreationTool continually checks whether the mouse is pointing to an EditPart. If so, the target Activity provides feedback by moving the Connection's endpoint to one of its ConnectionAnchors. The tool also sends the part an updated ConnectionRequest by invoking the part's getCommand() method.

As before, the request is sent to the target part's ActivityPolicy, which updates the PathCommand created by the source part. This update involves setting the Command's target field equal to the target Activity and setting the targetName field equal to name of the target's ConnectionAnchor.

If the user clicks a second EditPart, then the tool changes the state from STATE_CONNECTION_STARTED to STATE_TERMINAL. It also erases the dummy Polyline-Connection and begins creating the connection.

6: PathCommand executes

The PathCommand's execute() method creates the Connection. First, it sets the Path's source, sourceName, target, and targetName fields equal to the source Activity, the name of the source's ConnectionAnchor, the target Activity, and the name of the target's ConnectionAnchor, respectively. Finally, it informs the source and target that they're the source and target of a new connection.

Both the source and target Activities fire PropertyChangeEvents, and their ActivityParts respond by invoking refreshSourceConnections() and refresh-TargetConnections(). Since these parts have Path objects without PathParts, this method creates PathParts using the PartFactory.

Now that you have a thorough understanding of Tools, Actions, Requests, EditPolicys, and Commands, it's time to work with the class that brings them all together. The next section deals with the EditorPart.

D.10 Introducing the EditorPart

If you've come this far, you have our respect. Learning how GEF operates is difficult, but you're near the end of the road. We're now going to discuss the object that brings everything together: EditorPart. This section will cover this class and the GraphicalViewer that does most of the work. We'll finish by showing the final code for the FlowchartEditor.

D.10.1 Working with EditorParts and GraphicalEditors

Graphical components in the Eclipse Workbench are divided into *views* and *editors*. Views, which extend the `ViewPart` class, organize and display information about the Workbench. Editors function by allowing the user to manipulate and save files; they descend from the `EditorPart` class.

Both `EditorPart` and its superclass, `WorkbenchPart`, are abstract classes with abstract methods. Therefore, if you're seeking to build an Eclipse editor, you must provide code for each of these methods, shown in table D.6.

Table D.6   Abstract methods of the `WorkbenchPart` and `EditorPart` classes

Method	Function
`WorkbenchPart.createPartControl` `(Composite)`	Specifies the `Composite` control that provides the editor's appearance
`WorkbenchPart.setFocus()`	Gives the focus property to the editor
`EditorPart.init(IEditorSite,` `IEditorInput)`	Initializes the editor with the given location and input (file)
`EditorPart.isDirty()`	Returns whether the editor content has changed
`EditorPart.doSave` `(ProgressMonitor)`	Specifies actions when editor content is saved to its file
`EditorPart.doSaveAs()`	Specifies actions when editor content is saved to a new file
`EditorPart.isSaveAllowed()`	Specifies whether the `SaveAs` operation is enabled
`EditorPart.gotoMarker()`	Changes the selection based on the presence of markers

The two most important of these are `init()` and `createPartControl()`. The Workbench calls `init()` when the user opens a file with the supported extension. Then, to display the editor, the workbench calls `createPartControl()`. Like the `createContents()` method of a JFace `Window`, this method embodies the editor's appearance within a `Composite` object.

The nature of this `Composite` determines how the editor looks and acts. For text editors, this is one large `Text` box. Graphical editors use a `Canvas`, but there's much more to a graphical editor than this object. To provide added functionality, GEF supplies an `EditorPart` subclass, `GraphicalEditor`.

The documentation recommends using the `GraphicalEditor` class as a reference, but we'll directly integrate one in our flowchart editor. This class provides a number of important capabilities to the editor, such as an `ActionRegistry`, a

CommandStack, an EditDomain, and a SelectionSynchronizer to coordinate selections across multiple viewers. Its most important feature is the GraphicalViewer, which accomplishes the main work of a GEF editor.

D.10.2 *Understanding the GraphicalViewer*

Earlier, we mentioned that JFace Viewers serve as adapters for Widgets and can simplify and extend the capabilities of their underlying components. Therefore, you can think of a GEF editor as a GraphicalViewer on top of a Canvas object. It handles events, keeps track of the user's selections, and creates the basis for the editor's EditPart hierarchy.

Our editor's Viewer extends GraphicalViewerImpl, a concrete class that implements the GraphicalViewer interface. The best way to see how this object works is to examine its methods, shown in table D.7.

Table D.7   Important methods of the GraphicalViewerImpl class

Method	Function
createControl()	Constructs the Canvas beneath the graphical editor
createLightweightSystem()	Builds the Draw2D object to handle events and Figures
setRootEditPart()	Creates the EditPart that activates all its children
setRootFigure()	Specifies the top-level Figure for this editor
setContents()	Specifies the top-level Model class for the editor (Chart)
getEditPartFactory()	Finds the class to create an EditPart based on its Model
setRouteEventsToEditDomain()	Transfers Events from the LightweightSystem to the EditDomain
addDragSourceListener()	Keeps track of components being moved
addDropTargetListener()	Keeps track of components being dropped
setKeyHandler()	Keeps track of the user's keystrokes
addSelectionChangedListener()	Listens for changes in the user's selection
findObjectAtExcluding()	Determines which EditPart was selected by the user
getSelectedEditParts()	Obtains a list of the EditParts in the selection

The first two methods create the structure underlying the GEF editor. First, the createControl() method builds the SWT Canvas object. Afterward, it creates a LightWeightSystem to hold the editor's Draw2D Figures. These objects also provide a channel through which the Viewer can receive Events.

The next two methods provide a basis for the editor's MVC structure. First, the
setRootEditPart() creates a new top-level parent for the EditPart hierarchy. It's
important to understand that this is *not* a part that we've created previously. It
doesn't perform event handling or specify EditPolicys; it does interact with the
editor's Layers, but its main purpose is to manage child EditParts.

Another purpose of the RootEditPart is to specify a Figure to create when set-
RootFigure() is invoked. Again, this isn't a Figure that we've coded. The nature of
this Figure depends on the RootEditPart. In our case, because we're using a Scal-
ableRootEditPart, the Viewer creates a new Viewport with a LayeredPane.

The next two methods continue this MVC development. The getContents()
method initializes the Viewer by providing the top-level Model class of the Viewer.
In our case, this is a Chart. The class returned by getEditFactory() uses this
Model to create a new EditPart, or a ChartPart for our editor. This EditPart is
then added as a child of the Viewer's RootEditPart.

The next four methods handle events in the Viewer. The first method directs
Events from the LightWeightSystem to the editor's EditDomain. The Viewer creates
Listeners for DragEvents and DropTargetEvents and also provides a KeyHandler to
respond to keyboard actions. It's important to note that the Viewer doesn't
respond to Events itself, but sends them to the object best suited to handle them.

The last three methods in the table deal with the Viewer's management of selections. The Viewer listens for the user's selections and calls the findObjectAtEx-
cluding() method to see if a selection location matches that of an EditPart. If so,
the EditPart is added to the List of EditParts returned by getSelectedEdit-
Parts(). Even though the SelectionTool responds to the user's selection, it gets its
information from the Viewer.

D.10.3 *The FlowchartEditor*

Now that you understand how GraphicalEditors and GraphicalViewers operate,
we can present the complete code for the FlowchartEditor. This class extends the
GraphicalViewerWithPalette class, which is just a GraphicalEditor with the Composite split into two sections. The code is shown in listing D.28.

Listing D.28 FlowchartEditor.java

```
package com.swtjface.flowchart;

import java.io.*;
import java.util.EventObject;

import org.eclipse.core.resources.*;
import org.eclipse.core.runtime.*;
```

```java
import org.eclipse.swt.SWT;
import org.eclipse.ui.*;
import org.eclipse.ui.actions.ActionFactory;

import org.eclipse.gef.*;
import org.eclipse.gef.dnd.TemplateTransferDragSourceListener;
import org.eclipse.gef.editparts.ScalableRootEditPart;
import org.eclipse.gef.palette.PaletteRoot;
import org.eclipse.gef.ui.parts.*;

import com.swtjface.flowchart.actions.FlowchartContextMenuProvider;
import com.swtjface.flowchart.dnd.FlowchartDropTargetListener;
import com.swtjface.flowchart.editpart.*;
import com.swtjface.flowchart.model.*;
import com.swtjface.flowchart.palette.*;

public class FlowchartEditor extends GraphicalEditorWithPalette
{
  public FlowchartEditor()
  {
    DefaultEditDomain defaultEditDomain =
      new DefaultEditDomain(this);
    setEditDomain(defaultEditDomain);
  }

  Chart Flowchart;

  protected void setInput(IEditorInput input)          ◁┐ Setting editor's
  {                                                       │ initial chart
    super.setInput(input);

    IFile file = ((IFileEditorInput)input).getFile();
    try
    {
      InputStream is = file.getContents(false);
      if(is.available()!=0)
      {
        ObjectInputStream ois = new ObjectInputStream(is);
        Flowchart = (Chart)ois.readObject();           ◁┐ If file contains
        ois.close();                                     │ chart, use it
        setTitle(file.getName());
      } else
          Flowchart = new Chart();                      ◁┐ If file is empty,
    }                                                     │ create new chart
    catch (Exception e)
    {
      e.printStackTrace();
      Flowchart = new Chart();
    }
  }

  protected Chart getChart()
  {
    return Flowchart;
```

```
}

public void setChart(Chart chart)
{
  Flowchart = chart;
}

protected void createOutputStream(OutputStream os)
  throws IOException
{
  ObjectOutputStream outStream = new ObjectOutputStream(os);
  outStream.writeObject(getChart());
  outStream.close();
}
```

Convert existing chart to output stream

```
public void doSaveAs()
{}

public void doSave(IProgressMonitor monitor)
{
  try
  {
    ByteArrayOutputStream out = new ByteArrayOutputStream();
    createOutputStream(out);
    IFile file = ((IFileEditorInput)getEditorInput()).getFile();
    file.setContents(new ByteArrayInputStream(out.toByteArray()),
      true, false, monitor);
    out.close();
    getCommandStack().markSaveLocation();
  }
  catch (Exception e)
  {
    e.printStackTrace();
  }
}
```

Set file contents with output stream

```
private boolean savePreviouslyNeeded = false;

public boolean isDirty()
{
  return isSaveOnCloseNeeded();
}

public boolean isSaveAsAllowed()
{
  return true;
}

public boolean isSaveOnCloseNeeded()
{
  return getCommandStack().isDirty();
}
```

```java
private boolean savePreviouslyNeeded()
{
  return savePreviouslyNeeded;
}

private void setSavePreviouslyNeeded(boolean value)
{
  savePreviouslyNeeded = value;
}

protected void configureGraphicalViewer()          ◁┐  Create initial objects
{                                                   │   for Graphical Viewer
  super.configureGraphicalViewer();
  getGraphicalViewer().setRootEditPart
    (new ScalableRootEditPart());
  getGraphicalViewer().setEditPartFactory(new PartFactory());
  ContextMenuProvider provider =
    new FlowchartContextMenuProvider(getGraphicalViewer(),
      getActionRegistry());
  getGraphicalViewer().setContextMenu(provider);
  getSite().registerContextMenu
    (provider, getGraphicalViewer());
  getGraphicalViewer().setKeyHandler(new
    GraphicalViewerKeyHandler(getGraphicalViewer())
      .setParent(getCommonKeyHandler()));
}

protected void initializeGraphicalViewer()
{                                                              Set top-level Model for
  getGraphicalViewer().setContents(Flowchart);     ◁┘         Graphical Viewer
  getGraphicalViewer().addDropTargetListener(      ◁─────┐    Tell Graphical
    new FlowchartDropTargetListener(getGraphicalViewer()));  Viewer where
}                                                            to create new
                                                             Models
private PaletteRoot root;

protected PaletteRoot getPaletteRoot()
{
  if (root == null)
    root = FlowchartPalette.getPaletteRoot();
    return root;
}

protected void initializePaletteViewer()
{
  super.initializePaletteViewer();
  getPaletteViewer().addDragSourceListener(
    new TemplateTransferDragSourceListener(getPaletteViewer()));
}

// Part 4: Allow the user to interact with the environment
private KeyHandler sharedKeyHandler;

protected KeyHandler getCommonKeyHandler()
```

```
  {
    if (sharedKeyHandler == null)
    {
      sharedKeyHandler = new KeyHandler();
      sharedKeyHandler.put(KeyStroke.getPressed(SWT.DEL, 127, 0),
        getActionRegistry().getAction                  Associate Delete key
          (ActionFactory.DELETE.getId()));              with Delete Action
    }
    return sharedKeyHandler;
  }
  public void commandStackChanged(EventObject event)
  {
    if (isDirty())
    {
      if (!savePreviouslyNeeded())
      {
        setSavePreviouslyNeeded(true);
        firePropertyChange(IEditorPart.PROP_DIRTY);
      }
    }
    else
    {
      setSavePreviouslyNeeded(false);
      firePropertyChange(IEditorPart.PROP_DIRTY);
    }
    super.commandStackChanged(event);
  }

  public void gotoMarker(IMarker marker)
  { }
}
```

Whew! As shown by the annotations, this class performs three tasks. The first involves file operations. Once the user starts the editor by selecting a *.fcf file, the editor converts it into an ObjectInputStream and attempts to convert this into a Chart object. If the conversion succeeds, then this Chart is used to initialize the GraphicalViewer. Otherwise, if the file is empty, the editor constructs a new Chart object. Similarly, when the user wants to save the Chart to a file, the editor converts it into an ObjectOutputStream and then to a file. Notice that the editor constantly monitors the CommandStack to see if the contents are *dirty*, which means they've been changed since the last save.

The next task involves configuring and initializing the GraphicalViewer and PaletteViewer. The editor provides the GraphicalViewer with its RootEditPart, its EditPartFactory, ContextMenu, and KeyHandler, and initializes it with the Chart.

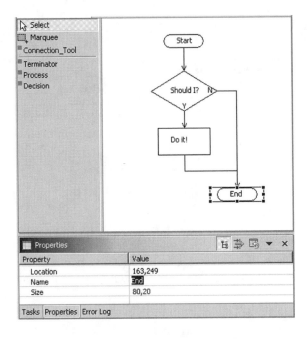

Figure D.15
The flowchart editor in full

To enable the user to drag template objects from the palette, the editor provides a `TemplateTransferDragSourceListener` for the `PaletteViewer` and a `Flowchart-DropTargetListener` for the `GraphicalViewer`. It also initializes the `PaletteViewer` with the `PaletteRoot` created in the `FlowchartPalette` class.

Finally, the editor manages user input. This means creating a `KeyHandler` and making sure the Delete keystroke creates a `DeleteAction`. The editor also responds to `Command` execution by firing a `PropertyChangeEvent` whenever the `CommandStack` changes.

And that finishes our flowchart editor. With luck, your application should resemble figure D.15.

D.11 *Other GEF aspects*

Despite the lengthy presentation, the GEF provides a number of important features that we failed to mention. We'll talk about these subjects in this final section.

D.11.1 *Accessibility*

We're ashamed that we failed to make the flowchart editor accessible, especially since the GEF makes accessibility so easy. GEF EditParts interact with accessibility tools by creating an AccessibilityEditPart() method and making it available. This new EditPart responds to AccessibilityEvents and AccessibilityControlEvents by providing information concerning the part's name, description, state, and children. AccessibleAnchors make it possible to create and remove Connections through the keyboard.

D.11.2 *Grid layout*

One of the most interesting features of a GEF editor is the possibility of adding rulers and a grid to the GraphicalViewer. This lets the user force the editor's Figures to position themselves according to the grid's points, a process also called SnapToGrid. Once the GridLayout is specified, Actions such as the ToggleSnapToGeometryAction cause EditParts to change their location in response to SnapMoveRequests and SnapResizeRequests.

D.11.3 *Zooming in and out*

Another interesting capability lets the user increase or decrease the size of a selected portion of the editor through zooming. This is accomplished by a ZoomManager, which is associated with the GraphicalViewer and fires a ZoomEvent when the user changes the zoom level. This Event results in a ZoomInAction or ZoomOutAction, which causes the Viewer to enlarge or reduce the component's graphics. These Actions can also be performed through the Workbench by adding their RetargetActions.

D.11.4 *Kudos to Randy Hudson*

The inspiration for our flowchart editor was the Logic Editor created by Randy Hudson, technical lead for IBM's GEF development and the driving force behind its improvement. Like a latter-day Prometheus, he took this powerful tool out of IBM's cloistered research group and made it freely available for us commoners.

We'd like to doff our hats to Mr. Hudson for his hard work in both developing and supporting this toolkit, and to you, gentle reader, for your patience in learning how it works.

index